Learning Digital Identity
Design, Deploy, and Manage
Identity Architectures

Phillip J. Windley

Beijing · Boston · Farnham · Sebastopol · Tokyo

Learning Digital Identity

by Phillip J. Windley

Published by O'Reilly Media, Inc., 1005 Gravenstein Highway North, Sebastopol, CA 95472.

O'Reilly books may be purchased for educational, business, or sales promotional use. Online editions are also available for most titles (*http://oreilly.com*). For more information, contact our corporate/institutional sales department: 800-998-9938 or *corporate@oreilly.com*.

Acquisitions Editor: Jennifer Pollock	**Indexer:** Judith McConville
Development Editor: Sarah Grey	**Interior Designer:** David Futato
Production Editor: Beth Kelly	**Cover Designer:** Karen Montgomery
Copyeditor: nSight, Inc.	**Illustrator:** Kate Dullea
Proofreader: Piper Editorial Consulting, LLC	

January 2023:   First Edition

Revision History for the First Release

2023-01-10:   First Release

See *http://oreilly.com/catalog/errata.csp?isbn=9781098117696* for release details.

978-1-098-11769-6

[LSI]

Table of Contents

Foreword

Three weeks ago I was sitting in a ring of concentric circles with over 320 people at the opening of one of the most unusual and fascinating conferences you will ever see: the Internet Identity Workshop (IIW). In the front row was Phil Windley, who—along with Kaliya "IdentityWoman" Young and Doc Searls—founded IIW 18 years ago.

If 18 years sounds like a good run for an annual industry conference, it is. But IIW is not an annual conference. It happens twice every year.

That's right—November 2022 was the 35th edition.

What is so urgent and important about the problems of digital identity on the internet that an average of 250 people have flown from all over the world to gather in-person 35 times over 18 years to work on solutions?

This book is the answer. Let me explain.

When most people hear the term "digital identity", they think of two things: the persistent pain of logging in with usernames and passwords and the bane of identity theft.

Is digital identity about those things? Absolutely. Is it limited to those things? Absolutely not.

In fact, for those experts gathering at IIW every six months, what is at stake is the very future of the internet. Why? The answer can be summarized by this 2021 quote from Thales Group (*https://oreil.ly/d9olg*):

> Trust is the most important currency in the digital world. Digital identities are how this trust is conveyed and embedded, and therefore their importance to our online society cannot be overstated.

In short, digital identities are the key to how we can solve the fundamental trust issues with today's internet. I doubt most readers need any convincing about the scale or severity of those problems. Some—like misinformation, ransomware, and Elon Musk's struggle to verify Twitter accounts—are regular front-page headlines. What most readers will not appreciate, however, is the depth or complexity of these challenges. In fact, Phil needed to devote an entire chapter (Chapter 3) just to explain the eight fundamental problems that need to be solved.

That's why I'm glad Phil and O'Reilly have put the emphasis on learning digital identity. Like the proverbial iceberg, the parts that are visible to everyday internet users are only the very tip. A full understanding of the subject requires not just diving below the surface, but also going backward in time to appreciate how and why the internet identity landscape has evolved so rapidly in the last 20 years—and why it will continue until we finally have an "identity layer."

In my talks about this evolutionary progression, I describe it as having three major "eras": centralized, federated, and decentralized. Phil and I first met at the Digital Identity World conference in 2003, when federated identity was just catching on and everyone was hopeful it would solve username/password hell.

The hot topic at that conference was how these new federated systems could be truly "user-centric", i.e., serve the interests of individuals, not just companies. Doc Searls introduced Phil and I to Kim Cameron, who had recently become Chief Identity Architect at Microsoft (a position he would hold for the next 20 years). The following year, Kim began publishing his Seven Laws of Identity[1] to help establish the "ground rules" for a user-centric internet identity system. These seven laws, widely debated in the blogosphere (when that was still a thing), have stood the test of time so well that Phil devotes an entire chapter to them (Chapter 4).

The following spring, Phil, Kaliya, and Doc hosted the inaugural Internet Identity Workshop. Under the guidance of Kaliya and Heidi Nobantu Saul, IIW used Open Space (*https://oreil.ly/o4r3B*) technology to self-organize sessions about every facet of the relationship life cycle that Phil covers in this book—naming, identifiers, discovery, privacy, integrity, cryptography, authentication, authorization, and access control—as well as every major identity standard of the last two decades, including SAML, OpenID, OAuth, UMA and SCIM.

Most of all, IIW was ground zero for the third era of internet identity—decentralized. The topic of how blockchain technology might be leveraged for user-centric identity first arose at the spring 2015 IIW. By fall there were a half-dozen IIW sessions on the topic. The next spring, "self-sovereign identity" (SSI) was in full force. In subsequent years, almost the entire focus of IIW shifted towards the topics Phil covers in the

---

1 Doc Searls published a wonderful retrospective (*https://oreil.ly/uGaXQ*) on these laws after Kim passed away in 2021.

latter half of this book: decentralized identifiers (DIDs), digital wallets and agents, digital credentials, and decentralized digital trust and governance frameworks.

At long last, there are real signs of traction. In the summer of 2021, the European Union announced the EU Digital Identity Wallets initiative to equip all EU citizens by 2024 with a government certified digital wallet and digital ID credential. The Canadian province of British Columbia issued its own digital wallet app (iOS and Android) based on the Hyperledger Aries open source code (Ontario and Quebec are expected to follow suit). Bhutan (the country best known for measuring Gross National Happiness) is preparing a National Digital Identity Act that will enshrine decentralized digital identity as the law of the land.

All of which makes this book more timely than ever. As I watched Phil make his traditional announcement of the day's sponsors in opening circle of IIW three weeks ago, I realized how extraordinary it is for someone who has had that front row seat for two decades to be sharing a comprehensive picture of everything he's learned over that period. And not just as an observer—over that same period Phil has taught as professor of computer science at BYU, founded a startup in the space, and maintained the most prolific blog on the topic.[2]

Bottom line: if you really want to learn about digital identity, you could not have found a better starting point. Dive in!

— Drummond Reed
Director, Trust Services, Gen Digital
Coauthor, Self-Sovereign Identity *(Manning 2021)*
Coeditor, W3C Decentralized Identifiers (DIDs) 1.0
Steering Committee Member, Trust Over IP (ToIP) Foundation

---

2 Phil Windley's Technometria (*https://www.windley.com*); I teased Phil that I've run out of space in my browser for all the bookmarks I have to his digital identity articles.

Preface

On December 2, 1942, beneath the viewing stands of the University of Chicago's Stagg Field, Enrico Fermi and his team initiated the first human-caused, self-sustaining nuclear chain reaction in history. Once humans knew how nuclear chain reactions work and how to initiate them, an atomic bomb was inevitable. Someone would build one.

What was not inevitable was when, where, and how nuclear weapons would be used. Geopolitical events of the last half of the 20th century dealt with the when, where, and how of that technology, as do many of the international questions of our day.

A similar, and perhaps just as impactful, discussion is happening now around technologies like artificial intelligence, social media, online surveillance, and digital identity. The choices that developers, architects, product managers, founders, and others make, day to day, change the future. My great hope is that the material in this book will help inform you of the important issues surrounding digital identity, so that you can make better decisions that result in better online experiences for us all.

But this book is also practical. I published my first identity book, *Digital Identity*, in 2005. Coincidentally, that year marked the beginning of a sea change in the field. Web 2.0 was all the rage, and organizations were looking for new identity tools and protocols to underlie their fledgling platforms and services.

That same year, Doc Searls, Kaliya Young, and I started the Internet Identity Workshop (IIW). We, and most of the attendees, were working on projects that needed what we called user-centric identity. We thought that using URL-based identifiers for people was the answer to the internet's identity problems. We imagined that we'd hold a couple of meetings, come up with a solution, and move on to other problems. Now, 18 years and 35 meetings later, IIW is still going strong, with solutions to new digital identity problems still being proposed, debated, and accepted (or not).

In this book, I will teach you what digital identity is, why it's hard to get right, what makes a good identity system, what technologies provide its foundation, how it's done today, and where it's going. You'll learn why digital identity is at the heart of every online service and interaction, and why that position makes it one of the most important technologies you can work on.

Who Is This Book For?

The primary audience for this book is product managers, architects, and developers who can use its ideas to lay a firm foundation for their own work, based on the principles of digital identity and an understanding of the architectures and technologies that are available to solve identity problems. This book will give you a good grounding in the base-level technologies and protocols that play important roles in digital identity systems. *Learning Digital Identity* will give you a fresh perspective on the role identity plays in creating usable and compelling digital products.

A secondary audience for this book is chief information officers (CIOs), chief information security officers (CISOs), chief privacy officers (CPOs), risk managers, security engineers, and privacy professionals, who will read it to understand the terminology, concepts, and architectures. More importantly, I hope they come to see the potential of identity systems to make their business more secure, agile, and appealing. In this book you will learn the specific identity architectures that are possible and determine how those architectures impact the usability, availability, reliability, security, and privacy of your digital services and products.

Conventions Used in This Book

The following typographical conventions are used in this book:

Italic
> Indicates new terms, URLs, email addresses, filenames, and file extensions.

`Constant width`
> Used for program listings, as well as within paragraphs to refer to program elements such as variable or function names, databases, data types, environment variables, statements, and keywords.

`Constant width bold`
> Shows commands or other text that should be typed literally by the user.

`Constant width italic`
> Shows text that should be replaced with user-supplied values or by values determined by context.

O'Reilly Online Learning

O'REILLY® For more than 40 years, *O'Reilly Media* has provided technology and business training, knowledge, and insight to help companies succeed.

Our unique network of experts and innovators share their knowledge and expertise through books, articles, and our online learning platform. O'Reilly's online learning platform gives you on-demand access to live training courses, in-depth learning paths, interactive coding environments, and a vast collection of text and video from O'Reilly and 200+ other publishers. For more information, visit *https://oreilly.com*.

How to Contact Us

Please address comments and questions concerning this book to the publisher:

O'Reilly Media, Inc.
1005 Gravenstein Highway North
Sebastopol, CA 95472
800-998-9938 (in the United States or Canada)
707-829-0515 (international or local)
707-829-0104 (fax)

We have a web page for this book, where we list errata, examples, and any additional information. You can access this page at *https://oreil.ly/learning-digital-identity*.

Email *bookquestions@oreilly.com* to comment or ask technical questions about this book.

For news and information about our books and courses, visit *https://oreilly.com*.

Find us on LinkedIn: *https://linkedin.com/company/oreilly-media*

Follow us on Twitter: *https://twitter.com/oreillymedia*

Watch us on YouTube: *https://youtube.com/oreillymedia*

Acknowledgments

I'm indebted to hundreds of people who have helped me learn digital identity over the past 25 years. Here are a few who deserve special thanks.

Kelly Flanagan has been my good friend, mentor, and cheerleader for most of my professional career. Steve Fulling is another great friend who was my business partner for many years in several adventures. They have both provided unflagging technical, financial, and emotional support for my identity explorations. Troy Martin and I had many profitable discussions about personal learning systems, which led to my interest in self-sovereign identity.

Kaliya Young and Doc Searls are my cofounders at Internet Identity Workshop. They and the participants at IIW have made working on digital identity fun, informative, and fulfilling. Heidi Saul, IIW's producer, makes the semiannual Internet Identity Workshop event possible.

In addition to being my IIW cofounder, Doc is also a great friend and trusted advisor. Many of the ideas in this book have their roots in discussions with him. I'm grateful for his wisdom.

Drummond Reed and I have never worked for the same company, but we have worked closely together for almost two decades on the problems of identity, personal data, and privacy. I'm grateful for his cheerful optimism and careful guidance.

Kim Cameron and Craig Burton, who both died this past year, were two of the "OGs" of the identity space who nevertheless continued to influence and guide its development over many years. They both had tremendous influence on my thinking and taught me important lessons (about both identity and life). Kim's ideas on the identity metasystem and Laws of Identity appear in Chapter 4 and provide a framework for analyzing the concepts, protocols, and architectures I discuss later.

I've had many technical discussions with people about the topics in this book that taught me important concepts and explained difficult ideas. Here are a few that stand out. Daniel Hardman and I had helpful discussions on zero-knowledge proofs, correlation, the time-value of privacy, and minimal disclosure. Sam Curren helped me understand the nuances of verifiable credential presentations and has been a trusted colleague for 15 years. Sam Smith is a source of insight on many digital identity topics, but I am most grateful for his ideas about privacy, self-certifying identifiers, and reputation. Nathan George is my go-to person for almost any question on details of cryptographic protocols and artifacts based on them. Jason Law's clear explanations of cryptography, privacy, and credentials were critical to the development of my understanding of self-sovereign identity. Lastly, I am grateful to Joe Andrieu for the best definition of digital identity I've ever heard (you'll have to wait until Chapter 2 for it!).

My wife, Lynne, and my children, Bradford, Alexandra, Jacob, Joseph, and Samantha, have put up with much travel, near-constant writing, and many meetings in my quest to understand and help solve the problems of digital identity. They've also all had a hand in running IIW and making it work. Their love and support have been indispensable.

The people at O'Reilly have made writing this book not only possible, but fun. A special shout-out to my editor, Sarah Grey, for making me look good. Her edits greatly increased the understandability of the book, and her advice got me through some of the rough spots.

Credits

Figure 9-11 is adapted with permission from a graphic produced by the DHS Science and Technology Directorate.

Figure 10-5 is from DIF and used with permission.

Table 16-2 is adapted from a table in Chapter 10 of *Self-Sovereign Identity* by Drummond Reed and Alex Preukschat (Manning).

In Memoriam

In memory of Kim Cameron and Craig Burton, two identity pioneers who taught me much and influenced the world for good through their work, professionalism, and kindness.

CHAPTER 1

The Nature of Identity

Cogito, ergo sum.

　　—René Descartes

The Peace of Westphalia, which ended the Thirty Years' War in 1648, created the concept of Westphalian sovereignty (*https://oreil.ly/1UMsp*): the principle of international law that "each state has sovereignty over its territory and domestic affairs, to the exclusion of all external powers, on the principle of non-interference in another country's domestic affairs, and that each state (no matter how large or small) is equal in international law."[1]

The ensuing century saw many of these states begin civil registration for their citizens, in an effort to turn their sovereignty over territory into governance over the people living in those lands. These registrations, from which our modern system of birth certificates springs, became the basis for personal identity and legal identity in a way that conflated these two concepts.

Birth certificates are a source of legal identity and a proof of citizenship, and thus the basis for individual identity in most countries. Civil registration has become the foundation for how states relate to their citizens. As modern nation-states have become more and more influential (and often controlling) in the lives of their citizens, civil registration and its attendant legal identity have come to play a larger and larger role in their lives. People present proof of civil registration for many purposes: to prove who they are and, springing from that, their citizenship.

Even so, Descartes did not say, "I have a birth certificate, therefore I am." When most people hear the word *identity*, they think about birth certificates, passports, driver's

---

1　"Nation-States and Sovereignty" (*https://oreil.ly/rzjfM*), History Guild, accessed October 5, 2022.

licenses, logins, passwords, and other sorts of credentials. But clearly, we are more than our legal identity. For most purposes and interactions, our identity is defined through our relationships. Even more deeply, we each experience these independently as an autonomous being with an individual perspective.

This dichotomy reflects identity's dual nature. While identity is something others assign to us, it is also something deep inside of us, reflecting what Descartes actually said: "I *think*, therefore I am."

A Bundle of Sticks?

Another way to think about the dual nature of identity is to ask, "Am I more than a set of attributes?" Property rights are often thought of as a *bundle of sticks*: each right is separable from the rest and has value independent of the rest. Similarly, identity is often considered a bundle of attributes, each with independent value. This is known in philosophy as *bundle theory* (*https://oreil.ly/ZiUVH*), originated by David Hume.

Bundle theory puts attributes into a collection without worrying about *what* ties them together. As an example, you might identify a plum as purple, spherical, 5 centimeters in diameter, and juicy. Critics of bundle theory question how these attributes can be known to be related without knowing the underlying substance—the thing itself.

Substance theory, on the other hand, holds that attributes are borne by "an entity which exists in such a way that it *needs no other entity to exist*," according to our friend Descartes.[2] Substance theory gives rise to the idea of persistence in the philosophy of personal identity (*https://oreil.ly/7iueB*). People, organizations, and things persist through time. In one sense, you are the same person you were when you were 16. But in another, you are not. The thing that makes you the same person over your lifetime is substance. The thing that makes you different is the collection of everchanging attributes you present to the outside world over time.

I'm no philosopher, but I believe both viewpoints are useful for understanding digital identity. For many practical purposes, viewing people, organizations, and things as bundles of attributes is good enough. This view is the assumption upon which the modern web is built. You log into different services and present a different bundle of attributes to each. There is no substance, at least in the digital sense, since the only thing tying them together is you—a decidedly nondigital entity.

This lack of a digital representation of you, that you alone control, is one of the themes I'll return to several times in this book. At present, you are not digitally embodied—your digital existence depends on other entities. You have no digital

---

2 Substance theory has many more proponents than Descartes, but his definition is helpful in thinking through identity's dual nature.

substance to connect the various attributes you present online. I believe that digital identity systems must embody us and give us substance if we are to build a digital future where people can operationalize their online existence and maintain their dignity as autonomous human beings.

Identity Is Bigger Than You Think

At first blush, digital identity seems pretty simple: the service you're building needs to know who the person at the other end of the connection is. Set up an account, give them a username and password, and let them log in. Collect any necessary attributes into a nice, tidy bundle and store them in the account. Job done.

I've seen plenty of examples of this kind of thinking over the 25 years I've been working on digital identity. I've succumbed to it myself. Years ago, every company offering an online service would start from this premise, build a simple identity system, and move on. Then they'd shake their heads as more and more of their development resources got sucked into solving the new problems that always seemed to crop up when the identity system couldn't support some new feature.

Today, most companies buy their identity systems. Identity and access management (IAM) barely existed as a market category in 2005 but is now a multibillion-dollar industry. Yet digital identity is still growing, with new concepts, products, and services appearing seemingly daily.

The lesson? *Identity is bigger and more complicated than you think.* Throughout this book you will see examples of identity that go well beyond the traditional notions of login and access control. Privacy, trust, authenticity, confidentiality, federation, authentic data, identity for things, and identity ecosystems are a few of the areas this book discusses.

Identity is the foundation for all but the most trivial online services. Suppose a workflow that you're building needs a signed attestation that certain work has been performed and includes the details about the work. The result is a secure, digital, machine-readable, auditable record of what's occurred. The workflow requires that this attestation is authentic. How do you ensure that?

The document might be considered authentic if it's signed by someone or something that's been *authenticated*, if the cryptographic processes have the fidelity necessary to *inspire confidence in the result*, and if there's some process that *establishes the provenance of the document*.[3] Authentication, confidence, and provenance are all based on identity.

---

3 Provenance takes into account where the document came from, who wrote it, the source of the data used to generate it, and how it's been transmitted.

Beyond services, many documents we use every day have identity-related purposes. A movie ticket (an example I'll use several times in this book) is an identity document that identifies the holder as someone entitled to a seat in a specific theater at a given time. Furthermore, it's designed so that the ticket taker recognizes that it's authentic.

What about an invoice? An invoice identifies a payment that's being requested by a specific party for a specific service. It has an identifier and can be recognized as authentic because of the workflow it's part of. An invoice identifies a transaction taking place inside a larger relationship.

These examples, and millions more, are all part of digital identity—yet they aren't about logging into an account to retrieve some attributes. As you'll learn in this book, however, they have much in common.

No Universal Identity Systems

Some people combine the mistaken assumption that identity is simple with the myopic view that identity is just about the process for tying legal identifiers to people. The result is a search for a universal identity solution. Universal identity systems are attractive because digital identity is hard and inconvenient. The siren song of a universal identity system calls developers and users alike with its promise to simplify online interactions, only to dash them upon the rocks of very real complexity.

Over the years, I've had many people pitch me that their product is a universal solution for digital identity because it provides the means to concretely tie a body (literally, through biometrics) to a legal identifier. While this can reduce fraud, identity systems that do this are almost always privacy disasters because they must collect lots of personal information to be universal. The result is a honeypot of personal information that hackers find too attractive to ignore. More worrisome, a single universal identifier provides the means for computers to correlate the activities of people across a large variety and type of systems, creating a universal dossier that allows governments and companies to surveil and even control them. Universal identifiers are a 20th-century technology that has no business being used in the digital age.

I hope that the examples from the last section have at least got you thinking about all the places that identity plays a role in your organization and, more importantly, your life. Because identity, in one form or another, is foundational to nearly every transaction, relationship, and interaction, identity systems are *polymorphic* (they have many forms). Consequently, universal systems, which, by definition, have a single form, always end up solving only some of the problems. *Universal identity systems do not exist.*

But all is not lost for those hoping for a better online identity experience, reduced fraud, and increased functionality. The internet provides a useful analogy. Think of all the ways messages are exchanged online: email, instant messaging, web pages, and video are just the more familiar ways that the internet facilitates the flow of messages between computers. But the internet is not a universal messaging system. Each of these message types has a different form and purpose. Rather, the internet is a system for building messaging systems on a common infrastructure. Similarly, protocols and standards can provide us with a *system for building identity systems*.

The Road Ahead

Learning digital identity requires that you understand important concepts and context, so you begin to think about identity holistically. Accordingly, the first part of this book deals with definitions of, problems concerning, and laws governing digital identity. Next you will learn about relationships, trust, privacy, and cryptography—concepts necessary for the discussions that follow.

The second part of this book describes the technologies, methodologies, and protocols necessary for digital identity. These include staples like naming, discovery, authentication, federation, and access control.

The third part of the book presents cryptographic identifiers, verifiable credentials, architectural patterns for digital identity systems, identity wallets and agents, and identity on the Internet of Things. We'll compare solutions, using concepts we developed early on, and see how different architectures are used to build identity systems that support authentic data and trustworthy online relationships.

Finally, I'll discuss policies and governance, two crucial concepts for building identity systems—and ecosystems—that work. I'll conclude with a look at how the concepts, protocols, technologies, and architectures discussed in the book can provide a foundation for digital identity that enables lifelike online interactions in preparation for a digital future we can live with.

CHAPTER 2

Defining Digital Identity

The family therapist Salvador Minuchin declared, "The human experience of identity has two elements: a sense of belonging and a sense of being separate."[1] This is as good a description of digital identity as it is of our psychological identity. A digital identity contains data that uniquely describes a person or thing but also contains information about the subject's relationships to other entities.

To see an example of this, consider the data record that represents your car, stored somewhere in your state or country's computers. This record, commonly called a title, contains a vehicle identification number (VIN) that uniquely identifies the car. In addition, it contains other attributes of the car such as year, make, model, and color. The title also contains relationships: most notably, the title relates the vehicle to a person who owns it.[2] In many places, the title is also a historical document, because it identifies every owner of the car from the time it was made, as well as whether it's been in a flood or otherwise salvaged.

While fields as diverse as philosophy, commerce, and technology define identity, most are not helpful in building, managing, and using digital identity systems. Instead, we need to define identity functionally, in a way that provides hooks for us to use in making decisions and thinking about problems that arise in digital identity.

Joe Andrieu, principal at Legendary Requirements, writes that "identity is how we recognize, remember, and respond to specific people and things. Identity systems acquire, correlate, apply, reason over, and govern information assets of subjects,

---

1 Salvador Minuchin, *Families and Family Therapy* (Cambridge, MA: Harvard University Press, 2009), 47.

2 We'll discuss how digital relationships are supported by digital identity in detail in Chapter 5.

identifiers, attributes, raw data, and context."[3] This definition is my favorite because it has proven useful over the years in thinking through thorny identity issues. I'll use it throughout the book.

The identity record for a car includes attributes that the system needs to recognize it: in this case, the VIN. The title also includes attributes that are useful to people and organizations who care about (that is, need to *respond* to) the car, including the owner, the state, and potential buyers. The government runs a system for managing titles that is used to create, manage, transfer, and govern vehicles (or, in Andrieu's formulation, *remember* them). The system is designed to achieve its primary goal (to record valuable property that the state has an interest in taxing and regulating) and secondary goals (protecting potential buyers and creating a way to prove ownership).

Digital identity management consists of processes for creating, managing, using, and eventually destroying digital records, like the one that contains your car title. These records might identify a person, a car, a computer, a piece of land, or almost anything else. Sometimes they are created simply for inventory purposes, but the more interesting ones are created with other purposes in mind: allowing or denying access to a building, the creation of a file, the transfer of funds, and so on. These relationships and the authorized actions associated with them make digital identities useful, valuable, and sometimes difficult to manage.

The Language of Digital Identity

The world of digital identity has its own nomenclature. Most of the terms are familiar but are used in specific ways. This section introduces some of that terminology.

A *subject* is a person, organization, software program, machine, or other thing in some record. One of the key purposes of an identity system is to *authenticate* that the subject is who they claim to be and *authorize* requests to access a resource. A *resource* might be a web page, a piece of data in a database, or even a credit card transaction. To gain access to the resource, the subject lays claim to an *identity record*. For people, this is usually called an *account*. Throughout this book, I'll use the word *entity* to generically refer to the subject of an identity record, such as people, places, things, and organizations.

I dislike using words like *subject* or *user* when speaking about people if it can be avoided. I think many of the problems we have with online privacy and surveillance are in part the result of technologists dehumanizing the people for whom they're building systems. Similarly, I dislike when people use the word *identity* when what they really mean is an account, identity record, or identifier. The problem is that *identity* means

---

3 Joe Andrieu, "Five Mental Models of Identity" (*https://oreil.ly/eAmS8*), Rebooting the Web of Trust 7, accessed January 27, 2022.

many things. We're better off being accurate in what we're talking about. Your account at Amazon isn't your identity. Your identity is much more complex and nuanced than what can be recorded in a single database record, or even a collection of them. So, while there are identity systems, records, accounts, and so on, there's really nothing that is "an identity."

In this context, an identity record is a collection of data about a subject that represents attributes, preferences, and traits:

Attributes
Attributes describe information about a subject, specifically of characteristics that are acquired. For a person this might include a drug allergy, purchase, bank balance, credit rating, dress size, age, and so on.

Preferences
Preferences represent desires and defaults such as preferred seating on an airline, favorite brand of hot dog, encryption standard used, default currency, and so on.

Traits
Like attributes, traits are features of the subject, but they are inherent rather than acquired. Attributes may change at any time, but traits change slowly, if at all. Examples of traits include a person's eye color or how and where a company was incorporated.

Since the distinction between attributes, preferences, and traits rarely makes a difference in the design of an identity system, I'll typically use the term *attributes* to mean all three unless there's a specific need to distinguish among them.

One of the primary purposes of an identity system is to authorize specific actions. This process is shown in Figure 2-1 and is broken down as follows:

1. To use an identity record to justify accessing a resource, a requester must present an *identifier* and authentication factors along with the request. *Authentication factors* are proof that a subject has the right to assert that they control a particular identifier. Authentication factors can take many forms, including a simple username and password, an X.509 certificate, cryptographic artifacts, or biometrics.

2. A *policy enforcement point* (PEP) receives the request and authentication factors. The PEP is whatever system is responsible for receiving and processing the request. The PEP authenticates the factors, perhaps using a separate authentication server. *Authentication*, as the name suggests, establishes the authenticity of the factors. Identity architects will choose the appropriate level of authentication based on the risk that attends accessing the resource and the confidence needed about the authenticity of the request. If the authentication server is run by another organization, it is typically called an *identity provider* and the PEP is called the *relying party*.

3. Once the identifier and factors are authenticated, the PEP makes an *access request* to an access control system called the *policy decision point* (PDP). The request includes an identifier for the requested resource and for the requester.

4. The PDP retrieves the *security policy* for the resource, which could be a machine-readable document of some kind or just a chunk of code that encodes the policy.

5. The PDP uses the policy and information from the identity record associated with the asserted identifier to access an *account store*. The account store associates identifiers with attributes. The sets of attributes for a given identifier are sometimes called *claims* since they are statements about the entity to whom the identifier refers. The PDP uses the attributes and security policy to determine the entitlements and permissions for this request. *Entitlements* are the services and resources to which an identity is allowed *access*, such as a credit limit, disk space, or bandwidth allocations. *Permissions* are the actions that the requester is allowed to perform with respect to the resource, such as withdrawing funds, completing a purchase, or updating a record. Again, the specifics of how this is done vary from system to system; the entitlements and permissions might be hardcoded or dynamically determined.

6. When the PDP transfers this information back to the PEP, it does so in an *authorization decision assertion* (ADA). Depending on the systems architecture, the ADA might range from a simple Boolean value returned from a function call to a structured JavaScript Object Notation (JSON) or XML document containing not only the decision ("yes" or "no") but also justifications for the decision.

7. The PEP allows or denies the access, depending on the contents of the ADA.

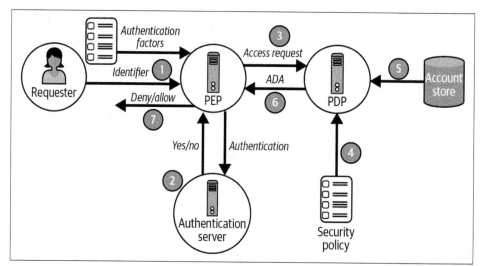

Figure 2-1. The interaction between policy enforcement points and policy decision points

The PEP, authentication server, and PDP may be separate systems or just functions in a single system, depending on how complex the digital identity infrastructure is, but it generally will perform all these functions.

Identity Scenarios in the Physical World

The concepts and words I used in the last section can seem intimidating, but most are perfectly understandable given our everyday experience in the physical world. To see how, consider a common transaction: buying beer at a US convenience store.

When a customer (the subject or entity) wants to buy beer (perform an action on a resource), they are required to submit proof that they are of legal drinking age, usually by presenting a driver's license. A driver's license is a *credential* containing claims asserting that the subject has certain attributes and traits and permissions that authorize the holder to drive a car (perform an action). The clerk (PEP) examines the license to see if it looks real (determines the authenticity and validity of the credential) and uses the picture (embedded biometric authentication factor) to see if the person presenting the license is the same person who owns it (authenticates the license). Once certain that the license is authentic and is being presented by the person to whom it was issued, the clerk reads the birth date (an attribute) from the license and determines whether the person is over 21 (consults a security policy determined by the state and makes a policy decision about permissions associated with the identity for a particular resource).

Now, suppose the person pays with a credit card (a separate identity credential). The clerk has just seen the driver's license and thus can establish the validity of this credential by matching the name on it to the name on the driver's license (attribute matching). The clerk runs the card through the point-of-sale terminal, which transmits to the bank the cardholder's name, credit card number, and expiration date (identity attributes) and requests credit (authorization request) in the amount necessary to buy the beer (the resource to be accessed). The bank (PDP) determines whether the customer is entitled to credit in the necessary amount and sends a credit authorization (ADA). Upon receiving this, the clerk completes the transaction.

In later chapters, I'll discuss these terms and processes in detail and see how they apply in less familiar scenarios.

Identity, Security, and Privacy

Digital identity is sometimes thought of as a subtopic of computer or information security. Certainly, digital identity is an important foundation for security, but it has greater utility than just protecting information. I've already discussed how digital identity enables important relationships. At the same time, information security is about more than authorization and authentication. The goal of information *security* is to protect information from unauthorized access, destruction, or alteration. Firewalls, for example, provide security but are not necessarily about identity.

The concept of *privacy* commonly holds that a subject (usually a person more often than an organization) should have the freedom to determine how information about them is collected and used. The relationship is circular: privacy is built upon a foundation of good information security, which depends on a good digital identity infrastructure. This relationship is shown in Figure 2-2.

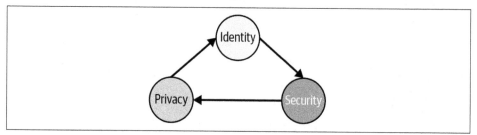

Figure 2-2. The identity–security–privacy triangle

Chapter 8 provides a more detailed and nuanced discussion of privacy than the one given above. Information security, beyond the concepts that it has in common with identity, is beyond the scope of this book.

Digital Identity Perspectives

We usually speak of identity in the singular, but subjects, especially people, have multiple identities. From an internal point of view, these seem like different facets of our singular identity, but other entities have a specific view that corresponds to only a subset of our internal view. For example, my bank sees a certain set of attributes for me: my credit card numbers, account numbers, credit score, and so on. My employer sees a different subset that overlaps only in a few points, such as name, Social Security number, and the bank account I give my employer for depositing my paycheck.

My multiple identities represent different perspectives on who Phil Windley is and what attributes I possess. Most of these attributes are stored in various formats in myriad databases. When I was chief information officer (CIO) for the State of Utah, I learned that the state government had over 250 different databases in which portions of my digital identity might be stored, depending on the specific relationship that database was meant to support. These multiple identities, or *personas*, as they are sometimes called, are tied together by a few common data elements (called *correlating attributes*). These systems use correlating attributes—my name, address, Social Security number, and birthday—as keys for accessing them, however imperfectly.

Tiers of Identity

Andre Durand, the founder and CEO of Ping Identity, introduced the concept of "tiers of identity" back in 2002.[4] Figure 2-3 shows a schematic of three tiers. At the bottom is Tier 1, labeled "My Identity." Tier 1 consists of traits associated with the subject that are both timeless and unconditional: my name is Phillip John Windley, I have blue eyes, and so on.

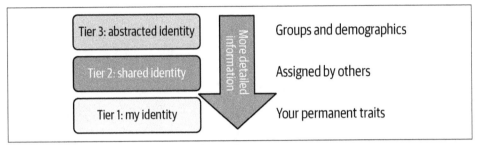

Figure 2-3. Identity tiers and their relationship

Tier 2, labeled "Shared Identity," consists of attributes assigned to us by others. These attributes are shared because they are used to identify the individual but are issued temporarily based on some kind of relationship. Your wallet is filled with Tier 2 identities: your driver's license, your employee badge, your credit card, your health insurance card, and your library card are all examples of identity information that is assigned to you. Once the relationship that defines the identity is terminated, the attributes associated with it are no longer useful.

The topmost layer, Tier 3, "Abstracted Identity," establishes group identity. For example, I could be identified as "Utahn," "white male over 60," or a member of any number of other demographic groups. Companies may classify me as a "frequent flier" or a "first-time customer." All these groupings identify me in some way, but only abstractly. Tier 3 is largely about marketing.

Tier 2 identity relationships may happen with your consent or not, but most are welcome because they are based on a relationship that probably has value to you. Tier 3 relationships, on the other hand, are usually forced on us. For example, email spam is a Tier 3 identity issue, as are telephone solicitations and even TV advertisements. Online surveillance (a topic I'll return to in Chapter 8) is one of the defining realities of the modern Web 2.0 experience. Tier 3 identities are inaccurate, imprecise, and nonspecific, so they rarely meet a real need for their subjects, for whom the benefit is so small as to be inconsequential. Most people perceive Tier 3-based relationships as

---

4 Andre Durand, "Three Tiers of Identity" (*https://oreil.ly/xreyT*), *Digital ID World*, March 16, 2002.

bothersome and resent them. However, companies realize significant benefit from such relationships and invest large amounts of money collecting and managing them.

Locus of Control

Another way to view digital identity is in terms of its *locus of control*—who or what controls the relationship. Control has several factors, including:

- Who initiates the relationship?
- Who owns the identifier (in other words, who can take it away)?
- Who sets the rules governing interactions?
- Who determines how attributes are shared?

Figure 2-4 shows this dimension, arraying three broad categories along the axis of the degree of *autonomy* that the identity system provides participants.

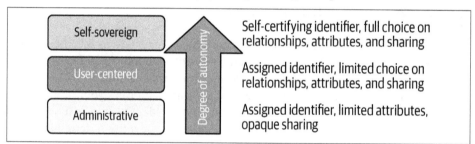

Figure 2-4. Sovereignty and autonomy

At the bottom of the diagram, with the lowest level of autonomy, is a category I call *administrative*. The vast majority of identity systems in use today are administrative, built and operated for the purpose of an organization. The organization determines its system's rules of operation, what attributes are allowed, how they are used, and whether and where they can be shared. Often the sharing is opaque, with the person who is the subject having little insight into how the identity system is being used or by whom.

In 2004, with the rise of Web 2.0 and its seemingly insatiable appetite for accounts, identity professionals began talking about identity systems, called *user-centered*, that would give people a higher degree of autonomy (the middle category of Figure 2-4). From those discussions, protocols such as OpenID and OAuth were born. These gave rise to *social login*, the ability to federate an account from one service, often a social media account, to another. Using your Twitter account to login to Medium is an example of this. Social logins are *user-centric* because the person chooses what account to use (from a small list) and is redirected from the *relying party* (such as Medium) to the *identity provider* (in this case Twitter) to approve the account sharing. Autonomy is limited in this model because the acceptable identity providers are chosen by the relying party, and the account being used as the foundation (Twitter) is still administrative, with all the limits that implies.

Since 2015, many people have been building a new model called *self-sovereign identity* (SSI). In contrast to administrative and user-centered identity systems—with the basis for the relationship being identifiers and interactions dictated by one side—parties in an SSI-based relationship exchange identifiers that can be mutually authenticated using cryptographic means. This relationship provides a trustworthy channel for exchanging protocol-mediated messages that can be tailored to the needs of the interaction.

The word *sovereign* can cause confusion, since most people either associate it with foreign affairs and nation-states or assume it means "the individual has complete control." Neither meaning is correct in this context. Sovereignty is about relationships and boundaries (discussed more in Chapter 5). When we say a nation is sovereign, we mean that it can act as a peer to other sovereign states, not that it can do whatever it wants. Sovereignty defines a boundary, within which the sovereign has complete control and outside of which the sovereign relates to others within established rules and norms (what we call *protocol* in technology).

SSI describes the same situation. An SSI system defines what the entity (person or organization) can control, along with rules of engagement for its relations with other entities. For example, an SSI system might give entities complete control over what attributes they share in response to queries about them. But sovereignty doesn't mean that a party relying on an attribute has to accept it. The relying party's sovereignty allows it to determine what attributes satisfy its demands and which don't. But sovereignty means that all powers are reciprocal: anyone can reject the claims others choose to present to them. The key to sovereignty is that all entities are peers. All parties to a relationship have the same powers and rights. The beauty of sovereignty isn't complete and total control but rather a situation where both parties have autonomy about what they request, share, and consent to.

Throughout this book, I'll come back to autonomy and discuss how different architectures support differing degrees of sovereignty.

Reimagining Decentralized and Distributed

Identity systems have specific topologies that affect their properties. I teach a course at Brigham Young University every year called "Large-Scale Distributed Systems." As I discuss distributed-system topologies with the class, there are always questions about *distributed* systems versus *decentralized* systems. The diagram shown in Figure 2-5 was used by Paul Baran of RAND Corp. in 1962 to explain centralized, decentralized, and distributed systems.[5] The diagram is frequently reproduced in articles and presentations on decentralization, and it always strikes me as an attempt to place the ideas of centralized, decentralized, and distributed computing on some kind of continuum.

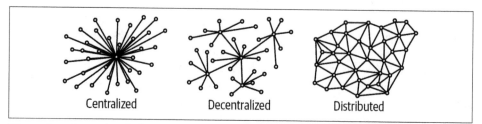

Figure 2-5. Centralized, decentralized, and distributed systems on a continuum

I prefer to use the term *decentralized* as the researcher Rohit Khare does: to describe systems that are under the control of different entities and thus can't be coordinated by fiat.[6]

Plenty of systems are distributed *and* under the control of a single entity. Almost any large Web 2.0 service will be hosted from different data centers, for example. What distinguishes the internet, email, and other distributed systems is that they are also designed to work across organizational boundaries. There's no central point that controls everything.

Consequently, I propose a new way of thinking about this, shown in Figure 2-6, that substitutes a two-dimensional graph for the linear one in Figure 2-5.

Figure 2-6 classifies systems along two axes:

Location
> The location axis determines whether the components are *colocated* or *distributed*. This could be either physical or logical depending on the context and level of abstraction.

Control
> The control axis determines whether the components are under the control of a single entity or multiple entities. A central control point could be logical or abstract, so long as it can effectively coordinate nodes in the system.

---

5 Paul Baran, *On Distributed Communications Networks*, RAND Corp. Report P-2626, September 1962.

6 Rohit Khare, "Extending the REpresentational State Transfer (REST) Architectural Style for Decentralized Systems" (*https://oreil.ly/Ec5-v*) (PhD diss., University of California, Irvine, 2003), accessed April 11, 2022.

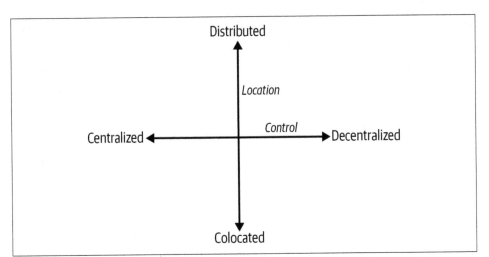

Figure 2-6. A two-dimensional conceptualization of the relationship between location and control in computer systems

We could extend this with a third axis that classifies systems by topology, as shown in Figure 2-7. In a *hierarchical* system, nodes are distinguished by superior-inferior relationships; in a *heterarchical* system, nodes have peer relationships.

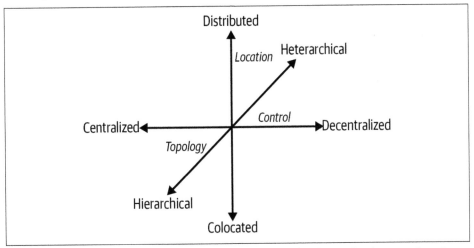

Figure 2-7. A three-dimensional conceptualization of the relationship between location, control, and topology in computer systems

To help you understand this distinction, here are a few examples of well-known systems and which octant of the graph they fall into:

- A supercomputer is usually centralized, colocated (due to latency issues), and hierarchical.
- DNS is a decentralized, distributed, hierarchical system (see Chapter 10).
- Facebook's Open Graph is a centralized, distributed, heterarchical system.

I will use these terms often as I discuss digital identity system architectures.

A Common Language

The language of digital identity helps us talk about the goals, operations, and outcomes of identity systems in ways that ensure accurate communication. Throughout the rest of this book, I'll use this language to discuss various identity architectures.

CHAPTER 3

The Problems of Digital Identity

Fixing the internet's identity problem is hard. Because the internet is missing an identity layer, every website, service provider, and application has solved the problem in a unique way. As a result, people are subject to cognitive overload, friction, increased costs, loss of privacy, and even outright fraud. Innovators have proposed numerous systems, protocols, and standards over the past 20 years. While most of them fixed specific issues, none has offered a holistic solution.

Several years ago, I attended a presentation by Andy Tobin of Evernym (now Gen Digital) in which he enumerated five problems (*https://oreil.ly/59RxN*) that make digital identity more difficult than identity in the physical world. I've since added a few to Andy's list. In this chapter we'll consider the differences between identity online and in the physical world to understand why digital identity is so difficult. In Chapter 4, we'll consider laws (in the sense of "laws of physics") that can help us design systems to overcome these problems.

Tacit Knowledge and the Physical World

Perhaps the most significant difference between the physical and the digital world is that our knowledge of the natural world is mostly tacit, while all our knowledge in the digital world is explicit.[1] In *The Tacit Dimension* (University of Chicago Press), Michael Polanyi describes the idea of tacit knowledge with a simple statement: "We can know more than we can tell." For example, we know how we walk, talk, ride a bike, and drive a car, but we cannot really explain the exact mechanisms we use to do

---

[1] I'm grateful to Doc Searls for a detailed conversation about this topic and his deep thinking about why it matters in understanding the problems of digital identity.

any of these—at least, not in the detail necessary to transfer those capabilities to someone else. They must learn them for themselves.

In the digital world, however, all the detail necessary to complete any task needs to be laid out and subjected to the logic of programming. This difference is profound and hard to explain, because we call the physical world "real" and the digital world "virtual." Consequently, we understand and operate in the physical world tacitly, but in the digital world we must make everything explicit.

When we walk down a street or go into a store, we have a clear tacit understanding that everyone we encounter is both real and named in some way, but anonymous—literally, nameless—to us (unless we happen to already know them). But this anonymity doesn't prevent us from recognizing, remembering, and reacting to others because we tacitly form an identifier for them of some sort (we can't explain it of course).

Staying anonymous until another party needs to know more about us is a grace of civilization. Being able to "recognize, remember, and react" is also an exercise of tacit knowing for which the explicit remains optional until it's required. That region of optionality—a tacit one—is why it would be absurd and creepy for everyone to walk around with a name badge, or to constantly present others with everything about us: our driver's license, birth certificate, tax records, habits, recent locations, or other facts that have become objects of extreme curiosity for online systems. Online surveillance has become controversial as well because that level of curiosity is at extreme variance from our experience of the physical world. In the physical world, we use long-standing assumptions, traditions, and other norms to maintain civil society, all of them based on tacit knowledge of how things are: knowledge that mostly goes unexplained but is well understood. Again, we know more than we can tell.

But *telling is required in the virtual world*, which needs explicit statements of what is so and what is not. Digital identity systems attempt to do that, but it is not easy, as we will see. Let's explore some problems that we need to solve.

The Proximity Problem

Proximity is the primary problem digital identity systems must contend with. The proximity problem is as old as the familiar *New Yorker* cartoon by Peter Steiner that says, "On the Internet, nobody knows you're a dog."

Recall that our functional definition of *identity* is the ability to recognize, remember, and respond to (or interact with) some entity. As embodied beings we are equipped to recognize people, things, and places using our senses. We naturally, and tacitly, remember them for later use and can react to or interact with them using our bodies or devices under our control.

Online, we possess none of the familiar sensory signals for knowing others because we are interacting with them virtually and at a distance. To cope, organizations have built *administrative identity systems* that serve their own narrow needs for identifying and recalling data about their customers, employees, or citizens. But the reverse is not true. People lack capabilities for knowing others online except in the fragmented ways allowed by organizations and their platforms.

The Autonomy Problem

As a result of our dependence on administrative identity systems, we lack the autonomy we possess in physical interactions as embodied beings. This isn't to say we act without limits, but that we largely interact with other entities independently, without having to be inside some administrative system. One way to think about autonomy is to imagine boundaries. Autonomy implies that there is some realm within which you can act independently—without another's permission.

People have limited autonomy, very few natural rights, and little leverage in current online identity solutions because each organization builds its administrative identity system for its own convenience, making design choices to maximize the legibility of people for its purposes and skewing the balance of power in its favor. The result is that people have nowhere to stand online. We are not *digitally embodied*. Almost every interaction we have online is intermediated by some organization's identity system and controlled by its rules—we are always within someone else's realm, never our own. We exist online through their grace.

This lack of autonomy means that people often cannot solve problems on their own in the ad hoc ways people solve problems in the physical world. Consequently, we cannot operationalize our digital existence and become full-fledged participants in the digital realm like we do in the physical.

The Flexibility Problem

Closely related to the autonomy problem is one of flexibility. The creators of current digital identity systems usually have very narrow purposes in mind. Many of the identity solutions in use today are limited by fixed schema or attribute sets. For example, GOV.UK Verify (*https://oreil.ly/Rd1PU*) is a universal identity assurance system for UK citizens, but it has a limited data set. And it's impossible for GOV.UK to reasonably expand the schema to cover all use cases (relationship types), even if it were inclined to do so. There are simply too many.

Our real lives are messy. Billions of people have trillions of separate relationships. This requires extreme flexibility. We are infinitely diverse, as are our circumstances. None of us presents the same picture of ourselves to everyone or every organization because each of our relationships is unique and our identities are fluid. The methods that we use to recognize, remember, and respond to others depend highly on context.

The Consent Problem

Also related to autonomy is the problem of consent. Not only do the operators of the various identity silos we are compelled to use collect our data, they also share it with others without our consent. Sometimes this is done in service of the *subject*, but often it's done to further the bottom line of the organization that controls the identity system.

We can have consent problems in the physical world as well, but two things limit their extent. First, data collection and surveillance are harder to do. Second, robust legal frameworks have been developed over centuries about how information collected in the physical world can be used. Consent is another area where the physical world's reliance on largely tacit measures must give way to explicit measures in the digital one. The Internet of Things (IoT) further blurs the lines on consent and privacy issues as digital devices (such as cameras, microphones, doorbells, thermostats, and so on) intrude into physical spaces. Consent is an area where getting it right in the digital space could afford increased privacy in the physical space.

The Privacy Problem

Computers are very good at pattern matching. Consequently, identity has very different implications for online privacy than for interactions in the physical world. When you hand your driver's license or identity card to a bartender to establish your legal age, you would be surprised and perhaps disturbed if they could remember all the details on it such as your address and birth date. And imagine if they could remember not just your data but also that of every customer they ever encounter. Computers, on the other hand, can be programmed to retain a perfect record of all the information they encounter until their operators delete it. They can also be programmed to correlate information from multiple sources to assemble personal profiles that go well beyond data collected from any single encounter or any single correspondent.

Current digital identity systems rely on vast collections of data, often collected without a subject's knowledge (and thus consent). The data is replicated repeatedly in different systems, creating a global data ecosystem. Third parties use universal identifiers like Social Security numbers, national ID numbers, and phone numbers to correlate identity information, again without the person's knowledge. Universal identifiers are at the root of many privacy problems. We will return to privacy and discuss it in depth in Chapter 8.

The (Lack of) Anonymity Problem

Anonymity relates closely to privacy. In real life, we often interact with others—people, institutions, and things—with relative anonymity. Our relationships with them are *ephemeral*, lasting only for the life of the encounter. If I go to the store and buy a Coke with cash, no exchange of identity information is necessary. Even if I use a credit card, it's rarely the case that the entire transaction happens under the administrative authority of the identity system that the credit card represents. Only the financial part of the transaction takes place in that identity system. This is true of most interactions in real life.

In the physical world, as this chapter has discussed, we act as embodied, independent agents. Our physical presence and the laws of physics have a lot to do with our ability to tacitly function with workable anonymity across many domains. In contrast, in the digital world, very few meaningful transactions are done outside the reach of some administrative identity system. There are several reasons for this:

Continuity
> While web sessions can be pseudonymous, they are often correlated across multiple independent sessions and devices when we log in. This supports, for example, online shopping carts that persist not only across time but also on different devices.

Convenience
> So long as the customer is authenticating, the system might as well store additional information like addresses and credit card numbers so it can complete transactions without requiring that the customer enter the same information over and over.

Trust
> There are some actions that should be taken only by certain people, or by people in certain roles or with specific attributes. Once a shopping site has stored my credit card, for example, I ought to be the only one who can use it. Identity systems provide authentication mechanisms as the means of knowing who is at the other end of the wire so that the system knows what actions they're allowed to take. This places identifiers in context so they can be trusted.

Surveillance
> Unfortunately, identity systems also provide the means of tracking individuals across transactions for purposes of gathering data about them. This data gathering may be innocuous or nefarious, but there is no doubt that it is enabled by identity systems in use on the internet.

In real life, we do without identity systems for most things. You don't have to identify yourself to go to the theater to watch a movie, or log into some system to sit in a restaurant and have a private conversation with friends. Many of our in-person interactions are effectively anonymous because they are transient: the theater ticket-taker cares only that we have a ticket for the movie we want to see. Given the right design, many more online interactions could use such transient, ephemeral relationships than they do today.

The Interoperability Problem

Most human beings have a similar set of capabilities for recognizing, remembering, and interacting with other people, organizations, places, and things in the physical world. Consequently, I don't have to wonder if I'll be able to talk to my friend at lunch or place my order with the server.

Online, the situation is more complex. While some things—email is an excellent example—are functionally interoperable thanks to standards, protocols, and common code, others are not. There is no widely accepted messaging protocol, for example. Instead, the modern messaging experience is fragmented into dozens of different apps. Most of us have several of them.

Moreover, every app on your phone presents a different user experience and is largely independent of every other app. My wife, Lynne, recently called me and asked a seemingly innocuous question: "How do I share this video?" Ten years ago, the answer would have been easy: copy the URL and send it. But this question is much harder to answer now. To answer it, I first had to determine which app she was using and then, since I wasn't that familiar with it, open it and search through the user interface to find the share button.

Interoperability is important for more than identity, but the foundational nature of identity means that the lack of interoperability is acutely felt. With myriad identity silos, people are faced with inconsistent user experiences. More importantly, people can't carry context from system to system. A friend or colleague in one system might have a different identifier in another, making it hard to consistently recognize and remember our friends or colleagues from system to system.

The Scale Problem

There are 4.88 billion people online,[2] each with dozens, even hundreds, of relationships. There are also an estimated 12.3 billion devices on the IoT, each an active endpoint with its own connections. Experts expect that figure to increase by several

---

2 See "Digital Around the World" (*https://oreil.ly/Vn5ph*) from DataReportal, accessed November 15, 2021.

orders of magnitude. Consequently, a general-purpose identity system needs to account for many trillions of relationships between the many billions of people, organizations, and things that make up the online world. No single, centralized system can do this.

Digital identity currently relies on hubs of identity information. We log in using Facebook or Google—huge *identity providers*. But for every place that uses one of these big identity providers, there are dozens that will never use social login systems. Many businesses are leery of giving up control of their customer information to another business that might decide next week to change things up. I don't think it's any accident that this is the same concern that was holding back online services in the days of CompuServe and Prodigy.

Scale is easier to manage when the architecture is decentralized and is mediated by protocol. The internet scales because it uses an encapsulating protocol that allows anyone, anywhere to connect their local network to it and exchange packets with anyone else. Long-term answers to the scale problem of digital identity will require similar architectures.

Solving the Problems

Taken together, the problems of digital identity present the colossal design challenge that makes digital identity hard. They are at the root of many of the frustrations and harms people experience online. But they are not intractable. This book will present patterns, protocols, and systems for tackling these problems and creating digital identity systems that work. The next chapter describes a conceptual architecture and set of laws to guide our work.

CHAPTER 4

The Laws of Digital Identity

Solving the problems of digital identity discussed in the last chapter requires building something more abstract and general than the one-off, context-specific identity systems (the ones that give you an "ID") that we find on the internet today. Almost every identity system you use is *administrative*, meaning it was created for the operator's own administrative purposes. Being administrative, every one of these is different from every other one—giving you as many "IDs" as there are administrative systems to deal with. The world had a similar situation with networks in the 1980s, and we solved it with a *metasystem*, a system of other systems, that unified and transcended all the world's separate, independent, and exclusive networks. This metasystem is called the internet.

The internet is a monument to abstraction and generality. Rather than being a communications system, like the telephone, the internet is a communications metasystem: that is, a system for building communications systems. Using encapsulating protocols—TCP and IP—that give everybody and everything a single and simple way to communicate across all those separate networks, the internet provides a unifying structure. This allows anyone to create whatever system they need by defining protocols. These new protocols, riding on top of TCP/IP, may be proprietary or open, special- or general-purpose. Every new protocol adds a new kind of message that the internet can communicate, changing and enriching its nature. Yet because they are built on a common protocol, they can serve a specific niche without sacrificing the underlying interoperability or modularity.

Similarly, an identity layer for the internet must also be a metasystem. An *identity metasystem* is a collection of interoperable identity systems. The identity metasystem provides the necessary building blocks and protocols for anyone to build an identity system meeting their specific needs that is interoperable with other identity systems similarly built. An identity metasystem is a prerequisite for an online world where identity is as natural as it is in the physical world. As we'll see in later chapters, an identity metasystem removes friction, decreases cognitive overload, and makes online interactions more private and secure.

An Identity Metasystem

In 2005, Kim Cameron, Microsoft's chief identity architect, published "The Laws of Identity" (*https://oreil.ly/cjdgN*), a landmark paper laying out seven important principles for how digital identity should work. Cameron describes an identity metasystem that can provide the missing identity layer:

> Different identity systems must exist in a metasystem. It implies we need a simple encapsulating protocol (a way of agreeing on and transporting things). We also need a way to surface information through a unified user experience that allows individuals and organizations to select appropriate identity providers and features as they go about their daily activities. The universal identity metasystem must not be another monolith. It must be polycentric (federation implies this) and also polymorphic (existing in different forms). This will allow the identity ecology to emerge, evolve and self-organize.

From Cameron's description, we can identify six important features:

Encapsulating protocol

Protocols describe the rules for a set of interactions. Protocols are the foundation of interoperability and allow for scale. By defining how interactions happen, they mitigate the proximity problem. An encapsulating protocol allows other protocols to be defined on top of it. For example, the Internet Protocol (IP) is a protocol that encapsulates the User Datagram Protocol (UDP) and the Transmission Control Protocol (TCP). Thus, the encapsulating protocol enables a flexible set of interactions that can be adapted for specific contexts and needs and take place at a distance.

Unified user experience

Part of the beauty of the tacit nature of identity in the physical world is that we don't have to switch apps or learn an entirely new way of interacting for each context. Traditionally, digital identity systems have not offered this kind of consistency. A unified user experience doesn't mean a single user interface. Rather the focus is on the experience. Unified user experiences let people know what to expect. As a result, they can intuitively understand how to interact in any given context. Unified user experiences increase user autonomy, increase privacy, and support consent since users better understand the interaction.

User choice

By allowing people to select appropriate service providers and features, a metasystem allows for autonomy, anonymity, and flexibility. No single system can anticipate all the scenarios that come up as people live their lives. A metasystem allows context-specific scenarios to be built and can even support ad hoc interactions that no one anticipated.

Modular

An identity metasystem can't be a single, centralized system with limited pieces and parts. Rather, the metasystem will have interchangeable components that are built and operated by various parties. Protocols and standards enable this. Modularity is a prerequisite for substitutability and choice, as is interoperability.

Polycentric (decentralized)

An identity metasystem is decentralized to enable autonomy and flexibility and to support better privacy. No single system can anticipate all the various relationships. And no single actor should be allowed to determine who uses the system or for what purposes. Furthermore, decentralization gives the metasystem the ability to scale as needed.

Polymorphic (different data schema)

The information human beings and systems need to recognize, remember, and react to various people, organizations, places, and things is context-dependent and varies widely from one situation to the next. The content carried by an identity metasystem must be flexible to support these varied interactions and support user autonomy.

The internet is full of identity systems for specific contexts, designed to administer identity for a specific service or application. Over the past two decades, developers, security researchers, and identity experts have made numerous attempts to share identity information between different contexts. The success of these efforts has been limited to federating identity data between close partners or simple authentication efforts (such as Google Sign-in). None has developed into a unifying metasystem with these properties, because they can't. Cameron's Laws of Identity help us explore why that is so and give us important design principles to follow in building an identity metasystem.

The Laws of Identity

The Laws of Identity describe seven objectives that an identity system must meet to function as a metasystem. A system meeting these seven laws can be widely accepted and used in many contexts. Each law gives rise to architectural principles that guide the construction of the metasystem. Understanding the laws can help eliminate a lot of bad designs before architects and engineers waste too much time on them. They can also be used to evaluate real-world identity systems. Chapter 22 will discuss the concept of *legitimacy* and how the Laws of Identity, along with governance and policy for an identity system, provide a basis for how broadly the system is adopted.

In writing about these, Cameron uses the word *law* in the scientific sense of a hypothesis about the world resulting from observation that can be tested.[1] Testing the laws involves using them to evaluate the successes and failures of identity systems. They are not *propositions* (proven from first principles) or *axioms* (self-evident truths). They are not legal or moral laws. Neither are they philosophical.

The sections that follow discuss the seven laws individually. Each starts with a statement of the law in italics, as defined in Cameron's paper.

User Control and Consent

Technical identity systems must only reveal information identifying a user with the user's consent.

—Kim Cameron, "The Laws of Identity"

In recent years, the idea of giving people more control over their digital identity has come to be known as *self-sovereign identity* (SSI), as I discussed in Chapter 2. Recall that SSI implies autonomy. Moreover, sovereignty is *inalienable*, meaning that it can't be transferred to another, taken away, or denied. To be inalienable is to be sovereign: to exercise supreme authority over one's personal sphere. Administrative identifiers— what others choose to call us—are alienable. Relationships are alienable. Many attributes are alienable. Who we are (our *substance*, as I called it in Chapter 1), and our right to choose how we present ourselves to the world, is inalienable. The distinction between the inalienable and the alienable, the self-sovereign and the administrative, is essential. Without this distinction, we are constantly at the mercy of the various administrative regimes we interact with.

Other labels, like *decentralized, user-centric*, and *self-managed*, have been used to describe systems that give users control, but one can imagine decentralized, user-centric, or self-managed systems that do not provide autonomy, privacy, or other desired features. None of these terms necessarily implies autonomy—the person acting for themselves. *Self-sovereign* does not suffer from those limitations.

An identity metasystem creates boundaries of control, assigns control over various activities to different roles, and distinguishes between the alienable and inalienable. *User control* creates the digital boundary between an entity and all those who observe that entity, as well as a center where all attributes, relationships, and information about an entity can be housed.

---

1 He also sometimes joked that by calling them "laws" he could outmaneuver lawyers and risk managers, who had an inherent respect for something called a law.

Minimal Disclosure for a Constrained Use

> The solution which discloses the least amount of identifying information and best limits its use is the most stable long-term solution.
>
> —Kim Cameron, "The Laws of Identity"

Hardly a week goes by without news of a data loss at a major organization that threatens the identity information of hundreds of thousands, even millions, of people. The bad news is that data breaches are a fact of life. We'll likely never get rid of them completely. The good news is that the amount and sensitivity of the data lost is something we can control.

Organizations often overcollect data about people and store it on the premise that it might be needed at some point. Even the data they do need could be reduced with an identity metasystem that makes the "just in time" transfer of data less onerous.

An identity metasystem can't stop organizations from overcollecting data or storing it beyond when it's needed. That's an organizational policy and, increasingly, a regulatory issue. But the metasystem can support minimal disclosure and make it simple to get data when it's needed, making it easier to argue for collecting less data.

Different types of information can be more identifying or less identifying. For example, a Social Security number (SSN) is more identifying than a one-off, unique identifier. Less identifying information is the least likely to identify an individual across several contexts. This information need not be just a single, highly correlatable identifier like an SSN but could be a collection of information that, taken together, can be used to identify an individual.

A good example is a system that needs to know a person's age. Traditionally such systems ask the person for their birthday, but they really only need to know the age. A birthday, when combined with information like zip code and gender, is more likely to be uniquely identifying than an age. The identity metasystem can make answering questions even less identifying by supporting the ability to answer questions like "Is this person over 21?" instead of "What is this person's age?" Asking questions in the form of predicates on attributes can significantly reduce the amount of information that is disclosed and how identifying that information is. There are orders of magnitude more people who are over 21 than there are who were born on any specific day.

Justifiable Parties

> Digital identity systems must be designed so the disclosure of identifying information is limited to parties having a necessary and justifiable place in a given identity relationship.
>
> —Kim Cameron, "The Laws of Identity"

Digital identity matters because people, organizations, and things need to have digital relationships with other people, organizations, and things. Clearly, everyone who is party to the relationship has a justifiable reason to know some things about others in the relationship. But not everything.

The law of minimal disclosure says that any information shared should be just what is needed and nothing more. The law of *justifiable parties* says these disclosures should be made only to entities who have a need to know. For example, suppose a dozen people are planning a party for Bob. If Alice needs to know Bob's age, minimal disclosure says she shouldn't ask him for his birthday. *Justifiable parties* says she should ask on a direct message channel, not in the group chat. Similarly, identity systems should be built so that only the parties who are involved in the transaction and have a need to know see the data that the system transmits.

With this law in mind, consider *social login*. When Alice logs into Bravo Corp's site using Google, Facebook, Apple, or some other service, she visits the website for Bravo Corp, the relying party (RP), and is redirected to, say, Google, the identity provider (IdP), where she logs in. (For a refresher on these terms, see Chapter 2. For more on social login, see Chapter 13.) The IdP sends a cryptographic token back to the RP, indicating Alice has provided the right credentials; it might also send back other identity data they have about Alice.

Do social logins break the law of justifiable parties? You could argue that the IdP is a justifiable party, since its authentication service is needed to complete the transaction. Clearly, Alice and the RP have consented to this arrangement, so we might consider that evidence that they see the IdP as a justifiable party.

Remember that one of the purposes of these laws is to inform identity system architectures and help us analyze where they might be effective and where they might be exploited, cause harm, or fail. In the social login scenario, the IdP doesn't just see that Alice is logging into Bravo Corp: it also knows about *everyone* who logs into Bravo Corp using its login service. They see many other places Alice logs into. Bravo Corp also learns something about Alice they don't necessarily need to know: that she has an account at Google. As a result, many people avoid social login and continue to use usernames and passwords where they can. They don't want the social login companies surveilling them.

Still, given its popularity, it would seem that social login has succeeded. But its use is far from universal. Regulated financial services companies, for example, do not use social login. I don't know all the reasons they might not want or be able to use it, but the foundational reason is that they don't consider the social login companies to be justifiable parties to the relationship they want to have with their customers.

An important implication of justifiable parties is that identity systems should make participants aware of the parties in any identity exchange. Social login does that—clearly—by redirecting the subject to the IdP. Some federated identity systems do not. Instead, they transfer information about the subject behind the scenes. This is sometimes called the "phone home" problem because the RP connects to the IdP directly. Meaningful user control requires the transparency implicit in the law of justifiable parties.

You also can't talk about justifiable parties without discussing ad networks—which, like almost everything online, are based on identity systems. At the heart of the ad network identity system is the *cookie*, a simple correlation identifier built into the HTTP protocol. A *correlation identifier* is a unique string that can be used to link requests. HTTP cookies are generated by the server and stored on the browser. Whenever the browser makes a request to the server, it sends back the cookie, allowing the server to correlate all requests from that browser. (Chapter 11 discusses cookies and correlation in greater depth.)

Consider how (simple) ad tracking works. When you see an ad on Acme Corp's website, it's being served from a server owned by an ad company that Acme Corp has an agreement with. The ad server plants a cookie in your browser. Now you visit Bravo Corp's website, which includes ads from the same ad server. Your browser dutifully reports the ad server cookie back to the ad server along with the information that the ad was on Bravo's website. The company running the ad server now knows you were on both sites (along with lots of other metadata). Rather than correlating requests on a single site, they are using cookies to correlate your activity across the web.

To get a feel for how pervasive ad tracking is, I recommend spending a few minutes with the Fou Analytics Page X-Ray (*https://oreil.ly/mVfSc*). Page X-Ray follows the cookies and trackers in a page to tell you more about how you're being tracked. If you x-ray *wired.com* (*https://oreil.ly/zBX1y*), for example, you'll see a massive amount of data sharing by trackers, cascading and fanning out across at least five layers consisting of hundreds of other parties—nearly all of which are involved in showing ads to that visitor. All these parties likely believe that their involvement is justifiable and involves minimal disclosure for a constrained use, but many people would disagree and are increasingly concerned with the impact ad networks have on online privacy.

Directed Identity

> A universal identity system must support both "omni-directional" identifiers for use by public entities and "unidirectional" identifiers for use by private entities, thus facilitating discovery while preventing unnecessary release of correlation handles.
>
> —Kim Cameron, "The Laws of Identity"

Identity systems depend on identifiers (discussed further in Chapter 10). Identifiers take many different forms, but the law of *directed identity* categorizes them into two types: omnidirectional and unidirectional. More commonly, we call these *public identifiers* and *peer or private identifiers*, respectively.

The value of a public identifier is that it is easily resolvable by anyone.[2] Public identifiers should be invariant and well known. In fact, their permanence is a feature. Public identifiers are designed to make it easy to discover information about the entity to which the identifier is bound.

URLs are the most common form of public identifier. They are based on DNS domain names, another common type of public identifier. Phone numbers and email addresses, alas, are also public identifiers. They too are relatively permanent, and most people like that they're invariant because of the huge hassle of informing all your contacts when they change.

On the other hand, the value of a peer identifier is that it is not public. Like any identifier, it still must be resolved to be used, but that resolution happens using some nonpublic system or method. Peer identifiers should not be reassignable, to avoid the confusion that can occur if they are reused, but they needn't be permanent. Many will be ephemeral.

A username (if it's not an email address) is an example of a peer identifier. You use it with a single site. Nothing requires that you use the same one everywhere; with a good password manager you could have a different username everywhere you go online. Of course, many sites will only let you use an email for a username.

Peer identifiers have significantly better privacy protection than public identifiers, since they don't leak correlatable information in every transaction. Many of the biggest privacy problems the world faces are rooted in universal identifiers like SSNs, phone numbers, national ID numbers, and so on.

Using public-key infrastructure (PKI) certificates to secure web connections is another example of an identity system with public identifiers (further discussed in Chapter 9). PKI certificates link an identifier to a public key. In this case, the

---

2 *Resolve* may seem like a funny word to use with identifiers. I'm using it as a general term because what you do with any given identifier depends a great deal on the context in which it is used.

identifier is the domain name in the certificate. Used in this way, certificates have proven to be a very successful identity system for organizations and websites.

On the other hand, PKI-based certificates for *people* have been a miserable failure. The person possessing the private key can use the PKI certificate to authenticate at websites or log into remote machines. Early web standards envisioned using certificates for authenticating at websites. The Netscape browser and web server supported this functionality. The expense of getting PKI certificates, which was quite high at the time, likely contributed significantly to the failure of this effort. But there was also significant concern over the privacy implications of people having one permanent identifier that they used all over the web.

Browser cookies are an interesting case. As we saw above, ad networks exploit cookies to surveil people as they use the web. An unintended consequence of the way HTTP cross-domain references and cookies work is that while they were intended to be peer identifiers, they ended up serving as public identifiers.

Cryptographic identifiers, like public keys, can function as peer identifiers if a new key pair is created for every relationship. This might seem daunting, but software can manage the keys, and recent developments in decentralized identifiers make management of large numbers of peer cryptographic identifiers easier. This makes directed identity much more feasible. Chapter 9 discusses public-private keys in detail and Chapter 15 discusses cryptographic identifiers.

Identifiers seem simple at first, but implementing them correctly can be difficult, as the case of cookies shows. Identity design can have a big impact on the usability, privacy, and flexibility of an identity system. An identity metasystem must support both public (omnidirectional) and peer (unidirectional) identifiers. In short, the law of directed identity tells us that the identity metasystem can't use a single, universal identifier.

Pluralism of Operators and Technologies

> A universal identity system must channel and enable the inter-working of multiple identity technologies run by multiple identity providers.
>
> —Kim Cameron, "The Laws of Identity"

The law of *pluralism of operators and technologies* tells us we need more than one identity system. The world is full of identity systems, each built for a specific context and purpose: Cameron refers to this as the "identity ecology."

At first this law might seem inconsistent with other laws, especially the law of *consistent experience across contexts*, which will be introduced later in this chapter. If users must have control and a consistent experience, irrespective of the identity context, doesn't that imply a ubiquitous and pervasive system? Resolving this dilemma requires that you understand the relationship between the identity metasystem and the identity systems built on it.

Recall that a metasystem has an encapsulating protocol upon which other protocols can be built. Further, the metasystem is decentralized and polymorphic, meaning it can carry different kinds of data. The identity metasystem provides a stable, universal base for building identity systems. Because it satisfies the Laws of Identity, the systems built on top of it satisfy them as well.

Passports, driver's licenses, national ID cards, employee badges, business licenses, credit cards, and professional licenses are all unique identity systems designed for a specific context to achieve a specific purpose. Thinking you could design just one system to replace all of these with some universal identity system would be ridiculous. But they all achieve user control and a consistent user experience because they use an underlying metasystem of sorts—the way credentials work in the physical world.

But we can go further than that. A movie ticket is an identity system. No, it doesn't identify *who* you are, but it does identify *what* you are: one of N people allowed to occupy a seat in a specific theater at a specific time. In this view, any venue ticketing system is an identity system. So are prescriptions, invoices, receipts, and systems for titling cars and land. Each is designed to identify someone or something and convey some right or record some transaction. And all of them use a common, underlying pattern to provide a consistent experience and user control.

Most organizations, even small businesses, design and deploy identity systems—even if they don't recognize that's what they're doing. Most of them are not digital. But as the internet comes to mediate more and more of our lives, many of them will be. An identity metasystem must support them all.

Human Integration

> The universal identity metasystem must define the human user to be a component of the distributed system integrated through unambiguous human-machine communication mechanisms offering protection against identity attacks.
>
> —Kim Cameron, "The Laws of Identity"

When I started the Internet Identity Workshop with Kaliya Hamlin and Doc Searls in 2005, the theme we chose was "user-centric identity." This was a shift; in the preceding years, identity discourse had primarily focused on enterprises and their internal needs, as organizations of all stripes felt the need to build identity solutions for their specific contexts. The term *user-centric* indicated a design philosophy that would swing the pendulum back in the other direction, integrating people and their needs with the identity systems they used.

Phishing attacks, fraud, complexity, and friction are the results of not considering how humans participate in an identity solution. Take phishing, for example. In a phishing attack, the intruder poses as a legitimate organization, application, or website to steal authentication factors such as usernames and passwords (see Chapter 11). Phishing doesn't attack the technical infrastructure of the identity system; it attacks the people using it. Phishing can happen over email, voice, Short Message Service (SMS), page hijacking, and even calendars. Quick response (QR) codes are sometimes used in phishing attacks where a legitimate QR code was simply stickered over with a fraudulent one.

QR code phishing is a good example of a common phishing technique: link manipulation. The manipulated links might be in web pages, emails, or SMS messages, but the idea is to make it look legitimate to fool the target into clicking on it. The new link usually leads to a page designed to look like the real thing but with some nefarious intent, like stealing a password, credit card numbers, or other personal information. Another kind of attack is social engineering, where phishers trick targets into thinking they need to take some action like revealing a password, passing on an access code, or even transferring funds.

Bad links, fake web pages, and con artists may not seem like the stuff of identity, but they happen because designs for identity systems often end at the computer screen and ignore the human component. The law of *human integration* says that designers need to extend their designs to consider how, when, and where people use identity.

As an example of where human-integrated design can mitigate this problem, consider web authentication. The usernames and passwords used for authentication are a primary attack vector in phishing. Web authentication reestablishes a session between the user's browser and the site over and over again. This constant need to reestablish sessions is confusing; most people view it as a complex process standing between them and what they want to do. That makes it a weak point that phishers can exploit. Identity systems could be designed to counter this by creating a mutually authenticated connection that is difficult for attackers to intercept. This takes a tricky and error-prone task away from human users and replaces it with a task that is easier to understand.

Human integration requires profoundly changing how people experience identity systems, making those systems predictable and unambiguous enough to support informed decisions. In short, the design of identity systems must take people into account to provide *good* experiences.

Consistent Experience Across Contexts

> The unifying identity metasystem must guarantee its users a simple, consistent experience while enabling separation of contexts through multiple operators and technologies.
>
> —Kim Cameron, "The Laws of Identity"

The law of *consistent experience across contexts* says that people's experiences should be *consistent* from context to context. Providing a consistent user experience makes up for the digital world's lack of tacit knowledge by allowing people to build up routines and muscle memory in its place. Designing a great user experience for one identity context is insufficient if you're then using a good but completely different one for a different identity context.

One of the most familiar examples of consistent user experience is the automobile. My grandfather, who died in 1955, could get in a 2022-model car and safely drive it with only a little instruction. The user experience (not just the interface) for a car is largely the same as it was 70 years ago. There are other examples, including email, the windowed user interface, and even the venerable QWERTY keyboard.

One of the underappreciated features of web browsers is the consistent user experience that they provide. Tabs, address bars, the back button, reloading, and other features are largely the same regardless of which browser you use. There's a reason why "Don't break the back button!" has been common advice for web designers over the years. People depend on the web's consistent user experience.

Alas, apps have changed all that by freeing developers from the strictures of the web. No doubt there have been some excellent uses of this freedom, but what we've lost is consistency in core user experiences. That's unfortunate. Moreover, the web—and the internet, for that matter—has never had a consistent user experience for authentication. (At least not one that has caught on.) Consequently, the user experience is very fragmented.

Anyone familiar with the modern world of websites and applications knows the subtle frustration of performing a slightly different authentication ceremony for each site or application you use. The username and password input boxes are in different places, perhaps behind a "Log In" button. The password box might not appear until the username is input. The rules around acceptable password length and characters can be maddeningly complex. The site might use multifactor authentication (MFA), but there's no consistency there: my phone has five MFA apps installed that I use regularly, in addition to sites that use SMS or email for MFA. And this is just for authentication.

You may not have thought about it as an identity-system design issue before, but anytime a website or application asks for information like your personal profile information, addresses, or even credit card information, you are transferring attributes—

identity data. Each of these interactions is different for every website and application. Even different applications from the same company often do it differently. Password managers have taken some of the sting out of these problems, but they are still frustrating. Worse, inconsistent user experience is the source of much of the fraud that is rife online.

The law of *consistent experience across contexts* is closely tied to the other laws and the metasystem, which must provide a single way for people to establish safe channels with other people, organizations, and things. The metasystem's encapsulating protocol provides a consistent method for requesting, selecting, and proffering identity information. Even though millions of individual identity systems might be built on top of the identity metasystem, the user experience in each is consistent because the metasystem is responsible for establishing safe channels where any kind of identity information can be exchanged.

There's a saying in security: "Don't roll your own crypto." I think we need a corollary in identity: "Don't roll your own interface." A consistent user experience helps ensure that consent is unambiguous and that the user knows which parties are participating in the exchange.

Fixing the Problems of Identity

An identity metasystem provides three primary capabilities that allow it to be used as the basis for building context-specific identity systems:

Relationships
> The metasystem provides a means for people, organizations, and things to have relationships with each other. These relationships are mutually authenticated, secure, and as private as possible for the use case.

Secure messaging
> The metasystem supports secure messaging between the parties to support relationships and allow them to confidently conduct identity transactions.

Trustworthy claim exchange
> The metasystem provides the means for parties that have relationships in the metasystem to use messaging to exchange polymorphic claims (messages about attributes) reliably, confidently, and securely.

Appropriately designed, a metasystem with these properties can conform to the seven laws and ensure that any identity system built on it does as well. An identity metasystem with the properties described above and designed to be consistent with the Laws of Identity provides the means to fix the problems of identity described in Chapter 3.

Let's look at how:

Proximity

Secure *claim exchange over a mutually authenticated channel* provides digital relationships that mitigate the problems caused when connections are distant.

Autonomy

A metasystem that conforms to the laws of *user control, minimal disclosure,* and *justifiable parties* gives participants autonomy by establishing boundaries and allowing each participant to create and manage secure relationships with other participants in the metasystem and ensures that the data is shared by choice.

Flexibility

A metasystem that is *decentralized, polymorphic,* and *modular* ensures that people and organizations can use the metasystem to build whatever context-specific identity system they need.

Consent

A metasystem that conforms to the laws of *user control and consent, justifiable parties, human integration,* and *consistent experience* ensures that people unambiguously know what they are sharing and with whom.

Privacy

A metasystem that provides *secure, mutually authenticated relationships* and conforms to the laws of *minimal disclosure* and *directed identity* provides the means for reducing correlation across contexts and minimizing the amount of data that is shared.

Anonymity

A metasystem that supports *trustworthy claim exchange* and conforms to the law of *minimal disclosure* and *directed identity* can create ephemeral relationships and share and needed data without revealing who is participating in a permanent way.

Interoperability

A metasystem with an *encapsulating protocol* and conforming to the laws of *pluralism of operators and technologies* and *consistent experience across contexts* allows people to share claims outside of a specific use case. Identity systems built on the metasystem interoperate through consistent technology and user experience.

Scale

A metasystem that is *decentralized* and built on an *encapsulating protocol* scales by supporting millions of identity systems for different contexts and allowing anyone to build the identity system they need without sacrificing security, privacy, or user experience.

The coming chapters will explore concepts that lie at the core of digital identity, technologies that underpin the implementation of identity systems, and architectures that conform to the laws of identity. Along the way, I'll also discuss existing identity protocols, standards, and systems and evaluate them with respect to the laws.

CHAPTER 5

Relationships and Identity

We typically don't think of it this way, but every interaction we have in the physical world, no matter for what purpose or how short, sets up a relationship. So too in the digital world, although our tools for creating and managing them have been sorely lacking.

One of my favorite scenarios for thinking about identity is meeting a friend for lunch:

> You arrive at the restaurant on time and your friend is nowhere to be found. You go to the host to inquire about the reservation. She tells you that your reservation is correct, and your friend is already there. She escorts you to the table, where you greet your friend. The host seats you and leaves you with a menu. Within a few moments, the server arrives to take your order. You ask a few questions about different dishes. You both settle on your order and the server leaves to communicate with the kitchen. You happily settle in to chat with your friend while your food is being prepared. Later you might get a refill on a drink or order dessert. Eventually you pay with a credit card.

While you, your friend, the host, and the server recognized, remembered, and interacted with other people, places, and things countless times during this scenario, at no time were you required to identify yourself as a particular person. Even paying with a credit card doesn't require that. Credit cards say something about you: *what* you are rather than *who* you are. And while it does show your name and that you have an account with a bank, the brilliance of the credit card is that you don't need to have accounts with every place where you want credit. You simply present a token that gives the merchant confidence that they will be paid.

Here are a few of the "whats" identified in this scenario:

- The host
- Your friend
- The table where your friend is sitting

- Your server
- An adult over 21
- Guest who ordered the medium-rare steak
- Someone who needs a refill
- Excellent tipper
- Person who owes $79.35
- Person in possession of a Mastercard

You don't need an account at the restaurant for any of this to work. But you do need relationships. Some, like your relationships with your friend and with your bank, are long-lived and identified (they know *who* you are). Most are ephemeral and pseudonymous. While the server certainly "identifies" patrons, they usually forget them as soon as the transaction is complete. And any identification the server does make is usually pseudonymous ("the couple at table three" rather than "Phil and Lynne Windley").

As I've discussed, in the digital realm we suffer from the problem of not being in proximity to those with whom we're interacting. As a result, we need a technical means to establish a relationship.

The reason we build identity systems isn't to manage identities but to support digital relationships. Identities are important, but they are not the end goal. Understanding the nature of digital relationships can help you understand the kinds of identity systems that will meet their members' goals.

Identity Niches

Depending on who you ask, the average person has between 100 and 300 online accounts. My own password manager has more than a thousand entries. Identity expert Steve Wilson states that using federation schemes to create a few identities that serve all purposes is deeply flawed.[1] His point is that we have so many identities because we have lots of relationships.

All of our online relationships have a common root, but they are highly contextualized. Some are long-lived; some are ephemeral. Some are personal, some are commercial or civic. Some are important, some are trivial. Still, we have them. We adapt the information we share about ourselves, what many refer to as *identity data*, to the specific niche of a relationship, just as Galápagos finches have famously adapted

---

1 Stephen Wilson, "Identities Evolve: Why Federated Identity Is Easier Said Than Done" (*https://oreil.ly/ QM3ZB*), (May 18, 2011). Available at SSRN.

(*https://oreil.ly/Jy9Ho*) to their niches in response to evolutionary pressure. Once you realize this, the idea of creating a few online identities to serve all needs seems preposterous.

Not only has each relationship evolved for a particular niche, but it is also still constantly changing. Often those changes are just more of what's already there: for example, my Netflix account represents a relationship between me and Netflix. It's constantly being updated with my viewing data, but its structure doesn't usually change dramatically. However, some changes are larger. Netflix also allows me to create additional profiles so I can specialize the relationship for different members of my household. And when Netflix moved from DVDs to streaming, the nature of our relationship changed significantly.

Identity systems like Google Sign-in, Apple Login, or Facebook Login—called *federated* identity systems and discussed further in Chapter 13—ignore this important fact, attempting to create one account that can be used across multiple contexts. Organizations attempt to outsource their identity systems by using federation. But this doesn't offer a complete solution, because while you can outsource authentication (is the right person logging in?), you can't outsource the relationship the account is meant to support. Consequently, even if they use federation to outsource the authentication, they still maintain accounts to service each relationship.

Because you're not physically interacting with people in online transactions, your natural means of knowing who you're dealing with are useless. Recall our functional definition of identity as being how we recognize, remember, and respond to another entity. These activities correspond to three properties digital relationships must have to overcome the problems of digital identity:

Integrity
  We want to know that, from interaction to interaction, we're dealing with the same entity as before. In other words, we want the interaction to be secure and authentic.

Life span
  Sometimes we want relationships to be long-lived and identified. At other times, we create ephemeral, pseudonymous relationships for short-lived interactions.

Utility
  We create online relationships to use them within a specific context for specific purposes.

I'll discuss each of these in detail below.

Relationship Integrity

Without integrity, you cannot recognize the other party to the relationship. Consequently, all identity systems manage relationship integrity as a foundational capability. Federated identity systems improve on one-off, often custom identity systems by providing integrity in a way that reduces account management overhead for the organization, increases convenience for the person, and increases security.

A simple relationship has two parties: let's call them Alice and Bob. Alice is connecting with Bob; as a result, Alice and Bob have a relationship. Alice and Bob could be people, organizations, or things represented by a website, app, or service. (I'll treat them as people for this example.) Recognizing the other party in an online relationship means you know that you're dealing with the same entity each time you encounter them (or it).

In a typical administrative identity system, when Alice initiates a relationship with Bob, Bob's system uses usernames and passwords to ensure the integrity of the relationship. By asking for a username to identify Alice and a password to ensure that it's the same Alice as before, Bob has some assurance that he is interacting with Alice. In this model, Alice and Bob are not peers. Rather, Bob controls the system and determines how and for what it is used, the factors it requires for authentication, and what happens to the data it collects.

In federated identity systems, as you learned in Chapter 2, Alice is usually called the *subject* or *requester* and Bob is called the *relying party* (RP). When a requester visits the RP's site or opens an app, they are offered the opportunity to establish a relationship through an *identity provider* (IdP) whom the RP trusts—say, Google, Apple, or Facebook. The requester may or may not have a relationship with one of those IdPs. RPs pick well-known IdPs with large numbers of users to reduce friction in signing up. The requester chooses which IdP they want to use from the relying party's menu and is redirected to the IdP's identity service, where they authenticate to the IdP and are redirected back to the RP. As part of this flow, the RP gets some kind of token from the IdP that signifies that the IdP will vouch for this person. They may also get attributes that the IdP has stored for the consumer.

In the federated model, the IdP is identifying the person and attesting to the integrity of the relationship to the RP. The IdP is a third party acting as an *intervening administrative authority* because they are in the middle of the relationship, playing an administrative role. Without their service, the RP may not have an alternative means of assuring themselves that the relationship has integrity over time. On the other hand, in this model the person gets no assurance from the identity system about relationship integrity. For that they usually rely on Transport Layer Security (TLS),[2] which is visible in a web interaction but largely hidden inside a mobile app. Alice and Bob are not peers in the federated model. Instead, Alice is subject to the administrative control of both the IdP and the RP. Further, the RP (Bob) is subject to the administrative control of the IdP.

As you've seen, an alternative to the federated model is self-sovereign identity (SSI). In SSI, a relationship is initiated when Alice and Bob exchange *decentralized identifiers* (DIDs). For example, when Alice visits Bob's website, app, or service, she is presented with a connection invitation. When she accepts the invitation, she uses a software agent to share a DID that is created for that relationship. In turn, she receives a DID from Bob. This is called a *connection,* since DIDs are cryptographic and thus provide a means for both parties to mutually authenticate. Alice likely doesn't see all this activity; rather, it's carried out behind the scenes by software she uses.

Because the participants in SSI mutually authenticate, their identifiers are self-certifying. This means that, in contrast to the federated model, the SSI relationship has inherent integrity without the intervention of a third party. By exchanging DIDs, both parties also exchange public keys. They can consequently use cryptographic means to ensure they are interacting with the party who controls the DID they received when the relationship was initiated. In SSI, Alice and Bob act as peers, since they both have equal control over the relationship.

In addition to removing the need for intermediaries to vouch for the integrity of the relationship, the peer nature of relationships in SSI also means that neither party has access to the other's authentication credentials. *Mutual authentication* means that each party can authenticate the other, each managing their own keys. Neither ever needs to share their private key with another party. This architecture significantly reduces the risk from security attacks that steal credentials, since no administrator has access to the credentials of everyone using the system. I'll discuss this more in Chapter 11.

Relationship Life Span

Whether in the physical world or digital, relationships have life spans. One of the biggest failings of modern digital identity systems is our failure to recognize that people often want, even need, short-lived relationships.

Think about your typical day for a minute. How many people and organizations do you interact with in the physical world with which you establish a permanent

---

2 TLS is the protocol used to secure interactions on the web. We'll discuss it in detail in Chapter 9.

relationship? Imagine if whenever you stopped in at the convenience store for a cup of coffee, you had to create a permanent relationship with the coffee machine, the cashier, the point-of-sale terminal, and the customers in line ahead of and behind you. Sounds ridiculous. But that's what most digital interactions require. At every turn we're asked to establish permanent accounts to transact and interact online.

There are several reasons for this. The biggest one is that many websites, apps, and services want to send you ads (at best) or track you on other sites (even worse). Unneeded, long-lived relationships are the foundation of the surveillance economy that has come to define the modern online experience.[3] A more pedestrian reason is simply that systems for quickly creating, then forgetting, short-lived digital relationships are scarce.

There are some services with which I *want* a long-lived relationship. I value my relationships with Amazon and Netflix, for example. But there are many things I just need to remember for the length of the interaction. I recently ordered some bolts for a car-top carrier from a specialty web store. I don't order these bolts all the time, so I just wanted to place my order and be done. I wanted an ephemeral relationship.

The Internet of Things will increase the need for ephemeral relationships. When I use a digital credential to open a door in a building I rarely visit, I don't want the hassle of creating a long-term relationship with it; I just want to open the door and then forget about it.

Digital relationships should be easy to set up and tear down. They should allow for the relationship to grow over time if both parties desire. While they exist, they should be easily managed, providing all the tools for the needed utility. Unless there's a long-term benefit to me, I shouldn't need to create a long-term relationship. And when a digital relationship ends, it should really be over.

Anonymity and Pseudonymity

Ephemeral and short-term relationships lead us to anonymity and pseudonymity. When people use the word *anonymous* to describe physical-world interactions, they almost always are talking about what is, technically speaking, *pseudonymity*. When you interact with the barista at the coffee shop, it's anonymous in the sense that they don't know your name. But they do recognize and remember you over the span of the interaction and may even know you're a regular customer—that's technical pseudonymity. True anonymity is unrealistic for most online services since they must use some kind of identifier for at least the length of the session. The user is not

---

3 "Surveillance economy" was coined by Shoshana Zuboff in her book *The Age of Surveillance Capitalism.* Chapter 8 discusses this in more detail.

anonymous, because the service can distinguish between different users. Thus, in the identity field, we're almost always dealing with pseudonymity.

In a pseudonymous system, users are uniquely identified, but other identifying information is not shared. Pseudonymous systems give subjects a unique identifier with which attributes, rights, and privileges can be associated. *Pseudonymity* is a term usually reserved for people, since the unique identifier and its associated attributes, rights, and privileges constitute an identity record as we've defined it. Pseudonymity implies that no one besides the subject can tie this record to others that the subject might have.

Businesses should ask, "What identifying information do we absolutely need?" early in the design process for an online service. I say "businesses" because this is almost always a business decision, not a technology decision. Ideally, each attribute you request should also be linked to a documented need for the data as well as the benefit that the customer will receive by giving the data.

This rule is not followed as often as it should be. You've probably filled out web forms that ask you for more data than you think the company needs to provide the service. You probably resented it. Adding insult to injury, it's likely that the company never made any use of that data, for your benefit or not. Collecting unnecessary data alienates customers and clutters forms, so don't do it.

Fluid Multi-Pseudonymity

As we've discussed, in the physical world, we often interact with others—both people and institutions—with relative anonymity. Most relationships in the physical world are ephemeral. In real life, we do without identity systems for most things. You don't have to identify yourself to the movie theater to watch a movie. In real life, we act as embodied, independent agents. Our physical presence and the laws of physics have a lot to do with our ability to operate with functional anonymity across many domains. In contrast, most digital relationships are created under the purview of an administrative identity system.

Online, we've accepted long-lived relationships with full legibility of patrons as the default. Some of that is driven by convenience. I like storing my credit cards and shipping info at Amazon because it's convenient. I like that they know what books I've bought so I don't buy the same book more than once (yeah, I'm that guy). But what if I could get that convenience without any kind of account at Amazon at all?

There's no technical reason we need long-lived relationships for most of our web interactions. That doesn't mean we won't want some for convenience, but they ought to be optional, like the loyalty program at the supermarket, rather than required for service. Our digital lives can be as private as our physical lives if identity system architects build identity systems that allow it. We don't have to allow companies to surveil us. And the excuse that they surveil us to provide better service is just that—an excuse. The real reason they surveil us is because it's profitable.

I like what philosophy professor Kathleen Wallace says: "Selves are not only 'networked,' that is, in social networks, but are themselves networks."[4] While I've defined functional identity as how we recognize, remember, and respond to specific people and things, Wallace's insight looks at identity from the perspective of the person, organization, or thing. We are multiple selves, changing over time—even in the course of a single day. Identity system architects must remember this as they design identity systems. Emil Sotirov calls this idea *fluid multi-pseudonymity*.[5] I like that term because I think it accurately describes how identity works.

The architectures of traditional, administrative identity systems do not reflect the fluid multi-pseudonymity of real life, so they are mismatched with how people actually live. I frequently see calls for someone, usually a government, to solve the online identity problem by issuing everyone a permanent "identity." You've seen that the varied nature of our relationships exposes the folly of this idea. Linking every body (literally) to some government-issued identifier and a small number of attributes will not make the problems of identity disappear—in fact, it will exacerbate them.

These calls don't often come from within the identity community. Identity professionals understand how hard this problem is and that there's no single identity for anyone. But even identity professionals use the word *identity* when they mean "account." All of us, in the physical world and online, have multiple relationships. Many of those are pseudonymous. Many are ephemeral. But even a relationship that starts out as pseudonymous and ephemeral can develop into something permanent and better defined over time. Any relationship we have, even one with an online service, changes over time. In short, our relationships are fluid, and each is different.

Relationship Utility

Obviously, we don't create digital relationships just so we can authenticate the other party. Integrity is a necessary, but insufficient, condition for an identity system. This is where most identity models fall short. You can understand why this is so given the evolution of the modern web. User-centric identity systems were needed once the web gave people reasons to visit places that they didn't have a physical relationship with, like an ecommerce site. Once the identity system had established the integrity of the relationship, at least from the website's perspective, we expected HTTP would provide the rest.

---

4 Kathleen Wallace, "You Are a Network" (*https://oreil.ly/GAkP2*), *Aeon*, May 2021, accessed February 2, 2022.

5 Tweet (*https://oreil.ly/w6X3s*) from August 28, 2021, accessed February 2, 2022.

Most traditional identity and access management (IAM) systems don't provide much beyond integrity and access control. Once a service has established who or what you are, it knows just what resources to let you see or change. But as more and more of our lives are intermediated by digital services, we need more utility from the identity system than simple access control. The most that an IdP can provide in the federated model is integrity and, perhaps, a handful of attributes in a static, uncustomizable schema. Making matters worse, these attributes are usually self-asserted, significantly reducing the confidence the RP can place in them. Rich relationships require much more than that.

Relationships are established to provide utility. An ecommerce site wants to sell you things. A social media site wants to show you ads. Thus, their identity systems, built around the IAM system, are designed to do far more than just establish the integrity of the relationship: they want to store data about you and your activities. For the most part, this is welcome. I love that Amazon shows me my past orders, Netflix remembers where I was in a series, and Twitter keeps track of my followers and past tweets.

The actual identity system is much larger and more specialized than the IAM portion. All the account or profile data these companies use is properly thought of as part of the identity system that they build and run. As I discussed in Chapter 2, identity systems acquire, correlate, apply, reason over, and govern the information assets of subjects, identifiers, attributes, raw data, and context. That's a big scope.

Regardless of whether they outsource the integrity of their relationships using a federated authentication system (and notice that none of the companies I list above do), companies still have to keep track of their relationships with customers in order to provide services. They can't outsource this to a third party because the data in their identity system has evolved to suit the needs of the specific relationship. Rip out the identity system from a Netflix or an Amazon and it won't be the same company anymore.

This leads to a simple but important conclusion: *You can't outsource a relationship.* Online apps and services decorate the relationship with information they observe and use that information to provide utility to the relationships they administer. Doing this, and doing it well, is the foundation of the modern web.

That's why companies will always need to build, manage, and use identity systems. Their identity systems are what make them what they are—there is no "one size fits all" model. Over the course of this book, we will explore in detail the concepts, processes, architectures, and features of identity systems in support of online relationships that are fit for purpose and evolve to meet the changing contexts of their participants.

Transactional and Interactional Relationships

If we start with the premise that we build identity systems to manage relationships, you might rightly ask what kind of relationships are supported by the identity systems that we use. Put another way, what kinds of online relationships do you have? If you're like me, the vast majority are transactional. *Transactional relationships* focus on commercial interactions: usually buying and selling, but not always that explicit. Transactional relationships look like business deals. They are based on reciprocity.

My relationships with Amazon and Netflix are transactional. That's appropriate and what I expect. But what about my relationships on Twitter? You might argue that they are between friends, colleagues, or even family members. But I also classify them as transactional.

My relationships on Twitter exist within Twitter's administrative control; Twitter facilitates those relationships in order to monetize them. Even though you're not directly participating in the monetization and may even be unaware of it, it nevertheless colors the kind, frequency, and intimacy of your interactions. Twitter's platform and product decisions facilitate and even promote the kinds of interactions that provide the most profit to them. Your attention and activity are the product in the transaction. What I can do in those relationships depends wholly on what Twitter allows. All the relationships you have on a social media platform are subordinate to the relationship you have with the platform itself.

If you accept this argument, you will agree that the bulk of our online relationships are transactional or at least commercial. Very few are what we might call *interactional relationships*—except for email. Email is one of the bright exceptions to this landscape of transactional, administrated online relationships. If Alice and Bob exchange emails, they both have administrative, transactional relationships with their respective email providers, but their interaction does not necessarily take place within the administrative realm of a single email provider. Let's explore what makes email different.

The most obvious difference between email and many other systems built to support online relationships is that email is based on protocols. Recall the importance of protocol from our discussion of the Laws of Identity. As a result of being based on a protocol:

The user chooses (and might even control) the email server.
> With an email client, you have a choice of multiple email providers. You can even run your own email server if you like.

Data is stored on a server "in the cloud."
> The mail client needn't store any user data beyond account information. While many email clients store email data locally for performance reasons, the real data is in the cloud.

Email client behavior is the same regardless of what server it connects to.
> As long as the mail client is talking to a mail server that speaks the right protocol, it can provide the same functionality.

The client is fungible.
> I can pick my email client based on the features it provides without changing where I receive email or with whom I can exchange email.

I can use multiple clients at the same time.
> I can use one email client at home and a different email client at work and still see a single, consistent view of my email. I can even access my mail from a web client if I don't have my computer handy.

I can send you email without knowing anything but your email address.
> None of the details about how you receive and process email are relevant to me. I simply send email to your address.

Mail servers can talk to each other across ownership boundaries.
> I can use Gmail, you can use Yahoo! Mail, and the email still gets delivered.

I can change email providers easily or run my own server.
> I receive email at *windley.org* even though I use Gmail. I used to run my own server. If Gmail went away, I could start running my own server again. And no one else needs to know.

The parties exchanging email interact as peers.
> Neither exists within the other's system or is subject to its control.

Email supports almost any kind of relationship imaginable.
> Email's flexibility is its hallmark and the reason it refuses to die, despite many pundits' predictions.

In short, email was designed to follow the architecture of the internet and functions according to the metasystem properties I outlined in Chapter 4. Email is decentralized and *protocological* (that is, it uses protocols). Email is open—not necessarily open source, but open in that anyone can build clients and servers that speak its core protocols, Internet Mail Access Protocol (IMAP) and Simple Mail Transfer Protocol (SMTP). As a result, email maximizes freedom of choice and minimizes the chances of disruption.

Why discuss email in a book about digital identity? Because the features and benefits that email provides are the same ones every online relationship needs. These properties allow us to use email to create interactional relationships. The important insight is that systems that support interactional relationships can easily support transactional ones as well, where necessary. But the converse is not true. Systems for building transactional relationships don't readily support interactional ones.

Email has obvious weaknesses: most prominently, it doesn't support mutual authentication of the parties to a relationship, so it suffers from problems like spam and phishing attacks. But email's support for rich relationships is a primary reason it is still used, despite the rise of social media and work platforms like Slack and Teams.

Promoting Rich Relationships

Relationships are the heart of digital identity. The architecture of an identity system must provide integrity, an appropriate life span, and the needed utility for the specific relationships it's meant to support. At the same time, systems should conform to the Laws of Identity. Protocol-based architectures can provide the properties discussed in Chapter 4 while allowing the flexibility to build rich online relationships that feel more lifelike and authentic, provide better safety, and allow people to live effective online lives.

CHAPTER 6

The Digital Relationship Lifecycle

When I was in grade school, our class captured a caterpillar and placed it in a jar with some leaves to see what would happen. You have probably done this too. Of course, in time, the caterpillar spun a cocoon, and the little jar became pretty boring. But our teacher encouraged us to keep watching, and one morning, we were thrilled to see a large moth in the bottle. This simple experiment clearly illustrated to me that the moth and the caterpillar were the same creature at different stages of its life.

Scientists use lifecycles to connect the seemingly unconnected. I'm a big fan of using lifecycles to analyze information technology problems for the same reason. Lifecycles help define all the phases of a problem or project so that they can be dealt with holistically rather than piecemeal. They're also useful for categorizing activities associated with the process.

Digital relationships have lifecycles, as shown in Figure 6-1, regardless of whether those relationships are long-term, short-lived, or ephemeral. Understanding how the digital relationship lifecycle plays out on every system, and in the enterprise as a whole, is crucial when creating a strategy for managing relationships.

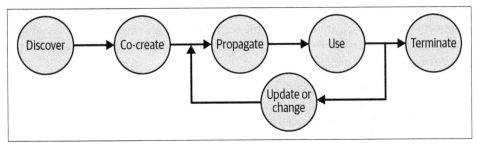

Figure 6-1. Digital relationship management lifecycle

Briefly, a digital relationship starts out with one entity *discovering* another. If they desire a relationship, it is *created*. The relationship is *propagated* to any relevant systems and then it is *used*. As we discussed in the last chapter, relationships *change* or are *updated* over time, and these changes must be repropagated for use. At some point, when the relationship has served its purpose and is no longer needed, it is *terminated*. Next, I will discuss each phase in more detail.

Discovering

Discovery is the initial phase of the lifecycle. You might think of this as a marketing function if you're just concerned with how customers find a service or digital product. But it becomes more interesting—and complicated—once you expand your thinking to include things like the following:

- How do friends find each other online?
- How does your phone find the digital door lock it has to connect with?
- How can you find the *right* identifier for a particular company?
- How can you find out what a given identifier refers to?
- How do you find the right place to interact with a specific entity (such as a website, an API, or a Bluetooth connection)?

Chapter 10 will discuss discovery in detail.

Co-Creating

After we discover the entity that we wish to establish a relationship with, we need to create the relationship. I call it "co-creating" because a relationship always involves at least two parties, and all the parties to the relationship have to take part in its creation. Creating a relationship is a ceremony where each party has a role and follows a script. The nature of the ceremony depends a great deal on the type of relationship.

Returning to our restaurant example from Chapter 5: a number of short-lived or ephemeral relationships are created in the course of a meal. The reason it feels so natural is because we are all familiar with the many ceremonies that happen over the course of a restaurant meal.

When you are creating an account on a website or in an app, the ceremony requires the person creating the account to enter information in a form of some kind and possibly set up multifactor authentication, but the bulk of the effort is borne by software on the business side.

Provisioning is the process of preparing an IT system to provide service to a client, customer, or other user. In a digital relationship, provisioning means creating the account record and populating it with attributes. Many of these attributes are provided by the person creating the account. They include standard information such as name, location, email, and phone, as well as things more specific to the system. For example, the account system in Twitter includes a "profile" that records a banner, profile picture, bio, and so on.

Provisioning can result from an administrator's actions or a user's (called self-service). When a new employee joins a company, for example, accounts are provisioned on several systems so that they can be assigned an office, get on the payroll, get a computer, get a badge, become part of the health plan, and so on. This may require separate actions by different administrators or be linked so that one request causes them all to happen.

We're all familiar with self-service provisioning—we see it every day on the web and in smartphone apps. It's perfect for services that are delivered over a network, and it works well when there is little need to verify physical credentials (other than perhaps a credit card).

The explosion of social media has given rise to platform-mediated relationships where people create an account on a platform—say, Twitter, Facebook, or LinkedIn— and then follow or connect with one another inside the platform's system. Some of these relationships (like Twitter follows) are asymmetrical because they don't require both parties to participate at the same level. Others (like Facebook friendships) are symmetrical: the relationship features are shared by both parties. These relationships are subordinate to the relationship with the platform itself and are generally easy to create.

Sometimes relationship creation is much less formal. When two people exchange email or Bitcoin addresses, they are forming a relationship that is then supported by tools like contact managers and digital wallets.

Propagating

When I was chief technology officer (CTO) of iMall, we built a large ecommerce system that allowed small merchants to sign up for an account and then create a full-service online store. The system had a self-service account management system that allowed merchants to provision an account. The identity information was then propagated so that the system could create directories and files on numerous systems, add records to databases on other systems, and even establish a merchant banking account through an outside partner. This propagation of identity information was critical to the overall functioning of the system.

Human resources systems have similar features to support *zero-day start* functionality, in which the enterprise links its systems for assigning offices, setting up payroll, and so on, so that on their very first day the employee has access to all the resources, physical and virtual, that they need to be productive.

For simple systems, the propagation is as easy as writing the account information to a directory. More complex systems may share an identity directory for use by multiple systems (see Chapter 10). IT architecture has moved beyond the idea of a single *system* or *record* that served as the single repository of data (account or otherwise). In today's distributed IT systems, such a single source of truth would result in tightly coupled systems that are prone to failure and performance problems. Instead, modern systems keep data in multiple repositories that must be kept in sync.

Propagation must occur after each change to the identity records, and it must happen reliably. Because modern distributed systems often can't use transactions (atomicity across multiple independent actions) to ensure data consistency, this can be a challenge. Distributed systems limit strong consistency (usually via transactions) to the smallest part of the system possible and use eventual consistency and recovery everywhere else.

To see why, consider the example I gave in the opening paragraph of this section. Suppose you create an account. The system creates directory records, files, and database records on multiple systems, only to discover that your payment has been declined. The system is in a state of partial completion and backing out to a clean state is often nontrivial. The more actions involved in a single propagation, the more difficult this problem becomes. So, the payment and an initial provisioning message may be protected inside a transaction; that way, if the payment fails, the provisioning message is never sent.

There may be numerous systems involved in provisioning the account. If one of them fails because it's offline or the message is lost, the system must have the means to note the inconsistency and recover through compensating actions. The design and implementation of distributed systems is beyond the scope of this book, but modern identity systems are usually distributed and must be architected as such.

Using

The use phase is probably the most obvious of all the phases in the lifecycle. Once the relationship has been created and propagated, its creators can use it to support the relationship's utility. This might be as simple as consulting an account to authenticate and authorize user actions against resources, or it could include more complicated actions such as billing, payroll, updating timelines, or even feeding AI agents that service the relationship.

Updating or Changing

Regardless of the nature of the relationship between entities, the attributes it uses will be updated from time to time, either because one party's base attributes change (for instance, a new home address) or because roles and assignments change. These updates don't change the structure or schema of the underlying systems supporting the relationship; these attributes are designed to be updated.

At other times, the nature of the relationship might change to support new business opportunities, add new features, or change the kind of relationship (such as moving from a free service to paid). Sometimes relationships that start out as short-term become long-term. When the relationship changes, new fields might be added to the record schema, or the account may need to be propagated to entirely new systems.

Relationships might include things, not just people and organizations. In these cases, it's possible that the entire entity referred to by the account is changed. As an example, consider upgrading the departmental laser printer. When the new printer is installed, its name and IP number may be the only attributes that remain the same. And yet, its role is still "department laser printer." This action would also result in changes that, after completion, must be repropagated to the affected systems.

Maintaining identity-related information is one of the costliest activities that IT help desks deal with from day to day. People frequently lose or forget passwords. They change roles or move. The more things users can do on their own, the less onerous this is for all parties to a relationship.

Terminating

Just as important as creating a relationship is terminating it at the end of its lifecycle. One employee of a company whose identity systems have won some acclaim told me that the company's sophisticated identity management system had ensured he was ready to begin work the same day he started. Ironically, two years after he quit, his voicemail still functioned. This company was doing a good job creating relationships but had fallen down on terminating them.

Leaving a voicemail account active may not be a big deal, but leaving a departing employee with access to a sensitive system could be catastrophic. Failing to terminate a relationship properly can lead to confusion, access to critical data by outsiders, and even fraud or theft. Leaving old accounts active is a dangerous security hole for two reasons. First, the employee may continue to use company resources after they've quit. More worrisome, these accounts are prime places for hackers to crack into corporate systems because they are unmonitored and strange activity won't raise any eyebrows.

Lifecycle Planning

You've learned in this chapter that the digital relationship lifecycle applies to relationships regardless of their length. Even an ephemeral relationship must be discovered, created, propagated, used, and terminated. Planning for each phase is critical to designing a digital identity infrastructure that meets the needs of everyone in the relationship. This planning can't simply be done at the abstract level but must extend to each subsystem that participates in delivering service. For example, a company's customer relationship management and the enterprise resource planning systems have different accounts as well as unique needs in each stage of the lifecycle. But they also need to cooperate in creating, propagating, and terminating relationships. Chapter 16 and Chapter 17 will discuss different architectures for identity systems and the nature of the relationships they support.

CHAPTER 7

Trust, Confidence, and Risk

Доверяй, но проверяй.[1]
—Russian proverb

Trust is at the heart of all relationships. Trust is the basis for society. We trust our spouse to lock the door when they leave the house. We trust our coworker to email a document for us. We trust the bank to not lose our money. We trust the airline pilot to fly us safely to our destination. Without trust in people and institutions, life is difficult to navigate.

In their excellent paper "Risk and Trust,"[2] Nickel and Vaesen define trust as the "disposition to willingly rely on another person or entity to perform actions that benefit or protect oneself or one's interests in a given domain." Unstated in this definition is that trust necessarily entails the trustor being vulnerable to the trustee. Trust entails an inherent risk.

By building relationships in the digital realm, we are creating a digital society, one where trust is necessary. Relationships imply a shared domain, context, and set of activities. We often rely on third parties to tell us things relevant to a relationship. Our vulnerability, and therefore our risk, depends on the degree of reliance we have on another party's performance. Relationships can never be "no trust" because we create them expecting to rely on the other parties in them. Bitcoin and other cryptocurrencies can be described as low- or no-trust precisely because the point of the system is to reduce reliance on any relationship at all—not relying on the other party to

---

1 Trust but verify.

2 Philip J. Nickel and Krist Vaesen, "Risk and Trust," in *Handbook of Risk Theory*, ed. Sabine Roeser et al. (New York: Springer, 2012).

the transaction and certainly not on any third party. In contrast, most online interactions do rely on a relationship and, therefore, trust to some degree.

Because of the proximity problem, digital relationships are potentially risky. In "Blockchain as a Confidence Machine: The Problem of Trust & Challenges of Governance,"[3] the authors argue that "trust and confidence are distinct phenomena: trust depends on personal vulnerability and risk-taking, whereas confidence depends on internalised expectations deriving from knowledge or past experiences." The *risk* is that the trustee is an independent agent who may not perform to the trustor's expectations. *Confidence*, on the other hand, focuses on assurance, not risk.

As Figure 7-1 illustrates, to the extent our confidence in another person, institution, or system increases, our trust can decrease because our risk and vulnerability have decreased. In contrast to trust, *confidence does not require that the trustor be in a vulnerable position* because some aspects of the relationship are predictable, reducing uncertainty. We can gain predictability, and thus confidence, in relationships from past experience, from evaluating the degrees of freedom the other party has, or from evaluating statistical and other evidence.

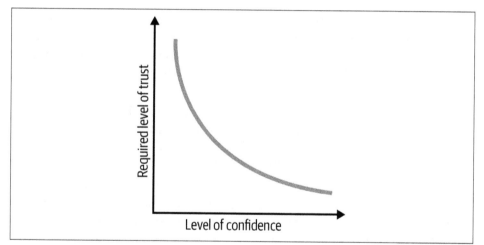

Figure 7-1. Trust and confidence have an inverse relationship

Confidence doesn't necessarily involve complete mastery of the systems or institutions you interact with. For example, you can have confidence that the airplane you're flying in is safe without understanding the technical systems involved or knowing how to fly yourself. Even if you've never flown, you have a general knowledge that planes don't usually crash and thus can gauge the risk as being very low.

---

3 Primavera De Filippi, Morshed Mannan, and Wessel Reijers, "Blockchain as a Confidence Machine: The Problem of Trust & Challenges of Governance," in *Technology in Society* (2020), 62.

But the plane example also points out the nuanced relationship between trust and confidence. Our confidence that the plane won't crash is undergirded by our trust in the various participants in the airline ecosystem. You cannot personally know about or verify them all, so you must trust that others are doing the right thing and ensuring air travel is safe. In other words, our confidence in one thing may depend on our trust in other things.

As I discussed in Chapter 5, the primary reason people need identity systems is to support relationships. A good identity system gives you confidence that the person at the other end of the relationship is the same one you initiated the relationship with. As you interact in a digital relationship, you gain experience and gather evidence. This reduces our need to trust the relationship because our vulnerability and risk decrease commensurately. An identity system can help parties to the relationship gather, manage, and analyze that evidence.

In the influential book *Trust: The Social Virtues and the Creation of Prosperity*,[4] Francis Fukuyama argues that public values, especially trust and confidence, shape the direction of national economies. Among other things, Fukuyama shows how trust and confidence reduce transaction costs and, ultimately, economic friction. Similarly, a digital society based on digital relationships requires a digital identity infrastructure to establish confidence and trust.

Risk and Vulnerability

In digital relationships supported by an identity infrastructure, the problems of digital identity present many risks, including:

- Are the identity credentials being presented held by the correct entity?
- Is the system Alice is talking to the one she wants to talk to?
- Will Alice's communication be unaltered and private?
- Is the access-control policy sufficiently and consistently protecting valuable assets?

I could go on.

Risk can be managed actively or passively. Some organizations and people are very risk averse. Others are more tolerant of risk, especially when the cost of reducing risk is high. Even so, most people and organizations want to reduce the risk attendant to digital relationships and increase their confidence in the outcomes. Risk management is a well-established practice in most businesses. Businesses don't try to measure trust

---

4 Francis Fukayama, *Trust: The Social Virtues and the Creation of Prosperity* (New York: Free Press, 1996).

in a system or approach; instead, they quantify the risk of a particular business process and balance that risk with the expected rewards or returns.

Risk and vulnerability depend on the domain and life span of the relationship. Short-lived and ephemeral relationships within a specific domain often have quantifiable risks that can be mitigated by creating policy, increasing our confidence, and reducing the trust you need to have. Consider an electronic door lock, with which you might establish an ephemeral relationship each time you need to use the door. If the lock can establish the authenticity of the identifier accessing it and know through policy that the identifier is allowed to unlock the door, then there is little risk.

But is the identifier being wielded by the person it is assigned to? Here you may need to trust a policy that tells employees not to let others use their employee ID card. Or you may be using a verifiable credential that gives you confidence through cryptography that the identifier is being used by the person it was issued to. Whether you can tolerate the risk of someone loaning out their card (and thus access to the door) depends a great deal on what the door protects. This again speaks to the domain of the transaction.

Relationships that are intimate, long-lived, and have broad responsibility are often very vulnerable to actions taken by one or more of the parties to the relationship. For example, the executive assistant to a company CEO often needs very broad access to company systems and considerable discretion about how resources are used in order to do their job. The risks are large and difficult to mitigate. Consequently, the CEO is left to trust that this person won't abuse their position through maliciousness, ineptitude, or negligence. While identity systems can reduce some of the risk inherent in this scenario, the breadth of the domain makes it impossible to significantly reduce the level of trust invested in this person.

When you create a policy for digital identity systems that control the actions available to holders of specific identity credentials, you're setting out objectives based on several factors, including:

- The circumstances of the transactions involved
- The business requirements
- The degree of risk that the business is willing to bear in those circumstances
- The cost the business is willing to pay to reduce the risk to an acceptable level

These objectives drive the level of trust required, the confidence our risk-reducing measures can buy, and the amount of evidence you need to collect to attain sufficient confidence.

Looking at risk in a particular domain for specific relationship types provides a strategy. For each domain, you must be able to measure the risk that the digital identity

---

infrastructure will fail to perform as required. Answering these questions requires a detailed understanding of the systems and processes that make up the digital identity infrastructure, including detailed assessments of interactions with partners and their ability to perform as required. You must know where in the process you can establish confidence and where you remain vulnerable. Furthermore, you must quantify the potential losses and their probabilities.

Often, for domains that have been in place for some time, you can use historical measurements to determine the expected level of risk. This assumes that the processes used to manage the digital identity infrastructure include monitoring and tracking the system and its outcomes. The level of detail available for these analyses will depend on the system's architecture and the maturity of the policies that govern it, topics I will discuss in detail in later chapters.

Fidelity and Provenance

The interconnected relationship of trust and confidence may feel hard to grasp without some additional structure. Figure 7-2 shows a mutually supportive relationship, with trust on the top and confidence on the bottom.

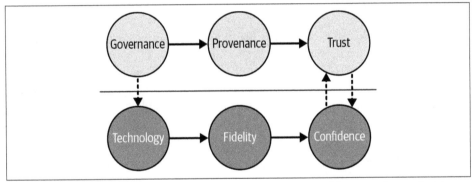

Figure 7-2. The relationship of fidelity and provenance to confidence and trust in identity systems

Trust depends on something I call *provenance*. Provenance includes various considerations that trust depends on, including:

- The trustee's reputation or moral standing
- The trustee's desire to maintain their reputation or brand
- The institutional context of the trust relationship
- The trustor's level of optimism
- How and from where data is collected

Provenance depends on *governance*,[5] which might include the following:

- Technical, financial, human resource, and other policies set by the trustee or trustor[6]
- The operating rules, roles and responsibilities, and legal validity of a policy
- The regulatory and legal structures within which the trust relationship exists
- The trustee's and trustor's personal rules and standards

The bottom layer of Figure 7-2 shows that confidence depends on what I broadly call *fidelity*. Fidelity includes the kinds of things that can give us confidence in digital relationships, including:

- How authentication factors are generated and stored
- The presence (or absence) of multifactor authentication
- Whether data is transmitted on a protected channel
- The protocols used for the authentication ceremony
- The cryptographic strength of verifiable credentials or other mechanisms used to transmit attributes

Fidelity is largely a matter of the specific digital identity architecture, technologies, and algorithms used to create, maintain, and service the digital relationship. Examples include OAuth, FIDO (Fast Identity Online), TLS (Transport Layer Security), digital certificates and public-key infrastructure (PKI), zero-knowledge proofs, and digital signatures. These will all be discussed in greater detail in later chapters.

Note that the diagram also includes a dotted arrow from *governance* to *technology*. How effective a given technology is in providing fidelity (and thus establishing confidence) usually depends on how it is deployed, maintained, and used. For example, while using TLS to secure a web connection can give confidence in its confidentiality, its effectiveness depends on what kind of digital certificate is being used, who issued it, what their policies are, and the strength of their security—all issues of governance.

Trust Frameworks

Governance needs a sustainable ecosystem. If the governance is entirely contained within an organization, the long-term viability of that organization determines the sustainability of the governance that creates provenance to provide the needed trust.

---

5 Chapter 22 discusses the details of governance.

6 Policy is the topic of Chapter 21.

Other ecosystems extend beyond a single organization and require other means to be viable. This may take the form of a nonprofit or other organization supported by interested parties. For example, whether or not schools, employers, and others trust the transcripts provided by US universities depends on a provenance process called *accreditation* that is administered by third-party agencies. We can observe the processes these third parties use and judge the competencies of graduates of the universities they accredit.

This arrangement, where a third party provides governance (and sometimes technology) to transfer trust between two parties in a relationship, is called a *trust framework*. Credit card companies are perhaps the best-known and most widely used trust frameworks in the world. Platform companies like Uber and Grubhub are other examples.

Figure 7-3 shows the relationships in the Visa trust framework. When I present my Visa card to a merchant, they have no relationship with me and likely no relationship with my bank. Even so, they fully expect to be paid. The trust framework provides this result using a mix of governance and technology.

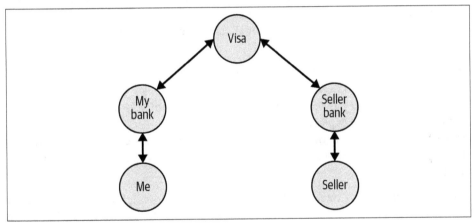

Figure 7-3. The relationships in a credit card trust framework

The relationship I create with the merchant is probably short-lived. But it provides the trust and confidence needed to conduct the transaction because of the long-term relationships represented in the trust framework. The merchant and I both have legal relationships with our respective banks. These banks both have legal relationships with Visa. Visa creates policies and rules to govern the transaction. At the same time, Visa depends on and mandates the use of technologies within the credit card network (much of which is provided by other parties) to create as much confidence as possible that the transaction is not fraudulent and to transfer funds from my account at my bank to the merchant's account at their bank.[7]

The Visa network is sustainable because Visa, the banks, and third-party processors each get a cut of any transaction on the network. This is a nice arrangement when it's possible, but often trust frameworks must do something else to remain viable, like charging a direct fee for service.

The Nature of Trust

Recall that trust is the "disposition to willingly rely on another person or entity to perform actions that benefit or protect oneself or one's interests in a given domain." For example, when you give your credit card to the waiter at a restaurant, you are expressing trust that the waiter will use the credit card to process a transaction that will pay for your meal. You expect that that transaction will be the only one processed and that the waiter won't steal the credit card number. You have confidence in the credit card system itself, but you must trust the waiter.[8] The only time I've ever had my credit card number stolen was in a restaurant, and yet I still blithely hand my credit card over to any waiter who comes along. There is clearly risk, but I take it because I'm convinced that the risk is small, largely due to credit card company policies that limit my liability.

Trust is something an entity grants to or withholds from others—it is a disposition, sometimes a conscious decision. Most of us don't consciously think about the risk of using a credit card to pay for a meal; we evaluate it intuitively based on a variety of factors: our previous experience, the way the restaurant looks, and, perhaps most importantly, our trust in the governance of the credit card companies. There's no doubt that trust is linked to risk when you consider who you're willing to trust with what.

Trust is based not just on the entities involved in the transaction but also on their roles and the context of the transaction. Alice might trust Bob to fix her car but not to babysit her children. She can adjust trust or revoke it completely at any time. This leads to some important properties of trust:

- Trust is transitive only in very specific circumstances. For example, if Alice trusts Bob's taste in music and Bob trusted Carol to select songs for the last party, Alice may be willing to trust Carol to pick the songs for her party.

---

7 To learn more about the founding of Visa and the ideas that helped it succeed, see Visa founder Dee Hock's *One from Many: VISA and the Rise of Chaordic Organization* (San Francisco: Berrett-Koehler, 2005).

8 If you're reading this in Europe, you're probably shaking your head at a process that allows the waiter to take the card to the machine rather than bringing the machine to the card. That's a good example of how technology, policy, and practice can impact trust by reducing risk and increasing confidence.

- Trust cannot be shared. If Alice trusts Bob and Alice trusts Carol, it doesn't necessarily follow that Bob trusts Carol.

- Trust is not symmetric. Just because you trust me doesn't mean that I trust you.

- Trustworthiness cannot be self-declared. This is so self-evident that the phrase "trust me" has become a cliché sure to get a laugh.

In digital relationships, trust is generally linked to a specific identifier and the attributes associated with it. I may have several email addresses, for example, and even though they all belong to me, people may see them in different contexts and trust a request sent from my work address more than they do one from my personal account.

Coherence and Social Systems

A collection of digital relationships forms a social system for accomplishing some goal. Some are small, others are global. Social systems that are enduring, scalable, and generative require coherence among participants. Coherence allows us to manage complexity. Coherence is necessary for any group of people to cooperate. The coherence necessary to create the internet came in part from standards, but more from the actions of people who created organizations, established those standards, ran services, and set up exchange points.

Coherence enables a group of people to operate with one mind about some set of ideas, processes, and outcomes. Trust and confidence play important roles in establishing coherent social systems. Identity systems have different architectures depending on their purpose, but all must establish coherence among participants. People have four ways of creating coherence in social systems: tribes, institutions, markets, and networks.[9] Consequently, all identity systems will fall into one of these four patterns. Let's look more closely at them:

"Tribes"
>   Startups and families, for example, both work as "tribes" or communities. When there's only a small set of people, collective action and leadership make rules and put incentives—and disincentives—in place. The relationships in communities are usually interactional rather than transactional. Through interactions that follow the rules and norms of the community, our initial trust turns into confidence in other members of the community. Coherence is the result.

---

9 For more about these four societal organizational models, see David Ronfeldt's RAND Corporation 1996 paper "Tribes, Institutions, Markets, Networks" (*https://oreil.ly/6R6hx*) and John Robb's commentary (*https://oreil.ly/5T-ZB*) on it.

Institutions

As a company grows, it becomes an institution that relies on rules and bureaucracy to establish confidence and create coherence. Families rarely grow into institutions (except among the very rich), but startups sometimes do. The relationships in institutions are both transactional and interactional, depending on the institution's purpose and organization. While good leadership is important, institutions are more about the organization than the personalities involved. Tribes and institutions are usually centralized—someone or some organization is making it all happen. In addition, institutions rely on hierarchy to govern interactions, reduce risk, increase confidence, and achieve coherence.

Markets

Markets are decentralized—and they are heterarchical rather than hierarchical. Rules and ad hoc ceremonies, perhaps evolved over time through countless interactions, govern interactions and establish confidence. Market relationships are almost exclusively transactional, regardless of how friendly they might be. Market forces driven by economic opportunity give participants incentives to abide by the rules. Market participants are also bound by institutions (such as the rule of law) to behave in certain ways. Competition among private interests (hopefully behaving fairly and freely) allows multiple players with different agendas to process complex transactions around a diverse set of interests. Nevertheless, most market relationships begin with trust and proceed to confidence over time.

Markets don't displace institutions but sit alongside them in a symbiotic relationship that mirrors the interplay between trust and confidence, establishing coherence in complex ecosystems. Although markets coexist with and depend on trust in laws, regulations, and institutions like banks and regulatory bodies, they also depend on the confidence that a functioning market instills in the economy at large.

Networks

Networks are also decentralized but based on peer relationships. Moreover, the rules of interaction are set in *protocol*—formalized ceremonies. Protocol provides a template for interactions that reduces market risk and increases network effects. Network relationships might be interactional or transactional, depending on the protocol. But protocol alone is not enough. The internet is probably the best and biggest example of a networked organization. Defining a protocol doesn't string cable or set up routers. There's something more to it. As with tribes, institutions, and markets, one form of organization doesn't supplant another but augments it. So too with networks. The internet is the result of a mix of institutional, market-driven, and network-enabled forces. These set up a complex web of trust and confidence in other actors in the network. The internet has endured and functions because these forces, whether by design or luck, are sufficient to create the coherence necessary to turn the idea of a global, public, decentralized communications system into a real network that routes packets from place to place.

Most identity systems rely on institutional control, patterns, and methods to create coherence, from employee portals based on company-run identity and access management systems to social login systems like Google Sign-in. Decentralized, networked identity systems, in contrast, use protocol to create coherence and enable autonomous interactions.

Trust, Confidence, and Coherence

A digital relationship is worthless if its participants cannot establish the trust and confidence needed for it to fulfill its purpose. Relying on confidence is better than relying on trust, but very few systems that need digital relationships will be able to get by on the fidelity of their architectures alone. Most will also need some level of trust —and the governance that trust requires. When building digital identity infrastructures, remember that you're attempting to enable a social system of digital relationships, simple or complex, that will succeed or fail based on the coherence that the design engenders and the degree of trust and confidence the relationships inspire.

CHAPTER 8

Privacy

"You have zero privacy anyway. Get over it."

These famous words were uttered by Scott McNealy, then CEO of Sun Microsystems, in 1999.[1] Despite McNealy's brutal pronouncement, privacy is still very much something identity professionals, product managers, architects, developers, company officers, and many others need to worry about.

Privacy is the place in identity where technology, policy, and the law meet. For example, in the early 2000s, General Motors set out to create a company-wide telephone directory, something companies have been doing for a hundred years, and put it online. It took *two years*. GM's hang-up was not technical but legal: GM has employees in many countries, each with its own privacy laws, some much stricter than those of the United States. Privacy turned a seemingly simple project into a two-year ordeal.

More and more organizations are appointing chief privacy officers, high-level officers who ensure that data about people is protected or (to take the cynical view) at least reduce the risk of being fined or sued over it. Privacy is a big deal. People believe that *their* identity data should be private. They don't necessarily believe that everyone else's data should be private, but they want to protect their own information.

What Is Privacy?

Ask 10 people what privacy is and you'll likely get 12 different answers. People's feelings about privacy depend on their context and experience. Long before computers existed, people cared about privacy and debated it in terms of government intrusion:

---

1 Polly Sprenger, "Sun on Privacy: 'Get Over It'" (*https://oreil.ly/TEt6e*), *Wired Magazine*, January 1999, accessed February 23, 2022.

in 1890, future US Supreme Court justice Louis Brandeis defined it (*https://oreil.ly/b8c1Z*) as "the right to be left alone."

The march of technological progress has made people more aware of privacy and presented new challenges. Today, private companies probably have much more data about you than your government does. Platforms are valued based on how well they display ads to their users, leading to widespread surveillance—usually without users knowing the extent or consequences.

This discussion requires a clear definition of privacy. The International Association of Privacy Professionals (IAPP) defines (*https://oreil.ly/ED69B*) four classes of privacy:

Bodily privacy
> The protection of a person's physical being and any invasion thereof. This includes practices like genetic testing, drug testing, or body cavity searches.

Communications privacy
> The protection of the means of correspondence, including postal mail, telephone conversations, electronic mail, and other forms of communication.

Information privacy
> The claim of individuals, groups, or organizations to determine when, how, and to what extent information about them is communicated to others.

Territorial privacy
> Placing limitations on the ability of others to intrude into an individual's environment...including workplaces, vehicles, and public spaces. Intrusions of territorial privacy can include video surveillance or ID checks.

While bodily and territorial privacy can be issues online, communications and information privacy are the ones most likely to have a digital identity component. To begin a discussion of online privacy, I first need to be specific about what I mean by "online conversations."

Each online interaction consists of packets of data flowing between parties. For our purposes, consider this exchange of packets a *conversation*. Even a simple Internet Control Message Protocol (ICMP) echo request packet and response constitutes a conversation as I'm defining it—the message needn't be meaningful to humans.

Conversations have content and *metadata*—or information about the conversation. In an ICMP echo, there's *only* metadata—the TCP and ICMP headers,[2] which include information like the source and destination IP addresses, TTL (time to live), type of message, checksums, and so on. In a more complex protocol, say SMTP for email, there is content—the message—in addition to metadata.

---

2 ICMP packets *can* have data in the packet, but it's optional and almost never set.

Communications Privacy and Confidentiality

Communications privacy is concerned with metadata; *confidentiality* is concerned with content. Put another way: for a conversation to be private, only the parties to the conversation should know who the other participants are or any other metadata about the conversation. This distinction between privacy and confidentiality isn't often made in casual conversation, where people often say they want privacy when they really mean confidentiality.

Defined in this way, online privacy might appear impossible. After all, the internet works by passing packets from router to router, all of which can see the source IP address and must know the destination IP address. Consequently, at the packet level, there's no online privacy. But the bigger picture is more nuanced.

Consider the use of Transport Layer Security (TLS) to create an encrypted web channel between the browser and the server. (I'll go into detail about encryption in Chapter 9.) At the packet level, the routers *will know* (and the operators of the routers *can know*) the IP addresses of the encrypted packets going back and forth. If a third party can correlate those IP addresses with the actual participants, then the conversation isn't private. That may or may not matter.

Beyond the host name and information needed to set up the TLS connection, all the rest of the headers are encrypted. This means other metadata in the same conversation—the headers—is private, including cookies and the URL path. Someone eavesdropping on the conversation could find out the server name, but not the specific place on the site to which the browser connected. For example, suppose Alice visits Utah Valley University's Title IX office (where sexual misconduct, discrimination, harassment, and retaliation are reported) by pointing her browser at *uvu.edu/equityandtitleix*. If Alice uses a TLS connection, an eavesdropper could learn that Alice connected to Utah Valley University, but not that she connected to UVU's Title IX site, because the URL's path (*/equityandtitleix*) is encrypted.

Extending this example, you can easily see the difference between privacy and confidentiality. If the Title IX office were located at a subdomain of *uvu.edu*, say *titleix.uvu.edu*, then an eavesdropper *would* be able to tell that Alice had connected to the Title IX website, even if the conversation were protected by a TLS connection. The content that was sent to Alice and that she sent back would be *confidential*, but important metadata showing that Alice connected to the Title IX office would *not be private*.

This example introduces another important term to this discussion: *authenticity*. If Alice goes to *uvu.edu* instead of *titleix.uvu.edu*, then an eavesdropper cannot easily establish the authenticity of who Alice is speaking to at UVU—there are too many possibilities. Depending on how easy it is to correlate Alice's IP address with Alice, an eavesdropper might not be able to reliably authenticate Alice either. So, while Alice's conversation with the Title IX office through *uvu.edu* is not *absolutely private*, it is *functionally private* because you can't easily authenticate the parties to the conversation from the metadata alone.

Information Privacy

When Alice connects with the Title IX office, she might transmit data by filling out forms or even just by authenticating, allowing the site to identify Alice and correlate other information with her. All of this is done inside the confidential channel provided by the TLS connection, but Alice will still be concerned about the privacy of the information she's communicated.

Information privacy quickly gets out of the technical realm and into policy. How will Alice's information be handled? Who will see it? Will it be shared? With whom and under what conditions? These are all policy questions that affect the privacy of the information that Alice willingly shared. Information privacy is generally about who controls disclosure.

Communications privacy often involves the involuntary collection of metadata—*surveillance*. Information privacy, by contrast, usually involves policies and practices for handling data that has been voluntarily provided. Of course, there are places where these two overlap. Data created from metadata becomes *personally identifying information* (PII), subject to privacy concerns that might be addressed by policy or subject to regulatory control. Still, the distinction between communications and information privacy is useful.

Transactional Privacy

The intersection of communications and information privacy is sometimes called *transactional* or *social privacy*.[3] Transactional privacy is worth exploring as a separate category because it is always evaluated in a specific context—for example, purchasing a book at Amazon. Thus, it speaks to people's real concerns and their willingness to trade off privacy for a perceived benefit in a specific transaction. Transactional privacy concerns are often more transient than people's general concerns about privacy.

The modern web is replete with transactions that involve both metadata and content data. The risks of this data being used in ways that erode individual privacy are great. And because the mechanisms are obscure—even to web professionals—people can't make good privacy decisions about the transactions they engage in. Transactional privacy is consequently an important lens for evaluating people's privacy rights and the ways technology, policy, regulation, and the law can protect them.

---

3 I have seen the term *transactional privacy* used to describe the idea of people selling their own data outright. That is not the sense I'm using; I'm speaking more generally of transactions that take place online.

With privacy, we rarely deal with absolutes. You could achieve absolute digital privacy by simply never using the internet, but that also means being absolutely cut off from online interaction. Consequently, privacy is a spectrum, and each of us must choose where we should be on that spectrum. I'll discuss some of the trade-offs later in this chapter.

Correlation

In the previous section, I observed that privacy is reduced if the IP addresses can be correlated with one or both parties in a conversation. This is not at all far-fetched: my home IP address has been the same for years, even though technically it is dynamically assigned. My internet service provider (ISP) pins it for convenience. As a result, anyone I communicate with on the internet can record my IP address. But what can they do with it?

You probably know that you can look up an IP address and find out which ISP controls the block of addresses it falls within. The ISP is unlikely to give out information such as which customer is assigned a specific IP address without a court order. But that doesn't stop companies from using it to identify you.

For example, Amazon knows my name, address, and other information when I'm logged in because I gave it to them. They also can see my IP address and connect the two, especially if it rarely changes. As a result, even if I'm not logged in, they could use my IP address to know, with reasonable certainty, who I am. They wouldn't let me make purchases based on that; IP addresses are not reliable enough identifiers. But they could, for example, use it to continue to show me products they think I might buy.

Amazon might not sell the information that Phil Windley uses a specific IP address to other companies, but many companies will, especially ad networks. As a result, my name, address, and other information are undoubtedly correlated with my IP address in numerous company's databases. Correlation allows you to enrich data by linking data sets together.

People frequently share data with one party and other data with another, naively thinking that the two data sets cannot be correlated. But most data we share contains good, reliable correlators like email addresses or phone numbers. If you use the same email address at different sites or routinely disclose your phone number, data brokers can use these correlating identifiers to link other data about you from several otherwise independent records.

Privacy, Authenticity, and Confidentiality

Earlier in this chapter, I used the words *authenticity* and *confidentiality*. *Authenticity* allows parties to a conversation to know to whom they are talking. *Confidentiality* ensures that the content of the conversation is protected from others. Privacy, authenticity, and confidentiality create a tradespace (*https://oreil.ly/LLnJb*), because you can't achieve all three at the same time.[4] Since confidentiality is easily achieved through encryption, we're almost always trading off privacy and authenticity. Figure 8-1 illustrates these trade-offs.

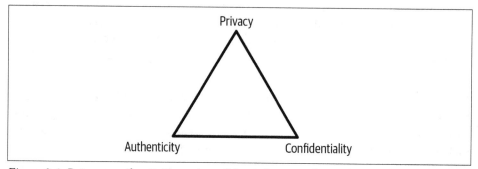

Figure 8-1. Privacy, authenticity, and confidentiality must be traded against each other

Authenticity is difficult to achieve in concert with privacy because it affects the metadata of a conversation. Authenticity often requires others besides the parties to a conversation potentially knowing who else is participating—that is, it requires nonrepudiation. Specifically, if Alice and Bob are communicating, not only does Alice need to know she's talking to Bob, she might also need the ability to prove to others that she and Bob were communicating.

As an example, modern banking laws include provisions known as Know Your Customer (KYC) and Anti-Money Laundering (AML). KYC requires that banks be able to identify the parties to transactions. That's why, when you open a bank account, they ask for numerous identity documents. The purpose is to enable law enforcement to determine the actors behind transactions deemed illegal (hopefully with a warrant). So, banking transactions are strong on authenticity but weak on privacy.[5]

Authenticity is another way of classifying digital relationships. As we discussed in Chapter 5, many relationships are (or could be) ephemeral, relying more on *what* you are than *who* you are. Recall the example of a movie ticket that doesn't identify who

---

4 I first learned about the trade-offs between privacy, authenticity, and confidentiality from Sam Smith at a Utah Self-Sovereign Identity meetup.

5 Remember, this doesn't mean that banking transactions are public, but that others besides the participants *could* know who participated in the conversation.

you are but does identify what you are: one of N people allowed to occupy a seat in a specific theater at a specific time. You establish an ephemeral relationship with the ticket taker, they determine you have a valid ticket, and you're admitted to the theater. This relationship, unless the ticket taker happens to know you, is strong on privacy but weak on authenticity, and it doesn't need much confidentiality either.

A credit card transaction is another interesting case that shows the complicated nature of privacy and authenticity. You have two relationships here: one with the merchant and another with your bank. To the merchant, a credit card says something about *what* you are (someone with sufficient credit to make a purchase) rather than *who* you are—it's strong on privacy, relatively weak on authenticity.[6] To be sure, the merchant does have a permanent, correlating identifier for you (the card number) but is unlikely to be asked to use it outside the transaction.

Because of KYC, however, you are well known to your bank, and the rules of the credit card network ensure that you could be identified by transaction for things like chargebacks and requests from law enforcement. So, this relationship has strong authenticity but weaker privacy guarantees.

The trade-off between privacy and authenticity is informed by the *law of justifiable parties* (see Chapter 4), which says disclosures should be made only to entities with a need to know. Justifiable parties doesn't say everything should be maximally private, but it does say that we need to carefully consider our justification for increasing authenticity at the expense of privacy. Too often, digital systems opt for knowing *who* when they could get by with *what*. In the language I'm developing here: they create authenticated, permanent relationships at the expense of privacy, when they could use pseudonymous, ephemeral relationships and preserve privacy.

Trust is often given as the reason for trading privacy for authenticity—but as the previous chapter discussed, this is often the result of a mistaken understanding of trust. What many interactions really need is confidence in the data being exchanged. As an example, consider how a bar ensures that a patron is old enough to drink. The bar could create a registry and have everyone who wants to drink register by providing several identifying documents, including birth date. Every time you order, you'd authenticate, proving you're the person who established the account and allowing the bar to prove who ordered what and when. This system would rely on *who* you are.

But that isn't how bars do it. Instead, your relationship with the bar is ephemeral. To prove you're old enough to drink, you show the bartender or server an ID card that includes your birthday. They don't record any of the information on the ID card; they

---

6 Recall from the discussion in Chapter 7 that the purpose of the credit card network's trust framework is to reduce the need for an authenticated relationship between the customer and merchant. Each has an authenticated relationship with their respective bank, not each other.

just use the birthday to establish *what* you are: a person old enough to drink. This system favors privacy over authenticity.

The bar use case doesn't require trust (which is, remember, the willingness to rely on someone else to perform actions on the trustor's behalf) in the ID card holder.[7] But it does require confidence in the data. The bar needs to be confident that the person drinking is over the legal age. Both systems provide that confidence, but one protects privacy, and the other does not. Recognizing that we need confidence more than trust allows us to reduce the use of authenticity for better privacy. In contrast, systems that need trust generally need more authenticity and thus have less privacy.

In general, a digital relationship needs authenticity when there is a need for legal recourse and accountability. Different applications will judge the risk inherent in a relationship differently and hence have different trade-offs between privacy and authenticity. I say this with some reticence since I know that, in many organizations, the risk managers are incredibly influential with business leaders and will push for accountability where it might not really be needed, just to be safe. I hope identity professionals can provide cover for privacy and arguments for why confidence is often all that is needed.

Functional Privacy

Pitting privacy against accountability might feel like a Hobson's choice, where good privacy is impossible if you want to prevent fraud. Fortunately, the outcome is not nearly as bleak as it might appear at first.

I've shown that authenticity is often driven by a need for accountability.[8] Understanding accountability helps navigate the spectrum of choices between privacy and authenticity. KYC and AML regulations require that banks be able to identify the parties to transactions. This is a bias toward authenticity at the cost of privacy. (There are nuances; the bank collects this data but doesn't need to use it unless there's a question of fraud or money laundering.)[9] In a technical sense, the nonrepudiability of bank transactions makes them less private, but there aren't a lot of people who are concerned about the privacy of their banking transactions. The authenticity associated with those transactions is provisional or latent. Transactions are revealed to outside parties only when legally required, and most people don't worry about that. From

---

7 The bar needs to trust the *issuer* of the ID card—a different discussion that we'll take up in Chapter 22.

8 Beyond accountability, a number of businesses make their living surveilling people online or are remunerated for helping collect data that informs that surveillance. I'll discuss that later in this chapter.

9 Note that I said *need*. I'm aware that banks likely use it for more than this, often without disclosing how they're using it.

that perspective, transactions with provisional authenticity are private enough. I call this *functional privacy*.

I discussed movie tickets as an example of an ephemeral transaction that doesn't need authenticity to function and thus is private. But consider another example where an ephemeral, nonauthenticated transaction is not good enough. A while back our family went to the ice-skating rink. We bought tickets to get in, just like at the movies. But each of us also signed a liability waiver, which the skating rink required to reduce its risk. That waiver meant that the transaction was much less private. Unlike the bank, where I feel confident my KYC data is not being shared, I don't know what the skating rink is doing with my data.

This is a situation where minimal disclosure doesn't help me. I've given away the data needed to hold me accountable in the case of an accident. No promise was made to me about what the rink might do with it. The only way to hold me accountable and protect my privacy is for the authenticity of the transaction to be made *provisional through agreement*. If the skating rink were to make strong promises that the data would be used only if I had an accident and threatened to sue, then even though I'm identified to the rink, my privacy is protected except in clearly defined circumstances.

Online, the rink could make this provisional authenticity even more trustworthy using cryptographic commitments and key escrow (see Chapter 9). The idea is that any data about me that's needed to enforce the waiver would be hidden from the rink, unchangeable by me, and revealed only if I threaten to sue. This adds a technical element and allows me to exchange my need to trust the rink for trusting the escrow agent, which might be more manageable than trusting every business I interact with. Escrow services could be regulated as fiduciaries to increase trust.

Provisional authenticity works when the data is needed only in a low-probability event (such as a personal injury lawsuit). Often, however, companies actively use data to provide utility in the relationship. For example, I provide my address to Amazon so they can ship me things. In these cases, confidentiality agreements (essentially nondisclosure agreements, or NDAs) are the answer to providing functional privacy while also providing the authenticity needed for accountability and utility. These agreements can't be the traditional contracts of adhesion where, rather than promising to protect confidentiality, companies force people to consent to surveillance.[10] Rather, agreements should be written to ensure that data is always shared with the same promise of confidentiality that existed in the root agreement.

---

10 Adhesion contracts, like the terms and conditions documents to which websites ask people to consent, are "take it or leave it" agreements where one party has substantially more power than the other and does not offer the opportunity to negotiate terms.

Provisional authenticity and data NDAs are important tools for protecting functional privacy without giving up accountability and relationship utility. Functional privacy and accountability are both necessary for creating digital systems that respect and protect people.

Privacy by Design

Privacy by Design (PbD) is set of principles intended to guide architects, product managers, and developers. The principles were published in 2009 as a framework (*https://oreil.ly/9p_pf*) by Ann Cavoukian, who was then the Information and Privacy Commissioner for the Province of Ontario, Canada. Since their publication, the principles have been adopted by organizations like the International Assembly of Privacy Commissioners and Data Protection Authorities and the IAPP. The European Union's General Data Protection Regulation (GDPR) also incorporates PbD.

Despite some criticism that they are too vague to offer solid design advice, the principles are important high-level guides for identity professionals. They apply to a wide variety of design problems, from individual product features to entire ecosystems. Architects should contextualize them for each use case to develop project-specific guidance.

The sections below discuss each of the seven principles in turn, quoting the text of the PbD framework in italics, followed by a discussion.

Principle 1: Proactive Not Reactive; Preventive Not Remedial

The Privacy by Design (PbD) approach is characterized by proactive rather than reactive measures. It anticipates and prevents privacy invasive events before they happen. PbD does not wait for privacy risks to materialize, nor does it offer remedies for resolving privacy infractions once they have occurred—it aims to prevent them from occurring. In short, Privacy by Design comes before-the-fact, not after.

The overarching goal of PbD is to make designers think about privacy ahead of time, building it into the technology and workflow of a system or product instead of trying to layer it on after the fact. The *proactive* principle states this clearly: think about privacy up front.

This principle might be applied to incorporate privacy-related user stories in project requirements. For example:

- As a shopper, I want to be able to control data sharing from the app so that I can decide who sees my data.

- As a site member, I want to limit which other members can view my posts so that I can protect myself from abusive comments.

- As an author, I want to be able to delete things I've written so that I can control my body of work.

These examples show how the general *proactive* principle can be used to create product requirements that increase the product's respect for privacy. User stories help identify the various actors and what actions they can take. By analyzing those interactions, the design team can identify risks to privacy, as well as trade-offs where authenticity is being correctly or incorrectly required.

PbD also implies the need to think through the data being collected; assess the privacy implications and burdens on people, partners, and the organization itself; and create policies and practices that guide architecture and system operations. I'll discuss these more in the *visibility* principle below.

Principle 2: Privacy as the Default Setting

We can all be certain of one thing—the default rules! Privacy by Design seeks to deliver the maximum degree of privacy by ensuring that personal data are automatically protected in any given IT system or business practice. If an individual does nothing, their privacy still remains intact. No action is required on the part of the individual to protect their privacy—it is built into the system, by default.

People say they value privacy, but it's hard to think about in the middle of an urgent transaction. Every morning my newsfeed has at least one article about how to change the settings in an app or on a device to protect privacy. Even accounting for the click-bait scaremongering of these headlines, it's nearly impossible to determine how those apps' and devices' many settings impact privacy without a detailed understanding of their design.

The *default* principle flips this idea, telling designers that *they* are responsible for understanding the privacy implications of settings (alone and in combination) and defaulting to those that best protect privacy.

The problem with this principle is that many apps, if they were private by default, couldn't make money. Apple recently added a feature to iOS that tells users whether an app is tracking them and gives them the option of allowing that to continue or not. As I write this, Facebook had projected in its 2021 fourth-quarter earnings call that this change would cost the company $10 billion in 2022. When the stock markets opened the next morning, its stock dropped 25%, wiping out $200 billion of Facebook's value (*https://oreil.ly/NRz-d*).

This illustrates that PbD goes beyond just product design. The *default* principle applies as much to an app's business model as it does to the way its settings are configured. If you're committed to privacy, you may have to forgo some business models or decline to work for companies with business models that don't respect it.

Principle 3: Privacy Embedded into Design

Privacy by Design is embedded into the design and architecture of IT systems and business practices. It is not bolted on as an add-on, after the fact. The result is that privacy becomes an essential component of the core functionality being delivered. Privacy is integral to the system, without diminishing functionality.

Sometimes an app or device is poorly designed from a privacy perspective and then patched with policy to fix the problem after the fact—for example, building an app that overcollects data, but then making a policy restricting how it can be used. While policy is important, it shouldn't be a substitute for good design.

Embedding privacy into a system means integrating privacy with other parts and features of the system in a holistic way. This allows designers to consider broader contexts and gives them more choices. For example, an app might use several APIs or authentication partners. By thinking about them at design time, designers can consider which trade-offs better protect privacy. Such designs should be auditable against standards and frameworks, including internal standards and principles.

After designers assess the trade-off between privacy and authenticity and make choices appropriate to the business model and architecture, the *embedded* principle ensures that user mistakes or administrator error or misconduct can't easily degrade those decisions.

Principle 4: Full Functionality—Positive-Sum, Not Zero-Sum

Privacy by Design seeks to accommodate all legitimate interests and objectives in a positive-sum "win-win" manner, not through a dated, zero-sum approach, where unnecessary trade-offs are made. Privacy by Design avoids the pretense of false dichotomies, such as privacy vs. security, demonstrating that it is possible, and far more desirable, to have both.

Good design often requires achieving some goals at the cost of not achieving others. The goal of design is to make the right trade-offs based on all the objectives that a product, service, device, or system must achieve.

The very real trade-offs between privacy and authenticity can't be ignored. Often, the need for authenticity is voiced as a security requirement. Designers should carefully vet those requirements and accommodate any legitimate need for authenticity. As I discussed earlier, there are methods you can use to achieve accountability and utility requirements while offering more privacy than a "security-first" stance would allow.

In Chapter 16 I'll discuss identity architectures that employ cryptography and other techniques to provide positive-sum designs that protect privacy, achieve accountability, and ensure full functionality.

Principle 5: End-to-End Security—Full Lifecycle Protection

Privacy by Design, having been embedded into the system prior to the first element of information being collected, extends securely throughout the entire lifecycle of the data involved—strong security measures are essential to privacy, from start to finish. This ensures that all data are securely retained, and then securely destroyed at the end of the process, in a timely fashion. Thus, Privacy by Design ensures cradle to grave, secure lifecycle management of information, end-to-end.

The *security* principle emphasizes the need for continuous attention to privacy throughout a product's or system's lifecycle. This means evaluating security over and over again and continuing to consider privacy as you update or maintain products and systems.

As you learned in Chapter 6, relationships, which are the heart of many systems, also have a lifecycle. Considering the security of relationship records is vital to protecting the privacy of participants in that relationship. The security principle tells designers to consider each phase of the lifecycle as they assess the security needs of the data their product collects, infers, and uses. Ultimately, when the relationship is terminated, that data must be treated securely as well. In an ideal situation, it can be simply deleted, but sometimes records retention laws or the demands of the business don't allow that. In those cases, secure data storage, combined with a good inventory of what is being stored and its retention requirements, is an important part of ensuring privacy.

Principle 6: Visibility and Transparency—Keep It Open

Privacy by Design seeks to assure all stakeholders that whatever the business practice or technology involved, it is in fact operating according to the stated promises and objectives, subject to independent verification. Its component parts and operations remain visible and transparent, to both users and providers alike. Remember, trust but verify.

A big part of PbD is ensuring that PII data is collected, stored, and managed according to reasoned policies and practices. *Visibility and transparency* are important in conforming to the *law of user control and consent*. At the start of any project involving PII, you should ask questions like:

- What kinds of identity data are we collecting?
- How is this identity data collected?
- Why was the identity data collected?
- Were special conditions on its use established? Were there agreements?
- Were affected individuals informed in a clear and easy-to-understand way about the collection and the policies and practices governing its use?

- Who is the data owner?

- Who is the custodian?

- Who uses the data? Why and how do they usually access it (remotely, via the web, from home)?

- Where and how is it stored? Is it stored on premises or in the cloud?

- How long should the data be kept? Is it routinely kept after that?

- Is any of the data stored on devices that are routinely transported off-site, such as laptops or smartphones?

- What information is transferred to third parties? Why is it transferred? Are the third parties held accountable for the promises our organization made about the data?

- Are there backups? If so, answer these same questions about the backups.

- Are there access logs for the data?

- Where are the logs stored?

- Are the logs protected?

- What other security measures (firewalls, intrusion detection systems, and so on) are used to protect the data?

The answers to these questions should be codified in a framework containing promises, objectives, guidelines, best practices, and policies that can guide development and maintenance of the system and its data. But that's just the start.

Many companies view their privacy framework as something they must do to keep their customers from being angry with them, because their industry demands it, or because someone convinced the CEO or CIO that they'd be liable if the company didn't have one. All of these may be true statements, but they're ancillary to the real reason to have a privacy framework: it provides a basis for the terms of service you're offering for whatever benefit the customer perceives.

For example, consider an online merchant that collects identity information from customers at various stages in a transaction, in return for which the customer receives some benefit. As a start, whenever a customer visits, the service installs a cookie on their browser so that the shopping cart works. The product managers realize that they can also use the cookie to recognize the customer the next time they return and even to track their shopping habits. When the customer buys something, the service collects PII such as their name, email, address, and credit card number, and can link the cookie to a customer profile. What should this online merchant's privacy policy say?

First, tell the truth. Tell customers what data you collect, why you collect it, and what you do with it. Second, be specific. In this example, the merchant might say, in part:

- We use cookies. Our shopping cart will not work without them.

- When you make a purchase, your personal information is stored in our system only if you give us permission by clicking the "Save my information" box on the checkout form. When you do this, we can serve you better by automatically filling out some forms for you when you shop.

- We use cookies to track our customers' shopping habits. We use this data to make our search tool better and to offer a better product selection. We may release information about our customers' shopping habits to partners and suppliers in aggregate, but your individual shopping habits will be released to a third party only with your specific permission, obtained in advance.

- Advertisements appearing on our system may use third-party ad response-tracking systems that use cookies to track ad click-through and to target those ads to specific customers.

A real privacy policy would be longer, and your lawyers will probably want to fill it with lots of other information. While it's a good idea to involve lawyers in the process, since it's ultimately a term sheet between you and your customers, make sure that customers can easily read and understand your privacy policy, or it won't do what you need it to do: inform them in clear language of the terms of your PII collection. *If it's not clear, consent is meaningless.*

Your goal is to create accountability around how PII is used. Accountability is a product of the following factors:

- Creating a privacy framework.

- Assigning the parties responsible for implementing and complying with each part of the framework.

- Creating open practices and processes that ensure transparency within and, where appropriate, outside the organization. You should be especially open with individuals about whom you've collected PII. Publish these practices and processes so customers can easily discover them.

- Audit (monitor, evaluate, and verify) to ensure compliance and provide redress mechanisms, both to people inside your organization and those outside who may be affected by noncompliance. Redress should include a means of appeal for adverse decisions.

On the subject of openness, you should also consider what parts of your codebase might be made open source or drawn from open source repositories to further enhance transparency about your practices.

Principle 7: Respect for User Privacy—Keep It User-Centric

Above all, Privacy by Design requires architects and operators to keep the interests of the individual uppermost by offering such measures as strong privacy defaults, appropriate notice, and empowering user-friendly options. Keep it user-centric.

Privacy concerns *personally* identifying information. I emphasize *personally* because too often it's easy to lose sight of the individual as we go about designing systems and products. One of the reasons I like including privacy in user stories as I gather requirements is because this ensures that people are central to privacy requirements.

The best PbD results occur when individuals are empowered to be active participants in privacy. There are three important practices you can implement to help with this effort:

Consent
> Inform individuals in clear and easy-to-understand ways about how their PII will be used and offer them the opportunity for meaningful consent. (*Meaningful* implies that the choices aren't "give us all your data" or "don't do business with us.")

Access
> Individuals should have access to their PII and the opportunity to amend or delete it as needed.

Accountability
> The organization should offer individuals the opportunity to learn about its policies and practices, review its compliance with its own policies and with relevant regulations, interact with the organization to bring problems to light, and appeal adverse decisions.

Chapter 14 through Chapter 19 will discuss technologies and architectures that go beyond mere user-centricity to self-sovereignty, where people are given tools that provide more control over their PII and how it's handled.

Privacy Regulations

PbD demonstrates the need for balance between technical and policy protections for PII. Technology alone cannot protect privacy, but policy without technical help leaves too much room for abuse that can be difficult to police. Beyond policy, regulation ensures consistent privacy protection across organizations within a jurisdiction.

General Data Protection Regulation

Adopted by the European Parliament in April 2016, GDPR is the big gun: the world's most comprehensive and far-reaching privacy regulation. Even though it's a European Union (EU) regulation, it applies to any company processing the data of EU residents (not just citizens), even if the data processing happens outside the EU. GDPR authorizes the European Data Protection Board to levy fines up to €20 million, or 4% of an organization's worldwide annual revenue—whichever is higher. As a result, GDPR got the attention of most companies around the world when it went into effect in May 2018.

GDPR is meant to ensure that products and services build in safeguards to protect data by design. It obliges organizations to protect data related to people. This focus on business is built into its language, in which *data controllers* and *data processors* (always businesses) are responsible for protecting data about a *data subject* (a person). GDPR speaks of *personal data* rather than *personally identifying information*, a distinction that broadens its applicability.

By the GDPR definition, *personal data* includes (but is not limited to):

- Name
- Home address
- Identification number (such as a US Social Security or employee number)
- Email address
- Sensitive data such as criminal, medical, and religious records
- IP and Media Access Control (MAC) addresses
- Cookies and other correlation identifiers
- Public keys

These last three are not often considered PII, since they can't always be used to identify an individual, but GDPR includes them as personal data.

Article 5.1-2 (*https://oreil.ly/3ThEf*) of GDPR holds data controllers responsible for complying with seven principles for processing personal data:

Lawfulness, fairness, and transparency
Personal data shall be "processed lawfully, fairly and in a transparent manner in relation to the data subject."

Purpose limitation
Personal data shall be "collected for specified, explicit and legitimate purposes" and not further processed in a manner that is incompatible with those purposes.

Data minimization

Personal data collection must be "adequate, relevant and limited to what is necessary in relation to the purposes for which they are processed."

Accuracy

Personal data collection must be "accurate and, where necessary, kept up to date."

Storage limitation

Personal data must be stored "in a form which permits identification of data subjects for no longer than is necessary" for the specified purpose.

Integrity and confidentiality

Personal data must be "processed in a manner that ensures appropriate security of the personal data, including protection against unauthorised or unlawful processing and against accidental loss, destruction or damage."

Accountability

The data controller is responsible for, and must be able to demonstrate, GDPR compliance with all these principles.

In addition, GDPR includes specific guidance on data security, when a company is allowed to process data, what constitutes consent, and when a data protection officer must be appointed.

Data protection is a prerequisite to privacy. But GDPR also includes a set of privacy rights (*https://oreil.ly/HOKC_*) for data subjects:

- The right to be informed
- The right of access
- The right to rectification
- The right to erasure (often called "the right to be forgotten")
- The right to restrict processing
- The right to data portability
- The right to object
- Rights in relation to automated decision making and profiling

As you can see, GDPR is far-reaching and supports several of the Laws of Identity, including *user control and consent, minimal disclosure,* and *justifiable parties.* Its extent, combined with its ability to levy fines based on where people live rather than where companies are located, means that it affects and will continue to affect data protection and privacy around the world.

Determining how best to comply with GDPR can be difficult. This situation involves two groups of people who don't often mix: lawyers and technologists. Like PbD, this gets much more difficult if your business model isn't easily aligned with individual data protection and privacy. But even when it is, the legal requirements will often force changes in your product that don't necessarily make sense from a product-design or application-engineering standpoint. Beyond the product itself, you will likely have to update or implement new policies, procedures, and processes that not only ensure you comply but allow you to demonstrate your compliance.

While GDPR is a big step in regulating data protection and privacy and will doubtless force more organizations to think about these important subjects, it does have some limitations. Like any regulation, GDPR cements a particular viewpoint about data protection into place. This can limit future innovation that doesn't fit the existing model well. For example, GDPR makes the person a mere data subject, and the data subject cannot be the data controller. Because GDPR sees these roles as mutually exclusive, it conflicts with models like self-sovereign identity that see the individual as a controller of personal data. Over time, these conflicts will need to be worked out, but regulations can be difficult and slow to change.

California Consumer Privacy Act

The California Consumer Privacy Act (CCPA), which took effect in January 2020, is the first major US privacy legislation enacted in the post-GDPR era. Because California is a large state with the fifth-largest global economy and an outsized presence of high-tech companies, CCPA is poised to have a similarly outsized global influence on data protection and privacy.

Like GDPR, CCPA aims to be a comprehensive privacy regulation granting people broad rights over their personal data. It is sometimes called "California's GDPR," but there are significant differences: CCPA focuses on businesses selling PII and requires customers to opt out rather than consent, and its potential fines for violating CCPA are much lower than GDPR's. Table 8-1 compares the two.

Table 8-1. Comparison of GDPR and CCPA

	GDPR	CCPA
Protects	Natural persons	Natural persons ("consumers") who are California residents
Rights	Requires consent and notice of the controller, its contact info, and the legitimate interest allowing collection	Requires opt-out and explicit notice of intention to sell data
Applies to	All organizations	For-profit businesses with annual gross revenue over $25M that process PII for more than 50,000 consumers or that derive more than 50% of annual revenue from selling PII
Legal basis	Legal grounds (legitimate interest) required to process data	Does not list positive legal grounds for processing
Scope	Organizations in the EU or doing business with people in the EU	Organizations doing business in California

	GDPR	CCPA
PII covered	All personal data processed by the organization	Opt-out for data sold or shared; excludes medical information (including clinical trial data), consumer reporting agencies, public data (lawfully made available), and data covered by other statutes (such as driver data)
Access	Controllers must provide access to collected data without undue delay	Applies only to data collected within the prior 12 months; limits access requests to twice annually
Enforcement	Up to 4% of global annual turnover or €20 million, whichever is higher	Up to $2,500 for each violation and $7,500 for each intentional violation
Civil remedies	Any violation can be used as a claim for civil remedies; no limit on damages	Only allowed when nonencrypted PII is accessed by unauthorized entities through theft, exfiltration, or disclosure in violation of a business's security obligations; limited to $100 to $750 per consumer per incident or actual damages, whichever is greater

As you can see from Table 8-1, CCPA has a narrower scope and much lighter penalties than GDPR. To date, it has had little impact on companies operating in the US, whereas GDPR has had a noticeable impact on ad revenues and by implication surveillance. But despite some important differences—some would say weaknesses—compared to GDPR, CCPA is the most comprehensive privacy legislation in the US. It is the beginning, rather than the end, of privacy legislation in the US; other states are bound to follow.

Other Regulatory Efforts

Beyond GDPR and CCPA, there are several notable laws and regulations affecting organizations. Table 8-2 shows some of the more prominent US and Canadian laws and regulations concerning privacy.

Table 8-2. Other notable privacy laws and regulations

Law/regulation	Description
Canadian Personal Information Protection and Electronic Documents Act	Applies to private-sector organizations across Canada that collect, use, or disclose personal information in the course of a commercial activity. PII can only be used for the purposes for which it was collected. Organizations must obtain consent to use it for another purpose.
Customer Identification Program (Patriot Act)	Requires financial services organizations in the US to collect and store customer data and verify it against government-owned lists of known or suspected terrorists.
Health Information Portability and Accountability Act (HIPAA)	Applies to any organization that manages health-care data in the US. Establishes a patient's right to control access to and use of personal health information (PHI). Requires that organizations control and safeguard PHI. Imposes technical standards for access control, auditing, data integrity, and security.
Gramm-Leach-Bliley Act	Applies to financial services organizations in the US. Requires physical, administrative, and technical measures to protect customer data. Data can be reused or disclosed only if the customer specifically opts in.

Law/regulation	Description
Children's Online Privacy Protection Act (COPPA)	Applies to PII about children under 13 years of age, including children outside the US. Outlines requirements for privacy policies and parental consent, and operator responsibilities for protecting the PII of minors.

All these regulations can have a direct impact on your organization's identity management plans. Some regulations, for example, set timeframes within which records must be retained. This clearly affects the design and implementation of digital identity infrastructures.

Another US federal law with indirect effects is the Sarbanes-Oxley Act of 2002 (*https://oreil.ly/_xDrK*). Sarbanes-Oxley applies to public companies and, among other things, requires annual reports on the effectiveness of internal controls and procedures, which are directly affected by identity management decisions about things like directories and access control. Consequently, public companies need to design and implement their digital identity infrastructure not only to comply with Sarbanes-Oxley requirements but also to minimize the cost of the auditing and reporting needed to comply where possible.

It's impossible to determine what laws and regulations affect your identity management strategy or what to do about them if you try to manage identity like most IT departments have traditionally managed security. These are business issues and require business input. For example, the Audit Committee of a company's board of directors will determine its ground rules for how to comply with Sarbanes-Oxley. Not understanding its directives to ensure that they're met would be a career-limiting act.

The Time Value and Time Cost of Privacy

We often talk about privacy like its value and cost never vary. In fact, people usually value privacy more for current information than they do for old information. Alice might not want her current address published but not care who knows the address of the apartment she lived in while at college. Similarly, the cost of making recent data private is usually lower than that of keeping data private over time. As time passes, more and more context builds up around data, making it harder to prevent its correlation with other information. Put simply, over time, secrets become harder to keep. This sets up the dynamic illustrated in Figure 8-2.

In the graph in Figure 8-2, there's a crossover point where the cost of maintaining the privacy of information is greater than the value of the privacy. To the right of that point, maintaining privacy is cost effective. To the left, it's cost prohibitive. This isn't meant to imply that you should do a cost-benefit analysis of individual data types and calculate some point where you just give up and publish it all. Rather, the point is that data management practices can shift the crossover point, making privacy more cost effective.

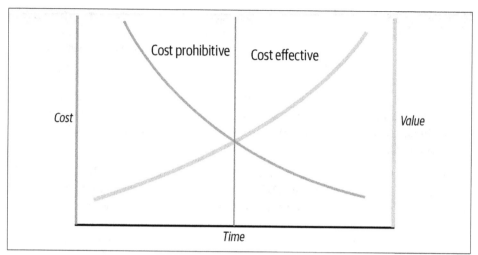

Figure 8-2. Time cost and time value of privacy

Figure 8-3 shows the same graph, but with two cost lines. The new cost line is lower and thus shifts the crossover point farther left, meaning we can keep data private longer at a reasonable cost or can maintain privacy on data that might have been cost prohibitive before.

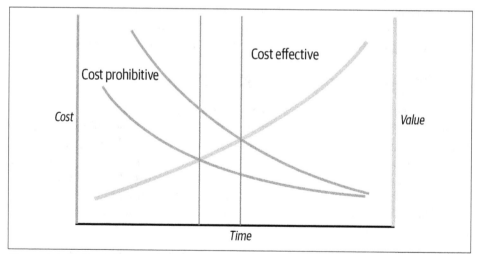

Figure 8-3. Shifting the crossover point left

How do you lower the cost? Keep less data that identifies people. This may seem obvious, but I'm always surprised by organizations that keep more data than they really need on the theory that it's cheap. They're only considering storage costs. When you factor in the costs of securing data and ensuring regulatory compliance, keeping PII gets much more expensive.

Keeping less data starts with collecting less data. This requires being thoughtful about product and site design, to collect only the PII that is necessary for business purposes. Regularly reviewing and purging data in different classes (depending on regulatory and business requirements) can also reduce the cost of keeping PII. In Chapter 15, I'll discuss techniques and technologies that support minimal disclosure, which can significantly reduce the amount of PII you collect without negatively impacting business needs.

Surveillance Capitalism and Web 2.0

In the opening chapter of her book *The Age of Surveillance Capitalism* (PublicAffairs, 2019), philosopher and social psychologist Shoshana Zuboff asks, "Can the digital future be our home?"

This question is perhaps one of the most important of our age. More and more of our lives are intermediated by digital systems. And yet those systems are not ours—they belong to the companies that provide them. Our experience on them is predicated on the goals, desires, and needs of those companies, not our own. I call these systems *administrative* because they are built to administer our experience in a particular domain for the administrator's specific purposes.

Zuboff makes several compelling arguments about why surveillance capitalism represents a significant threat to humanity's future. An overarching conclusion is that these companies, by putting everyone inside their administrative systems so as to make our lives *legible* to their surveillance, become tyrants:

> Tyranny is the obliteration of politics. It is founded on its own strain of radical indifference in which every person, except the tyrant, is understood as an organism among organisms in an equivalency of Other-Ones.

Contrary to what many might believe, obliterating politics is not a good thing. Politics is how decentralized, democratic systems achieve legitimacy and coherence. Getting rid of politics requires putting everyone and everything in the centralized administrative system of the surveillance capitalist—making them subject to the dictates of a tyrant who is radically indifferent to their autonomy, individuality, and humanity.

Living inside the administrative systems of Big Tech is like living inside an amusement park. It's not altogether unpleasant, but it's a far cry from authentic—stippled with moments of joy but devoid of real happiness and freedom. We are all treated identically and transactionally, despite pretensions to personalization.

Zuboff's conclusion that surveillance capitalism is a new "rogue" form of capitalism leaves little recourse but to regulate its ills. Not unreasonably, her prescription for this predicament is to protect, trust, and utilize democratic processes—to collectively push back, without letting our cynicism dissuade us or cause us to lose hope.

Cory Doctorow offers another remedy in his book *How to Destroy Surveillance Capitalism* (OneZero Books, 2020). In his view, merely regulating a big monopoly only further entrenches it, locking the world into the status quo. If we want to destroy surveillance capitalism, Doctorow argues, we must break it up and decentralize, making "big tech small again." Ultimately, the choice is between fixing Big Tech and fixing the internet. Doctorow argues for the second option.

Fixing the internet is hard but not impossible. Doctorow references Lawrence Lessig's *Code and Other Laws of Cyberspace* (Basic Books, 1999) saying, "Our lives are regulated by four forces: law (what's legal), code (what's technologically possible), norms (what's socially acceptable), and markets (what's profitable)." We can bring all four to bear on this problem.

Many people fear that breaking up Big Tech will diminish the fruits of the digital world we've come to enjoy and even rely on. Centralization, they say, is the only safe and efficient way to build messaging platforms, app stores, social networks, and so on.

This is where Lessig's other three forces come into play. The means exist to decentralize most of the centralized Web 2.0 platforms (in Lessig's words, it's "technologically possible"). The internet itself, and more recent decentralized networks like Bitcoin and Ethereum, show that large, decentralized systems can achieve legitimacy to accomplish global goals.

Returning to Zuboff's opening question: "Can the digital future be our home?" Fixing Big Tech just leaves us where we're at, with slightly fewer problems. It's a dead-end road that doesn't lead to a digital home. But fixing the internet, redecentralizing it, promises a future where we can live authentic digital lives that complement our physical lives.

Privacy and Laws of Identity

Privacy cannot be an afterthought. The stakes are too high. Beyond the regulatory and legal requirements, there are ethical and moral responsibilities. This chapter has introduced important ideas about where privacy intersects with identity, but privacy is bigger than what can be covered in one chapter. Identity professionals must be well versed in privacy to build identity systems that are not only functional but respect and protect the people who use them.

Many of the Laws of Identity (introduced in Chapter 4) have a privacy aspect:

- *User consent* speaks to the extent to which people control how and where data about them is shared.

- *Minimal disclosure* is about the amount of data that is shared, and whether the system overshares or overcollects data.

- *Justifiable parties* deals with who sees the data people share and whether their access to that data is justified.
- *Directed identity* addresses the amount of correlation that can occur from public global identifiers.

As you've seen throughout the first half of this book, the Laws of Identity and the features of the identity metasystem provide important means for solving the problems of identity discussed in Chapter 3. This chapter's discussion of privacy and its interplay with the Laws of Identity should convince you that how you think about, design, and protect privacy will have significant consequences for how well your identity system will support the relationships that allow people to live effective and safe online lives. Chapters 16 and 17 will discuss various architectures for identity and how they work toward or against Zuboff's vision of a digital future.

CHAPTER 9

Integrity, Nonrepudiation, and Confidentiality

Among the foundational concepts in digital identity are integrity, nonrepudiation, and confidentiality. *Integrity* ensures a message or transaction has not been tampered with. *Nonrepudiation* provides evidence for the existence of a message or transaction and ensures its contents cannot be disputed once sent. *Confidentiality* ensures that only the people or processes authorized to view and use the contents of a message or transaction have access to those contents. In some situations, these properties are unneeded luxuries, but in others, the lack of just one of these properties can lead to disaster. Understanding them, and when to use them, is crucial to a digital identity management strategy:

Integrity

Integrity is a fundamental requirement of a trustworthy identity infrastructure. Identity systems exchange credentials as well as messages and transactions regarding attributes, provisioning information, and other data. Trusting that the contents of these systems have not been tampered with is vital. As an example, consider a document representing identity credentials. To trust those credentials, we must be able to verify they are authentic and have not been changed.

Nonrepudiation

Nonrepudiation is the presentation of unforgeable evidence that a message was sent or received. If messages or transactions can be disputed, then important identity actions can be challenged and jeopardized. These disputes can take two forms. Consider that Alice and Bob are exchanging messages. In the first case, Alice denies sending a message to Bob that he claims to have received. Being able to counter Alice's denial is *Non-Repudiation of Origin (NRO)*. In the second case,

Alice claims to have sent Bob a message that he denies having received. Offering evidence to counter Bob's claim is *Non-Repudiation of Receipt* (NRR).

Confidentiality

Confidentiality can be achieved in several ways. The two most common are steganography and encryption. *Steganography* is the process of putting a message inside another message in such a way that observers do not know that it's there. For example, modifying the low-order bits in an image to transmit a message does not interfere with viewing the image and the presence of the message is difficult to detect. While steganography has some interesting uses, it cannot serve as the basis for confidentiality in most identity systems. *Encryption* is the process of transforming a message using a key so that anyone viewing the message without the key cannot determine its contents.

This chapter will focus on techniques, processes, and technologies for achieving these three important properties. The basis for all of these is cryptography. We'll discuss basic cryptography concepts and then apply these to solving problems of integrity, nonrepudiation, and confidentiality. While cryptography alone isn't the answer to the problems of identity, it provides important building blocks that we will use throughout the rest of this book.

Cryptography

Cryptography is the science of making the cost of discovery of hidden information greater than the value of the information itself. An important corollary to this statement is that there is no single cryptographic solution to every problem. With increasing needs for confidentiality, the methods become more involved, and the costs increase.

Understanding cryptography's limits is perhaps the most important thing you can know about it. Many people mistakenly think that cryptography is about absolute protection of data and are consequently upset to learn that someone has cracked a trusted cryptographic algorithm. While such news is certainly worth paying attention to, even easily compromised algorithms have uses in certain circumstances. The goal is to understand the challenges a problem presents and match those to the cryptographic method that solves them for the least cost, usually measured in compute cycles. The following sections will discuss several cryptographic systems, where they best apply, and common algorithms for implementing them.

Secret Key Cryptography

Secret key cryptography uses keys to transform a message in such a way as to render it unreadable to anyone without the proper key. Secret key cryptography is also known as symmetric cryptography (since the same key is used to encrypt and decrypt the message) or conventional cryptography.

Figure 9-1 shows a simple secret key transaction. Alice and Bob wish to share a message without divulging its contents to outside parties.[1] Alice uses her secret key to put the plain-text message through a process that transforms it into an encrypted message. Alice can send the message to Bob without fear that an outsider will be able to read it, as long as the eavesdropper does not possess the secret key. Later Bob puts the encrypted message through another process, using the same key, to recreate the plain-text message.

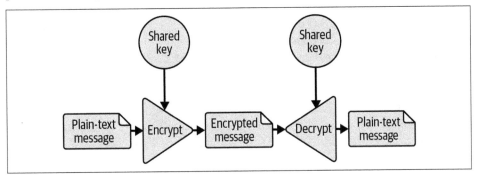

Figure 9-1. Encryption and decryption using a secret key

One of the most important factors affecting the strength of a secret key encryption process is the length of the key. There are a significant number of secret key algorithms which differ in their key length, their efficiency for encryption and decryption, and their vulnerability to attack. For most identity systems, the selection of a secret key algorithm is independent of other concerns and, consequently, it can be selected based on the requirements of the specific task at hand.

Well-known secret key cryptographic algorithms include Advanced Encryption Standard (AES), International Data Encryption Algorithm (IDEA), and Rivest Cipher 5 and 6 (RC5, RC6). In addition to selecting the algorithm, you will also usually need to select software that implements the algorithm. This is where it pays to get the advice and help of a cryptographer. One standard caution is to never implement your own crypto software.

---

1 Alice, Bob, Charlie, and others (*https://oreil.ly/qlayc*) are the cast of characters most papers on cryptography use to explain scenarios.

The process depicted in Figure 9-1 assumes Alice and Bob have agreed ahead of time on the secret key. One of them could choose the key and then transmit it to the other party using some alternative (often termed "out of band") form of communication, or they could meet to choose and exchange the key. The problem with both methods is that in both cases an attacker might steal the key. Key transmission is one of the primary weaknesses of secret key cryptography. Once the key is compromised, an attacker can decrypt and read any message encrypted with it.

To make matters worse, common attacks against cryptographic algorithms involve collecting large amounts of ciphertext that has been encrypted using the same key. To combat this attack, keys must be changed often, making key exchanges a frequent affair. The next section will discuss a concept that solves this problem.

Public-Key Cryptography

The challenge facing Alice and Bob is how to exchange keys. This is a big enough problem when just Alice and Bob are exchanging keys. Imagine the problems you'd have if you wanted to exchange encrypted messages with all the people in your organization and each of the subgroups. For example, if the development group wants to exchange messages in private, they need a key known to all of them that is different than any of the keys they use to exchange mail with each other. The management complexity of such a scheme is staggering. Fortunately, there's a cryptographic technology that does away with the need to exchange, store, and use secret keys. This technology is called *public-key cryptography*.

Public-key cryptography makes use of two distinct keys: the *public key* and *private key*. The private key is kept secret by its owner and is never divulged. The public key can be freely shared with other parties, even posted on a message board or website. The public and private keys are mathematically related to each other and are called a *key pair*. The mathematical relationship that the keys share enables a message encrypted by one to be decrypted by the other. Yet neither key can be used to decrypt what it has encrypted. Thus, a message that is encrypted with the public key can only be decrypted using its corresponding private key, and a message that is encrypted with the private key can only be decrypted using its corresponding public key. Because of this property, public-key cryptosystems are called *asymmetric*.

Figure 9-2 shows how Alice and Bob might use public-key cryptography to exchange a message. Because Bob's public key can be freely shared, he has posted it on his website. Alice downloads Bob's public key and uses it to encrypt her message. She then sends the encrypted message to Bob. Bob uses his private key to decrypt Alice's message. Only Bob's private key, which he has kept secret, can decrypt messages encrypted with his public key, thus ensuring that Alice's message has been kept confidential.

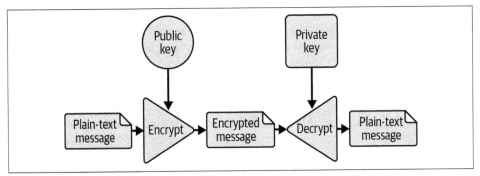

Figure 9-2. Public-key cryptography

Now, suppose that instead of encrypting her message with Bob's public key, Alice uses her private key to encrypt the message. Alice sends the encrypted message to Bob and Bob uses Alice's public key, which he can get from her site or in some other way, to decrypt her message and read it. Of course, everyone else also has Alice's public key. So, Alice cannot use her private key to send confidential messages to Bob. To send a confidential message to Bob, Alice uses Bob's public key to encrypt the message.

There are, however, good reasons for encrypting a message with a private key. Encrypting a message with a private key can provide message integrity and nonrepudiation. If Alice has kept her private key secret, anyone using Alice's public key to decrypt her message knows two things: (a) the message has not been tampered with in transit and (b) the message is truly from Alice. If the message has been changed, then Alice's public key will no longer decrypt it. If the message is encrypted with any key other than Alice's private key, her public key will not decrypt it. If a third party, Charlie, wants to impersonate Alice, he must have access to her private key.

Using a private key to encrypt a message creates a *digital signature*. Using a public key to decrypt a message that has been encrypted with a private key is called *signature verification*.

A key system is called *reversible* if a private key can decrypt messages encrypted with its associated public key and a public key can decrypt messages encrypted with its associated private key. Key systems where the private key can encrypt but cannot decrypt and the public key can decrypt but cannot encrypt are called *irreversible*. Reversible key systems can be used for confidentiality, integrity, and nonrepudiation. Irreversible key systems can only be used for integrity and nonrepudiation.

Hybrid Key Systems

Public-key cryptosystems are computationally more expensive than secret key algorithms. Public-key cryptosystems can take 100 to 1,000 times longer than secret key systems to encrypt or decrypt the same message. Consequently, public-key cryptosystems are rarely used to encrypt large amounts of data. Rather, they are used to negotiate a secret key between parties in the initial phase of communication. This is called a *hybrid cryptosystem* or *Diffie–Hellman key exchange* after a general scheme published by Whitfield Diffie and Martin Hellman in 1976.

Diffie–Hellman key exchange algorithms allow two parties that know each other's public keys to calculate a secret key using their own private key and the other party's public key. In our example, Alice and Bob have exchanged public keys. To create a shared secret, they also exchange a large prime number and another number smaller than the prime called the generator. Alice uses her private key, Bob's public key, the large prime, and the generator to create a secret key. This process is commutative and so when Bob uses his private key, Alice's public key, the prime, and the generator, he calculates the same secret key that Alice did. Charlie can know both public keys, the prime, and the generator and still not be able to calculate the shared secret because he doesn't have access to either private key.

Of course, if Charlie can somehow insert himself into the middle of the key exchange so that both Bob and Alice end up with his public key while thinking they've got the correct one, he can impersonate Bob to Alice and set up a shared secret with her and impersonate Alice to Bob and set up a shared secret with him. Afterward, he can sit in the middle of the conversation, reading the communication and forwarding Alice's messages to Bob and Bob's messages to Alice. This is called a *man-in-the-middle attack*. When Alice sends a message, it goes to Charlie, who decrypts it, reads it, reencrypts it with the shared secret he negotiated with Bob, and sends it on. Alice and Bob may never realize Charlie is snooping on their conversation. This kind of attack points out the need for trustworthy key exchanges, a topic we'll visit later in this chapter when we talk about digital certificates.

The most widely used hybrid key system is Transport Layer Security (TLS), the protocol that secures web pages. You might still hear people call it SSL (for Secure Sockets Layer), even though TLS is the preferred name. TLS is part of every major web browser and server. Recent campaigns to "encrypt everything" and tools to make it easier to use have pushed its adoption to even small websites.

TLS creates an encrypted channel between two applications. An encrypted channel automatically encrypts all the data being sent on the wire without any action by the user. TLS uses the public-key cryptosystem to negotiate a shared secret that is used to encrypt the communications. This negotiation is performed using Diffie–Hellman, giving both parties a shared secret without either having to send the secret over the wire. TLS sits below the application protocol and thus can be used to secure HTTP communications, email transport, or any other application protocol on the internet.

TLS 1.3, the latest version of the protocol, significantly simplifies and speeds up the creation of the shared secret and plugs several security holes in TLS 1.2. Figure 9-3 shows the Diffie–Hellman exchange in TLS 1.3.

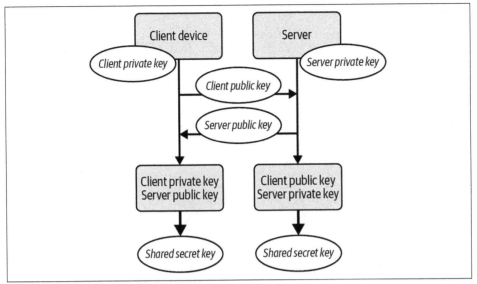

Figure 9-3. Diffie–Hellman secret key generation in TLS 1.3

In TLS 1.3, the client sends a public key with the initial HELLO message to the server. The server responds with its public key. Then each uses its own private key and the public key of the other to generate a shared secret using Diffie–Hellman. A different shared secret is negotiated for each session. The shared secret is then used to encrypt all further communications.

Public-Key Cryptosystem Algorithms

There are several public-key cryptosystems. Table 9-1 lists four of the common public-key algorithms, their type, and how they are primarily used. The choice of which algorithm to use depends on the task, the level of security needed for the task, relative efficiencies, and so on. Public-key cryptography schemes can be subject to nonobvious attacks that render them transparent, so it is best to employ a crypto-graphic expert when choosing which algorithm or scheme to use for a specific application.

Table 9-1. Public-key algorithms

Algorithm	Type	Primary usage
Digital Signature Algorithm (DSA)	Irreversible	Digital signatures
Elliptic Curve Digital Signature Algorithm (ECDSA)	Irreversible	Digital signatures
Rivest-Shamir-Adleman (RSA)	Reversible	Confidentiality, digital signatures, key exchange
Diffie–Hellman key agreement protocol	Reversible	Key exchange

In addition to selecting the algorithm, you will also sometimes need to select software that implements the algorithm. Good, open source implementations of important cryptographic algorithms are readily available, including libsodium, OpenSSL, and Hyperledger Ursa.

Key Generation

Both symmetric and asymmetric cryptographic systems must generate keys, usually large integers. If an attacker can guess how keys are being generated, then the attacker may not need to steal keys; they can simply generate duplicate keys as needed. Consequently, key generation is a critical factor in the security of a cryptographic system.

Randomness in keys is measured using *information entropy*, a concept introduced by information theory pioneer Claude Shannon in 1948. Analogous to thermodynamic entropy, high information entropy correlates to high disorder or randomness in a message. High entropy yields greater randomness and, all things being equal, more secure keys.

Keys are usually generated using some kind of random number generator (RNG). True RNGs are hard to come by since they involve measuring some physical phenomenon and then compensating for measurement errors. For example, Silicon Graphics developed an RNG system, called Lavarand, that used a wall of lava lamps to generate random patterns. The system is still being used by Cloudflare, a web infrastructure and security company.

For convenience, keys are usually generated using a pseudorandom number generator (PRNG). A PRNG uses a computational process that can produce sequences of seemingly random integers. The strength of the PRNG algorithm depends on the algorithm itself and the initial seed. PRNG algorithms used in cryptography are called "cryptographically secure" PRNGs. Don't implement your own RNGs and don't just blindly use the one built into a library or your operating system. This is another place where the guidance of a cryptographer can avoid security problems later on.

The information entropy of the initial seed determines the degree of unpredictability for the generated random numbers. If the attacker can guess the seed, then the attacker has access to all the keys the algorithm will generate. Since generating true randomness by observing natural phenomena can be slow, RNGs and PRNGs are often used together. The RNG is used to generate the initial seed and then the PRNG algorithm is used to generate keys for use.

Key Management

Key management is one of the harder parts of cryptography, especially as the number of keys grows. Key management is not primarily a technical activity, but one that involves governance, and, alas, politics. Creating good key management policies, training people on policies and best practices, and coordinating the activities of all those who need to use keys can be a challenging task. Many times, key management must conform to legal compliance requirements.

Like most management activities, key management can be thought of as a lifecycle with specific requirements and best practices for each step:

Generation

As we've discussed in the previous section, key generation is one of the places security can be compromised. As a management activity, *who, what, how,* and *where* are all valid questions to discuss. For example, can individual users generate keys, or is that an administrative activity? How are keys generated, and on what machines?

Exchange and distribution

Getting the keys into the hands of people or systems who use them is another place where security can be compromised. Even if you're using a hybrid system and generating secret keys as needed, the private keys must be distributed to the correct people and systems. Some key systems allow the derivation of keys from a master, making the distribution of keys to endpoints easier.

Storage

After keys have been distributed or exchanged, they must be stored in a secure manner. Enterprises often employ key management software for this purpose. Keys can also be stored in password utilities if the software is deemed secure enough. In many modern systems the CPU is paired with a Trusted Platform Module (TPM), which is a one-way cryptographic module that keys can be written to but not read from.

Use

Using keys involves removing them from storage and employing them in the algorithm of choice. Storage for some applications (e.g., Secure Shell [SSH]) may just be a file, but others might require more security. Private keys used in TLS, for example, must be stored on the web server or a TLS hardware appliance so they can be used for encrypting web sessions. In applications where a TPM is used, the TPM provides the cryptographic engine and keys are used inside the TPM but can't be read.

Destruction

Keys should be deleted when they are no longer needed or expired to prevent an accidental compromise. Deleting keys often involves more than using the operating system's "delete" command or dragging them to the trash. More secure processes may repeatedly overwrite the area of the disk where the keys were stored to prevent their being read despite being deleted.

Replacement

Keys should be rotated or changed at regular intervals to limit the risk of an undetected compromise of a key. The length of the interval depends on the risks and applications. Replacement can be challenging because it requires the reexchange or redistribution of the keys.

All of these are applicable for individuals and organizations of all sizes. The solutions may vary, but the need for securely generating and managing keys does not.

Message Digests and Hashes

Sometimes it is enough to be able to determine when a document or message has been changed, either maliciously or not, without suffering the computational overhead of encryption. A mathematical technique called a *message digest* (informally called a *hash*) can be used to show integrity in such cases.

A message digest is a fixed-length string of bits that is produced from a variable length message through a special mathematical function that has three important properties:

Irreversible

Feeding the message digest into another function should not produce the original document. This is a reasonable assumption of any algorithm that turns long strings into relatively short, fixed-length strings since there simply isn't enough information capacity in the short string to reproduce the longer one.

Noncorrelatable

Small changes to the original document should result in large changes to the new digest.

Unique

Finding two documents that produce the same message digest should be mathematically infeasible.

Irreversibility ensures that we can communicate the message digest without worrying that the contents of the message will be divulged. As an example, a common usage for digest algorithms is storing passwords in computer systems. In this usage, the user's password is passed through a message digest algorithm and then stored on the machine. When the user logs in and enters a password, it is passed through the same message digest algorithm and then the two digests are compared. If they match, the entered password is correct. In this way, passwords are never stored in the clear but can be used to authenticate users. Obviously, this method wouldn't be secure if the digest algorithm could be reversed.

Noncorrelatability protects against documents that are only slightly different from being identified as "related" by virtue of their hash values. Returning to our hashed password example from above, an attacker could deduce that two passwords were very similar if the digest algorithm were correlatable and use that information to break subsequent passwords more quickly after the first was cracked.

Uniqueness ensures that a different message can't be substituted for the one for which the message digest was created. This is important since we're relying on the digest to provide evidence of message integrity. If I can find a message that has a particular digest, I can substitute it for a message you have sent with that same digest, and no one will be the wiser. As an example of how this could create a problem, consider a common usage of message digests: ensuring the integrity of code distributions. If I can insert malicious code into a code distribution (for example, inserting code that emails any user's passwords to me) and then create the same message digest for the new distribution, you would download and install my malicious version of the code and never know about the switch.

Table 9-2 shows some message digest algorithms (also called *cryptographic hash functions*), their digest size in bits, and the developer or owner of the algorithm. Ronald Rivest (the "R" in RSA) is the inventor of MD2, MD4, and MD5. MD2 was developed in 1989 and optimized for 8-bit machines. MD4 and MD5 are built for 32-bit machines. MD5 is computationally more expensive than MD4 but provides better security. MD5 is used in a number of applications, from building hashes of passwords to integrity checksums of code distribution.

Table 9-2. Message digest algorithms

Message digest algorithm	Digest size (bits)	Owner
MD2	128	RSA Data Security, Inc.
MD4	128	RSA Data Security, Inc.
MD5	128	RSA Data Security, Inc.
SHA	160	US government
SHA-1	160	US government
SHA-2	224, 256, 384, 512	US government
SHA-3	224, 256, 384, 512	US government

SHA (Secure Hash Algorithm) and SHA-1 were developed by the National Institute of Standards and Technology (NIST) and specified in Federal Information Processing Standards (FIPS) 180 and 180-1. MD5 and SHA-1 have both been popular message digest algorithms.

MD5 has some discovered theoretical weaknesses, and consequently SHA-1 has been preferred over MD5 for some time. SHA-1 has also had reported weaknesses. Specifically, it has been compromised with collision resistance attacks. So, SHA and SHA-1 shouldn't be used in applications that require collision resistance like our password storage example.

These reported weaknesses by no means indicate that these algorithms are suddenly insecure, but they do show a need to migrate to alternatives. They also show why it's important to design identity systems so that the cryptographic functions can be easily changed out, and why systems that use encryption as well as the policies that govern them should be reviewed periodically.

SHA-3 is the latest NIST standard from 2015. SHA-3 is structurally different from earlier algorithms in the SHA family. NIST has not withdrawn SHA-2. SHA-3 can be directly substituted for SHA-2 in applications.

Digital Signatures

We've discussed how using a public-key cryptosystem in reverse can provide a sort of digital signature: if I encrypt a document with my private signature, anyone can decrypt it, but only with the matching public key. Provided I've kept my private key secure, this is strong evidence that I encrypted the document in question and can thus serve as a signature.

This methodology suffers from several disadvantages:

- The signed document is rendered unintelligible unless it is decrypted with the public key. This is annoying in applications where one might only occasionally want to check signatures.
- The signature and the document are inseparable. There's no way to send a signature under separate cover.

We can overcome these disadvantages if we combine public-key cryptography and message digests. Figure 9-4 shows the methodology schematically. Since a message digest is unique to a particular document (within certain cryptographic constraints), we can create a message digest of the document, or message to be signed, and then sign the digest rather than the message. The message remains in plain text and the signature and message are separable.

To verify the signature, we use the public key of the sender to decrypt the message digest and then apply the same message digest algorithm to the signed message. If the two message digests match, then the message is the same as the one that was signed by the sender.

Digital signatures, produced in this way, provide us with evidence of a document's integrity since changing the document, intentionally or not, would result in a different message digest being calculated by the receiver. The digital signature also provides us with nonrepudiation since it is evidence that the person who created the original digest had access to the identical document and, as long as they have maintained control of their private key, is the only one who could have produced the signature.

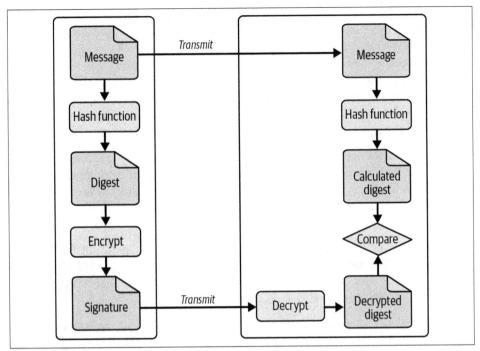

Figure 9-4. Digitally signing and verifying a message

When used for digital signature purposes, the private key is sometimes called the *signing key* and the public key is called the *verification key*. Technically, these keys operate in the same way as standard public key pairs; the terminology simply and clearly indicates which key is used for what purpose.

Digital Certificates

Public-key cryptosystems provide the underlying technology for creating identity systems that support confidentiality, integrity, and nonrepudiation. As we've seen, however, they are subject to several serious limitations:

- If you lose control of your private key, you can be impersonated, and your confidential documents can be read.
- If an attacker can convince me that their public key belongs to you, I'll accept whatever they tell me as coming from you.

The first problem is an authentication problem. We'll talk more about this in Chapter 11. The second problem can be mitigated in several ways. One of the most widely used is digital certificates and the *public-key infrastructure*. Another, decentralized identifiers, is discussed in Chapter 15.

A *digital certificate* is a data structure that associates identifying information with a public key. As we've seen, a public key is just a very long, seemingly random number. There's no way to look at a public key and tell who it belongs to. By combining a public key with other identifying information, such as a name, address, and so on, we can more easily identify the owner of the key and be sure that it's the right key. Of course, we will want to ensure the integrity of the digital certificate by having a trusted third party digitally sign it so that no one tampers with it and substitutes an alternate key. This trusted third party is the *issuer* of the digital certificate.

A digital certificate need not be issued to a person. In fact, most are not. Digital certificates can be issued to a variety of entities including individuals, companies, groups, organizations, government bodies, and things. The entity whose identifying information is associated with the public key in the certificate is called the *certificate subject*.

Digital certificates are created for different purposes with slightly different forms, called profiles. The most widespread use of certificates is in securing HTTP traffic in the TLS protocol. But they can be used for email, code signing, client-side TLS, and EMV (Europay, Mastercard, and Visa) payment cards, to name a few.

When a certificate is created, its data structure is populated and the issuer signs the certificate by creating a message digest of the information and then encrypting the digest with the issuer's private key. By signing the certificate, the issuer is making a statement that the public key contained in the certificate and the identifying information in the certificate belong together. The digital signature ensures the integrity of the certificate.

Digital certificates are not human-readable documents but rather data structures meant to be used by computer programs. However, with the aid of programs like OpenSSL, we can view the contents of a certificate. Here are the contents of the digital certificate I use on *windley.com* for TLS:

```
Certificate:
    Data:
        Version: 3 (0x2)
        Serial Number:
            58:e3:98:ba:6e:77:1e:86:09:42:74:65:98:97:62:c6
        Signature Algorithm: sha256WithRSAEncryption
        Issuer: C=GB, ST=Greater Manchester, L=Salford, O=Sectigo Limited,...
        Validity
            Not Before: Aug 18 00:00:00 2021 GMT
            Not After : Sep 18 23:59:59 2022 GMT
        Subject: C=US, ST=Utah, O=PJW, L.C., CN=www.windley.com
        Subject Public Key Info:
            Public Key Algorithm: rsaEncryption
                Public-Key: (2048 bit)
                Modulus:
                    00:f6:5b:88:1a:11:76:3a:12:44:df:eb:78:58:3a:
```

```
                76:12:c3:44:c6:a9:79:2a:62:43:22:40:ef:0d:a5:
                b4:1c:ec:25:ba:d1:21:00:2e:35:30:5d:ae:e4:61:
                d0:72:96:ba:0d:88:75:f4:cb:36:3f:9d:ad:4d:32:
                0c:4f:02:1b:89:ed:54:f3:d4:f6:24:b0:5f:5c:d3:
                e3:75:89:0f:ac:60:94:74:b3:02:04:57:03:ec:8f:
                1a:3b:f6:40:73:de:38:53:17:b5:d2:c4:d2:85:fb:
                02:2a:b1:fc:14:31:32:f4:86:89:5c:d4:1d:3b:4c:
                b0:d2:17:20:92:fa:d6:69:f9:d4:d7:40:11:92:c5:
                18:ba:92:c9:7e:02:5f:fe:34:4d:65:bd:af:21:b7:
                79:11:e3:38:89:6d:af:82:2a:7f:63:93:ef:1f:1f:
                78:24:e3:89:61:42:6a:7d:fb:36:a4:0a:ea:f7:6d:
                a4:ec:b9:5b:8c:78:4b:a2:a7:d5:8d:27:2d:42:62:
                6a:d6:2d:41:a4:d0:48:9a:1e:a3:79:3e:bf:a0:3b:
                98:0c:bb:3d:61:b8:87:5c:cb:23:6b:fe:b9:6a:d2:
                7a:b7:bc:53:a5:ec:c7:f3:0d:66:0c:36:0f:72:ac:
                12:38:70:0e:c6:3a:0a:a2:8a:37:7a:7d:1a:1c:9b:
                48:77
        Exponent: 65537 (0x10001)
    X509v3 extensions:
        X509v3 Authority Key Identifier:
            keyid:17:D9:D6:25:27:67:F9:31:C2:49:43:D9:30:36:44:8C:6C:A9:4F:EB
        X509v3 Subject Key Identifier:
            92:AA:60:A4:4F:D0:87:BC:56:4E:18:1F:12:AF:FB:BF:53:25:75:D9
        X509v3 Key Usage: critical
            Digital Signature, Key Encipherment
        X509v3 Basic Constraints: critical
            CA:FALSE
        X509v3 Extended Key Usage:
            TLS Web Server Authentication, TLS Web Client Authentication
        X509v3 Certificate Policies:
            Policy: 1.3.6.1.4.1.6449.1.2.1.3.4
              CPS: https://sectigo.com/CPS
            Policy: 2.23.140.1.2.2
        X509v3 CRL Distribution Points:
            Full Name:
URI:http://crl.sectigo.com/SectigoRSAOrganizationValidationSecureServerCA.crl

        Authority Information Access:
            CA Issuers - URI:http://crt.sectigo.com/...
            OCSP - URI:http://ocsp.sectigo.com

    X509v3 Subject Alternative Name:
        DNS:www.windley.com, DNS:windley.com
    CT Precertificate SCTs:
        Signed Certificate Timestamp:
            Version   : v1(0)
            Log ID    : 46:A5:55:EB:75:FA:91:20:30:B5:A2:89:69:F4:F3:7D:
                        11:2C:41:74:BE:FD:49:B8:85:AB:F2:FC:70:FE:6D:47
            Timestamp : Aug 18 17:54:22.678 2021 GMT
            Extensions: none
            Signature : ecdsa-with-SHA256
                        30:44:02:20:44:CE:BD:BA:85:3C:C2:36:59:B5:62:91:
```

```
                              4D:C5:20:26:0B:68:13:9C:C4:BB:BB:67:C3:66:FF:DA:
                              8F:5B:61:6E:02:20:74:CB:F5:E0:94:17:4E:AE:05:CB:
                              43:D4:65:B3:69:05:08:3A:DC:8F:E2:E2:07:11:06:33:
                              10:A3:D9:AA:52:6C
            Signed Certificate Timestamp:
                Version  : v1(0)
                Log ID   : 41:C8:CA:B1:DF:22:46:4A:10:C6:A1:3A:09:42:87:5E:
                           4E:31:8B:1B:03:EB:EB:4B:C7:68:F0:90:62:96:06:F6
                Timestamp : Aug 18 17:54:22.616 2021 GMT
                Extensions: none
                Signature : ecdsa-with-SHA256
                           30:46:02:21:00:DF:A5:D7:C2:5A:59:00:BF:E9:0C:80:
                           D8:BB:95:08:CE:38:C9:2D:CD:F7:34:26:84:38:6A:89:
                           C8:8E:B6:86:71:02:21:00:8B:CF:14:C2:F5:61:21:29:
                           47:F3:57:ED:BB:FA:41:32:CC:26:04:CD:EB:58:49:C9:
                           74:70:96:71:EA:87:BE:31
            Signed Certificate Timestamp:
                Version  : v1(0)
                Log ID   : 29:79:BE:F0:9E:39:39:21:F0:56:73:9F:63:A5:77:E5:
                           BE:57:7D:9C:60:0A:F8:F9:4D:5D:26:5C:25:5D:C7:84
                Timestamp : Aug 18 17:54:22.574 2021 GMT
                Extensions: none
                Signature : ecdsa-with-SHA256
                           30:45:02:20:5E:CA:3C:F4:54:AE:5C:BE:36:23:3C:6D:
                           C9:11:58:B9:15:F1:A8:45:31:FB:3B:9B:80:8D:14:78:
                           E7:94:AF:17:02:21:00:9A:87:A1:C2:1D:B2:04:3C:1E:
                           1F:C4:12:17:F8:B5:E2:41:63:F2:6F:BB:28:09:5F:E3:
                           21:81:82:B3:2F:C7:26
    Signature Algorithm: sha256WithRSAEncryption
        33:05:0a:11:bd:80:44:36:36:fe:1f:cf:be:93:d6:60:61:2e:
        bf:ae:10:90:73:96:67:4e:3c:fb:c4:dc:6e:46:5f:8e:50:79:
        9e:f5:b6:a4:52:0f:9f:df:02:cd:42:5f:e1:a1:73:38:90:f4:
        79:1f:b1:21:f9:93:bd:0b:70:54:91:3d:a0:2d:e9:96:45:b1:
        71:f4:e9:7a:0d:48:ef:7d:30:22:ff:ee:37:ba:46:08:7a:01:
        7f:48:a4:be:da:15:5a:63:93:09:38:2f:9b:f3:fb:70:eb:87:
        bc:3d:92:16:82:e3:a7:b8:5d:27:70:55:ef:c5:26:80:ce:5f:
        9e:b8:21:1d:e4:be:b3:c8:ba:03:52:07:b5:0f:ba:e9:ac:e2:
        b1:09:62:4f:1c:e0:b1:5c:98:26:4d:d9:94:04:35:2d:18:ed:
        62:2c:cc:4f:29:5c:ab:a0:59:bf:2c:61:98:f5:4a:0b:fe:80:
        57:2e:9f:e1:55:47:05:7a:85:5e:d4:99:d8:dc:51:56:f1:5c:
        9f:bc:66:c3:35:03:62:1f:7c:74:69:41:26:ff:80:ae:63:47:
        a4:bb:d8:00:e8:f0:cc:6a:44:89:53:e5:4f:28:30:e1:72:5c:
        8d:ec:7b:ef:c8:4e:f2:90:55:47:62:e9:31:6c:9e:d3:9b:f2:
        86:40:07:ed
```

There are several items in the certificate of interest to us. There are two main parts: the data block and the signature algorithm block. The data block tells us the certificate's serial number, who the subject of the certificate is, what signature algorithm was used, and who issued the certificate. The data block also contains the actual public key (2,048 bits in this case) and a list of extensions. The signature algorithm block contains the actual signed hash.

You probably noticed the string "X509" in several places in the data block. X.509 is part of the X.500 standard for directories. X.509 specifies the format of the data structure that holds the certificate information. Despite its origins as part of X.500, X.509 has taken on an independent life as a standard.

The X.509 specification defines ways to extend certificates to contain any data that the issuer deems important. Extensions take the form of key-value pairs. Each extension has an associated criticality flag that indicates to applications using the certificate whether they can safely ignore an extension that they don't understand. You can see several extensions in the certificate under the heading X509v3 extensions. Extensions give addition information to the user of the certificate. For example, the X509v3 CRL Distribution Points extension lists the URL where certificate revocation lists for this certificate can be retrieved.

You can see all this in a more readable version by going to www.windley.com and clicking on the lock icon in the address bar. On macOS, the result looks like Figure 9-5. This is more readable than the raw certificate data.[2]

From this we see that the signature algorithm is SHA-256 with RSA encryption and the public key is a 2,048-bit RSA key. These choices are made by the certificate vendor depending on the purpose of the certificate.

As we noted earlier, the certificate is a data structure and is encoded as binary data. Many of the uses for certificates, however, require that they be transmitted over networks. To make this possible, the data structure is serialized using an encoding algorithm called the *Distinguished Encoding Rules (DER)*. When serialized, the certificate takes the form of a string of octets and is suitable for transmitting over network connections. When the certificate is to be included in email and other text documents, the octet string is base64-encoded to create a stream of ASCII characters. Since it appears as a long, random-looking string of ASCII characters, many people confuse the encoded certificate with the public key itself. You can recognize base64-encoded certificates because they are, by convention, set apart with a beginning string "–BEGIN CERTIFICATE–" that serves as the header and an ending string "–END CERTIFICATE–" that serves as the footer.

---

2 If you're using Safari, select "Show Certificate" after clicking on the lock. In Chrome, select "Certificate" from the menu that appears. Other browsers will have the ability to inspect the certificate too, but it will be accessed and rendered differently.

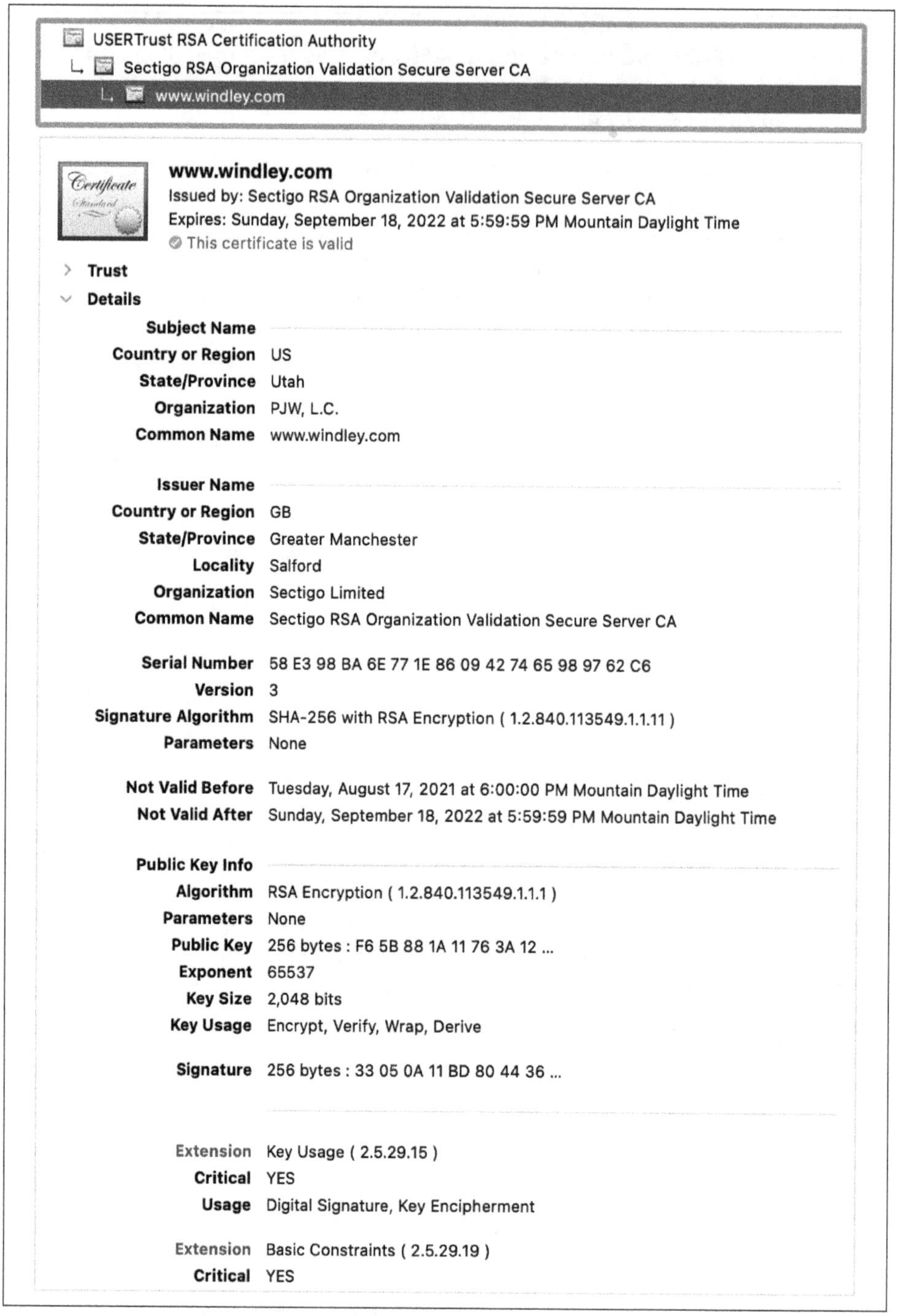

USERTrust RSA Certification Authority
  └ Sectigo RSA Organization Validation Secure Server CA
      └ www.windley.com

www.windley.com
Issued by: Sectigo RSA Organization Validation Secure Server CA
Expires: Sunday, September 18, 2022 at 5:59:59 PM Mountain Daylight Time
⊘ This certificate is valid

> **Trust**
∨ **Details**

Subject Name	
Country or Region	US
State/Province	Utah
Organization	PJW, L.C.
Common Name	www.windley.com
Issuer Name	
Country or Region	GB
State/Province	Greater Manchester
Locality	Salford
Organization	Sectigo Limited
Common Name	Sectigo RSA Organization Validation Secure Server CA
Serial Number	58 E3 98 BA 6E 77 1E 86 09 42 74 65 98 97 62 C6
Version	3
Signature Algorithm	SHA-256 with RSA Encryption (1.2.840.113549.1.1.11)
Parameters	None
Not Valid Before	Tuesday, August 17, 2021 at 6:00:00 PM Mountain Daylight Time
Not Valid After	Sunday, September 18, 2022 at 5:59:59 PM Mountain Daylight Time
Public Key Info	
Algorithm	RSA Encryption (1.2.840.113549.1.1.1)
Parameters	None
Public Key	256 bytes : F6 5B 88 1A 11 76 3A 12 …
Exponent	65537
Key Size	2,048 bits
Key Usage	Encrypt, Verify, Wrap, Derive
Signature	256 bytes : 33 05 0A 11 BD 80 44 36 …
Extension	Key Usage (2.5.29.15)
Critical	YES
Usage	Digital Signature, Key Encipherment
Extension	Basic Constraints (2.5.29.19)
Critical	YES

Figure 9-5. Browser rendering of a digital certificate used for TLS

Certificate Authorities

As we've discovered, a digital certificate associates identity information with a public key in a trusted package. Since the certificate issuer signs the certificate, we can easily verify that the information in the certificate has not been tampered with or otherwise modified. But how can we be certain that the identity data and public key are correctly associated? Put another way, the signature gives us confidence in the *fidelity* of the certificate, but how can we trust its *provenance*?

While anyone can issue certificates using OpenSSL or some other certificate issuance API, there are trusted issuers of certificates called *certificate authorities (CAs)*. The CA accepts and processes applications for certificates from entities, authenticates the information that the entity provides, issues certificates, and maintains a repository of information about the certificate and its subject.

The level and quality of the validation of information about the subject depends on the application. For example, TLS certificates have three levels of validation: domain, organization, and extended. In domain validation, the CA only checks that the organization has control over the domain in question. Organization validation checks that the organization is a legally registered business. Extended validation further validates the organization's information and location. Each level of additional validation takes more time and costs more money.

This hierarchy illustrates the organizational bias in the certificate industry. With the push to encrypt everything and get every website behind a TLS-mediated HTTP connection (`https`), certificate authorities like Let's Encrypt (*https://letsencrypt.org*) have sprung up to make getting a certificate easy and cheap (often free) by offering domain-validation certificates. The upside is that more and more connections are encrypted. The downside is that the certificate tells you little about the legitimacy of the website. Distinguishing a domain validation certification from an organization validation or extended validation certificate isn't easy. For example, if you look again at Figure 9-5, you'll notice nothing in the information that identifies the certificate type.

CAs provide the following services:

Certificate enrollment process
    This is the process whereby entities apply for a digital certificate.

Subject authentication
    The CA authenticates that the enrollee is really who they say they are. The level to which authentication is done depends on the level of assurance that is being promised by the certificate authority.

Certificate generation

As we've seen, certificate generation is not a computationally complicated process. What makes this task difficult is the need to do it in a completely secure manner.

Certificate distribution

Certificates and the private keys associated with them must be securely distributed to the enrollee.

Certificate revocation

When there is a question about the integrity of a certificate that has been issued (e.g., the private key has been compromised), the certificate is added to a revocation list.

Data repository

All of the information related to the enrollment and authentication, along with any other important information, must be kept, securely, for an agreed-upon length of time (e.g., 10 years, 100 years, etc.) in case information about the certificate and its use is questioned.

The CA typically publishes policies and practices related to the above activities in a *certification practice statement (CPS)*. These documents are typically understandable and not filled with too much legal jargon. Even so, they are lengthy; DigiCert's CPS (*https://oreil.ly/NYGPU*) is 80 pages long. Most users of digital certificates have never bothered to read the CPS. If you are using certificates for a regulated purpose and need to demonstrate compliance, you might need to have your legal department (or lawyer) ensure the CPS meets the regulatory requirements.

A set of standard extensions was added to version 3 of the X.509 specification to provide CAs more control over certificates. These include a *basic constraints* field that indicates whether the subject is a CA, a *certificate policy* field that contains a reference to the policy the CA issued the certificate under, and a *key usage* field that restricts the purpose of the key contained in the certificate. Since the key usage field is typically marked "critical," CAs can use it to limit the usage of the general-purpose keys they issue to specific tasks such as digital signing or nonrepudiation. The key usage field keeps keys from being used for purposes that their subjects did not intend for them. A cynic would also recognize that it also helps CAs sell more certificates.

Certificate Revocation Lists

Organizations often use digital certificates to control access to critical systems that must remain confidential. For example, the State of Utah uses digital certificates to control access to some of the systems used by the state police and other public safety officials around the state. A compromise to that system could result in the loss of sensitive data or worse, so the designers used digital certificates for authentication. A natural question is, "What happens if a user loses a certificate, or it is compromised in some other way?"

As we've seen, X.509 certificates have a period during which the certificate is valid. When the validity period has passed, the certificate is expired. Events can transpire, however, that make a certificate invalid before it has expired. Examples include the accidental disclosure of the private key associated with the certificate, a change in the identifying information contained in the certificate, or the compromise of the CA's private key. The compromise of a CA's private key would invalidate all the certificates that have been signed using that private key—quite a catastrophe for the CA and its customers.

When a certificate is prematurely terminated, we say the certificate has been *revoked*. Using a revoked certificate is usually in conflict with the CA's policy and could be risky since you can no longer rely on its integrity.

When a certificate has been revoked, the CA places the certificate on a *certificate revocation list* (CRL). The CRL is a data structure that contains identifying information about the CA, a timestamp, and a list of serial numbers of all the certificates that have been revoked. The CA signs the CRL to assert its authenticity and protect it from tampering. Whenever a certificate is used, the user should obtain the most recent CRL from the CA who issued the certificate and check to see that the certificate's serial number is not on the CRL. Of course, no one's going to do this unless the process is automated, a practice that is spotty at best.

CAs provide CRLs on a predefined schedule. The frequency of issuance depends on the level of assurance guaranteed by the types of certificates that are included. CRLs for low-cost certificates issued for lower-risk uses are not updated as frequently as more expensive certificates used for high-value transactions. The level of protection afforded by a particular class of certificate depends, in part, on the frequency of CRL issuance and how CRL status is to be obtained. There are three general ways that CRLs can be checked:

- The application using the certificate can ask the CA for the latest CRL. This is known as polling. The advantage is that the CRL is only transferred when it is needed. The disadvantage is that frequent polling can cause significant overhead to systems.

- The application can subscribe to a service from the CA that sends the CRL out on a predefined schedule. This ensures that the application always has the latest CRL, but an attacker may be able to block the CRL from reaching its destination and the application may be none the wiser.

- The application could query an online service provided by the CA or some other party. A protocol called Online Certificate Status Protocol (OCSP) is used for this. The advantage of this approach is that the application always has the latest information and only information relevant to the application is passed back (the status of a particular certificate).

Of course, all this is moot if the application does not check the CRL. Most browsers get a list of revoked certificates as application updates from time to time. A February 2021 test of popular browsers by SSL.com showed that revocation checking was spotty and mostly focused on high-priority and emergency incidents involving root and intermediate certificates.[3] This means that the browser might indicate that it is securely connected to a site using TLS even if the certificate at that site has been compromised and revoked. You can improve this by turning OCSP on (most browsers turn it off by default). If you turn it on, however, you'll discover why it is turned off by default: browsers often can't reliably get CRL information about some certificates and complain every time that happens.

Certificate revocation is one of the big holes in the use of digital certificates because many applications do not support it and CAs often make it difficult, or at least expensive, to access CRLs. This is probably of minor concern for web browsers. It is a greater concern when certificates are used in authentication schemes that control access to highly sensitive applications or protect sensitive data.

System designers often recognize that CRLs need to be part of the system but find the OCSP process is deemed too expensive—in computation or money. Ultimately, cost plays an important part in any identity system and the cost-risk trade-off can be difficult to quantify.

Public-Key Infrastructures

Public-key infrastructure (PKI) is the supporting infrastructure for digital certificates that provides policies, rules, agreed-upon standards, and interoperability guidance so that they can be widely used. PKI is a hierarchical, distributed system that provides security and scalability for global use of digital certificates.

We've discussed many of the standards and procedures that make up the public-key infrastructure, including algorithms, X.509 certificates, CPSs, CRLs, and OCSP. If there were only one CA, this would be enough and that CA would constitute the PKI. But that single CA would be a single point of failure. Consequently, PKI is designed to include many dozens of CAs around the world and provides methods for utilizing and establishing the veracity of certificates from each of them.

Figure 9-6 shows the hierarchical relationship that exists among CAs. In this schematic, there are two independent hierarchies of digital certificates and certificate

---

3 "How Do Browsers Handle Revoked SSL/TLS Certificates?" (*https://oreil.ly/Sr1f_*), accessed November 15, 2021.

authorities. The root of one tree is CA1, and CA2 is the root of the other; these are also known as *trust anchors*. Each of these root CAs has several subordinate CAs: CA3 and CA4 in the case of CA1. Consequently, the private key that CA3 uses to issue digital certificate DC2, for example, is signed using the private key associated with a digital certificate signed by CA1. The bidirectional arrow in the figure is meant to indicate that CA1 and CA2 have cross-certified each other, signing each other's digital certificates.

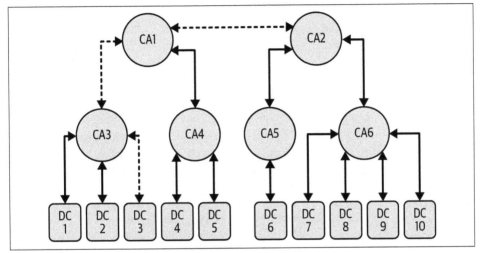

Figure 9-6. Hierarchical structures of CAs make up a PKI

When we want to check the integrity and veracity of digital certificate DC3, for example, we can use the digital certificate of CA3 to verify the signature on the certificate. We can further verify CA3 by checking to see that its digital certificate was signed by CA1, and we can check on CA1 by verifying its certificate was signed by CA2. The dashed-line arrows in the diagram represent this series of checks, which is called a *certification path*.

Whenever we are presented with a digital certificate, we can, in theory, discover its certification path as a way of checking its validity. The algorithm for performing a validity check is given in the IETF RFC 5280 specification. In practice, checking the certification path can be computationally expensive. Solving it once might not be overly expensive, but checking each time the application uses the certificate probably is. Most applications don't regularly check the full path each time but rather cache the result.

In practice, cross-certification between CAs is rare. Instead, applications usually check that the root certificate is from a known, trusted CA. How does a browser, for example, know which CAs to trust? An organization called Certificate Authority/ Browser Forum or CA/Browser Forum includes digital certificate companies, operating system vendors, browser vendors, and others with an interest in PKI. The CA/Browser Forum publishes guidelines governing the issuance and management of digital certificates. Browser and OS vendors use these guidelines to determine which root CAs they will include in their software.

Figure 9-7 shows the certificate validation path for the current certification used for TLS on *windley.com*.

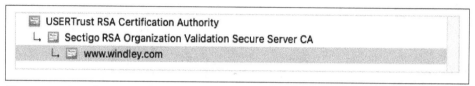

Figure 9-7. Certification validation path for windley.com

You can, if you're curious, check out the details for each of the certificates in the path. The certificate for windley.com is signed by a certificate from Sectigo, which is signed by a certificate from USERTrust. Windley.com's certificate is trustworthy because Sectigo says it is. Sectigo's certificate is trustworthy because USERTrust says it is. And USERTrust's certificate is trustworthy (on my laptop) because Apple says it is. If you use a different OS, they could decide to not include USERTrust's certificate, and then you would not see a lock in your browser when visiting windley.com. Of course, that would be devastating for USERTrust's business, so they work very hard to remain trustworthy according to CA/Brower Forum's guidelines.

MacOS stores the root certificates of CAs they trust in the Keychain. Windows 10 has a program called Certificate Manager. On Debian-based Linux systems, root certificates are stored in the */etc/ssl/certs* folder along with a file called *ca-certificates.crt*. Individual applications, including browsers, could, but usually don't, keep their own registries of trusted certificates. You can manually add certificates to your OS for development or other purposes. For example, I sometimes use an HTTP proxy for development to show the HTTP traffic on the wire. Using it for a TLS-protected site requires that I install a certificate that the proxy generates in the OS as a trusted certificate. In this way, the proxy can perform what amounts to a man-in-the-middle attack on my browser traffic.

Figure 9-8 shows a partial list of trusted root certificates listed in Keychain Access for macOS. I've highlighted USERTrust's RSA certificate. You can see that it doesn't expire until 2038. Root certificates are usually very long-lived because we don't rely on their expiration for protection. Instead, we assume the OS vendor, Apple in this case, will add, update, or remove certificates in OS updates when needed. Certificates further down the certification path have shorter expiration dates. The Sectigo RSA certificate expires in 2030, and the certificate for windley.com expires in 2022. TLS certificates typically expire in one year so that browsers don't have to rely as much on revocation, and CAs don't have to perform revocation, when a domain name changes ownership.

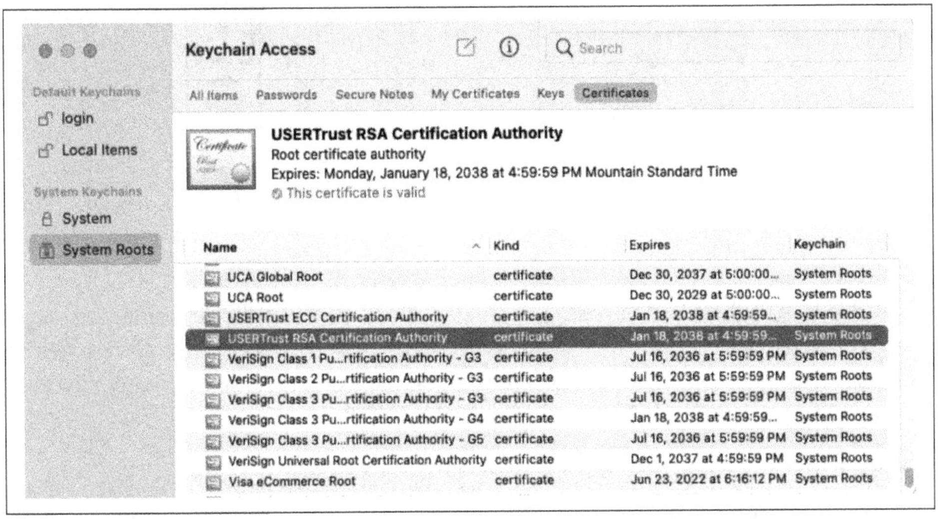

Figure 9-8. USERTrust RSA certificate stored in Keychain Access on macOS

Zero-Knowledge Proofs

Suppose Peggy needs to prove to Victor that she is in possession of a secret without revealing the secret. Can she do so in a way that convinces Victor that she really does know the secret? This is the question at the heart of one of the most powerful cryptographic processes we can employ in identity systems: *zero-knowledge proofs (ZKPs)*. Suppose, for example, that Peggy has a digital driver's license and wants to prove to Victor, the bartender, that she's over 21 without just handing over her driver's license or even showing him her birth date. ZKPs allow Peggy to prove her driver's license says she's at least 21 in a way that convinces Victor without Peggy having to reveal anything else (i.e., there's zero *excess* knowledge).

This problem was first explored by MIT researchers Shafi Goldwasser, Silvio Micali, and Charles Rackoff in the 1980s as a way of combatting information leakage. The goal is to reduce the amount of *extra* information the verifier, Victor, can learn about the prover, Peggy.

One way to understand how ZKPs work is through the story of the Cave of Alibaba, first published by cryptographers Quisquater et al.[4] as shown in Figure 9-9.

---

4 Jean-Jacques Quisquater et al., "How to Explain Zero-Knowledge Protocols to Your Children," in *Advances in Cryptology—CRYPTO '89: Proceedings*, Lecture Notes in Computer Science, vol. 435 (New York: Springer, 1990), 628–631. doi:10.1007/0-387-34805-0_60. ISBN 978-0-387-97317-3.

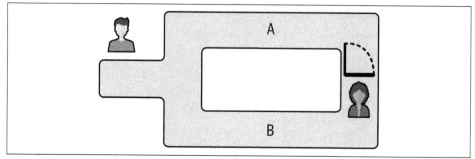

Figure 9-9. Peggy and Victor in Alibaba's Cave

The Cave of Alibaba has two passages, labeled A and B, that split off a single passageway connected to the entrance. Peggy possesses a secret code that allows her to unlock a door connecting A and B. Victor wants to buy the code but won't pay until he's sure Peggy knows it. Peggy won't share it with Victor until he pays.

The algorithm for Peggy proving she knows the code proceeds as follows:

1. Victor stands outside the cave while Peggy enters and selects one of the passages. Victor is not allowed to see which path Peggy takes.

2. Victor enters the cave and calls out "A" or "B" at random.

3. Peggy emerges from the correct passageway because she can easily unlock the door regardless of which choice she made when entering.

4. Of course, Peggy could have just gotten lucky and guessed right, so Peggy and Victor repeat the experiment many times.

If Peggy can always come back by whichever passageway Victor selects, then Victor can know with increasing probability that Peggy really knows the code. After 20 tries, there's less than one chance in a million (2^{20}) that Peggy is simply guessing which letter Victor will call. This constitutes a *probabilistic proof* that Peggy knows the secret.

This algorithm not only allows Peggy to convince Victor she knows the code, but it does it in a way that ensures Victor can't convince anyone else Peggy knows the code. Suppose, for example, that Victor records the entire transaction. The only thing an observer sees is Victor calling out letters and Peggy emerging from the right tunnel. The observer can't be sure Victor and Peggy didn't agree on a sequence of letters in advance to fool observers. Note that this property relies on the algorithm using a good PRNG with a high information entropy seed so that Peggy and third-party observers can't predict Victor's choices.

Thus, while Peggy cannot deny to Victor that she knows the secret, she can deny that she knows the secret to other third parties. This ensures that anything she proves to Victor stays between them and Victor cannot leak it—at least in a cryptographic way that proves it came from Peggy. Peggy retains control of both her secret and the fact that she knows it.

When we say "zero knowledge" and talk about Victor learning nothing beyond the proposition in question, that's not perfectly true. In the Cave of Alibaba, Peggy proves in zero knowledge that she knows the secret. But there are many other things that Victor learns about Peggy that ZKPs can do nothing about. For example, Victor knows that Peggy can hear him, speak his language, and walk, and that she is cooperative. He also might learn things about the cave, like approximately how long it takes to unlock the door. Peggy learns similar things about Victor. So, the reality is that the proof is *approximately* zero knowledge not *perfectly* zero knowledge.

ZKP Systems

The example of Alibaba's Cave is a very specific use of ZKPs, what's called a *zero-knowledge proof of knowledge*. Peggy is proving she knows (or possesses) something. More generally, Peggy might want to prove many facts to Victor. These could include propositional phrases or even values. ZKPs can do that as well.

To understand how we can prove propositions in zero knowledge, consider a different example, sometimes called the socialist millionaire problem. Suppose Peggy and Victor want to know if they're being paid a fair wage. Specifically, they want to know whether they are paid the same amount, but they don't want to disclose their specific hourly rate to each other or even a trusted third party. In this instance, Peggy isn't proving she knows a secret; rather, she's proving an equality (or inequality) proposition.

For simplicity, assume that Peggy and Victor are being paid one of $10, $20, $30, or $40 per hour. The algorithm works like this:

1. Peggy buys four lock boxes and labels them $10, $20, $30, and $40.
2. She throws away the keys to every box except the one labeled with her wage.
3. Peggy gives all the locked boxes to Victor, who privately puts a slip of paper with a "+" into the slot at the top of the box labeled with his salary. He puts a slip with a "−" in all the other boxes.
4. Victor gives the boxes back to Peggy, who uses her key in private to open the box with her salary on it.
5. If she finds a "+" then they make the same amount. Otherwise, they make a different amount. She can use this to prove the fact to Victor.

This is called an *oblivious transfer* and proves the proposition VictorSalary = Peggy Salary true or false in zero knowledge (i.e., without revealing any other information).

For this to work, Peggy and Victor must trust that the other will be forthcoming and state their real salary. Victor needs to trust that Peggy will throw away the three other keys. Peggy must trust that Victor will put only one slip with a "+" on it in the boxes.

Just like digital certificates need a PKI to establish confidence beyond what would be possible with self-issued certificates alone, ZKPs are more powerful in a system that allows Peggy and Victor to prove facts from things others say about them, not just what they say about themselves. For example, rather than Peggy and Victor self-asserting their salary, suppose they could rely on a signed document from the human resources department in making their assertion so that both know that the other is stating their true salary. In Chapter 16, we'll discuss verifiable credentials, a system that uses ZKPs to prove many different facts alone or in concert, in ways that give confidence in the method and trust in the data.

Noninteractive ZKPs

In the previous examples, Peggy was able to prove things to Victor through a series of interactions. For ZKPs to be practical, interactions between the prover and the verifier should be minimal. Fortunately, a technique called *SNARK* allows for noninteractive ZKPs.

SNARKs have the following properties (from whence they derive their name):

Succinct
    The sizes of the messages are small compared to the length of the actual proof.

Noninteractive
    Other than some setup, the prover sends only one message to the verifier.

ARguments
    This is really an argument that something is correct, not a proof as we understand it mathematically. Specifically, the prover theoretically could prove false statements given enough computational power. So, SNARKs are "computationally sound" rather than "perfectly sound."

of Knowledge
    The prover knows the fact in question.

You'll typically see "zk" (for zero-knowledge) tacked on the front to indicate that during this process the verifier learns nothing other than the facts being proved.

The mathematics underlying zkSNARKs involves homomorphic computation over high-degree polynomials. But we can understand how zkSNARKs work without knowing the complicated mathematics of homomorphic computation that ensures that they're sound. If you'd like more details of the mathematics, I recommend Christian Reitwiessner's Ethereum post "zkSNARKs in a Nutshell" (*https://oreil.ly/Iol7R*).

As a simple example, suppose Victor is given a `sha256` hash, H, of some value. Peggy wants to prove that she knows a value s such that `sha265(s)` `==` H without revealing s to Victor. We can define a function C that captures the relationship:

```
C(x, w) = ( sha256(w) == x )
```

So, `C(H, s)` `==` `true`, while other values for w will return `false`.

Computing a zkSNARK requires three functions: G, P, and V. G is the key generator that takes a secret parameter called `lambda` and the function C and generates two public keys, the *proving key* pk and the *verification key* vk. They need only be generated once for a given function C. The parameter `lambda` must be destroyed after this step since it is not needed again and anyone who has it can generate *fake* proofs.

The prover function P takes as input the proving key pk, a public input x, and a private (secret) *witness* w. The result of executing `P(pk,x,w)` is a proof, `prf`, that the prover knows a value for w that satisfies C.

The verifier function V computes `V(vk,` `x,` `prf)`, which is true if the proof `prf` is correct and false otherwise.

Returning to Peggy and Victor, Victor chooses a function C representing what he wants Peggy to prove, creates a random number `lambda`, and runs G to generate the proving and verification keys:

```
(pk, vk) = G(C, lambda)
```

Peggy must not learn the value of `lambda`. Victor shares C, pk, and vk with Peggy.

Peggy wants to prove she knows the value s that satisfies C for x `=` H. She runs the proving function P using these values as inputs:

```
prf = P(pk, H, s)
```

Peggy presents the proof `prf` to Victor, who runs the verification function:

```
V(vk, H, prf)
```

If the result is true, then Victor can be assured that Peggy knows the value s.

The function C does not need to be limited to a hash as we did in this example. Within limits of the underlying mathematics, C can be quite complicated and involve any number of values that Victor would like Peggy to prove, all at one time.

Blockchain Basics

Blockchains are one of the most exciting—and controversial—new technologies of the last decade.[5] They are increasingly being used in identity systems as people search for architectures that are more decentralized. And blockchains make use of many of the cryptographic techniques and algorithms we've discussed in this chapter, so they give us a good example to see how cryptography is used inside a larger, more complicated system with specific goals.

A blockchain-like protocol was first proposed by David Chaum in 1982. Stuart Haber and W. Scott Stornetta further advanced the concept of a secure chain of blocks in the early '90s and, along with Dave Bayer, improved and commercialized it in 1995 as Surety, Inc. Satoshi Nakamoto (whoever they are) conceptualized the first modern blockchain in 2008 as part of their design for a decentralized digital cash system called Bitcoin.

Decentralized Consensus

Whenever multiple computer systems are cooperating, they need a way to achieve consensus and make group decisions about values. If you've used Google Docs with other people in a simultaneous editing session, you've seen decentralized consensus in action. Multiple parties might try editing the same section at the same time. Eventually, they'll all see the same document because Google Docs is a way to achieve consensus on written documents with multiple authors.

Notice that I didn't say they'd all see the *right* document, because Google Docs doesn't have any way to know what "right" is. If you substitute "red" for the word "blue" and your coeditor substitutes "green" for the same word at about the same time, you will both eventually see either "red" or "green" in the document. But there's no guarantee which word will win out. Consensus isn't about finding the right value; it's about getting the *same value*.

Another takeaway from the Google Docs example is that I used the word "eventually" to describe the consensus result. Decentralized consensus mechanisms come to consensus over time. This makes sense when you consider inevitable network delays. If you can't live with eventual consistency, then your only other choice is to employ locks that block computation from happening while the various nodes in the system reach consensus.

---

5 I'm going to use the popular word "blockchain" as a general term for distributed ledgers rather than trying to distinguish architectures with various features.

Byzantine Failure and Sybil Attacks

There are many algorithms for reaching consensus in distributed and decentralized systems. The one Google Docs uses, for example, is related to a class of algorithms called *conflict-free replicated data types* (CRDTs). Another widely used algorithm is Leslie Lamport's Paxos algorithm.

CRDTs and Paxos are both designed to reach consensus despite nodes leaving or joining the system, network failures, and other problems we might expect in a decentralized system. But they are not built to resist malicious nodes that are actively trying to subvert consensus.

The Byzantine Empire was known for intrigue and political plotting. Thus, when Lamport was looking for an allegory to illustrate the problem of reaching consensus with participants who are acting in bad faith, he called it the "Byzantine Generals Problem," and failure where actors can report false values is known as Byzantine failure. While there are several excellent examples of algorithms that exhibit Byzantine fault tolerance, Bitcoin's blockchain uses one that is particularly interesting.

Say you want to create a digital currency like Bitcoin that has no central point of control. It's distributed, decentralized, and heterarchical. One of the primary problems is creating a ledger that tells everyone how much Bitcoin everyone else has, although:

- Some people may lie.
- Nobody is available to arbitrate disputes.

The classic way to solve the problem, described by Lamport in his 1982 paper[6] on the Byzantine Generals Problem, is to use majority voting. But voting doesn't work when bad actors can introduce new nodes at will. They simply overwhelm the voting system with votes in their favor. This is called a Sybil attack.

Bitcoin presents a classic Byzantine-Sybil consensus problem (i.e., maintaining a correct ledger) where some actors have impure motives and may come and go at will. Bitcoin and other blockchains achieve consensus in a decentralized system under these harsh conditions.

---

6 Leslie Lamport, Robert Shostak, and Marshall Pease, "The Byzantine Generals Problem," *ACM Transactions on Programming Languages and Systems* 4, no. 3 (July 1982): 387–389. CiteSeerX 10.1.1.64.2312. doi: 10.1145/357172.357176.

Building a Blockchain

Bitcoin's solution to the two problems listed above is a particularly ingenious algorithm. Let's explore how it works by designing our own crypto currency.[7] We'll call our hypothetical cryptocurrency "YCoin."

Problem 1: Sending money

The first problem we need to solve is how to send money. Suppose Alice wants to send one YCoin to Bob. Alice can create a message that says, "Alice sends one YCoin to Bob," and sign it with her private key.

As we learned earlier, this allows anyone with Alice's public key to:

- Verify that she (and only she) sent it.
- Protect themselves from Alice repudiating the transfer.

These are two critical properties. But what if Bob gets two such messages? Did Alice send him two YCoins? Or was the message accidentally duplicated?

Problem 2: Uniquely identifying coins

The problem of uniquely identifying coins is simple to solve. Alice can ensure that each YCoin she sends has a unique serial number.

The typical way to do this is to create a bank. The bank issues serial numbers (i.e., transaction IDs) and keeps track of who owns which serial numbers. The bank is entrusted to ensure the ledger is up to date and accurate. Institutions are one of society's methods for moving trust out of the personal realm so that strangers can transact with each other.

When Alice sends a YCoin with serial number 156 to Bob, he can contact the bank and ensure that the serial number is valid, that Alice is the current holder of the YCoin with serial number 156, and that no one else is claiming it. When he accepts it, the bank updates its ledger to show that Bob now owns YCoin 156.

Problem 3: Distributing the bank

But we want a solution with no central bank, so we need to do something more ambitious.

---

7 This iterative development was inspired by the arguments in Michael Nielsen's article "How the Bitcoin Protocol Actually Works" (*https://oreil.ly/OboKD*), accessed November 10, 2021.

Suppose that instead of checking with the bank when Alice sends him a YCoin, Bob checks with everyone else who has YCoins. Everyone is keeping track of who owns which YCoins in a shared, public ledger called the blockchain.

Alice and Bob are identified by their public keys. When Bob receives the message from Alice, he can use her public key to check that the message came from Alice and also check his copy of the blockchain to ensure Alice really owns YCoin 156. If she does, then he broadcasts Alice's message and his acceptance of the YCoin to the entire network. Anyone can use Alice's public key to validate her message.

Upon receiving Bob's message, everyone in the network updates their copy of the ledger to remove YCoin 156 from Alice's balance and add it to Bob's.

Note that at this point we can conveniently drop serial numbers. Since there's a single, shared ledger, we simply remove some amount (even fractional amounts are OK) of YCoin from Alice's record on the ledger and add it to Bob's. No serial numbers needed.

This all works great, unless Alice is dishonest (in other words, Byzantine).

Problem 4: Preventing double spending

What if Alice tries to spend the same YCoin with Bob and Charlie? You might think this is difficult since everyone would notice, but what if Alice takes advantage of a network partition or latency? She could convince both Bob and Charlie that they own the YCoin she's transferring and collect whatever she's exchanging it for before anyone notices there's a problem.

The answer, not surprisingly, is a two-phase acceptance algorithm. Rather than merely accepting Alice's transfer at face value, both Bob and Charlie broadcast the transaction to the entire network for verification. Other members of the network check to see if Alice has the coin and hasn't spent it.

In a double spending scenario, some network members would see Bob's transaction first and others would see Charlie's. Since the traditional answer to Byzantine failure is majority voting, only one of the transactions would be approved and the ledger will eventually be updated accordingly.

Problem 5: Stopping network hijacking

Alice can still double spend using the previous solution if she can take over the network by adding her own nodes that propagate her lies. That is, she can launch a Sybil attack.

Alice can succeed because validation is based on a voting system. Anyone with a node on the YCoin network can vote, and nodes can come and go as they please. Virtual machines and proxies make adding nodes cheap—potentially cheaper than the money Alice can make with fraudulent YCoin transactions.

We can make cheating more expensive by allowing validation only after the validator has expended a certain amount of effort—called *proof of work*—to show they aren't just a small virtual machine or network proxy.

Because Alice must do real work to validate her fraudulent transaction, she can only do so if she controls more than half of the computing power of the entire YCoin network. Provided there are many participants, this is impractical because it is too expensive.

In a proof-of-work scheme, before a node on the network can validate a transaction it must solve a cryptographic puzzle. The puzzle involves finding a value called a nonce such that when the nonce is appended to the YCoin message and hashed, the first n digits of the result are all zeros.

This sounds arbitrary but it has the clever property of allowing the amount of work to be adjusted according to the needs of the network at any given time by varying n. Larger values of n will require more computation to find a suitable hash.

Recall that hashing is irreversible. Consequently, the only way to search for a hash with a particular value is to try every possible computation. This is what is called *mining* in Bitcoin. Various parties compete to validate blocks by solving the cryptographic puzzle.

But if solving these cryptographic puzzles costs real money, why do nodes do it? One of Satoshi Nakamoto's clever design features was to reward miners for solving the puzzle. In our iterative development of a solution, we imagined solving the Byzantine fault problem with voting and the Sybil attack problem with proof of work. But that's not how real blockchains work. Instead, they solve both problems at the same time. So, only the miner who validates a block gets the reward.

Problem 6: Ordering transactions and handling disagreements

The YCoin network should agree on the ordering of transactions so we know, at any given time, who owns exactly what. This means that there's just one ledger even though there are many copies of it.

We call it a blockchain because it's literally a chain of blocks. Each new block contains a batch of new transactions. Rather than merely validating individual transactions, the network groups them into blocks, and as each block is validated, it is added to a chain so that everyone agrees on a precise order of blocks.

Digital signatures are used to sign the block. Before it's signed, the block is combined with a hash of the previous block so that anyone can validate the ordering cryptographically.

Under the right circumstances, the chain can be extended by two blocks at the same time, creating a fork and causing the problem we're trying to avoid. Some people would see one version of the ledger and others another. These ledgers would agree with each other except at the end.

The network can deal with forks by keeping track of them but agreeing to only extend the longest chain. Because of the probabilistic nature of the proof-of-work problem, one fork will get longer and become the winning chain, ensuring there's only one, linear chain that completely orders all transactions. In Bitcoin, once a block is six deep in the blockchain, it is considered "settled," since the probability another fork is going to be accepted is vanishingly small.

Other Ways of Countering Sybil Attacks

Proof of work is not the only way to deal with the Sybil attack in ledger systems. In fact, proof of work is controversial because the work is real, consuming large amounts of electricity and potentially contributing to climate change.

Another way to prevent Sybil attacks is called *proof of stake*. In proof of stake, nodes are still rewarded. But to participate, nodes are required to stake some amount of cryptocurrency against their good behavior. If the network algorithmically detects bad behavior, then some or all of the stake is forfeit. The Ethereum blockchain is moving from proof of work to proof of stake consensus in 2022, making it the largest blockchain to do so.

The third way to solve the problem is using what's broadly called *proof of authority*. Recall that the problem is that Alice can set up multiple nodes. Proof of authority requires each node to have approval to participate. There are various schemes for determining how approval is granted. Nodes might earn the right algorithmically in a kind of reputation system. Or they might be granted authority from some institution. We'll discuss this more in the next section.

Classifying Blockchains

There are numerous designs and architectures for blockchains. One way to classify them is by looking at how validation is done and how access is handled. As we just saw, transactions are validated when nodes add new blocks to the chain. Blockchains using proof of work or proof of stake can be classified as *permissionless*; no permission is needed to participate. Blockchains using proof of authority can be classified as *permissioned*, regardless of whether that authority is institutional or algorithmic.

Similarly, some blockchains restrict access, for reading, writing, or both, to specific parties. They are said to be *private* blockchains. Blockchains without such restrictions on access are *public*. Note that it doesn't make sense to be private and permissionless.

Figure 9-10 shows an access-validation matrix with a few examples in each box. There are dozens, maybe hundreds of blockchains that could be put in any of the three boxes. I've chosen a few examples for each box for discussion.

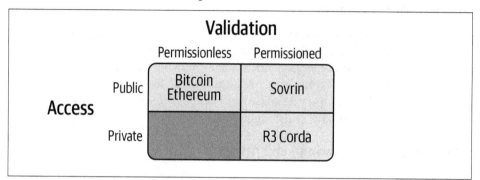

Figure 9-10. Classifying blockchains

Bitcoin and Ethereum are both well-known examples of *public-permissionless* blockchains. Anyone can run a node and anyone can inspect the ledger.

Sovrin Network is an example of a *public-permissioned* blockchain. Anyone can read and write to the network, but validator nodes are governed by a public governance framework maintained by the nonprofit Sovrin Foundation. Only organizations that agree to abide by the governance framework can run a validator node.

R3's Corda is an example of a *private-permissioned* blockchain. A group of organizations can run a Corda blockchain for their own purpose. Only members of the group can read and write to the blockchain, and validator nodes are chosen by the group's participants.

Should You Use a Blockchain?

As blockchain technology has become popular, it has been used by many groups and organizations for numerous purposes beyond cryptocurrency. As is the case with any new technology, some of those use cases are questionable. There might be other, less complicated and costly ways to achieve consensus than by using a blockchain.

The flowchart shown in Figure 9-11 can help evaluate whether a blockchain is the right answer for a particular problem.

Don't view the boxes on the left of the diagram as strict gates. Answering one "no" doesn't necessarily mean you don't want to choose a blockchain for your project. Instead, the prompts inside the boxes will force you to think about the choices you're making.

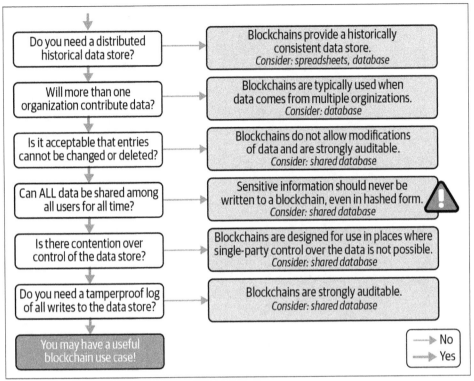

Figure 9-11. Should you use a blockchain?

The Limitations of PKI

Integrity, nonrepudiation, and confidentiality are important foundational properties in identity systems. Almost every activity in identity management relies upon one or more of these three concepts.

Public-key cryptography and PKI have suffered from overhype—being seen by some as the answer to every security problem that has surfaced over the years. For example, some have proposed the widespread adoption of digital certificates and PKI for authentication and authorization tasks. While the technology is theoretically up to the task, these schemes have usually collapsed under the weight of complexity, institutional policy, politics, and the sense that widespread adoption is too expensive or difficult to manage.

In coming chapters you'll explore authentication and authorization technologies that depend on public-key cryptography, ZKPs, and blockchains to solve many of the problems that have haunted identity systems for decades.

CHAPTER 10

Names, Identifiers, and Discovery

Names are one of the first things you think about when the subject of identity comes up. Of ccourse, identity is about more than names, but we name almost every object around us, so names become one of the most common attributes stored with an identity.

Once you've named a bunch of objects, you want to be able to find them. This is called *discovery*. Directories are one of the primary means of discovery. As a result, information technology systems are full of directories. There are directories for files, directories for email addresses, directories for domain names, and even directories for the processes on a computer. The simplest directories associate a name with something else, such as a file, address, IP number, or process.

This chapter will discuss names, identifiers, discovery, directories, and the role that these play in digital identity.

Utah.gov: A Use Case in Naming and Directories

When I was serving as CIO of Utah, directory issues seemed to take up a lot of my time and effort. When I became CIO, the state had been using the domain name *state.ut.us*. This domain name was not particularly easy to remember, and when you tacked on one or two subdomains to identify a department or agency, the effect was almost comical. For example, my email address was *pwindley@gov.state.ut.us*. The governor remarked that he could almost feel people start to dance to the rhythm when he told them his email address.

In addition to the official domain name, agencies in state government had gotten into the habit of registering domain names in the .org TLD (top-level domain) for every publicly facing website they launched. Utah managed over 100 domain names outside the official one. This created a huge problem in building brand awareness around the state's website and meant that it was impossible to know when you were on an official state website and when you were not.

Shortly after I came on board, I discovered that we owned the domain name *utah.gov*—much shorter, easier to remember, and more authoritative. (Only governmental entities in the US can get domain names in the *.gov* TLD.) By fiat and with the governor's support, I declared that Utah was moving to *utah.gov*. This isn't a strategy I'd recommend for endearing yourself to people, but it did accomplish the goal: within a month, we were using *utah.gov* as the domain name for our primary web presence and contemplating how to migrate the rest of the organization. There were two primary issues:

- *Utah.gov* represented a namespace that had been delegated to the State of Utah and within which we could manage things like server names and email addresses.
- The state had never had an enterprise strategy for naming, and each department and agency ran its own directory service for email and passwords—some ran many, with each division controlling their own directories.

The first problem called for the creation of a registration process and the appointment of a registrar through whom organizations within the state could reserve subdomains within *utah.gov*. The job of the registrar was to create namespaces within *utah.gov* and ensure that the names were unique, meaningful, and correctly recorded.

The second problem was more difficult. First we created a voluntary program through which people who wanted an email address at *utah.gov* could reserve a name. A simple program forwarded email sent to that name to their original email box. This was only temporary while we went through the difficult process of creating a naming procedure for assigning unique names (which would become email addresses) to each employee. We settled on a first initial/last name scheme with a series of fallback schemes for duplicates. The policy specifically prohibited names not associated with a person's real name to prevent people having email addresses like *dumbo@utah.gov* (unless their real name happened to be Doug Umbo, of course).

We also set up a metadirectory to aggregate the directories in the agencies to form a single large logical directory. This wasn't as easy as it should have been since software running many of the directories hadn't been updated for years and didn't support metadirectory linking. Thus, creating a single directory included upgrade projects for several directories around the state. Further, creating this logical directory from already existing directories meant that the names in those directories had to first be normalized according to the naming scheme we'd come up with earlier.

The use of multiple distributed directories had advantages in performance and local control but caused some difficulties in integration with other enterprise systems like the human resources (HR) system. The goal was to provision entries in the directory and even access control rights based on the employee's status within the HR system.

The technical problems faced in creating an enterprise directory pale in comparison to the political challenges. To begin with, I was asking many people to change their email address—some of which had been in use for many years. This has personal and organizational costs. Second, some people in power didn't want to change their email address. They got first pick of email addresses in case of a conflict. One executive director even insisted on having every possible permutation of her name and initials assigned to her to prevent anyone from accidentally sending mail intended for her to someone else with a similar name.

Ultimately, we were successful in establishing a single namespace within *utah.gov* for all email and logins. We even converted the state's many web servers to subdomains within the *utah.gov* domain. The effort took almost two years to complete, but once done, it enhanced our ability to brand the state's web services, increased confidence in the web presence, and gave people email addresses that they could distribute without having to break out the bongo drums.

Naming

Names are used to refer to things. Without names, we'd constantly be describing people, places, and things to each other whenever we wanted to talk about them. You do that now when you can't remember someone's name: "You know, the guy who was in the green shirt, with the beard, walking a dog?" Any given entity can have multiple names that all refer to the same thing. I'm Phil, Phillip, Phil Windley, Dad, and so on, depending on the context.

Naming is one of the fundamental abstractions for dealing with complexity. Names provide convenient handles for large, complex things—allowing them to be manipulated and referenced by a short, easy-to-remember string, instead of a longer, unwieldy description. Filenames, for example, let us pick a meaningful handle for what ultimately is a collection of bits located on a particular set of sectors on a particular set of tracks on a particular set of disks.

In computing, we use names for similar reasons. We want to easily refer to things like memory locations (variables), inodes (filenames), IP addresses (domain names), and so on. Names usually possess several important properties, including the following:

- Names should be unique within some specific namespace.
- Names should be memorable.
- Names should be short enough for humans to type into computing devices.

As Crosbie Fitch points out in his excellent treatise on identity,[1] names don't need to be globally unique, just unique enough. Names are identifiers we put on things that already have an identity. Names aren't the same thing as identity.

In computers, we often use the term *identifier* to refer to a name that is unique since the term *name* often refers to things that are not. For example, there are over 55,000 John Smiths in the United States. When we build systems that have a profile for a person, the name attribute will be their real name whereas their identifier, or ID, will be something that is unique within the system.

Names also disassociate the reference from the thing itself, so that the underlying representation can change without changing the name. Perhaps the most familiar example of this is domain names. The domain name *windley.com* points to some IP address. If I decide to change the machine hosting the services at *windley.com* to another one with a different IP address, it's easily done and everyone referring to the name will still end up at the right place. Indirection is a powerful mechanism for preserving identity across time since without it the name must change whenever the thing it references changes.

Namespaces

A namespace is the universe within which a name is guaranteed to be unique and defines where the name has meaning. Thus, namespaces are sometimes called "domains." A family name (usually) acts as a namespace wherein given names are unique and meaningful. In an email address, the name (the part before the @ symbol) is guaranteed to be unique within the namespace (the domain name after the @ symbol). Filenames are unique within the namespace of the directory they are in.

Namespaces can be flat or hierarchical. The usernames on a standalone computer are an example of a flat namespace. A filesystem is the most familiar example of a hierarchical namespace. Domain names are another familiar example of a hierarchical namespace. Figure 10-1 shows how hierarchical namespaces work in domain names and filesystems.

Hierarchical namespaces have some interesting properties:

- A path inside the hierarchy between the root node and a leaf node can be used to specify any entry in a hierarchical namespace.
- Some paths are referenced and written from root to leaf (e.g., filesystems) and some are referenced and written from leaf to root (e.g., domain names).

---

1 Crosbie Fitch, "Ideating Identity" (*https://oreil.ly/9KZwD*), July 11, 2007, accessed September 21, 2021.

- In some hierarchical namespaces, like domain names, names can be both nodes and leaves. For example, I can reference both *windley.com* and *www.windley.com* with windley serving as a node in one case and a leaf in the other.

- In other hierarchical namespaces, like filesystems, leaves and nodes are strictly differentiated—directories are not files (at least at a conceptual level).

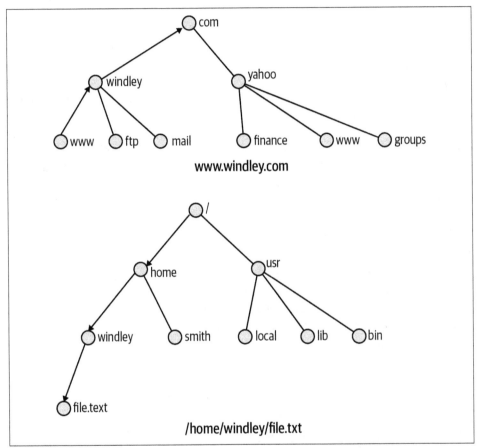

Figure 10-1. Hierarchical namespaces for domain names and filesystems

In many hierarchical namespaces, the hierarchy reflects some actual hierarchy in the physical world. Usually, however, the hierarchy in the namespace and the organization of the objects represented by the hierarchy do not have a one-to-one correspondence. For example, a filesystem is a hierarchy that exists entirely independent of the location of the bits on the disk and is strictly for the convenience of the user. With domain names, the hierarchy sometimes mirrors the physical world, but not always. For example, there really is an organization called Yahoo, Inc., that owns *yahoo.com*.

On the other hand, *windley.com*, *ftp.windley.com*, *www.windley.com*, and *mail.windley.com* all refer to the same machine.

Identifiers

Ironically, we often don't call the things we put in a namespace, names. We call them *identifiers* instead to avoid confusion between the name in the namespace and a person's name. Perhaps the best example of identifiers in use today are web addresses—URLs—that anyone who has used a browser has typed in.

Uniform Resource Identifiers: A universal namespace

We've all ordered something online that gets delivered via UPS or FedEx. One of the items in the confirmation email is a tracking number for the shipment. The tracking number is part of a URL to the package-tracking page at FedEx. Have you ever thought of this package-tracking page as the home page for that package on the internet? Every package shipped via FedEx, UPS, and most other companies has a home page that is named by the URL (Uniform Resource Locator) that is used to reference it. The URL is a unique location on the web, and that URL can be linked in another document or bookmarked for later reference—just like any other web page. The package's page is no different from any other page on the internet in that regard.

Uniform Resource Identifiers (URIs) are more general versions of URLs. Whereas URLs represent locations and, as such, typically correspond to real resources on the internet, URIs can be used to name things within a single, global namespace even when there's no web location associated with the name. The structure is the same, however, and so many URIs also function as URLs.

URIs are one of the most important features of the web. Without URIs, much of what we take for granted on the web wouldn't work. As a simple example, having a universal namespace created using URIs allows any document, anywhere on the web, to refer to any other document, anywhere on the web, without the authors of the two documents having to agree on the same software package or server beyond what's inherent in the web itself. In fact, Paul Prescod has said: "If there is one thing that distinguishes the web as a hypertext system from the systems that preceded it, it is the web's adoption of a single, global, unified namespace."[2]

Apart from their use to identify resources on the web, however, URIs have found their way into many other contexts, since the URI system represents a universal namespace. Giving off-web resources, such as database records, a URI makes them part of this same universal namespace and ensures that they can be uniquely distinguished from other resources.

---

2 Prescod, Paul, "Roots of the REST/SOAP Debate" (*https://oreil.ly/0ezrQ*), accessed September 22, 2021.

URLs and URIs can have five major components:

- A protocol identifier, called the "scheme," followed by a colon (e.g., *https:*, *ldap:*, *tel:*).

- An authority component, usually a domain name, indicating a unique namespace on the internet (e.g., *www.windley.com*)

- A path component indicating what specific resource in that domain is to be identified (e.g., */llp*).

- A query component following a question mark, usually giving resource attributes (e.g., *?ln=windley&lang=en*)

- A fragment component following a pound sign, indicating a subresource (e.g., *#top*)

Taken together, these components are written in the familiar fashion:

https://www.windley.com/llp?ln=windley&lang=en#top

There can be other components as well, including authentication information, port numbers, etc., but these five are the most common.

Cool URIs don't change

The URI is the public interface to a resource and, consequently, deserves great thought. One of the key factors that should be kept in mind when designing URIs is that they should not change—ever. This is not such a radical idea if you stop to consider that the URI is the name of the resource. In general, it's a bad idea to change the name of something since we cannot possibly know all the places where the name is being used and, consequently, cannot let them know when the name (the URI) changes. Thus, the URI should be chosen so that it is meaningful and unlikely to change. As the system is updated and maintained, the nonvolatility of the URIs should be preserved. Numerous tools and techniques exist to make this possible. URL rewriting is one of the most powerful, allowing servers to resolve URI references to almost any resource.

Designing the URIs for your information system should be one of the most important tasks of the design phase. It may seem unusual to think of designing URIs. After all, don't we just let the network folks tell us our domain name and let the path fall however it may? Not in a well-designed system. The previous section talked about the components that are typically part of a URL. All of them are usually under our control and should be carefully chosen.

In APIs, the issue of URL design is a topic of intense discussion, and there are many resources available that discuss principles of good API design, which in some ways is analogous to good URL design. API URLs represent the names of resource collections or items. Issues like versioning, pagination, and the proper use of query strings are all part of an API, and hence URL, design.

Don't construe this principle to mean that all resources need to be permanent. Just because URIs don't change doesn't mean that the resource always has to be available. Some resources are transitory and some that go out of existence. Even so, we shouldn't change their name. Think of the UPS tracking number we discussed at the beginning of this section. The package gets delivered, the resource is no longer needed, and so the URI for the package may not resolve. But UPS shouldn't reuse tracking numbers and hence doesn't change the URI representing it.

Uniform Resource Names

Uniform Resource Names (URN) are URIs with the *urn:* scheme. A URN is a persistent, location-independent identifier. Unlike URLs, URNs do not need to be resolvable. Like a URI, URNs have several primary components:

- A scheme of *urn:*
- A namespace identifier (e.g., *isbn:*)
- A namespace-specific string (e.g., *0596008783*)
- A resource component indicating parameters that can be used by a resolver (e.g., *?+method=a*).
- A query component, usually giving resource attributes (e.g., *?=ln=windley&lang=en*)
- A fragment component following a pound sign, indicating a subresource (e.g., *#top*)

A good example of where URNs can be useful is ISBN numbers used to identify books:

> *urn:isbn:0596008783*

This URN represents the book *Digital Identity* published in 2005. Of course, the book has multiple URLs. For example, the following URL is the same book on Amazon:

> *https://www.amazon.com/dp/0596008783*

And this URL is the same book at O'Reilly:

> *https://www.oreilly.com/library/view/digital-identity/0596008783/*

The URN in this example is abstract, naming the book as a concept rather than a physical thing. The URL is concrete, indicating a specific place online.

Zooko's Triangle

Zooko Wilcox-O'Hearn published a conjecture in 2001 widely known as "Zooko's triangle."[3] Zooko's premise was that identifiers can be any two of decentralized, secure, and human readable. These three properties are desirable for identifiers:

Decentralized
  Identifiers can be resolved to the correct value without reliance on a central authority.

Secure
  The system is hardened against attack by malicious actors.

Human readable
  Identifiers are relatively easy for humans to memorize and use.

Problems occur when trying to supply all three properties at once, though.

A Bitcoin address, for example, is secure and decentralized but hardly user-friendly, being a long string of seemingly random characters. An email address is human readable and relatively secure, but resolving it (either as an email address or an identifier) relies on a centralized service.

In recent years, people have used blockchain-based systems to create naming systems that refute Zooko's conjecture. The basic idea is to store a human-readable identifier and the value it resolves to on a blockchain. The result is secure and decentralized. The cost of meeting all three properties simultaneously is the complexity of the blockchain used to store the name-value pairs.

Despite this, however, it's important to keep Zooko's triangle in mind when planning an identifier scheme. Very few use cases can afford to ignore security. Consequently, we usually choose between decentralization and human readability. For many enterprise use cases, decentralization isn't important, and the expense of providing it can be avoided. For others, human readability isn't necessary because the identifiers are stored by computers and not intended for humans.

Discovery

You might have disagreed when I said URLs are names. URLs are a good example of Zooko's triangle. While URLs are globally unique, they aren't memorable, and most people hate typing them into things. If I'm looking for IBM, I'm happy to type *ibm.com* into my browser. But what if I'm looking for a technical report by IBM from

---

3 Zooko Wilcox-O'Hearn, "Names: Distributed, Secure, Human-Readable: Choose Two" (*https://oreil.ly/3e-nT*), 2001.

2012? Even if I know the URL, I'm not likely to type it into the browser. Instead, I'll just search for it using a few keywords. Most of the time that works so well that we're surprised when it doesn't.

We often distinguish between names, identifiers, and addresses. Let's recap:

- URIs are universal *identifiers*, as we've discussed.
- URLs are *addresses*. They are a form of URI, which also give the location of something.
- URNs are *names*.

Neither identifiers nor addresses are the same thing as a name, but these three things are often conflated and confused. When we don't have good names, or where names are impractical, discovery provides an alternative. The World Wide Web solved several important problems, but discovery wasn't one of them. As a result, Aliweb, Yahoo!, and a host of other companies or projects sprung up to solve the discovery problem. Ultimately Google won the discovery wars of the late '90s with a search engine that gave meaningful results on the first page.

Typing keywords into a search engine is a good example of discovery. Web pages don't have names, at least not that are globally unique. And even if they did, who'd be able to remember them all? But search engines allow us to discover the address of a web page using attributes of the page, including its content.

Discovery is a hard problem because whether we're talking about searching for web pages on Google, looking for an old high school friend on Facebook, or finding an API for a particular purpose, finding matches requires some level of understanding what the search target is about. In other words, discovery is often a semantic problem involving meaning, not merely a syntactic problem.

Determining relevance is an important goal of discovery. Discovery determines relevance using algorithms to find the meaning of metadata. One of the reasons search engines like Google succeeded is because they solved two problems. First, they automated the generation of metadata about web pages (e.g., Google web crawler). Second, they developed simple, fast algorithms for determining which addresses mattered most for any given set of metadata attributes (e.g., Google's PageRank algorithm).

Directories

Directories are one of the most widely deployed discovery tools. Most systems have multiple directories, for address books, password files, the list of authorized users for applications, and so on. IT departments maintain large, enterprise-wide directories. In fact, the average IT organization maintains dozens of different directories of all types.

Over the last decade, however, these directories have largely been absorbed into other tools, so we often don't see the directory as a standalone product. For example, if you use a cloud-based identity provider like Okta or SailPoint, there will be directories of users, but they will simply be part of the larger identity service.

A *directory service* is a network-aware directory that allows a directory to be centrally managed and at the same time supply directory information to distributed applications. While we typically think of directories associating information with people, directories are useful for a wide range of IT and business needs.

A directory service contains a structured repository of information, often with complex interrelationships. The structure is defined in a schema—the metadata that defines the overall relationship of each piece of data stored in each entry in the directory to the others. The schema specifies what properties can be associated with an entry, the allowed format or type of property, and whether it is optional or mandatory. Each entry in a directory is defined as an object with attributes, given as name-value pairs, that conform to the schema.

Standalone directories like Microsoft's Active Directory (AD) support complex, configurable schemas. Consequently, AD and others like it have been used in a wide variety of enterprise applications—many not directly related to identity. One of AD's primary uses is organizing IT assets like computers or printers in addition to users. In contrast, directories that are part of other services, especially those in the cloud, often have simple schemas that are not as flexible and designed to support just the features of the service they are part of.

As we've seen, it is not unusual for a namespace to be hierarchical, and so too with directories. The hierarchical structure of the directory is stored in the directory tree. The directory objects at the nodes of the tree are called container objects, which can contain other container objects, or leaves or terminal objects. For example, there might be a container object that represents the organization that holds other container objects for the major organizational departments, and so on until you get to the people, printers, offices, and other resources at the leaves.

A directory service provides methods for querying the directory and managing the entries. These methods may be accessed by client programs designed for human interaction, or by other programs that need access to the information contained in the directory.

Directories are not databases

From the description just given, it may be hard to distinguish a directory service from a standard database. Indeed, directories can be built inside databases, and many of the directories in use are just that. Still, directories are usually different from databases in some significant ways:

- Directories are usually hierarchical whereas databases are not. A directory can tell you all the people whose manager is Mary Jones and all the people who work in Salt Lake City, but it can't easily tell you all the people whose manager is in Salt Lake City—a trivial query with a relational database.

- Retrieval is more important than updating in a directory, and consequently, directories are optimized for reads over writes. Typically, about 90% of the accesses in a directory are retrievals or queries with the remainder being additions or updates.

- Directories are optimized for storing and managing many millions of small, relatively simple objects.

- Directories do not usually support transactions, meaning that operations on the directory cannot be coordinated with the operations of other applications so that they are atomic (i.e., all happen or none happen).

- Directories offer extensive support for matching, partial matching, filtering, and other query operations.

- Most directories have preconfigured schemas so that they are immediately usable for common purposes and are customizable only in very specific ways. Databases typically require considerable work on the schema before any data can be stored.

- Directories are usually simpler to manage than relational databases.

- Because queries and retrievals predominate, directories are easier to replicate for redundancy and performance reasons.

LDAP

No discussion of directories would be complete without talking about LDAP. LDAP, the Lightweight Directory Access Protocol, was created to provide simplified access to some of the functionality of an earlier, much more complicated protocol called X.500 (which we referenced in our discussion of digital certificates in Chapter 9). LDAP specifies an API for clients, something that X.500 lacked. Having an API allows standard software development kits (SDKs) to be created that contain much of the code necessary to use the directory service.

LDAP is a protocol that many different directories support. Because several applications understand LDAP, they can work with those directories. Support for interoperability between products from different vendors has been an important characteristic of LDAP.

The LDAP protocol includes operations for creating, retrieving, updating, and deleting entries from the directory. LDAP also provides search operators for discovering information in the directory.

Several native LDAP directory servers exist on the market. LDAP specifies a network-based server with a hierarchical namespace. LDAP also specifies a method for doing referrals to other directories so that multiple LDAP servers can cooperate to create a single virtual namespace from the namespaces of the individual servers. Most commercial directories are LDAP compliant, meaning they support the LDAP client API.

Domain Name System

The issue of discovery on the internet is more complicated than it is inside an enterprise. Whereas enterprise directories are under the control of a single organization that has the power to dictate policy and enforce naming, online systems must work cooperatively with other organizations not under their control.

The Domain Name System (DNS) is the best-known example of this and forms the basis for most online name systems. We've already seen, for example, how domain names form the basis of URLs.

When I first started using Unix in the mid-1980s, DNS was not widely used. Instead, we FTPed a *hosts* files from a computer at UC Berkeley, merged it with a local *hosts* file, and installed it in the */etc* directory. Mail addresses sometimes had an exclamation mark (!) in them to specify explicit internal routing from a well-known host to the local machine. We had machine names, but no global system for looking them up, or *dereferencing* them.

DNS changed all that by providing a decentralized naming service that based lookup on a hierarchy. DNS—the universal directory that maps domain names to IP addresses—is built around the hierarchical domain namespace that we discussed earlier. DNS is a decentralized, distributed, hierarchical directory and serves as the enabling infrastructure for a single, global directory of domain names. This directory is built from thousands of servers owned by thousands of organizations around the world. The architecture of DNS allows those machines to answer queries regarding domain name mappings efficiently and cooperatively and, at the same time, provide for delegated control over the mappings for any given namespace.

When a machine needs to resolve a domain name into an IP address, it queries a DNS server, looking to one of a few, often local, servers for the answer. The local server may know the answer because the query regards a local machine or because it regards a machine that the DNS server has recently looked up. If it does not, the hierarchical structure of the name is used to arrive at an answer.

Suppose that a distant machine is looking for *www.windley.com* (Figure 10-2). The machine contacts its DNS local server, but that server does not know the answer. The local server contacts one of the root DNS servers. The IP numbers for the set of root DNS servers are well known and built into DNS software bundled with the operating system. The root servers return the IP addresses for the TLD servers, in this case .com. The TLD server does not know the mapping for *www.windley.com*, but it does know the addresses of every DNS server for its domains. The TLD server refers the local server to the DNS server handling >*windley.com* and the local server contacts the DNS server handling *windley.com*. Since that server *does* know the address for *www.windley.com*, the address is returned to the local server, cached, and sent to the original requester. Of course, domain namespaces can be more than three layers deep and so can the associated servers. This process just goes on longer in those cases, but an answer is eventually returned if the mapping exists and the servers are properly configured and registered.

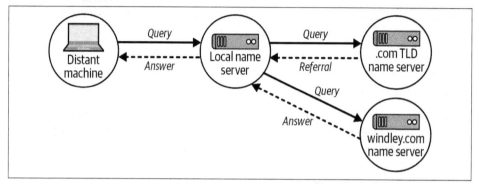

Figure 10-2. DNS query, referral, and answer pattern for www.windley.com

WebFinger

The Unix `finger` command allowed users of time-shared Unix systems to find out information about users. One of the interesting architectural features of `finger` is that it was a hybrid directory that used information the system knew as well as information the user provided to create the response. Users were responsible for creating files in their home directory that were used to give the person using `finger` information about the user.

WebFinger is a similarly architected system for the web. Although the Unix `finger` command and WebFinger are very different protocols, they both allow users to attach metadata to an identifier. The official specification says that "WebFinger is used to discover information about people or other entities on the internet that are identified by a URI using standard Hypertext Transfer Protocol (HTTP) methods over a secure transport."

A WebFinger query returns a JSON object called a JSON Resource Descriptor (JRD). The JRD for a person might contain things like their email address, telephone number, public key, and so on. For other kinds of entities, the data can include whatever information is relevant. For example, the JRD may contain the location of a printer, the capabilities of a server, the author of a blog post, and so on.

RFC 7033 is the specification that describes the WebFinger protocol. Entities in WebFinger are identified using a URI. For people (or more accurately accounts), the URL scheme `acct:` is used to create a URI. The format of the account URI is:

```
acct:<identifier>@<domain>
```

This may look like an email address, but note that this is a URI (i.e., we can tell because it uses the `acct:` scheme) so there's no requirement that it work as an email address.

WebFinger queries are made against a "well-known URI" for an identifier in the domain that the server represents. Well-known URIs are defined in a specification called RFC 5785 as "a URI whose path component begins with the characters `/.well-known/`, and whose scheme is `http`, `https`, or another scheme that has explicitly been specified to use well-known URIs." WebFinger has registered the well-known URI `/.well-known/webfinger`.

Queries for the JRD of a particular URI are made using WebFinger's well-known URI and a query string containing a key-value pair with the key resource identifying the subject URI as shown in Figure 10-3.[4]

Figure 10-3. WebFinger query for phil@windley.org

The returned JRD might look something like this:

```
{
  "subject": "acct:phil@windley.org",
  "aliases":
    [
      "https://phil.windley.org",
      "acct:phil@windley.com"
    ],
  "links":
    [
      {
        "rel": "http://openid.net/specs/connect/1.0/issuer",
        "href": "https://openid.windley.com"
      },
      {"rel": "http://kynetx.org/rel/well-known-eci",
        "property":
```

---

4 Note in Figure 10-3 and elsewhere in this section, I am not URL-encoding the query string for clarity even though this would be done in practice.

```
                {
                    "http://kynetx.org/rel/eci",
                    "76161abcd-18d4-00163-abcd12"
                }
        },
        {
         "rel": "http://webfinger.net/rel/profile-page",
         "href": "https://phil.windley.org"
        },
        {
         "rel": "http://webfinger.example/rel/businesscard",
         "href": "https://phil.windley.org/phil.vcf"
        }
        ]
    }
```

A JRD response contains name-value pairs:

Subject

A name-value pair whose value is the subject of the JRD. This value might be different from the value in the query if the subject has moved or there is a canonical identifier.

Aliases

A name-value pair whose value is an array of strings giving other URIs that also identify this entity. This name-value pair is optional.

Properties

A name-value pair whose value is an object with name-value pairs that identify a property (using a property URI) and a value. This name-value pair is optional.

Links

A name-value pair whose value is an array of objects with name-value pairs that give a relation type and (optionally) an href, set of properties, types, and titles. This name-value pair is optional.

Of course, you might not be interested in all this information when you make a query. The WebFinger specification allows the query to be restricted to certain relationship types of the subject resource in the query string. For example, the following query:

```
GET /.well-known/webfinger?
    resource=acct:phil@windley.com&
    rel=http://webfinger.net/rel/profile-page
```

would return the JRD:

```
{
  "subject": "acct:phil@windley.org",
  "aliases":
    [
```

```
        "https://phil.windley.org",
        "acct:phil@windley.com"
      ],
    "links":
      [
        {
         "rel": "http://webfinger.net/rel/profile-page",
         "href": "https://phil.windley.org"
        }
      ]
  }
```

The returned JRD contains only the relationship we asked for. Since there could be hundreds of relationship types for a complex entity, this reduces the amount of work the client must do to find relevant resource links.

Because WebFinger is based on HTTP, you can use redirects to service accounts in multiple domains from a single WebFinger server. For example, in the previous example `acct:phil@windley.com` is an alias for `acct:phil@windley.org`. The same WebFinger server could service deliver the appropriate JRD for both *windley.com* and *windley.org* using a redirect from those servers.

WebFinger does present some privacy and security concerns. In particular, the JRD could contain information that would allow for more sophisticated phishing attacks. The WebFinger specification states that "systems or services that expose personal data via WebFinger MUST provide an interface by which users can select which data elements are exposed through the WebFinger interface" and "WebFinger MUST NOT be used to provide any personal data unless publishing that data via WebFinger by the relevant service was explicitly authorized by the person whose information is being shared."

There is nothing that prevents WebFinger servers from only allowing access to information based on an authorization scheme or limiting what data is returned to different clients based on authenticated role or other authorization method.

WebFinger provides a good way to provide metadata and additional information about a resource. Used in conjunction with the `acct:` scheme, WebFinger allows a single, easy-to-remember identifier to be used to find additional information that might be identified only using a longer, more complicated identifier. For example, using `acct:phil@windley.org` might allow you to retrieve my complete vCard record or portions of my public calendar, which likely have more complex URIs.

Heterarchical Directories

You might have noticed that DNS and WebFinger have very similar architectures. Both allow a client to retrieve properties of a given identifier from decentralized sources. There is no centralized database of domain names or WebFinger URIs. Both systems allow for the records associated with an identifier to be maintained by the entity responsible for that information. This has advantages in both scale and accuracy.

But, while DNS and WebFinger are decentralized, they are still hierarchical (WebFinger's hierarchy is inherited from its dependence on DNS). Hierarchies have a significant limitation in that they introduce a single point of failure (SPOF) even in a decentralized system. In DNS, for example, there are a limited set of root servers. How well the root registry is architected can have a significant impact on its availability in the face of network failures or attacks.

The hierarchical structure of DNS has a further drawback in that it enables censorship. A despotic regime can limit access to certain TLDs or even proxy them and return different results for any given query. One of the key provisions of the Stop Online Piracy Act (fortunately never enacted) would have required DNS servers to censor websites deemed to be infringing on copyrighted material.

DNS is subject to SPOF and censorship despite being distributed and decentralized, The problem is in its hierarchical architecture. As we discussed in Chapter 2, the alternative to hierarchy is heterarchy. This section looks at directories that have a heterarchical architecture.

Personal Directories and Introductions

As we discussed, discovery is often used to get around the limitations expressed by Zooko's triangle. But discovery isn't the only way to solve the problem. Think about your house address. It's a long, unwieldy, difficult-to-remember string of digits and letters. There's no global way to resolve a person's name to their address. Put another way, there's no global directory (except maybe at Acxiom or the NSA) that maps names to addresses. Even the Postal Service in over 200 years of existence hasn't thought "Hey! We need to create a global directory of names and addresses!" Or if they have, it didn't succeed.

So how do people remember addresses? We exchange addresses with people and keep our own directories. We avoid security issues by exchanging or verifying addresses out of band. For most applications, this is good enough.

Address exchange is an example of the "introduction pattern," a powerful way to create distributed, heterarchical directories. So long as there is some trusted way to communicate with the party you're connecting to, long addresses aren't as big a problem as we might think. We resort to names and discovery when we don't have a trusted channel.

Personal directories are also how people exchange Bitcoins and other cryptocurrencies. I give you my Bitcoin address in a separate channel (e.g., email, my website, etc.). You store it in a personal directory on your own system. When you want to send me money, you put my Bitcoin address in your wallet. To make it even more interesting, since Bitcoin addresses are just public-private key pairs, I can generate a new one for every person, creating personal, peer-to-peer channels for exchanging money.

Personal directories are heterarchical since they are unranked. We each prefer our address book to others. The problem with personal directories is that they make global lookup difficult. Unless I have some preexisting relationship with you or a friend who'll make an introduction, a personal directory does me little good. One way to solve this problem is with systems that support global resolution of identifiers for other information like DNS but still are heterarchical. One such system is a distributed hash table.

Distributed Hash Tables

A distributed hash table (DHT) is a heterarchical directory with no central service. DHTs automatically heal when nodes fail. New nodes can also join at any time. DHTs form a ring in the address space with each node knowing about its successor and predecessor nodes. As a ring, you might object to me classifying a DHT as a heterarchical discovery mechanism. But the heterarchical classification is justified by the relationship of the nodes. They are peers and no node is more or less important than another. You can query any node and get the same answer.

A simple lookup algorithm is to linearly ask down the chain until the key is found, but that's slower than it needs to be, requiring on average $N/2$ queries. Instead, with an address space of N, a table of $\log(N)$ entries can give us sufficient data so that $\log(N)$ hops will get us the value associated with a particular key. This means that a DHT with a key space of 2^{128} entries—a very large space—can be queried in at most 128 steps. DHTs provide a fast and efficient decentralized directory system.

There are many DHT algorithms. The most popular may be Kademlia. For the example that follows we'll use the Chord algorithm since it's relatively easy to understand. Let's see how Chord manages lookup in Figure 10-4.

The variable m represents the logarithmic size of the address space. For simplicity, we'll let m = 5. With m = 5, we can support as many as 32 nodes in the system.

DHTs are sparsely populated. In Figure 10-4, only 9 out of 32 nodes exist. Each node is responsible for knowing the values associated with all the keys between itself and the previous node. So, in the figure, Node 18 is responsible for keys 15, 16, 17, and 18. Data can be replicated in other nodes so that the network can withstand nodes leaving unexpectedly.

The DHT in the example is much more densely populated than most DHTs, since with m = 128 or m = 160 we'd have lots of space (2^{128} or 2^{160} keys) and even millions of nodes would be a small fraction. In the DHT, each node knows its predecessor and successin in the ring. Thus, in our example, node 14 knows that it comes after 11 and before 18—like a doubly linked list.

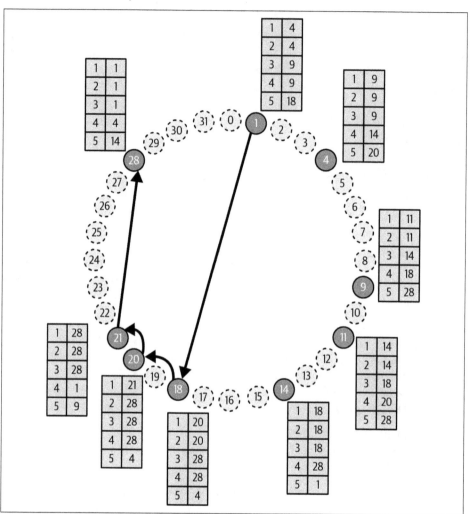

Figure 10-4. Chord DHT showing the lookup of key 26 from node 1

Chord uses a data structure called a finger table to hold information used for looking up keys. Each node keeps its own finger table with m rows. So, in the example in Figure 10-4, each node keeps information about five other nodes. Even in a system with an address space of 2^{160} possible nodes and millions of actual (populated) nodes, each node only needs a table with 160 entries.

Line i in node p's table shows the node that is a logarithmic number of hops from p using the formula succ($p+2^{i-1}$). Note that succ() here is the next node, not an increment. Study the finger tables for each node in Figure 10-4 and try to convince yourself that they are correct.

Looking up key 26 from node 1 involves forwarding the request to a series of nodes that are progressively and exponentially closer to the node responsible for that key. In the figure, no value in node 1's finger table is greater than 26, so we hop to the highest value, 18, taking the request halfway around the ring.

Since 20 < 26 < 28, node 18 forwards to 20. Similarly, since 21 < 26 < 28, 20 forwards to 21. Finally, 26 is less than any entry in 21's finger table, so the value in row 1, namely 28, is the node responsible for key 26.[5] Node 28 will respond with a value (if one exists) for 26.

Distributed hash tables provide a convenient, scalable way to create distributed directories of information. While they are not suitable for storing personally identifying information (PII), they are efficient and stand up well in the face of unreliable nodes. The primary disadvantages are that they are not immune to Byzantine and Sybil attacks. As a result, DHT usage is best limited to trusted environments where the node operators are identified and can be held accountable. For example, I have used a DHT for indexing a large number of processing nodes to distribute the load and avoid a SPOF. Since the DHT nodes could be run by a trusted entity, there was no danger of Byzantine and Sybil attacks.

Using Blockchains for Discovery

Directories require consensus about entries to be useful. If we don't agree on what a name means, then the directory is useless. Enterprise directories achieve consensus through centralized technology and policy. DNS achieves distributed consensus but using a hierarchy that, as we've discussed, is not as resistant to failure, attack, and censorship as we'd like.

We discussed the basic operation and features of blockchains in Chapter 9. Blockchains provide a way of creating consensus about shared information that is resistant to both Byzantine and Sybil attacks.[6] Other means of providing distributed consensus, like distributed hash tables, don't have blockchains' resistance to these attacks. Consequently, blockchains provide a unique solution to creating a decentralized directory.

Blockchains have some limitations that must be considered when using them as a directory, though:

---

5 Note that some lookups loop across the top. Tables use modulo arithmetic to stay within the address space.

6 I'm going to use the word "blockchain" in this section to refer generally to distributed ledgers of all kinds regardless of their specific architectural details.

- Blockchains are immutable. You cannot just delete an entry like you can in a traditional directory.

- Blockchains are expensive. Blocks are written after confirmation by third-party actors who are usually compensated in some way. The process and cost vary from blockchain to blockchain.

- Blockchains are space constrained. Most blockchains have limited capacity to store data based on the size of their blocks.

- Blockchains are not databases with built-in query languages. Most aren't even designed to function well as key-value stores.

- Blockchains are, usually, publicly accessible, so they are not appropriate places to store PII, even if that information is hashed or encrypted.

Considering these limitations, it may seem that using a blockchain as a directory is a bad idea, but with careful design, blockchains can be useful tools for discovery. The details of how to use a blockchain as a global, distributed registry vary depending on the blockchain's architecture and features. There are three general approaches to this.

The first approach is to augment an existing blockchain, usually Bitcoin, with other systems to support the needed features. Bitcoin was designed as a digital currency, and so its native capabilities are very much aimed at that use case. Bitcoin makes it easy, for example, to verify a specific transaction has occurred by checking the hashes of the block that holds the transaction and ensuring it is properly situated in the chain.

Sidetree is a protocol from the Decentralized Identity Foundation (DIF) that uses a blockchain to anchor a bundle of operations stored on some other content-addressable storage (CAS). Sidetree operates as a overlay network, with Sidetree nodes operating independently of the underlying nodes operating the blockchain and CAS. For example, ION is a system for storing, updating, recovering, and deactivating decentralized identifiers (DIDs) that uses the Sidetree protocol. ION uses Bitcoin and the InterPlanetary File System (IPFS) as the blockchain and CAS in a Sidetree-based system to implement the `did:ion` DID method.[7] Figure 10-5 shows the nodes of a Sidetree network and their relationship to the ledger and the CAS.

The advantage of this method is that ION can use well-resourced, decentralized infrastructures like Bitcoin and IPFS to provide the underlying functionalities without the implementers having to build them. The primary disadvantage is that overlay networks depend on the underlying systems. For example, the cost of using the ION net-

---

7 We'll discuss DIDs in detail in Chapter 14.

work depends on the value of Bitcoin at any given time, so fluctuations can increase (or decrease) cost.

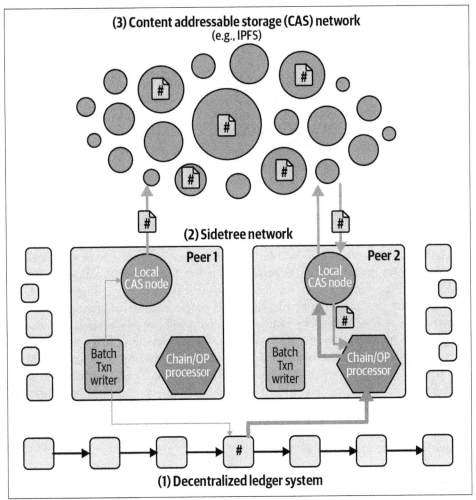

Figure 10-5. Sidetree is a network of nodes that interact with a public ledger (1) and a content addressable storage network (3)

The second approach applies to blockchains that support smart contracts. Smart contracts are programs stored on a blockchain, and the nodes operating the blockchain execute these programs on demand, in a trustworthy way due to the cryptographic nature of the underlying blockchain. Smart contract programming languages allow data to be persistently stored on and retrieved from the underlying chain.

The advantage of using smart contracts is similar to the advantages of the first method. Well-resourced, decentralized platforms for running smart contracts (e.g.,

Ethereum) exist and are operated by others. Smart contracts discovery systems operate on this public infrastructure. Smart contracts can be self-sufficient, meaning that they can collect money, carry out transactions, and distribute resources, including funds. The code for the contract is generally inspectable, providing transparency. Again, like the first method, smart contracts depend on the underlying infrastructure and how it operates.

The third approach uses blockchains specifically architected for the directory operations. For example, the Hyperledger Indy blockchain is designed to store information associated with verifiable credentials, including DIDs, credential schema, credential definitions, and credential revocation accumulators. Indy does this by coupling the underlying blockchain with a database to provide the key-value store. Indy transaction history can be replayed to build a state record—a Merkle Patricia trie is used to prove the values in the database match the transaction history.[8] The details of how this works are beyond the scope of this book,[9] but the result is a very fast, cryptographically trustworthy key-value store.

The biggest advantage of the custom blockchain approach to discovery is that all the necessary functionalities can be built into the code from the start, and needed changes can be made without worrying about the features or functionality of the underlying infrastructure since there isn't any. And that's also the biggest disadvantage: someone must operate the blockchain. If it's permissionless, getting the incentive structure right can be tricky and the blockchain will live or die based on how well designed the incentives are. In my experience, this is very hard. If it's permissioned, then an organization must be created to govern the operation of the nodes. Many may object to the structure of the organization or that there's any organization at all, since many in the blockchain world believe that real decentralization cannot be achieved in permissioned systems.

In Chapter 14, you'll learn that each of these methods has been used to implement the discovery mechanism for public DIDs.

Discovery Is Key

Discovery is one of the fundamental activities in any digital identity infrastructure. Many organizations can solve their most pressing identity management problems with a good directory strategy. As the world has become more interested in user-centric or decentralized identity solutions, discovery beyond the walls of the enterprise has become increasingly important. We'll explore specific ways this is playing out in upcoming chapters.

---

8 A trie is a type of search tree where the node's position in the trie defines the key with which it is associated.

9 For more information, see the Indy documentation (*https://oreil.ly/7hTME*).

CHAPTER 11

Authentication and Relationship Integrity

Authentication (often abbreviated as "authn") is the process we use to recognize other entities online.

As Chapter 5 discussed, online relationships depend on knowing that you're interacting with the same entity each time you connect. I've defined functional digital identity as recognizing, remembering, and responding to a person, organization, or thing online. Because of the proximity problem, we are forced to do this recognition without the familiar methods we use in the physical world. Put another way, the integrity of the relationship depends on the authenticity of each connection—being able to identify to whom or what you're connected.

Authentication prevents outsiders from gaining fraudulent access to a system. This also protects the requester from identity theft. Ensuring authentication is sufficiently robust is vital to the security and relationship integrity of a system.

Identification usually starts with declaring an identifier. Depending on the type of relationship and its uses, you may need to ensure the authenticity of that declaration. There are numerous methods for doing so.

The internet routes packets between machines. When email and other internet services were developed, their creators assumed that people were using a particular machine or domain, so no one needed a method for identifying people. This assumption is the reason emails are addressed to *someone@some.domain*. This worked well until the web caused an explosion in internet use. Suddenly many more people were using different services (sometimes hundreds) and needing accounts on almost all of them. These had to be easy to use—with so many passwords to track—but also balance the attendant security and privacy concerns. In short, an authentication crisis arose, with accounts too often under attack and personal data too often lost or inappropriately shared.

The foundational purpose of digital identity is architecting and installing an authentication system that maintains the integrity of the relationships it manages and mitigates these concerns. This chapter discusses critical factors in designing useful and usable authentication systems.

Enrollment

Enrollment initiates a new relationship. Specifically, *enrollment* is the process of creating an account for a person, organization, or thing (we'll call this entity the *requester*) and associating it with whatever authentication factors will be used to prove that the requester has control of the account. The most familiar enrollment process is registering a new account in an app or on a website. In this familiar flow, the requester picks an identifier (often an email address) and a password. After these are accepted, the requester may be asked to supply other attributes. But this is just the most common enrollment experience. There are many more. Let's explore a few of the important components of the enrollment process.

Identity Proofing

Identity proofing is the process of ensuring that an account is associated with a specific requester. The type and rigor of identity proofing depends on the relationship type. For many web accounts, there is essentially no identity proofing. To cut down on denial-of-service attacks, many enrollment processes use a CAPTCHA to ensure the requester is human.

CAPTCHA, which stands for "Completely Automated Public Turing test to tell Computers and Humans Apart" is undoubtedly familiar to you. A CAPTCHA is a challenge response system that is designed to protect against automated systems filling out forms that are meant for humans. Sometimes these ask you to identify all the pictures that have a specific quality (for example, they depict a boat) in an N by M matrix of pictures. Sometimes you're asked to type letters and numbers from an image that has them obscured in ways to make text capture difficult. CAPTCHAs can be attacked in various ways, such as outsourcing the image-recognition tasks to a real human, but they remain an important way to avoid denial-of-service attacks and mass enrollment for fraudulent purposes.

Often, if the account needs an email or phone number, identity proofing will include checking that these have been entered correctly and belong to the requester, usually by sending a one-time code to the email address or phone number and having the person enter it while logged in. Sometimes account services are unavailable until the email address or mobile number is proofed, but not always.

For many types of relationships, the identity proofing process is much more involved. When you are hired, for example, your employer will ask you to supply identity documents like birth certificates or passports, usually in person. Similarly, opening a bank account requires stricter identity proofing because of the Anti-Money-Laundering and Know-Your-Customer regulations you learned about in Chapter 8.

Since the data needed to support an employee-employer or a bank-customer relationship is much richer than that needed for establishing an account at an online retailer, the enrollment process is more involved. Historically, rich enrollment processes have happened in person, but that is changing with the increase in remote work: numerous companies now offer remote identity-proofing services.

Biometric Collection

Establishing an account often involves collecting biometric data in the form of photographs, fingerprints, handprints, voice prints, facial scans, and so on. Sometimes, as I'll discuss below, this biometric data is collected to strengthen the authentication process and ensure that only a specific person can authenticate for the account. But it has other purposes, too, such as a picture for an employee badge or fingerprints for a background check. These attributes, even when not used for authentication directly, are associated with the account and attest to the identity of the account controller (requester).

Attribute Collection

Attributes like name and address are often collected as part of the enrollment process. These provide basic information needed to service the relationship. Not all such information is necessarily collected at the time of enrollment. For example, to reduce friction, new shoppers at an online retailer may register for an account without supplying any other information. But when they check out, they are given the opportunity to save their shipping address or credit card information for future visits, augmenting the attributes associated with the account.

Incremental attribute collection is more common than you might think. Relationships are constantly changing. Often those changes are just more of what's already there. My Netflix account is constantly being updated with my viewing data—attributes that increase the utility of the relationship between me and Netflix.

Authentication Factors

Authentication requires proof that an identifier and the account it is connected to belongs to or is controlled by the requester providing that identifier. I use *proof* here in the broadest possible sense: the nature of the proof varies, depending on the degree of authenticity demanded by the relationship type and use.

You'll sometimes hear people describe authentication factors as *credentials*, but I will reserve that word to refer to cryptographic documents used to carry attributes.[1] Instead, I'll refer to the information people supply to authenticate simply as *authentication factors*.

Undoubtedly, you've heard of *two-factor authentication* (2FA) or *multifactor authentication* (MFA). These terms are meant to convey the strength of the proof of authenticity by indicating how many authentication factors were used. Authentication factors can be categorized as follows:

Knowledge factor
    Something you know

Possession factor
    Something you have

Inherence factor
    Something you are

Behavior factor
    Something you do

Location factor
    Somewhere you are

Temporal factor
    Some time you're in

I'll discuss each of these in more detail.

Knowledge Factor: Something You Know

This is the most familiar authentication factor because passwords are a knowledge factor, and they are ubiquitous. Personal identification numbers (PINs), like those used in automatic teller machines (ATMs), are an example. The *something you know* should ideally be a shared secret that only you and the authenticating service know, so your username or email isn't normally considered a knowledge factor. As you saw in Chapter 9, shared secrets suffer from several weaknesses, including the need to safely share the secret, their susceptibility to theft, and the ability to brute-force guess them. Reusing passwords; using short, well-known, or easy-to-guess passwords; and storing passwords insecurely are practices that exacerbate these problems.

---

1 Chapter 15 discusses verifiable credentials at length.

Password managers and smartphones make it more manageable to keep track of all the things you know. When used properly, they reduce some of these risks by allowing people to use longer, less easily guessed, and single-use passwords.

Possession Factor: Something You Have

Physical possession is a time-honored method of proving authenticity. In the Middle Ages, letter writers used signet rings with a unique, engraved symbol to create wax seals to prove the authenticity of a letter. Some examples of possession factors are:

- Physical keys
- ATM cards
- Identification cards
- So-called "magic links": hyperlinks with an embedded one-time code, emailed to the address associated with the account. Clicking on the link proves you control (possess) the email account. This can be done to prove the email address is valid when the account is initialized and then later used for authentication.
- Recovery passcodes: services generate a group of passcodes when you sign up and tell you to save them in case you need to recover your account.
- The one-time codes that some services send via SMS for authentication; the thing you possess is the SMS account.[2]

One way to create one-time codes that don't have to be delivered to the authenticating party is to use hardware devices like the RSA SecurID token. These devices generate a one-time code (generated using one of several open standards) that you can use to prove you possess a specific token. Tokens based on HMAC-based One-Time Password (HOTP) generate a code that does not expire until it is used, at which time the next code in the unique sequence is generated. Tokens based on Time-based One-Time Password (TOTP) generate a unique number that expires automatically after a set period (usually 30 seconds). Instead of producing a code you type into the login form, some hardware tokens use a cryptographic protocol built into a browser or application. I'll talk more about these later in the chapter.

Apps use possession of your smartphone as a means of authentication, often with the assumption you've protected it with a PIN or biometric. But software authentication

---

2 While this is very common, the National Institute of Standards and Technology (NIST) Digital Identity Guidelines (800–63B) recommends against using SMS for presenting one-time codes because the possibility of social engineering or compromise of the SMS number makes it less secure than other methods. See *Digital Identity Guidelines: Authentication and Lifecycle Management* (*https://oreil.ly/e89D9*), NIST Special Publication 800-63B, June 2017, accessed March 15, 2022.

apps can be used in lieu of service-specific hardware tokens to generate TOTP codes for services that accept them.

Inherence Factor: Something You Are

The more common term for the *inherence factor* is *biometrics*: measurements of something unique about your physical body. Fingerprints, handprints, retinal scans, voice scans, and facial scans are known as *morphological biometrics* because they have to do with the structure of your body. There are also *biological biometrics*, like DNA, blood scans, and other tests, that can yield unique data about you. When people talk about biometrics for authentication, they are almost always talking about morphological biometrics.

When you do an initial morphological scan to open an account, it is reduced to a data structure and stored. When you attempt to authenticate, an algorithm scans you again and compares the new scan with the stored one. The comparison is not an equality test, since any two scans will differ in some ways. Biometric algorithms are designed to take this into account and still yield accurate results.

Biometrics are popular because they offer good proof of authenticity while being convenient. Most people prefer to unlock their phone using their finger or face as opposed to typing in a pin or password.

Behavior Factor: Something You Do

Behavior factors are not used very often. The "picture password" in Microsoft Windows is an example of a behavior factor: requesters authenticate by drawing shapes, tapping on the right points on the screen, or making the right gestures on a pre-chosen image. Another example is typing behavior: people's typing is remarkably unique, especially on a relatively long phrase.

Location Factor: Somewhere You Are

A *location factor* is based on geofencing something that is accessed remotely and ensuring that the requester's location makes sense. Traveling with a credit card is a familiar example: if you fail to notify your bank you'll be out of the country, your charges may be declined because they don't fit a familiar pattern. We can do the same thing with IP addresses, network routes, Global Positioning System data, or ping latency to ensure that the requesting device is where it's expected to be. Location factors are not generally secure enough to be used for authentication on their own but are combined with other factors.

Temporal Factor: Some Time You're In

Like a location factor, a *temporal factor* is not something you'd use on its own to perform authentication, but it's evidence that a particular authentication falls inside or outside a recognizable pattern of common access times. For example, a system might notice if someone is accessing it after normal work hours. We can also combine time and location. If location changes more rapidly than is reasonable with modern transportation services, that can also be a red flag.

Relying on location and temporal factors can lead to unintended consequences. A friend of mine located in the US recently logged into his bank account from his phone and also from his laptop, forgetting he'd been using a virtual private network (VPN) on the laptop to access websites in Germany. This made it appear to the system that he was somehow in both the US and Germany at the same time. The bank assumed, wrongly, that his account had been hacked, locked him out, and started a fraud investigation. He spent several days sorting this out.

Authentication Methods

Authentication methods use authentication factors, alone or in combination. Presenting yourself to a remote service to be identified has two steps. First, you assert an identifier. Second, you use some combination of authentication factors to prove you control that identifier.

As you learned in Chapter 10, identifiers are (usually) subject to Zooko's triangle, which states that an identifier can have at most two of three desirable properties: decentralized, secure, and human readable. Most familiar authentication systems like those in mobile apps opt for human-readable identifiers without much thought for the others. Email addresses are perhaps the most common, since they are guaranteed to be globally unique and they're easy to remember. They might or might not be secure, depending on the email service the requester uses. This forces the service performing the authentication to depend on the security of some other system that is not under its control.

The remainder of this section will discuss four different categories of authentication methods:

- Identifier only
- Identifier and authentication factors
- Challenge-response
- Token-based

Identifier Only

Identifier-only authentication is really "no-factor authentication," since no authentication factors are used. The requester asserts an identifier, and the relying party accepts it without any further proof. Identifier-only identification is widespread; the most common such system is the browser cookie.

Most people don't think of cookies as an authentication system, but they *are* used to lay claim to a particular session. The *Hacker's Dictionary* defines a *cookie* as a handle, transaction ID, or other token of agreement between cooperating programs. The claim check you get from a dry cleaning shop is a good example of a cookie; the only thing it's useful for is making sure that you get your clothes back, which it does by relating two transactions that happen at different times.

On the internet, whenever a requester's browser makes a request to the server, the server generates and sends back an HTTP cookie, allowing the server to correlate all requests from that browser. The requester's browser stores the cookie for future use. These cookies serve the same purpose as the dry cleaning claim check: they tie transactions together that are otherwise difficult to connect.

To see how this works, suppose Alice uses her browser to visit a website she's never been to before: *foo.com*. The administrators for *foo.com* have configured their server to return a cookie with every HTTP response. So, when Alice visits the site, the server passes a cookie back to her browser. Alice's browser dutifully stores the cookie in a file on her computer used especially for this purpose. The next time she requests a page from *foo.com* (which could happen in the same browsing session or days or even weeks later), her browser sends back the cookie it received on the previous visit. This allows *foo.com* to correlate Alice's visits and create a session that spans individual HTTP transactions.

So, let's review what happens in this process:

1. The server asks Alice's browser to store some information as a cookie, knowing that it will be sent back verbatim when the browser makes its next request.

2. The server chooses the information in the cookie it gave to her browser.

3. Alice's browser doesn't add any information to the cookie, just passes it back.

4. Alice's browser stores the cookie in a special file that it, not the server, chooses.

5. The next time Alice retrieves a page from that website, her browser sends the string back to the server.

The cookie does not necessarily contain any information about Alice, but it could. Remember, the server chooses the string used for the cookie. The cookie is not a program, either; it can't be executed and has no ability to access other information on Alice's computer. It represents an identifier for the session, not necessarily for Alice. If it is stored on a public computer, for example, anyone using that computer will be in the same session, from the server's perspective. To make it Alice's identifier for the session, the cookie must be set when Alice is authenticated in some other way, then deleted or invalidated when she logs out.

Cookie-based correlation is foundational to the modern web. Because HTTP is a stateless protocol, every request looks like a different session. The ability to link together time-separated transactions is what allows a website to run a shopping cart, remember who you are, or fill in forms for you. Just like you wouldn't return to a dry cleaner who couldn't match customers with their clothes, websites without the ability to link transactions across time don't do much besides serve simple pages.

There is a dark side to cookies. As I've described them, they sound largely innocuous—but the devil is in the details. If Alice is shopping on *foo.com*, she wants the site to keep track of her session because that provides utility and convenience. But it turns out that most web pages are not a single chunk of HTML that the server sends down. They have lots of other things, like JavaScript files and images, embedded in them too. These other things don't have to be from the same server and are identified by their own URL. Each of those servers can set its own cookie as well. And since the cookies know where they were linked from, they can correlate activity across multiple websites.

This is how (simple) ad tracking works. When you see an ad on website A, it's being served from a server owned by an ad company with which website A has an agreement. The ad server plants a cookie in your browser. Now suppose you visit website B, which displays ads from the same ad server. Your browser dutifully reports the cookie back to the ad server, along with the information that the ad was on website B. The company running the ad server now knows you were on websites A and B (along with lots of other metadata). Rather than correlating requests on a single site, it's using cookies to correlate your activity across the web, well beyond the utility of a shopping cart or a chat server. It doesn't stop with your browsing history. The ad company learns other things about you from the sites you visit, and soon it can develop a comprehensive dossier. This is the basis for surveillance capitalism, discussed in Chapter 8.

Identifier-only authentication is a weak form of authentication because there's no way to ensure that the same entity is using the cookie from visit to visit. Not only might the cookie be on a shared computer, but cookies can be moved from one browser to another. Even with these problems, identifier-only authentication is useful in a variety of circumstances.

Identifier and Authentication Factors

We often classify authentication systems by how many different factors they use. Every authentication factor I've discussed here has unique security vulnerabilities that limit its effectiveness as a proof of authenticity. Combining factors can reduce those vulnerabilities, since the strength of one factor can compensate for the weakness of another.

Username/password is a *single-factor authentication* scheme: the password, something you know, is the only authentication factor used. As we've seen, the weakness of passwords is that the shared secret may become known to attackers through hacking. Using *two-factor authentication* (2FA), combining something you know, the password, with something you possess, like a one-time code from your phone, mitigates this limitation, since the hacker must gain access to your phone somehow in addition to stealing your password.

2FA is becoming more commonly available, even if it's not often required. You could even consider the one-time code from an authenticator app, combined with a password, to be *three*-factor authentication in some circumstances. Not only is the password a knowledge factor and the one-time code a possession factor, but using a biometric to access the authenticator app can provide a third factor, an inherence factor, in the overall proof of authenticity. The service could also use location or temporal factors. Consequently, the name *multifactor authentication* (MFA) has gained popularity in describing the general idea of combining factors.

Passwords

By far, the most common form of identifier and authentication factor is a username and password. If you're like me, you have hundreds of username/password pairs for various computer systems around the internet. By entering a username, you lay claim to an account, and the password is used to authenticate that you are allowed to do so. The system uses the account that the username represents to associate attributes with the account holder. In a web session, for example, the authenticating party is laying claim to a specific web session and the attributes the service has stored for them.

The flow for password registration and use is shown in Figure 11-1. With passwords and other factors like one-time security codes, the authentication factor (such as the password or one-time password, OTP) flows from the authenticating party to the authenticating service.

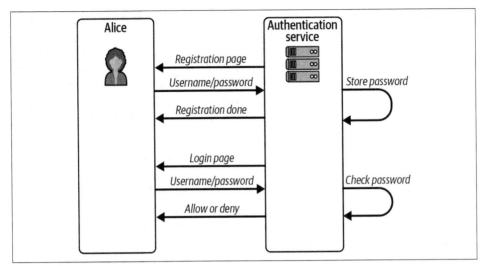

Figure 11-1. Password registration and use

Password management

The biggest advantage of username and password systems is their simplicity and familiarity. The largest drawback is their reliance on passwords. In theory, because passwords are secret (something you know), they are secure, and only the entity with the secret can reveal it to the authentication system. In practice, passwords suffer from several serious limitations:

- People can remember only a limited number of items with perfect accuracy (around eight, on average). Furthermore, they usually have multiple passwords to remember. As a result, people tend to create passwords that are short and simple. They also often use the same password for multiple accounts.

- Easy-to-remember passwords can be easily guessed by an attacker. Even passwords that have no relation to the requester can be effectively guessed if they are what are known as "dictionary words." The best passwords are long, random strings of characters, but people can't remember those.

- People (and even machines) can be tricked into revealing passwords to an attacker. One common method is creating fake login screens, a technique called *phishing*. Another is known as *social engineering*, in which the attacker contacts the account holder and tricks them into revealing their password by posing as an administrator or someone else the person trusts.

- People write passwords down or store them in files on computers. This makes them vulnerable to theft and misuse.

Many IT departments institute password aging policies that force users to change their passwords on a periodic basis to mitigate the dangers posed by loss or sharing. They also frequently enforce rules about password structure to make passwords less guessable. For example, the rules may disallow dictionary words, require passwords longer than eight characters, or require passwords to contain a mixture of letters, numbers, and punctuation. These policies often result in people giving up trying to remember their passwords and simply writing them down and pasting them to their monitors or sticking them in the pencil drawer.

When it's poorly implemented, password aging can be a detriment in other ways. Some password-aging implementations, for example, allow a person to immediately change their password back to the previous password, defeating the purpose. Also, many systems surprise the person with a requirement to select a new password when logging in. Faced with having to select a new password quickly, many people select simple variations on older passwords.

The best tool for making passwords better is a password manager, an app that provides a secure, convenient way to generate, store, and use passwords. Solving the memory problem means people can choose better passwords. But this tool doesn't answer other problems, like phishing, hacking, and social engineering.

Password reset

Managing passwords is a significant challenge for any service with many accounts. Password issues can make up 40% of all calls to an IT help desk—which can cost as much as $70 per call, making this an expensive proposition.[3] To mitigate password management costs, many organizations have implemented self-service password-reset systems that don't require knowing the old password.

Password reset services can work in various ways. One of the most common methods is to ask security questions that must be answered correctly before the reset proceeds. The questions can be canned ("What is your mother's maiden name?") or free-form, allowing the users to enter their own questions and answers when establishing their accounts. Another common technique is the so-called *magic link*, where a password reset link is sent to a verified email address associated with the account.

Biometric factors

As you've seen, inherence factors or biometrics tie an authentication to a specific person. This property allows biometrics to be used for identification, not just authentication. This can prevent account sharing. To understand the difference, consider the

---

3 "Resetting Passwords (and Saving Time and Money) at the IT Help Desk" (*https://oreil.ly/5lbN6*), Duo Security, accessed June 28, 2022.

problem of ensuring that a person receives a government entitlement like food assistance only once per month. By fraudulently obtaining usernames and passwords, crooks apply for entitlements under different names. Biometrics determine whether that specific person, rather than just someone with the right username and password, is known to the system and whether that person has previously been enrolled.

The flip side of this advantage represents the most significant *disadvantage* of inherence factors: biometric characteristics can be duplicated or cheated. Once a biometric identification characteristic is compromised, there is little recourse. You can't easily issue new irises or fingerprints to replace the compromised feature. This is not a hypothetical concern: the US Office of Personnel Management was hacked in 2015 and cybercriminals made off with the fingerprints of 5.6 million government employees.[4]

There are also privacy concerns if people are automatically identified without their knowledge. Some biometrics, like facial or iris scans, are easy to perform even at a distance, without people knowing.

You can significantly reduce these risks by using biometrics in ways that limit theft, such as storing the data locally on each device instead of keeping a large database of scans: collecting a large trove of biometric data would require hacking millions of computers rather than just one. In general, local biometrics present many fewer security and privacy concerns than global, general-purpose applications.

Another thing to keep in mind when considering biometrics is that there are individuals who don't fit into the standard patterns. Imagine a scenario in which a data center installs hand-geometry scanners at each of its doors and relies on them for perimeter security. These devices cannot successfully identify the hand geometry of individuals with polydactylism (one or more extra fingers), which occurs in 0.2% of the general population. If the data center hires a polydactyl individual, in the US and many other countries, it would be required to accommodate this disability. Most reasonable accommodations would create a special-purpose breach in the security wall or reduce the automation level of the authentication system.

Challenge-Response Systems

In challenge-response authentication, the system generates a random string of characters, and the requester is required to manipulate the string according to some predefined algorithm and send it back to the server. The algorithm may be secret or use cryptographic keys. Usually, some sort of computer performs the manipulation to make the algorithm more complicated and thus more difficult to guess.

---

4 "Hacking of Government Computers Exposed 21.5 Million People" (*https://oreil.ly/xqVOd*), *The New York Times*, July 10, 2015, accessed March 15, 2022.

The simple version of this uses shared secrets. Suppose Alice and Bob agree to meet at the zoo to exchange a package. They do not know each other by sight and agree to verify their identities by way of a spoken password, like in spy movies. The two parties approach each other, one says something, and the other responds with a predetermined response. This is a simple challenge-response system.

In a more sophisticated challenge-response system, Bob might be instructed ahead of time to add 3,133 to the number Alice gives him and repeat it back. Alice then gives Bob a number: say, 5,634. He responds with 8,767. Alice performs the same calculation, gets the same answer, and knows that Bob is the party she's to meet. She could distinguish between multiple parties by giving them different challenges: telling another party to reverse the number and add 3, for example.

Challenge-response systems have an advantage over identifier and authentication factor methods because their algorithms can be made so complex that they are nearly impossible to guess. The disadvantages are that the algorithm must be coded on a special-purpose device or run on the person's computer or smartphone and might be subject to loss or theft.

Challenge-response systems can also be built using a *cryptographic shared secret*. In this scheme, both the requester and the service know the secret key. The service generates a challenge phrase and sends it to the requester. The requester creates a message digest for the challenge phrase using the secret key and sends the result back to the service. The service calculates a message digest for the phrase with the shared secret key and compares it to the response. If they match, the service knows that the requester possesses the secret key, without ever having to send it across the network. If the message digest algorithm and the way it's combined with the password are not cryptographically sound, an attacker may be able to deduce the secret key from the network traffic.

As Chapter 9 discussed, shared secrets are problematic because they must be communicated securely, usually on a separate channel. When the shared secret must be rotated, the new secret must be communicated again. As you learned, asymmetric-key cryptography is a better fit for challenge-response systems. This is often done using digital certificates, but any asymmetric-key system can be used if both parties trust it. The challenge response proves that the requester controls the private key associated with the public key.

Figure 11-2 shows the flow for a generic challenge-response system using public keys. During registration, Alice sends the public key to the service. In the authentication portion, the service sends a challenge to Alice, who signs the response and returns it. The service uses the public key to determine if the signed response is valid and, if so, authenticates Alice.

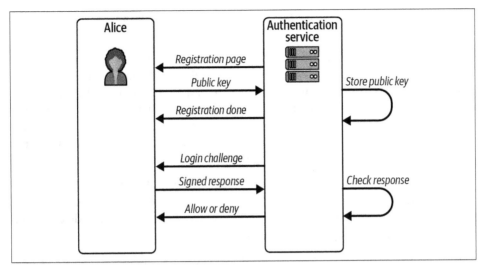

Figure 11-2. Key registration and challenge-response flow

Figures 11-2 and 11-1 shows an important difference between the challenge-response and identifier-authentication-factor flows. In the identifier-authentication-factor flow, Alice sends the secret (a password or OTP) to the service. In the challenge-response system, the secret is not exchanged during authentication. In an asymmetric-key-based challenge-response system, the secret never leaves Alice's device.

Digital certificates and challenge-response

Because digital certificates based on public-key infrastructure (PKI) aggregate identity attributes with a public key signed by a third party, they can easily be used for authentication. As you saw above, a public key can be used in authentication, with a digital-signing algorithm creating a message digest of the challenge. The certificate can serve as a trustworthy means of distributing the public key. By authenticating, the requester proves they are in control of the private key associated with the public key in the certificate. Once verified, the identifying information in the certificate can be assumed to belong to the certificate's subject, if the verifier trusts the certificate issuer.

Digital certificates have been a runaway success in securing exchanges between browsers and web servers using Transport Layer Security (TLS). Most websites now use TLS to authenticate the server to the browser or app and encrypt the conversation. In TLS, the challenge is a string that the client encrypts, using the public key in the server's certificate, and sends to the server. If the server has the private key associated with the public key in the certificate, it uses the string the client sent to generate a secret key. The client has also generated a secret key. The response is the establishment of an encrypted channel, using the secret key both sides have independently generated. By successfully setting up that channel, the client also authenticates the server.

Using certificates for client authentication is a different story. Microsoft, IBM, and other tech companies have invested millions of dollars building systems for creating, administering, and using client-side certificates for authentication. But outside of high-security applications, client-side certificates have not had much success. The primary problem is that they are complicated for users to manage and involve considerably more difficult concepts than simpler systems like ID and password systems. And managing private keys can be difficult.

A secondary problem is that commercially issued digital certificates cost money. They must be renewed regularly, and people frequently forget their access codes or lose the certificate entirely, leading to costly refreshes. This ongoing expense can deter organizations from adopting digital certificates as their primary authentication mechanism.

Client-side certificates also present a privacy problem. Because of the cost, most people would use only a few client-side certificates. Consequently, every place the client-side certificate is used has a strong single global identifier (the public key) that can be used to correlate activities across the internet—which is, as you learned, not privacy-friendly.

All this doesn't mean that digital certificates have no place in an authentication strategy, but you should understand why you're using them and compare the expected benefit with the additional complexity and expense. Certificate-based authentication has found the most success in special-purpose applications where security is of particular concern.

Chapter 14 will discuss cryptographic identifiers, a good alternative to client-side certificates for authentication that solves the cost, management, and privacy problems.

FIDO authentication

Fast Identity Online (FIDO) is a challenge-response protocol that uses public-key cryptography. Rather than using certificates, it manages keys automatically and beneath the covers, so it's as user-friendly as possible. I'm going to discuss the latest FIDO specification, FIDO2, here, but the older FIDO U2F (Universal Second Factor Framework) and UAF (Universal Authentication Framework) protocols are still in use as well. The FIDO Alliance, which governs the FIDO standards, uses the name *passkey* for FIDO2 credentials. You might also hear them called *discoverable credentials* or *resident credentials*.

FIDO uses an *authenticator* to create, store, and use authentication keys. Authenticators come in several types. *Platform authenticators* are devices that a person already owns, like a laptop or smartphone. *Roaming authenticators* take the form of a security key that connects to the laptop or smartphone using USB, NFC, or Bluetooth.

When Alice registers with an online service, her authenticator creates a new cryptographic key pair, securely storing the private key locally and registering the public key with the service. The online service may accept different authenticators, allowing Alice to select which one to use. Alice unlocks the authenticator using a PIN, fingerprint reader, or face ID.

When Alice authenticates, she uses a client such as a browser or app to access the service (Figure 11-3). The service presents a login challenge, including an account identifier, which the client passes to the authenticator. It prompts Alice to unlock the authenticator and uses the account identifier in the challenge to select the correct private key and sign the challenge. Alice's client sends the signed challenge to the service, which uses the public key it stored during registration to verify the signature and authenticate Alice.

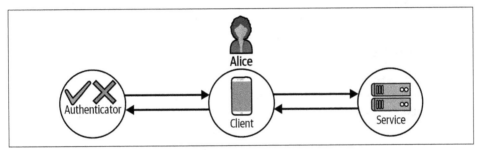

Figure 11-3. FIDO authentication flow

FIDO2 uses two standards. The *Client to Authenticator Protocol* (*CTAP*) describes how a browser or operating system establishes a connection to a FIDO authenticator. The *WebAuthn* protocol is built into browsers and provides an API that JavaScript from a web service can use to register a FIDO key, send a challenge to the authenticator, and receive a response to the challenge.

FIDO provides a secure and convenient way to authenticate users without resorting to passwords, SMS codes, or TOTP authenticator applications. Modern computers and smartphones and most mainstream browsers understand FIDO natively. While roaming authenticators are available, for most use cases, platform authenticators are sufficient. This makes FIDO an easy, inexpensive way for people to authenticate. The biggest impediment to its widespread use is probably that people won't believe something so easy is secure.

Token-Based Authentication

A movie ticket is a real-world example of a token. The ticket says nothing about its bearer, simply that the holder has the right to sit in a certain theater at a specific time. A season pass at an amusement park might be even less specific, indicating that the holder can access any ride whenever the park is open.

Similarly, an *authentication token* is a string that contains no usable information; it merely represents the power to do something.[5] As long as the token remains valid, the holder can access the service. Just as you can't get a movie ticket without handing over some money, authentication tokens are usually issued based on some other authentication activity and are associated with a specific account and permissions on the service.

Tokens have several advantages. First, even though they rely on other methods of authentication, they reduce the need to authenticate over and over. Second, tokens let you use an authentication service that's separate—even in a different domain—from the primary service. (As you'll see in Chapter 13, this has distinct advantages for identity federation.) Third, tokens are useful for granting time-bound or event-based access, because they can be set to expire and to allow refreshing or not, depending on context or circumstance.

Token-based authentication has proven useful in APIs because the service accessing the API, like a mobile app or single-page web application, is doing so repeatedly, sometimes without the requester being present to authenticate. The requester authenticates, and the mobile app or web application gets a token it can use for the access it needs. Tokens might remind you of cookies, and the two have some features in common, but tokens are generally designed to be cryptographically verifiable and usable in circumstances where cookies are not natively supported, like API access.

Classifying Authentication Strength

"Identity is the new perimeter" is a frequent refrain at conferences and in the trade press. If you're new to information security, you might not understand what this means. Back in the dark ages, security depended strongly on firewalls to prevent intruders from gaining access to corporate networks. This worked fine when most IT assets were on premises. But as more and more services have moved to the cloud, it's harder to put walls, virtual or not, around your IT systems. As a result, authentication has become the primary means of protecting people, money, and systems from attack. This is true for individuals as much as for enterprises.

---

5 As you saw in the section on factors, possession factors like those using TOTP are sometimes called *tokens*. The tokens discussed in this section are not hardware tokens.

I noted earlier that of the primary means of attack against authentication systems is called *phishing*. Phishing is essentially a man-in-the-middle attack that relies on the target not paying attention to clues that the site or app they're logging into is fake. In a phishing attack, the intruder poses as a legitimate organization, application, or website to steal whatever authentication factors are being used. Phishing relies on two things: setting up a fake login screen (or app) that mirrors the one from which the attacker is stealing authentication factors; and sending a notification to the target that entices them to open the fake site or app. The notification often comes as an email or text with a strong call to action.

Figure 11-4 shows how phishing works. Alice believes she's connected to the origin server, but her client is *actually* connected with a phishing server controlled by Malfoy. Malfoy uses the information Alice enters at his phishing server to log into the origin server. Some phishing attacks are extremely sophisticated, even mimicking second-factor collection mechanisms (like a page for entering an OTP sent via SMS or from a TOTP authenticator app). What usually gives them away is the URL: the phishing site might use a domain name that looks like the real domain name and often has a certificate so that the browser displays a TLS lock.[6] Still, people don't pay enough attention to URLs (and browsers sometimes hide them), making phishing a profitable online sport.

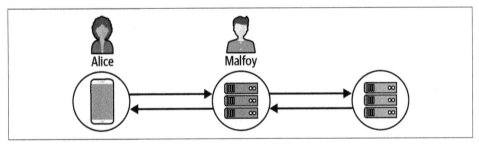

Figure 11-4. Phishing is a man-in-the-middle attack

The Authentication Pyramid

Figure 11-5 shows the strengths of various authentication methods as a pyramid.[7] Methods are progressively more secure as you move from the bottom of the pyramid to the top.

---

6 As you saw in Chapter 9, most digital certificates simply verify that a given public key is associated with a given domain name. They don't necessarily provide any useful information about the organization behind the domain name.

7 Damien Bowden first introduced me to this method of viewing the relative strengths of authentication schemes using a pyramid (*https://oreil.ly/XS-Q4*). Later, I saw the same concept from Intercede (*https://oreil.ly/WJOxo*). The authentication pyramid shown here is adapted from these to fit our discussion.

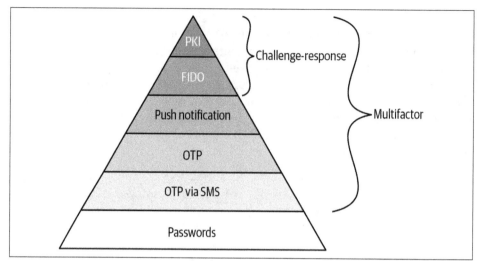

Figure 11-5. Authentication pyramid

Let's look at each method in more detail:

Passwords

Passwords, to summarize, are the least secure and most widely used of the methods in the pyramid. While they're familiar, they are inconvenient, costly, and the most common cause of breaches. Companies often make it worse by failing to hash passwords stored on their systems or forcing people to rotate their passwords.

OTP via SMS

MFA protects against password compromise; the most common second factor is an OTP sent via SMS or email, which has the advantage of simplicity. The chief disadvantage is that SMS and email aren't secure communication channels. NIST recommends against using SMS as a second factor.

OTP

FIDO authenticator apps and TOTP devices are both examples of OTPs not based on a code pushed through SMS. These are generally more secure than SMS-based OTPs but tend to be inconvenient. Some password managers make this easier by incorporating the OTP application and automating much of the work.

Push notifications

Some services or apps, like Google, are so popular that push notifications directly to the app make sense. When you log in, you get a notification on your phone asking if it's you; this is convenient because it's usually just a click on the screen.

This has the advantage of using a separate channel for the notification that is likely already authenticated.

All the methods at the bottom of the pyramid have the big disadvantage of being phishable, even push notifications. As shown in Figure 11-6, if Alice thinks she's at the real site, she'll push the "Yes, This Is Me" button on a push notification, and the origin server will receive it and assume Malfoy is Alice. There's a technique called *prompt bombing* that sends the target multiple push notifications—sometimes close together, sometimes spread out over days—on the theory that they'll eventually approve one of them. The only defense against phishing with these systems is wariness, suspicion, and care on the part of the person authenticating.

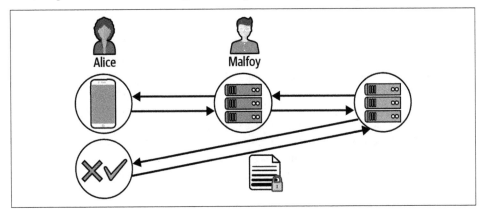

Figure 11-6. Phishing attack with a push notification

FIDO and PKI, the top two layers of the pyramid, are different. They are resistant to phishing when properly implemented and used because they're directly connected to the browser or app. Both are challenge-response systems based on asymmetric-key cryptography.

FIDO

When a client passes a challenge on to the FIDO authenticator, it uses the private key to sign the challenge and includes the URL to which the browser is connected. As shown in Figure 11-7, Malfoy can't instruct Alice's client to lie, so her client uses the phishing site's URL. When Malfoy passes the signed response to the challenge back to the origin server, it detects that the URL in the signed response is invalid and rejects the response, disallowing access.

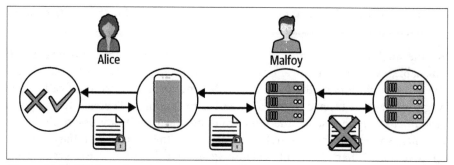

Figure 11-7. FIDO authenticator signing challenge

PKI

PKI, the infrastructure for digital certificates, works a little differently: through the client, not adjacent to it. I've placed PKI above FIDO on the pyramid because, done right, a digital certificate can include identity proofing that ties it to a specific entity. TLS uses the keys associated with certificates to create a shared secret to provide an encrypted channel. The client can authenticate the server and know that it controls the private key associated with the public key in the certificate. PKI-based authentication uses client-side certificates to the same effect. When both the server and client have certificates, they can mutually authenticate, and the phisher can't prove they control the private key used to sign the client's challenge.

Figure 11-8 shows the PKI certificate exchange between the client and server. Alice requests access to a protected resource on the server using her browser. The client and server exchange certificates; each can use the public keys in the certificates to authenticate the other using a challenge-response protocol. The certificate for the server contains the URL. Similarly, Alice's certificate has information about who is authenticating, allowing the server to validate her. Malfoy is left out because he doesn't have either Alice's or the server's private key.

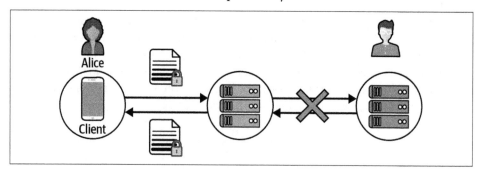

Figure 11-8. PKI certificate exchange

Authentication Assurance Levels

NIST's authenticator assurance levels classify the strength of various authentication methods used in US government systems.[8] Seeing how this agency views authentication assurance is instructive:

Authentication Assurance Level 1
> AAL1 requires a single factor. This could be passwords or just a hardware token. AAL1 doesn't count biometrics by themselves as an authentication factor; they must be associated with some physical authenticator.

Authentication Assurance Level 2
> AAL2 requires two factors: a password and hardware authenticator or a hardware authenticator and a biometric used to access it. In addition, AAL2 requires shorter reauthentication time, replay resistance, standards (FIPS 140 Level 1) for hardware tokens, and authenticator intent (which means that the system can't be triggered by malware without alerting the requester).

Authentication Assurance Level 3
> AAL3 requires a hardware token as one factor that offers authenticator intent, verifier *impersonation resistance* (protection against phishing), and verifier compromise resistance (the keys in the authenticator are destroyed if it is physically compromised).

These levels are primarily used by the US government and its contractors and vendors. But they can be a useful tool for understanding the strength of your own authentication system since they represent the collective wisdom of the team of identity and security professionals who collaborated to create them.

Account Recovery

No matter which authentication method you use, remember, it's only as secure as your account-recovery process. For example, if you are using FIDO but your system allows Alice to use passwords with an OTP to recover her account if she loses her authenticator, then your system is only as secure as a password with OTP.

Figure 11-9 shows the fallbacks for one of my Google accounts for my second factor. When I log in on my computer, if I click the link labeled *Try Another Way*, Google will let me use a FIDO security key that I have registered with the account; a one-time code (using email or SMS); an app push; a code from my TOTP authenticator app; or one of the backup codes I stored when the account was created.

---

8 NIST Special Publication 800-63B (*https://oreil.ly/hnRME*), *Digital Identity Guidelines: Authentication and Lifecycle Management*, accessed March 29, 2022.

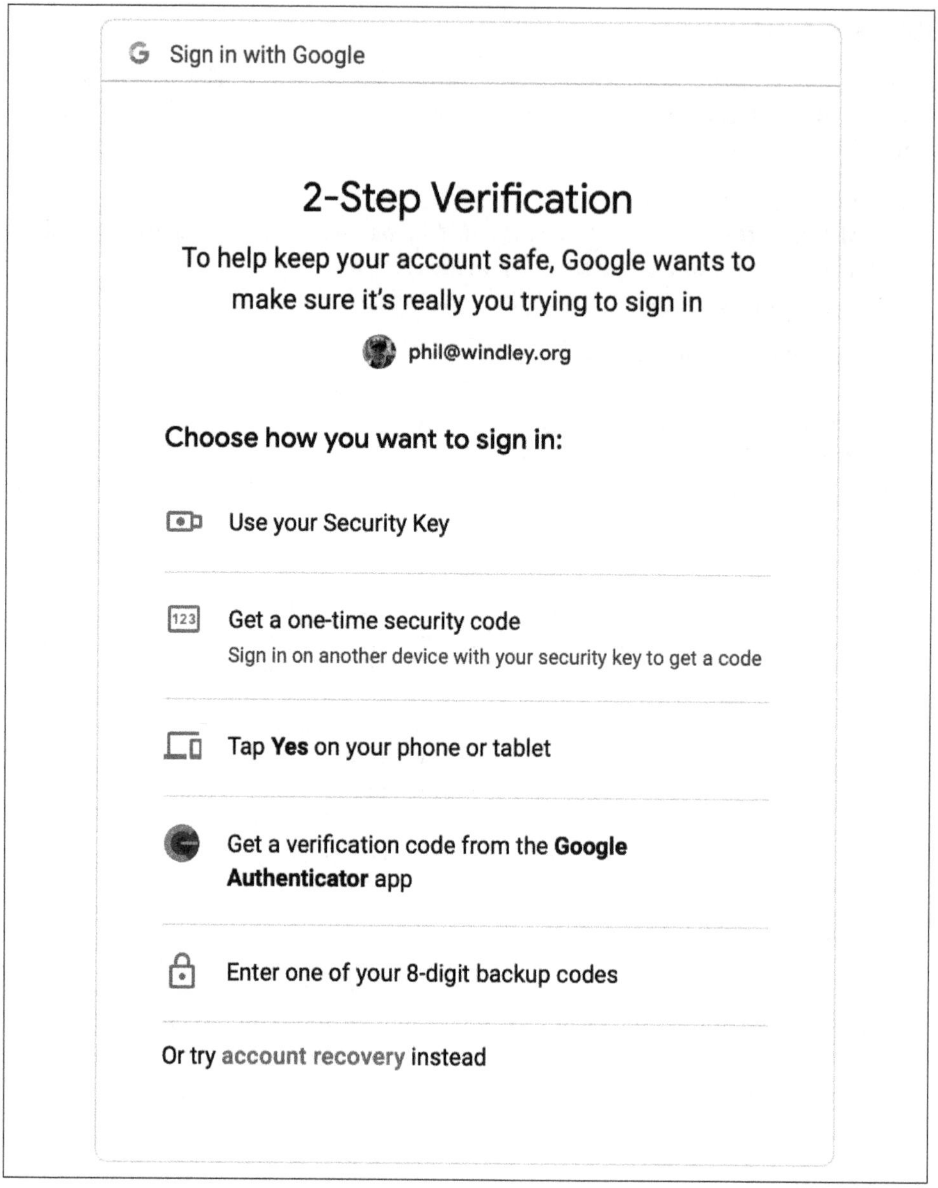

Figure 11-9. Second-factor options for Google

Since the one-time security code is SMS, my account is protected only to that level. The other methods might be more convenient for me in various circumstances, but my security isn't improved by having, for example, a FIDO security key. Google lets you tailor these options to some degree in the *Security* tab on the account page.

If I click *account recovery* on the screen in Figure 11-9, I see the screen in Figure 11-10(a). Since I have the Google app installed on my phone, when I check it, I see Figure 11-10(b) asking if it's really me. Clicking *yes* shows the screen in Figure 11-10(c). Picking the right number, 97, logs me in.

Figure 11-10. Account recovery for Google

Because I have the Google app, account recovery defaults to using a push notification. Google sends me several email notifications as part of this process. Of course, if my email is compromised, the attacker could choose to get the code via email and delete that message and the security notifications. To combat this, Google also notifies a second email address, controlled by you or someone you trust to be aware of suspicious activity. I'm the second account for my wife and my kids, so I see a lot of these. I always contact them using another channel to make sure it was them.

Google's doing all of this to keep accounts safe because it runs a large public system that billions of people around the world rely on. It involves defense in depth, good decisions about defaults, and a sophisticated account infrastructure. You can likely tailor your system's account-recovery processes more specifically to your account holders, making them simpler.

Authentication System Properties

This section describes nine important characteristics that authentication systems should have. You can use these properties to create an evaluation process for authentication systems in your organization. The most effective method is to prioritize these properties based on design criteria for the overall system, then evaluate different designs against the prioritized list.

Practicality

Practicality is probably the most important feature that any authentication system can have. From the requester's standpoint, the authentication system should be easy to use and nonintrusive. No one likes an authentication system that asserts itself too frequently or asks for authentication when none is needed. People also dislike using multiple authentication systems for multiple resources when they see those resources as related. For example, if your employee benefits are administered by an outside organization, you might have to access them using a different authentication process from the one you use to access your employer's self-service functions. This has been known to cause employees to grumble.

From the service or enterprise's viewpoint, the authentication system should scale well, provide the appropriate level of protection, and be cost-effective. Easy-to-use systems are a priority as well, due to high support costs. Organizations frequently manage authentication by several large, diverse groups, such as customers, employees, and the employees of partners and suppliers. They all need access to resources that the organization controls. Each of these groups has unique needs, and the authentication system should adapt to those needs.

Systems that require people to install new software—or, worse yet, new hardware (like biometric devices and smart card readers)—are difficult and costly to deploy and maintain. That doesn't mean they shouldn't be used when warranted, but it does need to be factored into the choice.

Appropriate Level of Security

Different applications require different levels of security. As we've seen, there are many ways to authenticate credentials with authentication factors. While the security of an authentication method is directly dependent on the number and type of authentication factors used, so is its cost. Good design will match the level of authentication to security requirements.

Evaluating authentication strength can be subjective. You need expert knowledge to evaluate the weaknesses of complex systems like cryptographic key systems. Comparing two systems and judging their relative strength is easier, provided they are not too similar. Deciding the relative strength of two different multifactor systems that differ only in policy details is much more difficult.

Locational Transparency

Smartphones, remote work, global customer bases, and international partners mean mobility is an important factor in modern IT systems. You often can't count on the requester being in a specific location. Using location as an authentication factor requires good prediction algorithms and flexibility.

Integrable and Flexible

Take care to ensure that the authentication system and various servers interoperate. New tools offer developers easy access to authentication, but it may not be as easy to create systems that *inter*operate. Most organizations never create an authentication system from scratch, but they will integrate various systems with it. Carefully choose vendors with appropriate SDKs, libraries, and APIs to maximize flexibility.

Appropriate Level of Privacy

The extent to which user data is kept private depends on the organization and the resources being protected. For example, in the US at least, companies can log and track employee access to company resources (including computers, smartphones, and email) to whatever extent the employer feels is appropriate. On the other hand, on a system that allows patients at a medical center to view their treatment records, the authentication mechanism must provide more privacy protection because of laws and regulations such as HIPAA.

Reliability

Reliability is crucial because the authentication system controls access to mission-critical resources. Reliability requires appropriate redundancy, operational excellence, configuration management, close monitoring, and proactive capacity planning. When other organizations use the authentication system, they may require a service-level agreement that stipulates specific uptimes and penalties for failing to meet them.

Auditability

Accountability requires that the system be auditable. Transactions logs are the heart of an auditable system: they make it possible to review and track authentication activities.

Logs can be made at various levels. Aggregate logs do not track individual transactions but aggregate data such as totals, averages, and trends. These can be useful for capacity planning and understanding the overall operation of the system. Detailed logs track individual actions and are required for some problems, like responding to security breaches. Authentication system logs provide an important resource for dealing with system intrusions but may be subject to legal and other regulations or policies.

If not properly protected, detailed logs can raise privacy and security concerns, even when the data they contain seems relatively innocuous. Traffic analysis is the art of deducing information from the patterns in messages. For example, if I know that the chief financial officer (CFO) always accesses certain company investor resources before announcing a big deal, and I have access to the authentication logs for those resources, I may be able to use that information to trade ahead of the market or, worse, conduct a targeted phishing attack (known as *spear phishing*) on the CFO's executive assistant to gain access to those resources.

Manageability

Manageability means that the operator of the authentication system can easily add, update, or delete accounts. The system should allow new classes of accounts and provide for different configurations among groups. Operators will add, renew, and delete certificates; maintain licenses; and update the system as new releases become available. The interfaces to the authentication system should be well documented.

Federation Support

Modern organizations have resources that must be accessed by diverse groups across other organizations. An authentication system that supports federation will allow those resources to be managed by their respective organizations. This requires trust in the partner organization and significant planning. It's crucial for the organization to agree with its partner's policies about resource access and its processes for verifying identity when it issues credentials. If they're going to trust the partner's authentication system to make authentication assertions, they must understand the policies surrounding that system and the system's relative strength. (I'll discuss federation in more detail in Chapter 13.)

Authentication Preserves Relationship Integrity

Authentication, or the way digital systems recognize people, organizations, and things online, is a fundamental function of a digital identity system and is required for relationship integrity. Integrity is a prerequisite for any authorization and access-control determinations.

CHAPTER 12

Access Control and Relationship Utility

Authentication provides evidence that the remote entity is authentic—the same entity who first created the account. This allows the system to recognize the other party at a distance and underpins relationship integrity. But identity requires more than merely recognizing the other party; the system must also remember them and react appropriately. The goal is to allow authenticated entities to take permissible actions and capitalize on the relationship. The utility of a relationship depends on allowing each party to act in ways that are appropriate and secure.

Consequently, *access control* is one of the most fundamental concepts in digital identity. Access control is the process of granting specific accounts access to a resource while denying access to others. Here are some examples:

- An email system grants each employee access to their email box but not to anyone else's. Email administrators are granted access to everyone's email accounts.

- The bank grants me access to my bank account but limits that access. For example, I can withdraw only up to some preset limit at the ATM. Certain bank employees have read access to the account in some situations and even write access in very controlled situations.

- The software I use to manage my website has access to the website and can create new files and delete or update existing ones. Anyone is granted access to the files for reading.

Crafting a set of permissions for an account also defines the nature of the relationships that it supports. Without restrictions on an email system, for example, the recipient can't be sure who their emails come from. Restricting the withdrawal amount at an ATM balances the inconvenience of not being able to get sufficient funds with the convenience of relatively light authentication requirements (for example, possessing the debit card and knowing the four-digit pin). Granting public access to my website provides me a relationship with a reading public. Remember that designing access policies determines the nature of relationships.

Access control requires determining a set of *authorizations* for a given account. The terms *access control* and *authorization* (often abbreviated as "authz") are often used interchangeably. Even the notion of granting access is too coarse-grained—in many cases, an administrator must determine what actions a subject is allowed to take on a resource. This chapter explores some of the issues, patterns, and technology surrounding access control.

Policy First

Access control is first and foremost a policy question. Access control technology is designed to automatically enforce access policies. Policy reflects security objectives, application architecture, implementation choices, generally accepted practices of industrial and professional organizations, regulatory and legal requirements, and, most importantly, organizational goals.

Here are some simple examples of access control policies:

- Everyone is allowed to read the website.
- Applications with a valid OAuth token can GET and POST to the application API.
- Alice is allowed to read and write the "orders" table in "sales" database.
- All members of the marketing department can read the marketing materials on the internal web server.
- HR employees who are managers or above can modify salaries during working hours if they are accessing the salary application from the corporate intranet.

I've purposely ordered this list so that the policies progress from simple and specific to complex and abstract. The first, for example, is relatively straightforward to implement. Some of these policies talk about the role rather than identifying specific people ("manager" is a role, for example).

The last policy assumes that the system can identify which employees work in HR, what their grade is, and when "working hours" are (a temporal factor). Are working hours from 8 to 5? Does it change with each employee? Can the system reliably tell who is accessing it from the corporate intranet (a location factor)? There are business and technology aspects to these questions. For example, the idea of working hours is a business concept, but can the access control infrastructure support locking users out of resources based on the time of day?

Responsibility

The most important questions in access control have to do with responsibility. There are typically three categories of classification: owners, custodians, and users.[1] The owner of the resource may be the person who created it, the head of the organization that owns it, or some other person or role. Ownership can be delegated or assigned. When you can't figure out who owns a resource, the natural default is the organization itself.

You might have noticed that these responsibility roles are like those used in data governance. This isn't an accident, of course. Access control is closely related to data governance. In many ways, access control represents the implementation of the policies made in the data governance process, providing the means for their enforcement.

Access control is more effective when data governance processes explicitly designate data owners. *Owners* have ultimate decision-making authority and responsibility for ensuring resources under their control are appropriately accessed. In government organizations, it is not unusual for owners to be designated in statute or by regulation. Your organization may not be as legalistic, but specifically designating owners and holding them responsible is an important part of information security.

Custodians manage resources from day to day. Every person in an organization might be a custodian for some set of resources. Custodians are responsible for ensuring that access control policies are enforced and that resources are available for authorized entities to use. Often the custodian and the owner are the same person—for example, when the resource is a document or other information created in the course of daily work. Someone other than the owner usually maintains larger resources, such as databases and websites.

Custodians play an important role in access control because they implement and monitor the access control policies that the owner specifies. Often, custodians are system administrators or technical operations personnel. Custodians have significant responsibility and are often entrusted with numerous resources. They usually have "superuser" powers and can access any resource under their purview. Consequently, it's important to choose custodians with care and build identity infrastructures that allow cross-checks and auditing of custodial actions.

A *user* is the person, group, corporation, software program, app, API, or other entity that wants access to resources. Users might be the customers or employees of the organization that owns the resource. They might also be the employees, or even the customers, of partners and suppliers. Users might be responsible for ensuring that a

---

1 I try to avoid the term *user* because it is usually better to use a more specific term, but for this discussion I am using the language of access control.

resource is protected while in use, becoming custodians for a time. Often, access control systems do not or cannot have the level of granularity needed to protect a resource completely, so it becomes the user's responsibility to act in accordance with the owner's instructions.

As an example, most document management systems can control access to the document itself but not individual parts of the document. The owner of a document might share it with a coworker with specific instructions about what sections can be modified and which cannot. The coworker, as a user of the resource, has responsibility to treat the document in accordance with the owner's instructions, but these cannot be enforced by an access control system.

Principle of Least Privilege

One of the fundamental ideas upon which access control policies are founded is the *principle of least privilege*. This principle says that users should be given no more access to resources than they need to accomplish necessary functions. Least privilege is a good guideline to follow in creating policy and makes some decisions easier. In practice, however, it has limitations that are not easily overcome by real-world access control systems, including the following:

- Fully implementing least privilege requires extremely fine-grained permissions. Essentially, every action that might ever be taken by any user on any resource needs a permission defined.

- The types and levels of authorization necessary to perform a given task may change over time.

- Any given individual will need different levels of privilege depending on the task they are currently performing.

These limitations have led to systems that implement least privilege imperfectly, sometimes to ill effect. I include examples of this later in this chapter. Even so, the principle of least privilege represents an ideal to shoot for as you build access control policies.

Accountability Scales Better Than Enforcement

The limitations of the principle of least privilege have led to an additional principle to guide the development of access control policies: accountability scales better than enforcement. The simplest access control policies to implement are based on trust and accountability. User actions are logged, and the logs are audited. When the logs show unauthorized access by a user, appropriate action is taken. Accountability is a log-processing problem that can be done offline by a separate system and thus scales very well.

As an example, consider the problem of documents shared by email. Companies generally have no idea whether one of their employees is using the corporate email system to send important, even vital, company secrets to their competitors. One approach to this problem would attempt to create some sort of access control infrastructure that uses access control and policies to govern what documents can be attachments in external email. This is largely impractical.

But a system to solve this problem based on accountability *is* practical. It is much easier to create a system that logs external email, notes any with attachments, and records the sender, date, and a hash of the document. The system may not be able to stop the document from being sent, but someone will at least know about it and be able to take the appropriate next steps.

Obviously, real-world scenarios cannot accept the risk of an access control policy based solely on accountability. But accountability can augment the access control policy to provide protections that are difficult or expensive using traditional permissions-based access control. Carefully consider what risk you can tolerate, because accountability-based systems are considerably cheaper to implement and operate than enforcement systems.

Authorization Patterns

Real-world systems live somewhere in between a perfect enforcement of least privilege and a system based solely on accountability. As computing and networking technology has matured, various access control schemes have been developed to try to balance these needs. These schemes represent broad philosophical frameworks that aid the development of access control policies as well as specifying implementations for a particular scheme.

In practice, most organizations use a hybrid approach to access control, where the resource owner tightly controls certain resources and custodians control other resources. For example, most organizations control access to the HR system in a very formal way, while allowing individual employees to determine who will see documents that they produce within some very broad guidelines.

Many of the patterns I'll discuss have been around for decades, but even though the resources may have expanded from files on a local disk to Lambda functions on Amazon Web Services (AWS), the concepts still apply.

Mandatory and Discretionary Access Control

The US Department of Defense was one of the first organizations to look systematically at access control on computer systems. Its 1983 publication *Trusted Computer System Evaluation Criteria* (commonly referred to as "the orange book" because of the color of its cover) defined two modes of access control: mandatory and discretionary.

In *mandatory access control (MAC)*, the owner or the owner's representative sets the policy, and custodians and users are obligated to follow it. In *discretionary access control (DAC)*, the custodian is left to determine what users will be granted access. Once granted access, the user becomes, in effect, a custodian, because they can grant access to other users.

Significant research has been conducted on military security standards, with some important discoveries. Among the most important is an undecidability result that showed that a DAC-based system initially judged to be safe, with respect to a specific policy, cannot be shown to remain safe over time. The takeaway is that user actions may eventually result in an unauthorized user being granted access.

Another important result involves what is known as "tapping-out information." Consider a system where there are two levels of access control: classified and unclassified. In any system with shared resources between access control levels (for instance, classified and unclassified documents stored on the same filesystem), it is impossible to keep users of classified information from sharing that information with unclassified users. In short, enforcing MAC on a shared system is impossible, because users with access to classified data can always find ways to encode classified information in system resources (such as by manipulating the presence of a particular file, or even just its size). Since these resources can be viewed by both sets of users, unclassified users can decode the message and see classified data.

Taken together, these results lead to a fundamental and important conclusion: *it is not possible to build a practical access control system that does not rely, to some extent, on trusting custodians and users to follow the policies.*

User-Based Permission Systems

Perhaps the best-known and most widely used access control scheme is a user-based permission system made popular by the Unix file permission system and continued today in Linux and (with some modifications) macOS. Figure 12-1 shows a schematic representation of how user and group permissions work in this system. The system is conceptually simple: both users and groups have access rights to resources directly, and users belong to groups.

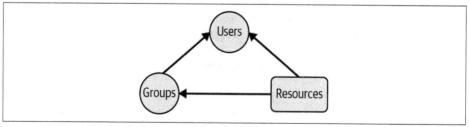

Figure 12-1. Permission hierarchy for users and groups

As embodied in the Unix filesystem, there are three permission levels: read (r), write (w), and execute (x). These permission levels are applied as attributes of the files and directories on the system. For simplicity, I'll just speak of files here, but the concepts also apply to directories.

Files belong to *owners*, specific users on the system, and *groups*, collections of users. Each of the permission levels can be set for the file's owner, the file's group, and everyone else. For example, it is possible to set permissions on a file so that it is readable and writable by its owner, read-only by its group, and not readable by anyone else. User-based permission systems are simple to use and administer and have served nicely for decades. Still, they suffer from the following drawbacks:

- Most users ignore groups altogether and few understand them, because user-interface issues in Unix make using groups problematic. For example, each user in a group can own files and, therefore, control the permissions. But when users create files meant for the group, they often forget to set group permissions correctly, resulting in a flurry of messages asking that the owner fix the group permissions.

- The group system is inflexible. Since only one group owns a file, it is difficult to create a set of files that can be accessed by multiple groups. The only way to do this is to create a third group and put everyone in the other two groups into the new group. But because groups cannot contain subgroups, if the membership of one of the subgroups is changed, the third group would not be updated automatically.

- Groups work best for long-standing file-sharing relationships. If someone wants to quickly share a file, there's considerable overhead in creating a new group, adding users to the group, and making the file owned by the new group. Also, on most systems, creating groups requires superuser authority, so most users can't do it.

- There are few tools for managing groups other than editing text files, and the commands that users must issue to set up group-shared directories are somewhat arcane, even for Unix experts.

- Because both users and groups have access to resources, merely deleting a group does not necessarily delete group members' permissions to access the resource. In fact, because the permissions are associated directly with the resource, it is almost impossible to determine what resources any given user has access to.

These drawbacks led system designers to search for something more flexible and easier to understand and use.

Access Control Lists

Access control lists (ACLs) are lists of specific users and groups who have access to a resource, designed to offer a more flexible permissions system that grants individual users access to specific resources. In filesystems, ACLs are stored as attributes of the files, encompass the standard file-permissions system, and expand it to enable specific users or groups to be designated as having a particular level of access.

Figure 12-2 shows a schematic representation of ACLs. The primary difference between this diagram and Figure 12-1 is the insertion of a permissions structure between the resources and the users and groups. Rather than users and groups being directly associated with a given resource, the resource has a set of permissions that includes both users and groups. This indirection gives ACL-based permission systems additional flexibility at the cost of some additional complexity.

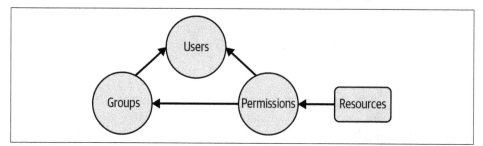

Figure 12-2. Permissions hierarchy for ACLs

One problem with ACLs is that permissions are stored as attributes of the resources and are thus distributed across the filesystem, making it difficult to manage individual user access. For example, when a user no longer requires access to a set of resources due to a change in a job or process, there is no single place where those permissions can be changed. You have to visit the resources one by one and remove permissions for that user.

Still, ACLs have proven to be a good solution for access control in cloud-based resources, and are used in AWS and Google Docs, among others.

Role-Based Access Control

Role-based access control (RBAC) is based on the idea that users are typically granted access to resources based on their role in an organization. Figure 12-3 shows a schematic representation of RBAC.

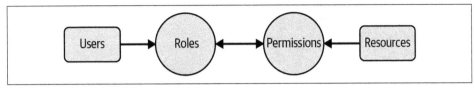

Figure 12-3. Permission hierarchy for RBAC

A key feature of the RBAC model is that *all* access is permissioned through roles. Contrast this with the user-based permission model shown in Figure 12-1. In the RBAC model, some authority, such as the HR department, assigns roles and the resource owner assigns permissions.

A second key feature of RBAC-based authorization is that roles can be hierarchical, as shown in Figure 12-4. If roles are created this way, assigning an employee a role as a developer also automatically assigns that person roles as a member of the engineering department and as an employee. In addition to being hierarchical, roles can be parameterized to aid in administration.

Role-based authorization schemes are based on three rules:

Role assignment
    All users of the system are assigned roles; users without roles cannot take any action.

Role authentication
    Before a user can take on a role, that role must be authenticated for them.

Action authorization
    A user can take an action only if that action is authorized for their current, authenticated role.

Group-based access control systems can be used to implement roles, but they often lack features that make RBAC easy to administer and more secure. Role-based authorization is more flexible than an authorization scheme based on simple groups and more secure than one in which users can be authorized independently of their group or role membership. Furthermore, role-based authorization makes it relatively easy to add and remove a user's access to resources as their organizational function changes, even if they change tasks day to day.

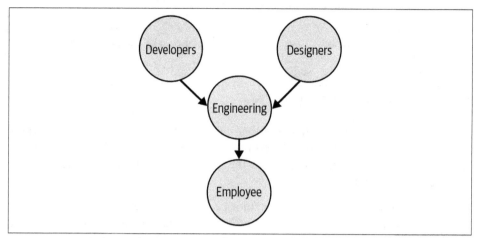

Figure 12-4. Role hierarchy for an engineering department

Attribute- and Policy-Based Access Control

The terms *attribute-based access control* (ABAC) and *policy-based access control* (PBAC) are usually interchangeable. The term PBAC emphasizes policy rather than attributes. RBAC can be seen as a special case of ABAC where the only attribute is the role. In RBAC, an assigned role is used to determine access to a resource. This is simple and relatively quick. For ABAC, the policy will potentially be evaluated with respect to many more attributes from various systems.

Compared to RBAC, ABAC is more flexible and multidimensional, but is usually more computationally expensive. A role is just one of many attributes an ABAC policy might use to make an access decision. For example, an RBAC policy may allow anyone in the role "dean" to access student accounts, whereas an ABAC policy might state that the resource can be accessed by anyone with the job title "dean" who is serving in the same college as the student when authenticated using MFA.

ABAC uses potentially complex Boolean rulesets to describe access control policies. A standard way to define these rules is using eXtensible Access Control Markup Language (XACML, a standard language for access control policies), which I will discuss in greater detail in the following sections. These rules take into account attributes of the party requesting access as well as information about the resource and the context, which could include any detectable environmental characteristic. The obvious ones are things like time of day or location but could include other factors. For example, a pharmaceutical company might not allow a sample door to be opened if the room temperature is above a certain amount, or if there's insufficient humidity.

Abstract Authorization Architectures

Authorization follows a set pattern that allows us to use an abstract architecture to discuss the common needs of authorization systems even though they may vary in their details. This abstract architecture was first described as part of the XACML specification, but it's general enough that it's used even when the system doesn't use XACML. These roles have since been codified by the US National Institute for Standards and Technology (NIST).[2]

Figure 12-5 shows the abstract authorization architecture in action:

1. Alice requests a protected resource.

2. The *policy enforcement point* (PEP) sees the request and sends it to a *policy decision point* (PDP) to verify if Alice is authorized.

3. The *PDP* retrieves access control policies relevant to the resource from a *policy administration point* (PAP).

4. The *PDP* uses information about the resource and the access control policy to retrieve relevant attributes about Alice and the resource from *policy information points* (PIPs), returning a "yes" or "no" answer to the *PEP*.

5. The *PEP* grants or denies access to the resource.

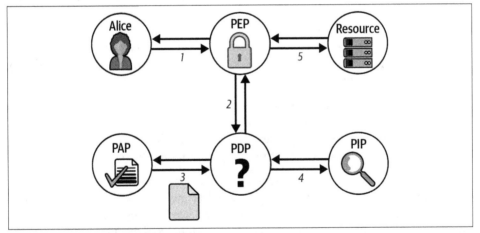

Figure 12-5. Abstract authorization architecture

The PEP is the point in the system where the user requests access to a resource. The PEP doesn't have to be separate from the system serving the resource. For example, if

---

2 *Guide to Attribute Based Access Control (ABAC) Definition and Considerations*, NIST Special Publication 800-162, January 2014.

Alice attempts to access a web page, the web server could serve as the PEP. The PDP is where the decision is made about whether Alice will be allowed to access the page.

When a PDP makes a decision about a particular subject's right to access a particular resource, the decision is called an *authorization decision assertion* (ADA). An ADA can take any form that the PEP and PDP agree on, but it is usually simple and light-weight.

The PDP is often part of the same system that houses the PEP, but it needn't be. PEPs are lightweight and are often positioned near the resource they protect (on a cloud-based service, for example). The PDP, on the other hand, is requesting policies and attributes from the PAP and PIP and might be better located near those services. The PAP, PEP, and PIP might be separate services or all running together.

Even when the PEP and the PDP are colocated in the same system or program, it is useful to see authorization as a coordinated effort between these two abstract systems. The PDP makes its determination of entitlements or permissions based on an access policy that has been set in advance.

Representing and Managing Access Control Policies

Access control policies help define the context within which systems are built and operated. However, merely writing a policy does not ensure that it's correctly promulgated and implemented throughout the IT infrastructure. I have seen access control policies written in English by the data owner, then translated through the data custodian to the technical team, which implements the policy in programming logic. Not only is this difficult to change, it's also hard to have confidence the code faithfully represents the data owner's wishes.

Worse, access control policies are often written in English and then implemented on dozens or even hundreds of different systems individually. Each of these systems has a proprietary configuration language. Compounding the problem, every time the access control policy changes, the entire configuration must be redone.

When an access control architecture allows policy decisions to be made independently from the specific resource being accessed (Figure 12-5), the system can treat access control policy as an artifact that can be reviewed, versioned, referenced, used, and maintained. Such an architecture needs a machine-readable policy language that can also be represented in ways that nontechnical business owners can understand. As illustrated in Figure 12-5, a policy language allows different PDPs to use consistent policies from a policy repository (PAP) without constant manual configuration and reconfiguration.

XACML is an OASIS Standard XML-based language for storing and sharing access control policies, currently in its third generation. It is widely used in ABAC systems by PDP and PAP. XACML is not the only policy language. Others include the policy language used by Open Policy Agent (*https://oreil.ly/OsEVE*) and the JSON-based access policies of AWS (*https://oreil.ly/RTuG3*). Most of the concepts are similar, however, so we'll use XACML as our example.

XACML is a rule-based language, supporting declarative, rather than imperative, policies. Policy rules can be created to allow fine-grained control over access. These rules can be based on items such as:

- Attributes of the requester (only people who work in accounting are allowed to access this document)
- The action to be taken (reading a document versus updating a document)
- The time of day (personnel can log in only during their shifts)
- The authentication mechanism (only allow entities authenticated with MFA)
- The protocol used for access (allow HTTPS access but not HTTP access for this resource)

These can be combined using Boolean connectives to create complex policies. For instance, they might allow users from accounting to update this document over HTTPS but allow users from other departments to read it anytime over HTTP.

Rules are the basic component of an XACML policy. In simplified terms, a *rule* contains a target, an optional condition, and an effect. The *target* defines the set or requests that the rule applies to. A *condition* further refines the applicability of the rule as a Boolean test. The *effect* defines the result of the rule if the target matches and the condition is true.

Rules are contained in a `<Policy/>` element. This can also contain a `<Target/>` element that defines the class of subjects, resources, and actions to which the entire policy is applied. As an example, review the following rule taken from the XACML 3.0 specification (*https://oreil.ly/vtzKZ*):

```
<Rule
  RuleId= "urn:oasis:names:tc:xacml:3.0:example:SimpleRule1"
  Effect="Permit">
  <Description>
     Any subject with an e-mail name in the med.example.com domain
     can perform any action on any resource.
  </Description>
  <Target>
    <AnyOf>
      <AllOf>
        <Match
          MatchId="urn:oasis:names:tc:xacml:1.0:function:rfc822Name-match">
          <AttributeValue
            DataType="http://www.w3.org/2001/XMLSchema#string"
```

```
        >med.example.com</AttributeValue>
      <AttributeDesignator
        MustBePresent="false"
        Category=
          "urn:oasis:names:tc:xacml:1.0:subject-category:access-subject"
        AttributeId="urn:oasis:names:tc:xacml:1.0:subject:subject-id"
        DataType="urn:oasis:names:tc:xacml:1.0:data-type:rfc822Name"/>
      </Match>
    </AllOf>
  </AnyOf>
  </Target>
</Rule>
```

In English, this rule states:

> Any user with an email name in the "med.example.com" namespace is allowed to per-
> form any action on any resource.

The XACML states that the subject-id attribute of the decision request must be a
Name-match (a specific matching function) to a literal value, med.example.com. If
the Name-match function returns true, then this rule Target is applicable and the rule
returns its effect, Permit.

XACML also has a concept called a *combining algorithm*, which allows multiple (perhaps conflicting) rules to be applied to a resource and some action taken as a result.
For example, if this rule were the only one in a policy that had a combining algorithm
of deny-overrides, then the overall effect of the policy would be to deny the request
unless this rule returned Permit.

Rules are evaluated in the context of a request. For example, consider the following
XACML request, again from the XACML 3.0 specification:

```
<Request xmlns="urn:oasis:names:tc:xacml:3.0:core:schema:wd-17"...
    ReturnPolicyIdList="false">
  <Attributes
      Category="urn:...:xacml:1.0:subject-category:access-subject">
    <Attribute IncludeInResult="false"
        AttributeId="urn:oasis:names:tc:xacml:1.0:subject:subject-id">
      <AttributeValue
        DataType="urn:oasis:names:tc:xacml:1.0:data-type:rfc822Name"
        >bs@simpsons.com</AttributeValue>
    </Attribute>
  </Attributes>
  <Attributes
      Category="urn:...:xacml:3.0:attribute-category:resource">
    <Attribute IncludeInResult="false"
        AttributeId="urn:oasis:names:tc:xacml:1.0:resource:resource-id">
      <AttributeValue DataType="http://www.w3.org/2001/XMLSchema#anyURI"
          >file://example/med/record/patient/BartSimpson</AttributeValue>
    </Attribute>
  </Attributes>
```

```
<Attributes
    Category="urn:oasis:names:tc:xacml:3.0:attribute-category:action">
  <Attribute IncludeInResult="false"
      AttributeId="urn:oasis:names:tc:xacml:1.0:action:action-id">
    <AttributeValue DataType="http://www.w3.org/2001/XMLSchema#string"
        >read</AttributeValue>
  </Attribute>
</Attributes>
</Request>
```

This <Request/> contains three attributes. The first contains the entity making the request: bs@simpsons.com. The second contains the resource to which the subject has requested access: file://example/med/record/patient/BartSimpson. The third contains the action the subject wishes to take on the resource, read.

The policy engine evaluates the rules in the context of the request and produces a response. In this case, the preceding rule would not match, since the subject-id is simpsons.com, not med.example.com as required in the rule's target. The response is also specified in XACML:

```
<Response xmlns="urn:oasis:names:tc:xacml:3.0:core:schema:wd-17"...>
  <Result>
    <Decision>NotApplicable</Decision>
  </Result>
</Response>
```

The PEP would deny access based on this decision.

XACML is a complete, declarative rule language, and there is much more to it than is covered in this simple example. Most people don't write raw XACML. Instead, they use a commercial or open source tool to write rules and policies that provides a human-friendly interface and generates XACML. People writing and reading rules still need to understand the overall concepts of how policies work, how subjects and resources are identified, the operation of the various matching functions, and conditional logic—but they *don't* have to be able to write XML.

Handling Complex Policy Sets

As presented in the last section, ABAC-based policy decisions seem simple to evaluate. When we're only analyzing one policy for one resource, determining who has access is straightforward. But computer systems comprised of multiple compute nodes, storage locations, and network endpoints are the norm. Each of these can have its own access policies, so determining who can access what is complicated. Hackers exploit this complexity to find ingress paths that aren't obvious. For example, policy may limit direct access to your database, but a weak policy for accessing the application server that uses the database might open an unintended path to your sensitive data.

Combatting this problem requires that you treat policies for what they are: code. Declarative code, to be sure, but still something that is executed. Versioning, formal reviews, testing, and static analysis are the tools developers commonly use to gain confidence that their code works correctly. Apply these same techniques to your policies, not only when they're developed, but any time they change.

Digital Certificates and Access Control

Chapter 11 showed how digital certificates can be used in an authentication infrastructure. Because the certificate is just a data structure that can be extended, it can also be used to store permissions and other authorization information, such as roles. The signature of the certificate authority ensures that these attributes can't be tampered with. The use of certificates in this way makes two important assumptions:

- The roles, permissions, and entitlements regarding the subject of the certificate are static, and thus can be encoded in a certificate that is updated infrequently.
- The chain of trust from the organization to the certificate authority is such that systems needing to use the permissions in the certificate can trust that they were set in accordance with the correct access control policy.

The inflexibility of this system is its chief drawback. Changing access control permissions requires revoking the old certificate and issuing a new one. Its primary strength is that permissions move with the certificate in a trustworthy way, negating the need for a complicated database infrastructure to store the permissions.

Maintaining Proper Boundaries

Authorization complements authentication to form the basis for access control. In many ways, authorization is the focal point around which identity systems revolve. Access control is the basis of a security principle called *zero trust*. Zero trust uses identity and access control systems to dynamically protect resources from unauthorized use instead of relying on static defenses like firewalls. As more and more of our lives are intermediated by information systems, boundaries are critical to living effective online lives. Access control systems are the basis for digital boundaries that support safe, functional relationships.

CHAPTER 13

Federated Identity—Leveraging Strong Relationships

Aadhaar, the Indian universal identity system, was launched in 2009 with the aim of giving every Indian citizen a biometrically authenticated identifier. Just scanning the irises and fingerprints of one billion people is a stupefyingly large task. The even *bigger* task is making it useful in Indian life.

I traveled to Bangalore, India, in 2018 to help run a workshop that I and the other Internet Identity Workshop (IIW) organizers helped plan.[1] By coincidence, the Digital Identity Research Initiative (DIRI) at the Indian School of Business sponsored an event the same week on Aadhaar. Attending the DIRI event help me learn more about Aadhaar, which is the foundation for many digital identity systems in India. In fact, *aadhaar* means "foundation" in Hindi.

The highlight of the week was visiting a village outside Vijayawada near India's east coast, thanks to an Aadhaar field trip that Omidyar Network organized for me and a few others. We talked with fertilizer distribution agents, farmers, families receiving food distribution, people running the distribution centers, an insurance office at a local hospital, and a bank officer. They showed us how Aadhaar was being used in their respective areas. We saw challenges but also heard positive stories from people in the trenches.

Aadhaar's goals are to reduce fraud, make taxation more efficient, and save money. The program has had a positive impact on the lives of Indian people, but there are

---

1 The workshop was an IEEE Digital Inclusion Through Trust and Agency (*https://oreil.ly/EVnD7*) event called *InDITA* since it was happening in India.

concerns as well, including privacy loss (through account linking) and exclusion (because of limitations in the biometrics, system malfunctions, or errors).

Aadhaar is an example of a *federated* identity system operated by the Unique Identification Authority of India (UIDAI). UIDAI is a government agency that issues each person a 12-digit identifier and links it to the biometric information for that person. Other government agencies use UIDAI's system to authenticate people. This is a classic federation pattern called *hub and spoke* that uses an *identity provider*, UIDAI in this case, and *relying parties*, including food and fertilizer distribution centers like the ones I visited, as well as other direct benefit transfer programs, health agencies, and banks. Figure 13-1 shows a woman using her fingerprint on an Aadhaar terminal to authenticate in a food distribution center. In fact, almost every government program uses or has plans to use Aadhaar for its digital services.[2]

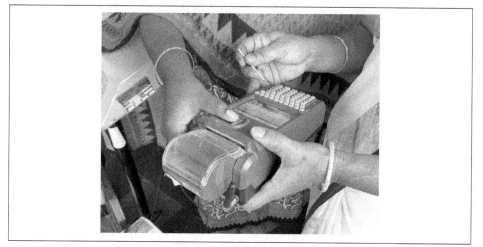

Figure 13-1. Scanning a thumbprint on an Aadhaar terminal (photo by the author)

Aadhaar is impressive for its sheer size and scope. But federated identity systems are very much the global norm in 2022. Nearly anyone who uses the web or apps on a smartphone has used one organization's identity system (like those of Google, Apple, Facebook, or GitHub) to authenticate to another organization's application or service. In this chapter, I'll discuss different types of federation and their underlying protocols.

---

2 Private companies, like mobile phone providers, tried to piggyback on Aadhaar by requiring customers to present an authenticated Aadhaar identifier as a condition of service, but a 2018 Indian Supreme Court ruling put a stop to that.

The Nature of Federated Identity

As I've noted throughout this book, the proliferation of identity accounts creates significant challenges. People have trouble remembering multiple usernames and passwords. Organizations are required to build and operate multiple identity-management systems. To address these challenges, *federation* links accounts across two or more systems. Federation has several advantages, including:

- Reducing friction and enhancing user experience by reducing the number of accounts needed to gain services from diverse resources

- Enhancing security by reducing the number of passwords people must remember, instead focusing resources, policy, and operations on just one authentication service

- Lowering costs because companies don't need to build as many authentication systems

Let's contrast federated identity with *centralized* identity. Using our terminology from Chapter 2, we can call centralized identity systems *colocated*, since the point is that the account system is in the same domain as the resource it protects. In centralized identity, each domain authenticates the entity requesting service separately. Centralized identity systems have become rarer as the world has become more networked. A small example of a centralized identity system is the account system on your personal laptop. You likely created accounts for yourself and maybe some family members when you set it up. The accounts serve a single domain: your laptop. Even in this simple example, however, most people link their laptop accounts to their Apple iCloud or Microsoft Live accounts, creating a federation between the account on the laptop and the account in the cloud.

Figure 13-2 shows a generic federation pattern. Alice authenticates with the system on the left, called the *identity provider* (IdP). She then accesses a service or resource from the system on the right, called the *relying party* (RP). There is an existing trust relationship between the IdP and the RP, so the RP has confidence that Alice has been properly authenticated. The method by which the trust relationship is established, along with its nature and extent, is the primary distinction between different kinds of federation.

The result of the federation example in Figure 13-2 is identity data being transferred from the IdP to the RP. The data may be transferred directly from the IdP to the RP— this is called a *back-channel presentation*—or transferred through Alice (using a redirect), called a *front-channel presentation*.

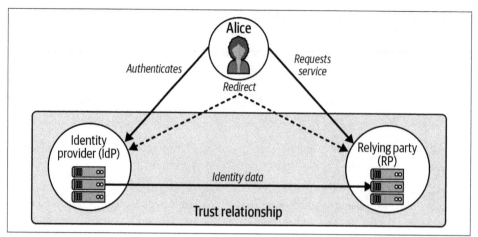

Figure 13-2. Generic federation pattern

Federation doesn't reduce the need for different systems to manage their own accounts. In Figure 13-2, the IdP and the RP both have an account for Alice. Federation *only reduces* the need for the RP to build, manage, and service an authentication system of its own. The nature of the relationships between Alice and the IdP and Alice and the RP will dictate different account structures and attributes. This is true even if the IdP shares some of Alice's attributes with the RP through the trust relationship. The RP shouldn't depend on Alice being in an active session with the IdP after she presents her identity data.

SSO Versus Federation

Single sign-on (SSO) and federation are related but not the same thing. All SSO systems use federation, but not all federated identity systems support SSO. You've likely experienced the difference at work.

The promise of SSO is streamlined experiences that don't ask you to authenticate over and over again. The reality is difficult to pull off in practice because of the technical limitations of identity systems, the limited will of many IT departments to do the hard work necessary to overcome those limitations, and security concerns.

Nevertheless, as the use of federation has grown, so have the opportunities for SSO. For example, when I use systems at Brigham Young University (BYU), where I'm an adjunct faculty member, I often don't have to reauthenticate as I move from system to system. But there are places where that breaks down.

For example, BYU uses a third-party benefits manager. I don't know all the reasons, but BYU and the benefits manager chose not to federate their systems, so I have a separate username and password at each. The benefits manager uses another company for retirement benefits. They have federated with each other, so I use the same username and password at the benefits manager's website as I do on the retirement website. And if I update my password at the benefit manager's site, it's updated at the retirement website. But I have to log into the retirement system's site every time I visit, even if I visit from the benefit manager's site and have already logged in there. The benefit manager and retirement manager support federation, but not SSO.

SSO is difficult with web and smartphone applications that are from different domains. For web applications, this is because cookies are used to manage authenticated sessions and the browser sends back cookies only for the domain it makes the request from. For example, BYU uses Canvas, from Instructure, as a learning management system. The URL that BYU faculty and students use for Instructure is *byu.instructure.com*, not *canvas.byu.edu*. As a result, even though Canvas is using BYU as an IdP, it is not SSO. While I might already be logged into BYU at *byu.edu*, the cookie storing the token that says I'm authenticated won't be sent to services in the domain *instructure.com*.

Federation in the Credit Card Industry

The credit card industry provides many excellent lessons about the move from centralized to federated identity management, as well as the challenges of implementing a federated model. I will use it to illustrate some ideas because it is the most widespread, familiar example of a federated identity system.

You may not have thought of Visa and Mastercard as identity systems. They are, of course, primarily concerned with payments, but at their foundations, they are sophisticated federated identity systems.

Let's look at an example. Bank of America launched the first multi-merchant credit card, BankAmericard, in 1958 as a way to extend small consumer loans to Bank of America customers at the time of a purchase. Any merchant could choose to participate. In essence, the bank functioned as a central clearinghouse, vouching to merchants for its customers' ability to pay. Before that, consumers had only had credit relationships directly with individual merchants. From an identity perspective, each of these independent credit accounts had its own identifiers and store of attributes.

BankAmericard was so successful that it attracted rampant competition. In 1966, five other California banks collaborated to issue a competing product, Master Charge, with a significantly larger customer base. In response, Bank of America began franchising BankAmericard to other banks across the US. This meant Bank of America no longer had direct relationships with all the merchants and consumers in the network. It had to establish mechanisms for merchants to verify cards through the card-issuing banks, and for the banks involved to settle transactions. What emerged was a federated financial network and an underlying federated identity system. Every bank controlled its own relationships with consumers and merchants. Federation allowed data about these relationships to stay in place at the issuing bank, using common policies and technologies for member banks to exchange information with each other.

Three Federation Patterns

Federations fall into one of three patterns:

Ad hoc federation
> *Ad hoc federation* is characterized by bilateral relationships between systems or organizations wishing to create a federated identity relationship.

Hub-and-spoke federation
> In the *hub-and-spoke* pattern, many RPs use a single identity provider.

Identity federation network
> An *identity federation network* allows many players to share identity information with each other without a central node. Nodes may act as both IdP and RP simultaneously.

All three patterns require standards, architectures, protocols, and governance. I'll discuss each pattern in turn.

Pattern 1: Ad Hoc Federation

Ad hoc federation is done between a few systems, inside the same organization or across organizational boundaries, usually to solve a specific problem. Before Bank of America launched BankAmericard in 1958, there were ad hoc credit arrangements that linked lenders to consumers through merchants (called *merchant-centric credit arrangements*). Ad hoc federations are usually bidirectional, but they can also be multiparty.

Ad hoc identity federation has been going on since networks were first invented and people on one system needed to access another. The example I gave above of Canvas using BYU as an IdP is an ad hoc federation. Every organization of any size has similar arrangements with various partners. The cloud and the rise of enterprise software delivered as a service have made ad hoc federation common.

Ad hoc federations typically use Security Assertion Markup Language (SAML) or OAuth (both discussed later in this chapter) to provide authentication services or share account data. You might run across some old federations (or just federations to old systems) that use LDAP to access directory information, but that's fading away. The challenge for organizations is that they will likely have to support multiple protocols, because the software they buy will have picked its own standard.

The biggest problem with ad hoc federations is that they don't scale well. Even with standards and protocols like SAML or OAuth, each federation must be set up independently, usually as a custom integration that must be designed, built, and maintained over time as systems change.

For federations that cross organizational boundaries, legal agreements must be put in place. These are often custom agreements involving legal departments on both sides. Even internal federations require governance, although it's not always recognized as such. Internal governance often takes the form of unwritten agreements between different parts of the organization. Don't let this happen. Documenting all internal federations will save you downtime, money, and heartache.

Pattern 2: Hub-and-Spoke Federation

Hub-and-spoke federation is one answer to the challenges of ad hoc federation. Hub-and-spoke federations are characterized by a single IdP and multiple RPs. The IdP is usually dedicated and functions as the single source of authentication for all the RPs.

In our credit card example, hub-and-spoke describes Bank of America's initial foray into credit, in which BankAmericard served as the only credit clearinghouse for Bank of America customers. A merchant who wanted to serve customers from multiple banks would need relationships with each. American Express and Discover still function as hub-and-spoke federations.

When organizations set up a hub-and-spoke federation, it's usually with a company-run identity service serving as the IdP and other systems within the organization acting as RPs. Most company-internal SSO, for example, relies on a hub-and-spoke federation. Various things get in the way of doing this perfectly: for instance, some of those internal systems may not use protocols that the identity service supports. Large organizations often have legacy ad hoc federations that are deemed too expensive to retool. And enforcing a single source of truth for something as foundational as identity information can be hard. Modern systems expect to have their own account structure.

The fallback is often to make the corporate identity service the sole means of authentication but still support multiple stores of identity information. These are synchronized using a variety of patterns. Reducing these ad hoc synchronizations is a laudable goal but can be expensive. As you've learned, identity is used to support relationships, and each system has specialized needs that go beyond whatever schema the identity service is configured with. As with ad hoc federation, it pays dividends to formalize the agreements between different services, even inside an organization.

Since 2005, hub-and-spoke federation between organizations has become extremely popular, driven by the development of protocols like OAuth and OpenID Connect (OIDC) and the increased use of APIs to provide services to outside organizations.

Aadhaar is a hub-and-spoke federation, as is the British government's GOV.UK Verify.

But hub-and-spoke identity federation goes well beyond national governments. Social login services like those through Facebook, Google, Twitter, Apple, and Amazon are based on OAuth 2.0 (which I'll discuss later in this chapter). The agreements between the IdP and RP are standardized, and RPs can use the IdP on a self-service basis. Most IdPs also have software development kits (SDKs) for a variety of languages to ease the developer burden and eliminate the need for the RP to set up its own authentication service. These benefits have made such services very popular.

If you've used social login to sign up for an app or service, you know that the RP app almost always maintains its own account information (sometimes called a *profile*). The need for this is obvious when you consider that many allow you to pick from among several IdPs. One of the weaknesses of many RP implementations of social login is that they don't allow for a single account to be linked to multiple IdPs—once you've picked, that's it. At BYU, the system detects when you log in with an identifier it hasn't seen before and prompts you to link that new identifier to your already established account (see Figure 13-3).

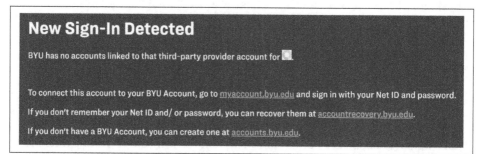

New Sign-In Detected

BYU has no accounts linked to that third-party provider account for █.

To connect this account to your BYU Account, go to myaccount.byu.edu and sign in with your Net ID and password.

If you don't remember your Net ID and/ or password, you can recover them at accountrecovery.byu.edu.

If you don't have a BYU Account, you can create one at accounts.byu.edu.

Figure 13-3. Catching new sign-ins so they can be linked to an existing account

Account linking is a best practice to make social login more usable for ordinary people. Personally, I usually don't use social login, because it's hard for me to remember which IdP I used for which site—and my password manager does a reasonable job of making the standard username-password bearable.

Over the last decade, a small number of powerful players have emerged as focal points of the identity domains that they control: Google, Facebook, Apple, Twitter, and Amazon. These IdPs wield enormous power. Smaller organizations seeking federation are left with little bargaining power, because the hubs set rules, often to their own advantage.

Bank of America: A Cautionary Tale

This is precisely the scenario that unfolded in the credit card industry after Bank of America franchised its credit card. The licensing strategy worked—to a point. Bank of America did gain a certain level of ubiquity with its card, but it also gained a system that seemed incapable of holding up under strain. The BankAmericard system was beset with security problems, delays, and outages.

What's more, the licensees were growing unhappy not only with the system but also with the licensing strategy itself. They saw the need for cooperation—for a credit card federation—but they did not enjoy being beholden to one large bank that was getting rich off their efforts and dictating the terms under which they were cooperating.

In the days when Bank of America controlled the system, it struggled under its technical and operational burdens. Having developed the credit card for its own use, Bank of America had neither the expertise nor the inclination to devote sufficient resources to the infrastructure necessary for interchange with other banks. Participating banks delayed processing payment requests to earn undeserved interest, distorted the "merchant discounts" and other processing fees they were entitled to retain, and squabbled over responsibility to cover fraud and other losses.

In social login, IdPs have kept federation simple—offering only authentication and perhaps a few self-attested attributes—to avoid disputes and keep others from gaming the system. IdPs, who sometimes compete in other areas with other members of the federation, never fully win the trust of those subject to their policies. As a result, social login has not been successful with some potential RPs. Banks, for example, are loath to use hub-and-spoke federation systems, because their authentication system and policies would be controlled by someone else.

Pattern 3: Identity Federation Network

The third pattern is federation within an identity network, an independent entity focused solely on the technical, administrative, and governance aspects of identity federation. In Chapter 4, I called this kind of system a *metasystem*: a system of systems. An identity network will typically gain support once a sufficient number of individual participants have become frustrated with the challenges of operating in an ad hoc multilateral environment, or when a hub-and-spoke network has begun to groan under its own weight.

Just two years after Bank of America began franchising BankAmericard, the situation had become so unworkable that the bank called its licensees to a meeting in Columbus, Ohio, to try to address the problems. The meeting quickly turned into a session of acrimonious finger-pointing. Finally, Dee Hock, vice president at a licensee bank in Seattle, stood up and suggested that the group form a committee to study the core problem in more depth. The participants immediately created the committee and appointed him chair.

Hock's committee recommended that the banks collectively create a new kind of organization that would be not only cooperative but also decentralized. Hock saw that the independent, competing organizations participating in the BankAmericard federation needed to cooperate on standards, rules, and processes for the cross-boundary use of a device (the BankAmericard). However, the federation could not persist over time if the organization couldn't address the needs of all issuers of the BankAmericard equally.

In response, the BankAmericard federation became independent in 1970. The result was a unique entity, initially called National BankAmericard Inc. but later rebranded as Visa. Visa is an autonomous organization that exists to coordinate the cooperation required from an ever-expanding membership, enabling them to issue and manage credit cards even as they compete. Visa took the islands of banks that had grown weary of the autocratic BankAmericard licensing system and brought them together under shared governance, with a common purpose and a new vision. It created a genuine network.

Visa's success illustrates the benefits of independent identity networks. Identity networks' core mission is handling challenges that are peripheral to any member of the network—such as ensuring the smooth interchange among participating institutions, selecting technical standards, defining liability responsibilities, determining common policies, managing security and fraud risks, enforcing privacy policies, resolving disputes among members, and interfacing with governments. When federation occurs through an identity network, the network can avoid the redundancy inherent in the ad hoc and hub-and-spoke models and devote its full attention to ensuring that the network scales effectively and serves the needs of all its members.

Identity networks can provide an ordered ecosystem for enterprises and individuals to interact, transact, and compete. As of 2022, only a few identity networks exist, and they are still in their early stages of adoption. The technologies, standards, protocols, and governance necessary for their growth are still young. Unlike credit card networks, where strong legal organizations took on the challenge of developing the technologies, standards, and governance, identity networks are developing the way the internet has: with multiple organizations playing roles in various parts of the process. Later chapters will discuss identity networks' technologies, standards, governance, and adoption in detail.

A secure, protected environment

By creating a quality-controlled environment for identity federation, the identity network both mitigates the risk of fraud or security breaches and reduces the likely damages of any breaches that do occur. The network is in a better position to design and implement monitoring, certification, tracking, and compliance mechanisms than any of its individual participants. Moreover, its ability to enforce its security standards ensures that there will be no weak links among network members: those who fail to adhere to policies can be subject to liability, recertification requirements, fines, suspensions, or even expulsion.

By pooling data and experience, the network can identify theft patterns and create effective protections against criminal activity more quickly and less expensively than any individual organization. Fraudsters tend to repeat attack patterns against various targets until those targets recognize and close their vulnerabilities. The common practices and information-sharing possible in an identity network give members a security advantage over organizations that do not participate in the federation.

An identity network also provides an environment perfectly suited to protecting the privacy of personal information online. In the identity network, access to personal information is permission-based, so no one company has a complete view of any individual's PII. Indeed, the distributed nature of the identity network ensures that no one party could ever know more than one piece of the identity puzzle without the individual's express consent. People can control access to their personal data, providing only what is absolutely necessary to gain access to a particular online resource.

What's more, when third-party authenticators authorize individual users and data is shared minimally and in zero knowledge,[3] companies will be able to take advantage of personal data without actually seeing it. The strong privacy protections that identity networks can establish and enforce also shield member organizations from the significant potential costs of failures to protect privacy, including fines, legal awards, and reputation damage.

Identity networks are more complicated than financial networks

Establishing a federated identity network, or identity metasystem, is not an easy task. Unlike a credit card network, which can extract a small fee from each transaction to fund its operation, members of federated identity networks must fund them out of pocket. Also, issues like liability are more fully understood in financial services networks, and it's relatively easy to charge higher fees for riskier transactions. What's more, there is a large body of legal knowledge about financial services that helps to establish the ground rules. These problems are yet to be solved for federated identity networks.

More importantly, the nature of identity transactions is more complex than that of financial transactions. Money is fungible—a dollar is a dollar. But attributes, authorizations, and permissions are not fungible. In fact, the whole point of many identity

---

3 Recall the discussion of zero-knowledge proofs in Chapter 9.

interactions is to *ensure* they are not fungible—we put great effort into ensuring that Alice cannot access a resource based on Bob's authorization.

Additionally, identity networks must handle far more types of identity transactions: the number is orders of magnitude greater than those in a financial network. For example, your driver's license is an identity document that contains a collection of attributes and some specific permissions (what kinds of vehicles you can legally drive). Your university transcript is a completely different identity document from a different type of institution, used for different purposes. An identity network should support transactions and the governance that goes along with them for both of these, and countless more. The metasystem discussion in Chapter 4 provides some guidelines for how an identity system can be built that accommodates this; Chapters 14, 15, and 16 will provide even more detail.

Addressing the Problem of Trust

Federated identity can operate only in an environment in which trust has already been established between parties. In an ad hoc federation, trust is established one bilateral agreement at a time. Each trust relationship is a custom creation. In hub-and-spoke federations, the trust relationship is created between the IdP and the RPs —generally as take-it-or-leave-it contracts of adhesion that RPs must agree to if they use the service. In a networked federation, trust is established through a common governance model that apportions or limits liability for players in specific ecosystems.

In each of these patterns, trust comes from the participants and the structure of their relationships; it cannot be created through technical specifications alone. SAML, for example, does not specify how much confidence should be placed in an identity assertion. Nor does it, or any other federated identity standard, directly address privacy policies. Each organization must decide what level of security precautions and privacy protections are sufficient, then negotiate baseline operational agreements with partners.

Federated identity cannot establish trust—it can only communicate it. Creating an environment in which digital identity can be strongly authenticated and used for high-value online transactions across identity domains is not simply a software engineering problem. It also requires well-established business, legal, and social processes.

Digital identity is not necessary for a single business process or relationship, but it is a fundamental element of a networked business. Ultimately, companies need trusted federated identity mechanisms that scale to different users, partners, and applications. An identity network is the only effective means to do so while ensuring that operational, legal, and security obligations are met.

Network Effects and Digital Identity Management

You've probably heard of Metcalfe's law (*https://oreil.ly/qPnIr*), which states that the value of a network grows as the square of the number of nodes. The reason is simple: the value is in the number of potential relationships, or links between nodes. Metcalfe's law informs digital identity architectures because the difficulty of managing an identity and access-management system is proportional to the number of potential relationships.

The internet uses a distributed, packet-switched architecture to manage the complexities arising from Metcalfe's network effects. No centralized architecture could have scaled to the size of today's internet. The only solution was to make each node smart enough to allow relationships between any two hosts on the internet to be established without any centralized coordination.

Efforts to create large centralized digital identity systems fail to appreciate three important lessons of the internet's distributed architecture:

Distributed architectures are more secure
> The distributed architecture and decentralized nature of the internet makes it difficult for attackers to break the network by concentrating their efforts in one place. In contrast, in a centralized system, the benefit of learning how to scam or break the system is very high, making it worthwhile for criminals to invest heavily in discovering a means of compromising the system.

Decentralized systems are less prone to commercial or political abuse
> No one wants their data to be under someone else's control because of the potential for it to be exploited. We put up with external control because the benefits are worth the risk. But problems like surveillance capitalism show the danger in centralized architectures.

Distributed architectures fail better
> A distributed architecture degrades gracefully, making it less susceptible to catastrophic failure. By contrast, once a key part of a centralized system becomes compromised, the entire system, along with all its connected data, is untrustworthy.

Numerous real-world examples show why centralization is more difficult in practice than in theory. For years, enterprise software vendors have claimed strong return on investment from integrating customer or supply chain data. Though enterprise resource planning, customer relationship management, and enterprise application integration have delivered some value, it has seldom been without significant pain and implementation expense. The rise of "software as a service" (SaaS) cloud offerings has exacerbated these integration and synchronization problems, which often come down to identity.

Beyond the IT challenges, centralized digital identity systems run into significant perceptual and user-behavior obstacles. People have no desire to do the work of putting all their information in one place. They don't necessarily want yet another username and password combination. Concerns that a single company could monopolize identity data, or that governments could use such a repository to gain access to personal data, inevitably dog centralized identity schemes.

Federation Methods and Standards

In discussing the problems of online identity in Chapter 3, I stated that because the internet is missing an identity layer, over the last several decades every website, service provider, and application has solved the problem in a unique way. This explosion of different authentication and authorization methods has created extreme interest in reducing the complexity of logging in. Consequently, the early 21st century has been a period of intense evolution in federated identity standards. Much of this evolution has played out in sessions at the IIW, which several of us started in 2005 to bring together various URL-based identifier schemes into a single standard. Despite dozens of meetings at IIW over the years, the work continues.

This section will discuss four mature identity federation standards that are widely used both inside organizations and online. All these standards are applied both inside and across organizations and are focused on the hub-and-spoke federation pattern, although they also frequently serve ad hoc federations. Chapter 14 and Chapter 15 will discuss emerging standards for networked federation.

The federation standards discussed below offer several important benefits, including:

- The federation partners (RPs) don't have to maintain expensive identity infrastructure or the support functions necessary to service accounts (such as password reset).

- People (and systems) establish fewer authentication relationships and thus don't have to remember as many passwords or store other authentication factors in as many places.

- The authentication flow is designed so that RPs never see the authentication factors. These are all contained on the IdP's system. Reducing the parts of the system that handle sensitive information increases security.

SAML

Identity and access management systems need a way of creating and distributing authentication and authorization assertions. The Security Assertion Markup Language, or SAML, is a standard that allows an IdP to pass authentication, authorization, and attribute information about a subject to an RP. The SAML specification calls the RP a *service provider* (SP), so that's the language I'll use in this section for consistency with the specification. The information the IdP sends the SP is contained in a *security token* that takes the form of a digitally signed XML message. SAML is primarily used for web-based, cross-domain SSO.

SAML 2.0 was ratified as an OASIS Standard in March 2005, replacing SAML 1.1. The standard is composed of four primary specifications:

Core
> The *core* specification defines the main SAML protocols, including assertion query and request, authentication request, and artifact resolution.

Binding
> The *binding* specification says how SAML is mapped onto various transport protocols (such as HTTP).

Profile
> The *profile* specification describes how SAML messages can be embedded in or used with other types of messages (like SOAP).

Metadata
> The *metadata* specification provides an extensible standard for identifiers, binding support, endpoints, certificates and keys, and other metadata.

Its support for different bindings, profiles, and metadata extensions makes SAML extremely flexible. Covering it in detail would require an entire book, so I'll focus on one of the most popular, the web-browser flow. But keep in mind that no matter which systems, transport protocols, messaging requirements, or specific metadata your application requires, you can probably use SAML.

The IdP is known as a *SAML authority* and responds to *SAML requests*. SAML responses are called *assertions*. There are three different types of assertions:

Authentication assertions
> When a SAML authority receives a request about a particular subject's authentication status, the result is returned as an *authentication assertion*. The authority asserts that subject S was authenticated by means M at time T. For example, "Subject Alice in company example.com was authenticated using a password over protected transport at time 2023-05-06T13:20:00-05:00."

Attribute assertions
> In addition to the authentication assertion, a SAML authority can be asked for attributes associated with the subject. These are returned as an *attribute assertion*. The authority asserts that subject S is associated with attributes A, B, etc., with values X, Y, etc. For example, "Subject Bob is associated with attribute Department with value Engineering and attribute Email with value *bob@engr.example.com*."

Authorization decision assertions

An authority can return an *authorization assertion* in response to a request about a subject's permissions with respect to certain resources. The authority asserts that subject *S* has (or has not) been granted permission for action *A* on resource *R* given evidence *E*. For example, "Subject *http://A.com/services/foo* is granted permission to read the file at *http://B.com/bar* as evidenced by assertions A1, A2, and A8."

Authorities can act as IdPs, producing assertions, and as SPs, consuming assertions from other authorities.

Assertions contain the following common elements:

- Issuer ID and issuance timestamp
- A globally unique assertion ID
- Subject, including a name and security domain, and optionally the subject's authentication data
- Optional, additional information (*advice*) provided by the issuing authority
- Conditions under which the assertion is valid such as the assertion validity period (such as `NotBefore` and `NotOnOrAfter`)
- Audience restrictions
- Target restrictions, such as the intended URLs for the assertion

The following example shows a SAML authentication request:[4]

```
<samlp:AuthnRequest
    xmlns:samlp="urn:oasis:names:tc:SAML:2.0:protocol"
    xmlns:saml="urn:oasis:names:tc:SAML:2.0:assertion"
    ID="aaf23196-1773-2113-474a-fe114412ab72"
    Version="2.0"
    IssueInstant="2023-12-05T09:21:59Z"
    Destination="http://idp.example.com/SSOService.php"
    ProtocolBinding="urn:oasis:names:tc:SAML:2.0:bindings:HTTP-POST"
    AssertionConsumerServiceIndex="0"
    AttributeConsumingServiceIndex="0">
  <saml:Issuer>https://sp.example.com/SAML2</saml:Issuer>
</samlp:AuthnRequest>
```

This request was issued by a service provider identified by the URI *https://sp.example.com/SAML2*. It requests an assertion containing an authentication statement. The SP doesn't usually identify the subject, leaving that task to the IdP.

The following XML is an example of a signed authentication assertion:

---

4 The SAML examples are adapted from the Wikipedia entry for SAML 2.0 (*https://oreil.ly/KkaJy*).

```
<saml:Assertion
    xmlns:saml="urn:oasis:names:tc:SAML:2.0:assertion"
    xmlns:xs="http://www.w3.org/2001/XMLSchema"
    ID="aaf23196-1773-2113-474a-fe114412ab72"
    Version="2.0"
    IssueInstant="2023-12-05T09:22:05Z">
  <saml:Issuer>https://idp.example.org/SAML2</saml:Issuer> ❶
  <ds:Signature
    xmlns:ds="http://www.w3.org/2000/09/xmldsig#">...</ds:Signature> ❷
  <saml:Subject> ❸
    <saml:NameID
      Format="urn:oasis:names:tc:SAML:2.0:nameid-format:transient">
      3f7b3dcf-1674-4ecd-92c8-1544f346baf8
    </saml:NameID>
    <saml:SubjectConfirmation
      Method="urn:oasis:names:tc:SAML:2.0:cm:bearer">
      <saml:SubjectConfirmationData
        InResponseTo="aaf23196-1773-2113-474a-fe114412ab72"
        Recipient="https://sp.example.com/SAML2/SSO/POST"
        NotOnOrAfter="2023-12-05T09:27:05Z"/>
    </saml:SubjectConfirmation>
  </saml:Subject>
  <saml:Conditions ❹
    NotBefore="2023-12-05T09:17:05Z"
    NotOnOrAfter="2023-12-05T09:27:05Z">
    <saml:AudienceRestriction>
      <saml:Audience>https://sp.example.com/SAML2</saml:Audience>
    </saml:AudienceRestriction>
  </saml:Conditions>
  <saml:AuthnStatement ❺
    AuthnInstant="2023-12-05T09:22:00Z"
    SessionIndex="b07b804c-7c29-ea16-7300-4f3d6f7928ac">
    <saml:AuthnContext>
      <saml:AuthnContextClassRef>
        urn:oasis:names:tc:SAML:2.0:ac:classes:PasswordProtectedTransport
      </saml:AuthnContextClassRef>
    </saml:AuthnContext>
  </saml:AuthnStatement>
  <saml:AttributeStatement> ❻
    <saml:Attribute
      xmlns:x500="urn:oasis:names:tc:SAML:2.0:profiles:attribute:X500"
      x500:Encoding="LDAP"
      NameFormat="urn:oasis:names:tc:SAML:2.0:attrname-format:uri"
      Name="urn:oid:1.3.6.1.4.1.5923.1.1.1.1"
      FriendlyName="eduPersonAffiliation">
      <saml:AttributeValue
        xsi:type="xs:string">member</saml:AttributeValue>
      <saml:AttributeValue
        xsi:type="xs:string">staff</saml:AttributeValue>
    </saml:Attribute>
  </saml:AttributeStatement>
</saml:Assertion>
```

There are several important elements in the assertion:

❶ `<saml:Issuer>` contains the unique identifier of the IdP issuing the assertion, `https://idp.example.org/SAML2`.

❷ `<ds:Signature>` contains a digital signature (redacted in the example) for the entire `<saml:Assertion>` element.

❸ `<saml:Subject>` identifies the authenticated principal using an opaque transient identifier, `3f7b3dcf-1674-4ecd-92c8-1544f346baf8`.

❹ `<saml:Conditions>` gives the conditions under which the assertion is to be considered valid, not before or after specific datetimes and only within `https://sp.example.com/SAML2`.

❺ `<saml:AuthnStatement>` describes the act of authentication at the identity provider, namely `PasswordProtectedTransport`.

❻ `<saml:AttributeStatement>` asserts a multivalued attribute associated with the subject, specifically that the attribute `eduPersonAffiliation` has values `member` and `staff`.

SAML Authentication Flow

Because the SAML standard is so flexible, there are many possible ways to use it. The most common use case is the authentication flow shown in Figure 13-4. Here, Alice is accessing a service provided by a third-party benefits provider her employer has selected. The flow has the following steps:

1. Alice uses a *user agent* (for example, a browser) to access a service provided by a service provider. The SP has a federation agreement with one or more identity providers (IdP). If there's more than one possible IdP, the request must include information that allows the SP to choose the appropriate IdP (for example, if the third-party benefits provider works with multiple employers, the request would need to identify Alice's employer).

2. The SP sends a response that redirects the user agent to the IdP (for example, using an HTTP 302 response). The response includes a SAML *authentication request*. The IdP in this example is being operated by Alice's employer.

3. The user agent relays the authentication request to the IdP identified in the redirect response.

4. If necessary, the IdP authenticates Alice. She may already be in an established session; if so, this step is skipped.

5. The IdP processes the authentication request and generates an assertion. The assertion is contained in the response to Alice's user agent as an *authentication response.*

6. The response is also a redirect, causing the user agent to relay the assertion to the SP.

7. If the assertion was affirmative, then the SP establishes a session in response to the request relayed in step 6. For a browser, this would typically be a cookie. At this point, we would say that Alice has *logged on* to the SP.

8. Alice requests a protected resource at the SP.

9. The SP responds with the protected resource because she has authenticated through the IdP.

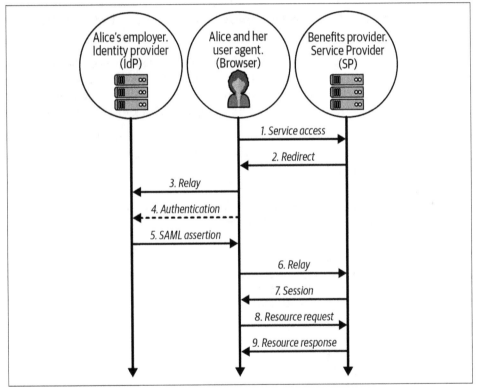

Figure 13-4. Typical SAML authentication flow

In the flow shown in Figure 13-4, the authentication ceremony is initiated by Alice. However, there are cases where the flow can be initiated by the SP or the IdP. If the SP initiates the flow, step 1 is skipped. If the IdP initiates the flow, steps 1 through 4 are skipped. For example, Alice might be on her employer's website and click a link to go to a third-party benefits provider. Rather than starting Alice at step 1, the employer website knows who Alice is and what she wants to access (because it's in the URL), so it could start at step 5, by generating an assertion and sending that as a redirect response to Alice's request.

SCIM

In Chapter 6, I discussed the lifecycle of digital relationships. Creating, propagating, updating, and terminating identity relationships is relatively straightforward in a single system. Federation makes these tasks more difficult. System for Cross-domain Identity Management (*https://oreil.ly/WYdQO*) (SCIM) is a standard for doing those important tasks.

Modern organizations usually have an IAM system that serves as a central repository (although not always a single source of truth) for identity data. They also use numerous on-premises and cloud-based systems to get work done. All of these need to get identity data from the IAM system and send identity data back to the IAM system.

SCIM identifies *users* and *groups* broadly as *resources* with standardized JSON schemas. It also provides a RESTful API for manipulating these resources. For example, a user resource looks like this:

```
{
  "schemas": ["urn:ietf:params:scim:schemas:core:2.0:User"],
  "id":"2819c223-7f76-453a-919d-413861904646",
  "externalId":"dschrute",
  "meta":{
    "resourceType": "User",
    "created":"2011-08-01T18:29:49.793Z",
    "lastModified":"2011-08-01T18:29:49.793Z",
    "location":"https://example.com/v2/Users/2819c223...",
    "version":"W\/\"f250dd84f0671c3\""
  },
  "name":{
    "formatted": "Mr. Dwight K Schrute, III",
    "familyName": "Schrute",
    "givenName": "Dwight",
    "middleName": "Kurt",
    "honorificPrefix": "Mr.",
    "honorificSuffix": "III"
  },
  "userName":"dschrute",
  "phoneNumbers":[
    {
      "value":"555-555-8377",
```

```
        "type":"work"
    }
  ],
  "emails":[
    {
      "value":"dschrute@example.com",
      "type":"work",
      "primary": true
    }
  ]
}
```

The resource identifies what schema it uses; gives a record identifier, a user identifier, and meta information; and includes numerous claims.

The REST operations that can be used with SCIM resources are:

Create

POST https://example.com/{v}/{resource}

Read

GET https://example.com/{v}/{resource}/{id}

Replace

PUT https://example.com/{v}/{resource}/{id}

Delete

DELETE https://example.com/{v}/{resource}/{id}

Update

PATCH https://example.com/{v}/{resource}/{id}

Search

GET https://example.com/{v}/{resource}?filter={attribute}{op}{value}
&sortBy={attributeName}&sortOrder={ascending|descending}

Bulk

POST https://example.com/{v}/Bulk

In the URLs, {v} is a version number and {resource} is a member of either Users or Groups.

IAM systems and services implement this API to use SCIM for exchanging identity data. Most popular IAM systems support SCIM, as do many on-premises and cloud-based service providers. SCIM provides a standard way of automating the relationship lifecycle, makes centralized account management tenable, and simplifies administrative tasks.

OAuth

OAuth was invented for a very specific purpose:[5] to allow people to control access to resources associated with their accounts, without requiring that they share authentication factors. OAuth differs from the other federation protocols I'm discussing in this chapter because its focus is access control, not just authentication.

A primary use case for OAuth is accessing data in an account using an API. For example, the Receiptify (*https://oreil.ly/qRbnv*) service creates a list of your recent listening history on Spotify, Last.fm, or Apple Music that looks like a shopping receipt. Figure 13-5 shows a receipt of my recent listening history.

Before OAuth, if Alice (the *resource owner*) wanted Receiptify (the *client*) to have access to her history on Spotify (the *resource server*), she'd give Receiptify her username and password on Spotify. Receiptify would store the username and password and impersonate Alice each time it needs to access Spotify on her behalf. By using Alice's username and password, Receiptify would demonstrate that it had Alice's implicit permission to access her data on Spotify. This is sometimes called the "password antipattern."

The password antipattern has several serious drawbacks:

- The resource server can't differentiate between the user and other servers accessing the API.

- Storing passwords on other servers increases the risk of a security breach.

- Granular permissions are hard to support since the resource server doesn't know who is logging in.

- Shared passwords are difficult to revoke and must be updated in multiple places when changed.

OAuth was designed to fix these problems by making the resource server part of the flow that delegates access. This design lets the resource server ask the resource owner what permissions to grant and records them for the specific client requesting access. Moreover, the client can be given its own credential, apart from those that the resource owner has or those used by other clients the user might have authorized.

---

5 In this book, when I say "OAuth" I'm referring to the newer OAuth 2.0 protocol, not OAuth 1.0a. You may still run into OAuth-1.0a-protected APIs, but OAuth 1.0a should not be considered for new developments.

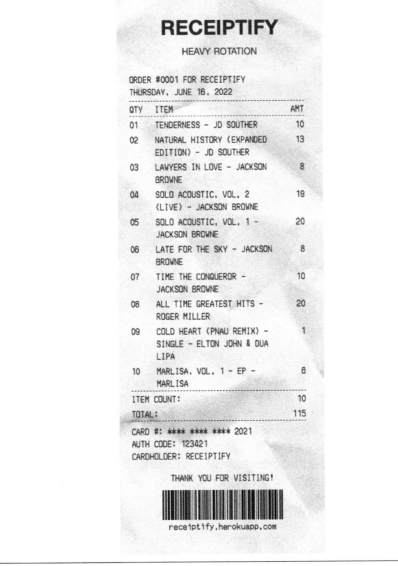

Figure 13-5. Listening history for June 16, 2022, from Receiptify

OAuth basics

OAuth is a protocol (*https://oreil.ly/iPhx9*) for access control. As such, it defines the interactions among several actors who play specific roles. The central figure in these interactions is the *resource owner*: the actor, almost always human, who controls *client* access to resources.[6] Figure 13-6 shows these actors and their relationships to each other.

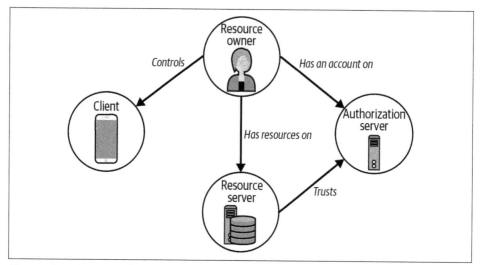

Figure 13-6. Actors in the OAuth protocol

The owner has resources on a *resource server* (RS), which protects the resources by controlling access. The server might be a cloud-based API or a connected device. The owner also specifies the *authorization server* (AS). The AS issues tokens that can be used to access resources on the RS. The RS and AS are often the same, but they needn't be. The interactions between these actors result in the AS granting the client an *access token* that it can later present to the RS to gain access to the protected resources. The client has registered with the AS and received a client ID and secret that it uses to identify itself to the AS during the OAuth flow.

Earlier I said that OAuth is an authorization protocol, not an authentication protocol. The access token is usually opaque and doesn't tell the client anything about the owner. Furthermore, the resource being accessed might or might not have identity information, and OAuth doesn't presume that the AS, RS, and client share any common identifier for the user other than the OAuth token. The next section will discuss

---

6 The client is the name the OAuth specification uses for the RP. Don't confuse the client with the browser, usually called a *user agent*. The web page or app, not the browser itself, is interested in accessing the resource.

OIDC, an authentication protocol based on OAuth that adds an identity layer for applications that need it.

There are two primary activities in OAuth: getting a token and using a token.

Getting a token

To get an access token, the client interacts with an AS. There are four ways to do this (called *flows*). They're formally called *authorization grant types*, but most people call them "OAuth flows." The different flows exist to accommodate different types of clients and access scenarios.

Authorization code grant
   The *authorization code grant* is the most used OAuth flow and what most people are talking about when they say "OAuth." If you've ever used social login, you've used this flow. Figure 13-7 illustrates the authorization code grant.

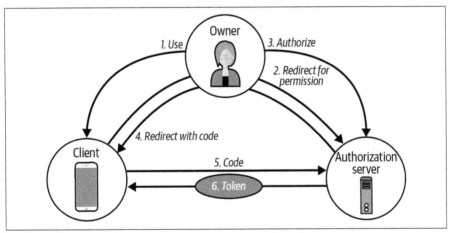

Figure 13-7. The authorization code grant flow in OAuth

In this flow, the owner uses a client (step 1) that needs access to the resource to function. The client asks the owner for permission to access the resource, by redirecting the owner (step 2) to the AS. There the owner sees a page called the *permissions screen*, which lists the permissions (called *scopes*) being requested by the client. The redirect includes information about the client in the form of the credentials that the client received when it registered with the AS. The owner can click "Accept" (or a similarly labeled button) to agree (step 3).

When the owner clicks on the "Accept" button to grant access, the response from the AS redirects the owner's browser to the client (step 4). The redirect URL contains a one-time, opaque code in the query string of the URL. The client can exchange this authorization code in a back channel, along with the client ID and secret it received when it registered with the AS, for the actual access token in a back channel (steps 5 and 6).

Obviously, this flow is only usable when the owner is present to interact with the AS *and* the client can allow the owner to interact with the AS via a web browser. Websites fit this description, as do desktop and mobile applications that can use an embedded browser.

Implicit grant

Like the authorization code grant flow, the *implicit grant* flow redirects the owner to the AS, where they sign in, and explicitly grants permissions to the client to access resources. The difference lies in what gets returned. Unlike the authorization code grant, the implicit grant returns the access token *directly* when the owner is redirected back to the client, skipping steps 4 and 5 in Figure 13-7.

The implicit grant is intended for clients that might not be able to keep the access token secret for some reason. Therefore, the access token returned usually has only limited permissions and is typically short-lived. It does not come with a refresh token (see below) for extending the grant's life.

Resource owner credentials grant

In the *resource owner credentials grant*, the client collects the owner's username and password (or other credentials as appropriate) and exchanges those for an access token. While this might feel like the password antipattern discussed above, in the resource owner credentials grant, the client doesn't store the username and password—but merely exchanges them. This might be desirable in a mobile app or other use cases where redirection isn't possible.

While many see this grant type as suboptimal, the fact that it doesn't rely on web redirection makes it suitable for connected devices that don't have web interfaces or sufficient processing power for engaging in complex HTTP interactions.

Client credentials grant

The *client credentials grant* uses the credentials that the AS gave to the client when it registered to gain access to resources in the client's own right. This is often useful for clients to "boot up" with an RS API, supply client information, or create accounts for the owner. Most API providers supply client IDs and keys as client credentials for people building applications on their platform. These IDs and keys can be used in a client credential grant for client-specific features of the API.

This grant also applies when an organization is using OAuth for access control but controls both the client and RS. For example, if an organization uses an administrative application to manage its systems, that application might use client credential grants to gain access to resources when it is not the owner of the data but needs administrative access for other legitimate reasons. Another use of this flow is situations where some resources on the RS are considered public, but the RS needs to ensure that only clients it knows are accessing the resource.

Refresh tokens

Access tokens are bearer tokens—anyone in possession of the token can access the resource on the owner's behalf. To protect against loss, tokens are usually granted with a time to live. The AS can simultaneously give the client a *refresh token* that it can use to renew the access token. Refresh tokens are never sent to the RS, only the AS. As a result, the RS can't save them and replay them later, a restriction that strengthens the owner's control over access to the resource.

The OAuth 2.0 specification does not require a specific token structure. Usually, access and refresh tokens are long, opaque strings that are useful only as keys into a data structure where the real information is stored.

OAuth scopes

As I noted earlier, the page that allows the owner to grant or deny permission might display what permissions the RS is requesting. This isn't freeform text written by a UX designer; rather, it's controlled by scopes. A *scope* is a bundle of permissions that the client asks for when requesting the token, coded by the developer who wrote the client.

Figure 13-8 shows the permissions screens that I, as the owner of my Twitter account, see for two different applications, Revue and Thread Reader.

There are several things to note about these authorization screens. First, Twitter is presenting these screens, not the clients (note the URL in the browser window). Second, the client is asking for quite different scopes for these two applications. Revue wants permission to update my profile as well as post and delete tweets, while Thread Reader is only asking for read-only access to my account. Finally, Twitter is making it clear to me who is requesting access. At the bottom of the page, Twitter warns me to be careful and to check the permissions that the client is asking for.

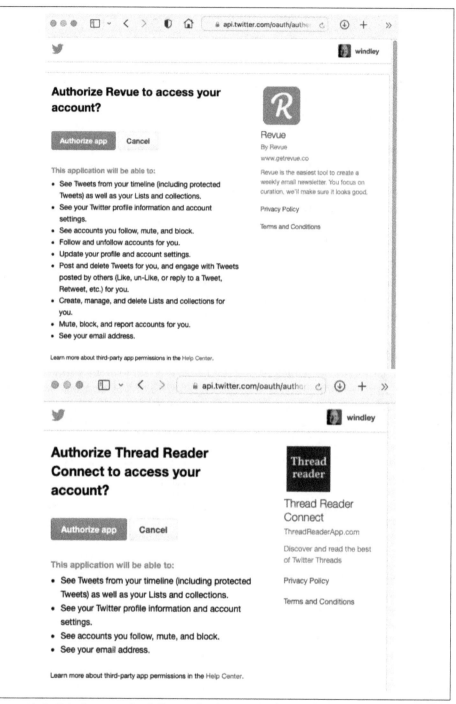

Figure 13-8. OAuth scopes for different third-party applications using the Twitter API

Using a token

Once the client has the access token, using it is straightforward. Figure 13-9 shows the standard interaction for using an OAuth token. The client presents the access token to the RS whenever it needs access to the resource.

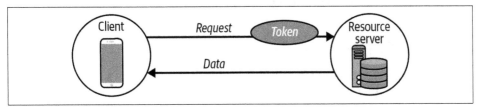

Figure 13-9. Using an access token

The standard interaction is for the client to present the access token in the HTTP Authorization header, prefixed with the string Bearer. This reminds us that the access token is indeed a bearer token. The RS will provide access to the resource in keeping with the permissions granted by the owner, regardless of who presents the token. Keeping the token secure is therefore paramount.

You might recall Figure 13-10: it appeared in Chapter 12's discussion of access control and introduced an abstract authorization architecture.

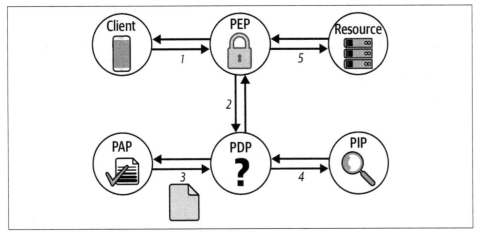

Figure 13-10. Abstract authorization architecture

We can make the following mappings between this abstract architecture and OAuth:

- The client (rather than Alice) is requesting access to a resource. Alice is approving access, but she doesn't show up in the abstract authorization architecture.
- The OAuth AS plays the role of the PAP and PDP. In many cases it would also serve as the PIP.
- The OAuth RS plays the role of the PEP.

Not shown in the abstract architecture is the resource owner, who interacts with the PAP to grant permission.

OpenID Connect

When my colleagues and I started IIW in 2005, people had proposed four different URI-based identity schemes, Simple eXtensible Identity Protocol (SXIP), Lightweight Identity (LID), Extensible Resource Identifier (XRI), and OpenID, so the time felt ripe for finding common ground and coming up with a single specification.

Over the next several years and a handful of IIWs, the proponents of those standards combined the best of each into a single specification, which came to be called OpenID. Eventually, the participants in these discussions formed the OpenID Foundation to oversee the specification and do additional work to implement and market it as an open standard for online authentication.

OpenID had two different versions, OpenID 1 and OpenID 2. Both put the identity owner in the middle of the flow, using redirects. While these standards enjoyed some popularity, they suffered from several problems:

- OpenID identifiers were based on URIs. They proved hard for people to remember, and attempts to fix the problem with one-click buttons for popular OpenID URIs meant login pages had to be plastered with the logos of every popular OpenID IdP. (This came to be called the *NASCAR problem.*)
- OpenID wasn't very friendly for APIs and mobile apps, a growing need in the late 2000s.
- OpenID didn't offer robust support for signing and encryption.

The last two problems led to the development of OAuth. Much of that work was done at IIW by the same people who'd worked on OpenID.

As I've discussed, OAuth is an authorization protocol, not an authentication protocol. It doesn't transfer anything other than the access token. The token carries an implicit identity—the resource owner granted permission, after all—but RPs frequently need more. Despite that limitation, all the major social media companies and many others started using OAuth for login in the late 2000s and early 2010s.

OIDC (*https://oreil.ly/5qtxL*) was a natural extension of OAuth. It solves the problems of OpenID 1 and 2, along with the limitations of using OAuth as an authentication system, by adding a layer on top of OAuth for moving identifiers and attributes. The OIDC flow is the same as OAuth's authorization code grant. The client adds an openid scope to the redirect (step 2 in Figure 13-7) to identify the flow as OIDC.

When the client receives the access token (step 6 of Figure 13-7) in an OIDC flow, it also receives an *identity token*. The OIDC identity token is a digitally signed JSON Web Token (JWT). The JWT contains claims about the resource owner in a JSON data structure, like this:

```
{
    "iss": "http://opeid.example.com",
    "sub": "alice",
    "aud": "1234abcdef",
    "exp": 1655506780,
    "iat": 1655506780,
    "name": "Alice Abrams",
    "given_name": "Alice",
    "family_name": "Abrams"
}
```

The JWT contains identifiers for the issuer (iss), the subject (sub), and the RP (aud). This JWT also has claims for full name (name), given name (given_name), and family name (family_name). Other claims can be added as well.

A JWT adds a header and signature to this and then encrypts and base64 encodes it to produce a string like this:[7]

```
eyJhbGciOiJIUzI1NiIsInR5cCI6IkpXVCJ9.
eyJpc3MiOiJodHRwOi8vb3BlaWQuQuZXhhbXBBs
ZS5jb20iLCJzdWIiOiJhbGljZSIsImF1ZCI6
IjEyMzRhYmNkZWYiLCJleHAiOjE2NTU1MDY3
ODAsImlhdCI6MTY1NTUwNjc4MCwibmFtZSI6I
kFsaWNlIEFicmFtcyIsImdpdmVuX25hbWUiOi
JBbGljZSIsImZhbWlseV9uYW1lIjoiQWJyYW1
zIn0.VesmKXMo96Ce4lEp9qhNhEKJ9V1fEBs
RarT6FXVlmys
```

This string (without line breaks) is the ID token. In addition to claims passed as part of the identity token, OIDC also defines a standard way for the RP to request additional attributes from the IdP using the access token.

Because many large internet companies were already acting as OAuth authorization servers, upgrading to OIDC was relatively easy. OIDC scales well and increases security by reducing the number of sites performing authentication and thus dealing with

---

7 You can use JWT.io to encode and decode JWTs and see how this works.

the attendant issues of securely setting, storing, and updating passwords. Furthermore, as those IdPs add additional features, like multifactor authentication or support for challenge-response protocols like FIDO, everyone gains from the increased security.

The very benefits I mentioned in the last paragraph have led to natural monopolies in the IdP space. Many of the most popular IdPs are in the business of tracking and monetizing people's online behavior. These models support that. The small number of IdPs makes correlating people's online activities easier. Furthermore, OAuth and OIDC put the IdP and RP in direct contact and use a single correlatable identifier.

As a result, while OAuth and OIDC have important uses and have made a big impact on online identity, they have not been universally adopted. For example, I don't know of any banks that are willing to give up their primary relationship with their customers to a third-party IdP.

Going back to the Laws of Identity (Chapter 4), you can see why this is the case. While OIDC is consistent with the laws of user control and consent, pluralism of operators and technologies, and human integration, it runs afoul of the laws of minimal disclosure, justifiable parties, directed identity, and consistent experience across contexts (since every RP and IdP is free to craft important features of the user experience to its own needs). Later I'll discuss alternatives to the OAuth and OIDC that attempt to better abide by the Laws of Identity.

Governing Federation

Anytime independent entities cooperate, you need governance. Since federation is, by definition, a cooperation between different entities, it implies governance of some kind. Federation doesn't work if the participants don't have confidence or trust in each other. Governance is the mechanism that allows us to trust that IdPs and RPs will behave in certain ways. Governance can include consequences for failure to comply.

Most SAML-based federation is ad hoc, and that shapes the nature of the governance. When an employer and a third-party benefits provider agree to federate identity data using SAML, they usually enter into a legal agreement. While the benefits provider, which does this frequently, will undoubtedly have contract templates, and most of the provisions will be straightforward, the very nature of legal contracts ensures that each will be slightly different.

Hub-and-spoke-style federations, like those that OAuth and OIDC promote, use *contracts of adhesion,* since one party (the AS or IdP) has most of the power in the relationship. If you want to use Google's (or anyone else's) API or identity services, they will set the terms and you'll agree. Take it or leave it.

Even so, since these federations are based on open, public specifications, creating and modifying those specifications becomes an important part of how the federation works and thus influences—even becomes part of—the governance mechanism for anyone using them.

Networked identity federation is still in its infancy, but networks extend the open governance of specifications to network operations. For example, the Sovrin Foundation has an extensive governance framework (*https://oreil.ly/GflMY*) including a master document that defines the foundation's purpose, core principles, and core policies; standardized legal agreements; controlled documents; and a glossary. There is also a set of controlled documents that contain policies managed by specific subgroups within the Sovrin Foundation. The process for creating all of these is open. The Trust Over IP Foundation is working on a templated governance stack (*https://oreil.ly/VZLzb*) that can be used to create governance for other identity networks. I'll return to policy and governance in Chapters 21 and 22.

Networked Federation Wins

Federated identity provides an important underpinning for an increasingly distributed internet. As companies link themselves more closely with their customers, employees, and partners, federated identity mechanisms must scale to accommodate new demands and counter a wide variety of threats. This explains the shift from internal, ad hoc federations to online federations between organizations of all stripes.

As the early history of the credit card industry demonstrates, ad hoc and centralized approaches to federated identity are difficult to scale and can be unstable. Just as Visa succeeded in creating a foundation for the explosive growth of the credit card industry by establishing a member-owned network for managing identity-related processes and systems, independent identity networks can create forms of federated identity that comply with all the Laws of Identity.

CHAPTER 14

Cryptographic Identifiers

As you learned in Chapter 10, identifiers are meaningful within a specific namespace. We need namespaces to confer context to the identifiers, because the same string of characters might be a phone number in one system and a product ID in another.

Take an email address like *windley@example.com*, for example. The identifier windley is contextualized by the mail domain *example.com*. If I just gave you the string wind ley, without any further context, you'd have a tough time associating it with anything in particular. If I said @windley, you might guess it was a Twitter handle—but the convention of putting @ before identifiers has become standard in other applications, so you can't be sure. Before you can be certain that I'm talking about a Twitter identifier, I must give you the entire URL: *http://twitter.com/windley*.

The context makes the identifier meaningful. You can use my Twitter identifier to view my profile or follow me. Most of the identifiers in common use are context first: the context (Twitter, in this example) already exists and the identifier gets created within that context, usually when someone creates an account and specifies an identifier. Because they are context first, traditional identifiers are controlled by the organization that controls the namespace. Twitter, for example, can suspend any account, making the identifier unusable or even assigning it to someone else. You have little recourse if that happens.

This becomes a larger problem when the identifier is assigned meaning outside its context. So long as my Twitter handle is just used within Twitter, if Twitter revokes my account, losing the identifier is just part of the hassle of losing my Twitter account. But what if I've used it at a third-party site, as part of an OAuth or OpenID Connect authentication? Now, when I lose control of my Twitter identifier, I might lose control of those other accounts as well.[1] My Twitter handle is administratively controlled by Twitter, not by me or the third-party site.

Given this relationship, an identifier without a namespace seems impossible. The problem isn't uniqueness. Universally Unique Identifiers (UUIDs) (*https://oreil.ly/yyue9*) , for example, are globally unique for practical purposes. In version 4 (variant 1) UUIDs, there are 128 bits. Six bits are fixed, but the remaining 122 bits are randomly generated, for a total of 2^{122} possible UUIDs. The possibility of a collision is extremely small. Software engineer Ludi Rehak estimates (*https://oreil.ly/-10In*) that in a sample of 3.26×10^{16} UUIDs there would be a 99.99% chance of having no duplicates.

The bigger problem is how to make the randomly generated identifier meaningful inside relationships *without* ceding administrative control of the identifier to some other context or authority. To understand why this is a problem, recall the example I've used several times of meeting a friend at a restaurant for a meal. In the digital world, you and your friend would likely identify yourselves to each other using an identifier controlled by someone else. If the restaurant provided you with identifiers and you and your friend used those to meet, then your relationship with your friend at the restaurant would exist in a silo, disassociated from other aspects of your relationship.

This chapter introduces *cryptographic identifiers* that are created *outside* a specific context. Cryptographic identifiers are controlled by their creator and contextualized for a given situation after creation, addressing these problems with traditional identifiers.

The Problem with Email-Based Identifiers

Many web-based identity systems have defaulted to using email addresses as identifiers. It's easy to see why. Everyone has one. And someone else has done the work of ensuring uniqueness since email addresses must be globally unique to function.

But email addresses are less than ideal as identifiers for several reasons:

- Email addresses have a different intended use (sending email), so an address might change for reasons unrelated to its use as an identifier.
- Email addresses are generally correlatable. If you use the same email address for all your account identifiers, it's easy to track and combine your activity at all those different places.

---

1 I'm going to talk about *control* of identifiers in this chapter without being specific about what that means. Chapter 17 will deal with identifier control and the trust basis for various identity architectures. Similarly, I will speak of the software that controllers use to control identifiers as *agents* in Chapter 18.

- Email addresses are generally administered by someone else who can take them away. Even if you use your own domain name, you're just renting that and may have to give up control in the future.

- Email addresses have limited global resolvability. All you can do is send an email message to the owner.

- Email addresses are reusable. If you stop using an email address, the administrator of the email system may reassign it, decreasing your security and privacy. For example, most password-reset processes send an email to the email address in the account. Whoever controls the email address can hijack the password-reset process and take over the account.

Decentralized Identifiers

Decentralized identifiers (DIDs) are a kind of cryptographic identifier that solves the problems outlined in the last section, and they provide one of the foundational technologies of self-sovereign identity. DIDs are defined by the DID specification (*https:// oreil.ly/PKVyN*) that was developed by the World Wide Web Consortium's Decentralized Identifiers Working Group.[2]

DIDs can be an identifier for anything, including people, places, organizations, and things. They are designed to be created without a context and then assigned to a context later. As such, they are globally unique outside of any context.

DID Properties

Properly implemented DIDs have these important properties:

Nonreassignable
> DIDs should be permanent, persistent, and nonreassignable. Permanence ensures that the identifier always references the same entity. As a result, DIDs are more private and more secure than identifiers that can be reassigned, such as domain names, IP addresses, email addresses, or mobile numbers.

Resolvable
> DIDs are made useful through resolution, meaning you can use the DID to look up more information about it. Resolution ensures that a DID is actionable. I'll discuss how DID resolution works in more detail below.

---

2 Version 1.0 of the DID specification was approved by the World Wide Web Consortium (W3C) on June 30, 2022.

Cryptographically verifiable

DIDs are designed to be associated with cryptographic keys. The entity controlling the DID can use those keys to prove ownership of the identifier. That can happen in several ways, the most common being a digital signature. When a DID is resolved to retrieve its associated DID document (more on this later), the result may be cryptographically signed to ensure its integrity. The resolution also provides one or more public cryptographic keys associated with the DID, which the owner can use to prove they are in control of the DID. Parties who have exchanged DIDs can mutually authenticate each other and encrypt their communication.

Decentralized

DIDs are designed to function without a central registration authority. Depending on the method specification for a given class of DIDs, they might also be created and updated outside the purview of any single party or entity, increasing censorship resistance. One method to censor someone is to revoke their identifiers. If no single party can take this action, censorship becomes harder. I'll come back to censorship several times in coming chapters.

DID Syntax

The syntax of a DID is simple and designed to support different decentralization methods. DIDs are Uniform Resource Identifiers (URIs). You learned about URIs in Chapter 10 where we primarily focused on how they have been used on the web, as URLs. Recall that a URI has several components. DIDs have the same components as a URI, even if they look somewhat unfamiliar, since we're so used to URIs used as URLs on the web.

A DID by itself, without a path, query, and fragment components of a URI, is a Uniform Resource Name (URN). Figure 14-1 shows the primary required components of a DID.

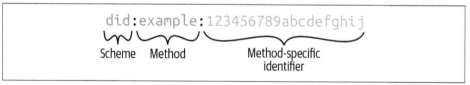

did:example:123456789abcdefghij

Scheme   Method   Method-specific
                            identifier

Figure 14-1. The syntax of DIDs

Each component of the DID is separated by a colon. The *scheme*, did, is fixed for all DIDs. It alerts any software that sees the identifier that it is a DID. The *method* specifies how the DID is created, updated, and resolved. In Figure 14-1, the method is example. The method functions as a namespace. The *method-specific identifier* is an alphanumeric string that is guaranteed to be unique within the context of the method. The method and identifier comprise the *authority* component of the URI (where you're used to seeing a domain name, in web contexts).[3]

DID Resolution

To be useful, identifiers' schemes must provide a way of discovering what the identifier means. Each DID method defines how discovery is performed for that specific DID method. Think of the method as a technology-specific implementation of the identifier operations that the DID specification requires. Different methods can support their own way of performing resolution using a specific blockchain or other storage system. The *method* outlines the way to create, retrieve, update, and deactivate the DID and its associated DID document. For example, the `did:indy:sov` method outlines how to create, lookup, and update the DID on the Sovrin ledger.[4] A resolver can use the method to find the routines necessary for interacting with a given identifier. Methods allow a variety of systems to serve as repositories for DIDs in an interoperable way.

The primary purpose of the method is to resolve a DID to a DID document (see the next section for a discussion of DID documents). *Resolution* is the act of looking up the DID document for a specific DID using the method given by the DID's method name. Taken as a whole, DID infrastructure functions as a global, decentralized key-value store where DIDs act as the keys and DID documents are the values.

The DID specification lists more than 100 possible methods, and others may be developed. While this might seem like something to be concerned about, I don't view it as a problem for three reasons. First, methods allow the specification to be flexible. Many methods differ from others for reasons specific to the use case. For example, a DID using the Ethereum blockchain method, `did:eth`, resolves to a smart contract that returns a DID document, whereas the `did:indy:sov` method looks up the DID document stored on the Sovrin ledger. Second, over time, a few DID methods will likely become primary and used for most applications. Finally, so long as the method can be used to resolve the DID, most applications should be able to support a wide range of methods without significant problems.

---

3 Technically, the augmented Backus–Naur form for RFC 3986 has a very specific definition of the authority component that wants a hostname and optional account and port information at that host. But logically, we can think of the method and identifier as the authority component, since they serve the same purpose.

4 The method name can have only one part: `indy`, in this case. Indy is an open source ledger project at Hyperledger that has several ledgers using its code. One of those is the Sovrin ledger. The DID specification allows methods to define subnamespaces, in this case `sov`. So, the method for the Sovrin ledger is `indy` and the subnamespace is `sov`. The combination of the method name and subnamespace tells the resolver how to resolve the DID.

While it's likely that these repositories will be decentralized, nothing in the specification forces that. Any storage system could potentially have a DID method associated with it. Beware that some repositories may not be able to fulfill the non-reuse and permanence properties that are expected of DIDs. For example, a `did:dns` method that resolves a DID using the Domain Name System (DNS) can't guarantee permanence because DNS names are not permanent.

DID Documents

DID documents describe the public keys, authentication protocols, and service endpoints that are necessary to initiate interactions with the identified entity, the *subject*. A DID document is a structured, key-value formatted document that contains the DID itself,[5] identified by the key `id`, along with several optional components. Here are the four most common:

- One or more public keys in a list, identified by the key `verificationMethod`
- Lists of protocols for authenticating control of the DID and delegated capabilities, identified by the key `authentication`
- A list of service endpoints, usually URLs, that allow discovery of how to interact with the subject, identified by the key `service`
- A timestamp indicating when the DID document was created, identified by the key `created`

DID documents that use the JavaScript Object Notation for Linking Data (JSON-LD) representation can use other forms of JSON-LD context to extend the DID document and aid in discovery.[6] For example, the data model could be extended to include the entity's Really Simple Syndication (RSS) feed by referencing a JSON-LD context that describes RSS feeds.

Most DID documents will contain at least one public key, one service, and metadata, in addition to the `id`. The following is an example of a minimal DID document, modified from an example in the DID specification (*https://oreil.ly/PKVyN*):

```
{
  "id": "did:example:123",
  "verificationMethod": [
    {
      "id": "did:example:123#key-1",
      "type": "Ed25519VerificationKey2018",
```

---

5 The document can be JSON, JSON-LD (a method for including semantic data and schemas inside JSON), or CBOR, which stands for Concise Binary Object Representation (*https://cbor.io*).

6 JSON-LD contexts are a way of providing a link to an external schema for the extension.

```
      "controller": "did:example:123",
      "publicKeyBase58": "H3C2AVvLMv6gmMNam3uVAjZpfkcJCwDwnZn6z3wXmqPV"
    },
    {
      "id": "did:example:123#key-2",
      "type": "JsonWebKey2020",
      "controller": "did:example:123",
      "publicKeyJwk": {
        "kty": "OKP",
        "crv": "Ed25519",
        "x": "r7V8qmdFbwqSlj26eupPew1Lb22vVG5vnjhn3vwEA1Y"
      },
    }
  ],
  "authentication": [{
    "id": "did:example:123#z6MkpzW2izkFjNwMBwwvKqmELaQcH8t54QL5xmBdJg9Xh1y4",
    "type": "Ed25519VerificationKey2018",
    "controller": "did:example:123",
    "publicKeyBase58": "BYEz8kVpPqSt5T7DeGoPVUrcTZcDeX5jGkGhUQBWmoBg"
  }],
  "service": [{
    "id": "did:example:123#edv",
    "type": "EncryptedDataVault",
    "serviceEndpoint": "https://edv.example.com/"
  }],
  "created": "2022-02-08T16:03:00Z",
}
```

The DID document is the root record for a decentralized identifier that can reference not only what's in the DID document itself but also any information from the service endpoints. This is accomplished by adding paths, query parameters, and fragments to the DID. The syntax of these is familiar to anyone acquainted with the syntax of a URI. Such a reference is called a *DID URL*.

Fragments are used to identify a particular part of the DID document. In the preceding DID document, there is only one service. Nevertheless, it can be selected using the following DID URL:

```
did:example:123#edv
```

By using a DID with paths, queries, and fragments, the DID functions like a URL. To convert the DID into a URL, you start with the URL given in the serviceEndpoint selected by the fragment and then append the path and query. For example, the following DID:

```
did:example:123/foo/bar?a=1#edv
```

is equivalent to the following URL (based on the preceding example DID document):

```
https://edv.example.com/foo/bar?a=1
```

Through service endpoints, DIDs provide a permanent, resolvable identifier for any internet service. For example, if one of the service endpoints in my DID document is for email, then I can change my email address at will and anyone holding that DID will still be able to reach me. All I need to do is to be sure to update the DID document when I change my email.

Indirection and Key Rotation

If you remember the discussion of public-key cryptography from Chapter 9, you might be wondering why we can't just use public keys as cryptographic identifiers. The short answer is: we can, but there are several problems. First, public keys are not resolvable, so there's no standard way to find the digital certificate associated with one. Second, they need the extensive public-key infrastructure (PKI) to establish trust, as discussed in Chapter 9. Finally, rotating the keys changes the identifier, making public keys impermanent.

Remember that the public key and private key are a pair and that authenticating the public key depends on keeping the private key secret. If the private key is compromised (or is even suspected of being compromised), the correct procedure is to rotate the key: generating a new public-private key pair. If you're using the old public key as an identifier, you now must tell everyone who is using that identifier to switch to the new one.

DIDs solve this problem using *indirection*: rather than using the public key as the identifier, the DID refers to the DID document that contains it. If the keys need to be rotated, the controller of the DID rotates the keys and puts the new public key in an updated DID document. When someone with the DID resolves it again, they will get the new public key.

How can you know that the new DID document is legitimate? Different DID methods have different ways to do this, but the most obvious way is to use the old key to sign the new DID document.[7]

Figure 14-2 shows the steps involved in generating a new DID document using this method. Suppose Bob needs a DID from Alice for something. Here's what happens next:

1. Alice generates a new DID.
2. She shares it with Bob.
3. Bob resolves the DID and retrieves the associated DID document and public key.
4. Bob stores the DID document.

---

7 There are some problems with this simple approach that I'll fix later in this chapter.

5. Later, Alice determines that she needs to rotate the key in the DID document. She does so, generates a new DID document, and signs it with the previous key.

6. Later still, Bob needs to interact with Alice again. He doesn't just use the stored DID document and key he retrieved earlier; instead, he resolves the DID again and gets the new DID document.

7. He can check its integrity by using the previous key to validate the signature on the new DID document.

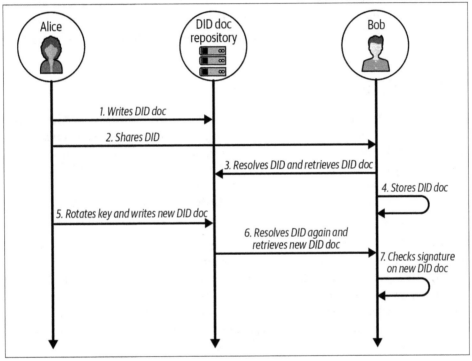

Figure 14-2. Rotating keys and generating a new DID document

Because you can rotate the keys in a DID document, transferring a DID from one controller to another is easy.

There are many reasons why a permanent identifier might need to be transferred. For example, parents are generally the guardians of their children. For guardianship and similar use cases, the DID identifies the child, but the parent controls the DID. Over the course of raising a child, a parent might make hundreds of DIDs for the child's various digital relationships. Some of these relationships are long-lasting and so the DID will be used for a long time. When the child gains their majority, they will want to control many of the DIDs their parents created. Because the DID document can be updated with a new key, the child can generate a new key, and the parent can generate a new DID document containing the child's key. The child now controls the DID.

People with power of attorney and caretakers of people with dementia are a few other examples of guardians. For more information on this, see the Sovrin Foundation's paper on digital guardianship (*https://oreil.ly/aqMf7*).

Beyond guardianship, there are other important use cases where the subject of a DID document is not the controller. Organizations of all kinds have human directors or owners. So do physical objects (your car) and natural things (your cat). All of these are subject to sale or transfer, and DIDs' ability to support the smooth transfer of control from one human to another is a significant advantage over other types of identifiers.

Autonomic Identifiers

In his paper introducing Key Event Receipt Infrastructure (*https://oreil.ly/GbHKz*) (KERI), which I'll discuss in a moment, Sam Smith coined the term *autonomic identifier*. The word *autonomic* comes from the Greek *auto* (self) and *nomos* (law) and means "self-governed" or "self-regulating." You're probably most familiar with this word from its use in describing the body's autonomic nervous system, which is responsible for the various processes in the body that we don't consciously control: circulation, respiration, and so on.

Autonomic is the perfect word for describing a class of identifiers that have self-governing capabilities. Traditional identifiers are governed by the owner of the context or namespace in which they are created. With DIDs, it is the DID method that describes how the identifier works. Most DID methods depend on some external system, like a blockchain or ledger, which I've referred to as a *verifiable data registry* (VDR). How much you trust a DID depends on your level of trust in the DID method it uses and, consequently, the VDR it is based on.

In contrast, autonomic identifiers are self-certifying. The basis for trusting them is rooted in cryptography rather than some external system. This sets autonomic identifiers apart from other identifiers and makes them especially useful in identity systems that prioritize reducing dependencies and increasing privacy.

Self-Certification

Self-certification means that the controller of an identifier can prove control without relying on a third party. Self-certification is an important property for a decentralized identity system that does not depend on external infrastructure. *Self-certifying identifiers* (SCIDs) are not new. They go as far back as 1991, when Marc Girault published a paper describing the use of self-certifying identifiers to reduce reliance on PKI.[8] Other efforts followed for self-certifying URLs and a self-certifying filesystem.[9]

The simplest form of SCID is a public key, since (a) anyone can create one and (b) only the person who controls the private key can make authoritative statements about it. As you learned in the discussion of DIDs, public keys have weaknesses when used as identifiers. DIDs correct those weaknesses by binding the key to the identifier using a DID document. You also learned that you can use the previous key to sign a new DID document when the keys are rotated, to create a trust chain between older and newer versions of the DID document. Figure 14-3 shows a chain of DID documents, with each signed by the previous key.

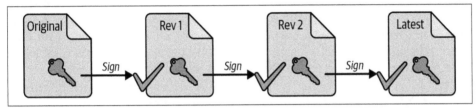

Figure 14-3. A chain of signed DID documents

A chain of signed DID documents might remind you of a blockchain, where each block is linked to the previous block using a hash of its contents and a signature. Unlike a blockchain, this chain of documents doesn't have the ability to withstand Byzantine attacks or prevent double spending. But for many DID applications that don't require public discovery and resolvability, this method can provide the necessary confidence in the integrity of the identifier. Because SCIDs depend only on cryptography for verification, with no central administrator or blockchain required, they are fully portable.

Whether or not the DID and DID document can be self-certifying depends on the processes used to do this—specifically the DID method. One of the primary questions the process needs to describe is how the chain works to provide self-certification and resolution. The rest of this section will describe two different ways for doing this. First, I'll discuss peer DIDs, a DID method designed to provide self-certifying DIDs that don't use a ledger. After that, I'll discuss KERI.

---

8 Marc Girault, "Self-Certified Public Keys," EUROCRYPT '91, Workshop on the Theory and Application of Cryptographic Techniques, Brighton, UK, April 8–11, 1991.

9 Michael Kaminsky and Eric Banks, "SFS-HTTP: Securing the Web with Self-Certifying URLs" (*https://oreil.ly/AqGz2*), MIT, 1999; David Mazieres, "Self-certifying File System" (*https://oreil.ly/3JwEb*) (PhD diss., MIT, 2000).

Peer DIDs

The proposed specification (*https://oreil.ly/c8EqI*) for peer DIDs define a DID method, did:peer, for creating self-certifying autonomic identifiers. Most DID methods describe DIDs that use a public blockchain, ledger, directory, or database to bind the identifier to the DID document. The public nature of the binding allows parties to resolve arbitrary DIDs and retrieve the DID document. If you trust the public DID repository, then you can have confidence in the binding.

Most relationships don't need to resolve arbitrary DIDs. For example, suppose Alice and Bob create a relationship by exchanging DIDs. They now have a mutually authenticated relationship based on the keys associated with their respective DIDs. Alice knows she can get Bob's DID document from him; Bob knows he can get Alice's DID document from her. Alice and Bob don't need a public DID repository for their digital relationship to work. What they need is a secure, trustworthy way to exchange DIDs, retrieve their respective DID documents, and get updates if either of them rotates the keys, changes service endpoints, or otherwise updates the DID document. The peer DID method describes the processes for doing these activities, so that people can have full control over their digital relationships.

Benefits of peer DIDs

Peer DIDs have several benefits over public DIDs for peer relationships, including:

Reducing cost
> Public DID repositories usually require payment to support their operation. Peer DIDs are completely supported by the computational resources of the parties in the relationship and are, therefore, free.

Increasing privacy
> The best way to reduce correlation and make it harder for third parties to discover the identities of participants in a conversation is to use a different identifier for each relationship. The cost of public DIDs puts a price on privacy and discourages using them without reserve. Peer DIDs are cheap, so it makes sense to create a new one for each relationship, or even different relationships with the same peer. For example, a student employee at a university might have a student-educator relationship with the university as well as an employee-employer relationship. Using a different DID for each relationship might make sense even though the parties are the same. Peer DIDs thus offer developers better tools for supporting privacy.

Increasing security
> Peer DIDs and the data associated with them are not stored in a single public repository, so there is no trove of data to protect. This reduces the benefit of an attack and reduces the incentives that lead to large data breaches.

Decreasing regulatory burden

As you learned in Chapter 8, GDPR and other regulations consider public identifiers—even opaque ones—to be personal data and thus subject to regulation. Peer DIDs are not stored in repositories controlled by third parties and thus not subject to regulations about such arrangements.

Reducing complexity

Peer DIDs are simpler than public DIDs because they don't need a complex VDR to store DID documents, with the attendant security, privacy, regulatory, and technical burdens.

Increasing scalability

Reducing costs, complexity, and technical infrastructure mean that peer DIDs can scale proportionally to the capacity of the participants in the relationship, not based on some public repository's capacity and limitations.

Reducing dependence on internet access

Peer DIDs work well in circumstances where connectivity is limited because they don't need to contact a public DID repository to resolve a DID. For example, consider a door lock in a basement corridor where WiFi and cellular service are spotty. Alice could create a relationship with the lock over Bluetooth or some other local networking technology and use that relationship to unlock the door when she needs access, even when she is offline.

Making peer DIDs trustworthy

The processes peer DIDs use for creating an identifier and associated keys are important but straightforward, since they depend on public-key cryptography. The peer DID process for updating the DID document is more interesting, since self-certification depends on it.

Figure 14-3 shows a simple method for creating a chain of DID documents. The problem is that if the device used to support the DID-based relationship goes offline, it could miss several updates to the DID document. Let's return to the example of Alice and her relationship with a door lock. Suppose Alice needs to pass through that door sporadically and infrequently over the course of many years. She or the lock could update their DID documents many times between her visits to the basement. The simple method requires complex negotiation and exchanging a lot of data for Alice and the lock to synchronize.

The peer DID specification, in contrast, describes a process for using change documents called *deltas* to detail any changes and a process for validating that a sequence of deltas are authentic. For this to work, agents handling peer-DID-based relationships must be able to answer questions about previous states, who authorized state changes, and when those state changes occurred. The agent needs persistent storage, called a *backing store*, to keep track of these historical details and the metadata surrounding them.

The following code example (from the peer DID specification) shows the JSON object, called a *change fragment*, that encodes a delta for a DID document.

```
{
    "change": <base64url encoding of a change fragment>,
    "by": [ {"key": <id of key>, "sig": <signature value>} ... ],
    "when": <ISO8601/RFC3339 UTC timestamp with at least second precision>
}
```

The change field is a sparse version of the DID document showing just the sections being changed. The by field is a tuple of key-signature pairs that establish the authenticity of the change; the when field says when the change was made. The current version of the DID document is the cumulative application of all the authenticated change fragments from the backing store to the original.

At the inception of a relationship based on peer DIDs, both parties will share the *genesis version* of the DID document. The format for sending the genesis version is a change fragment that contains the entire DID document. Figure 14-4 shows a chain of change fragments in which DID documents have been resolved over time as needed.

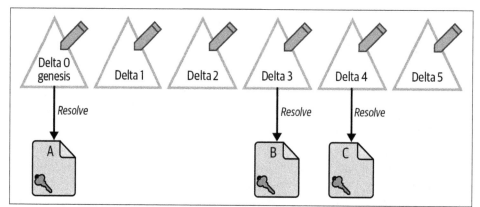

Figure 14-4. A chain of change fragments with resolved DID documents

One complication is that it's possible for two agents to make a change to the DID document for a given DID at the same time. This could happen, for example, when two agents of the same owner or controller rotate their keys at the same time. To avoid merge conflicts, the backing store is designed to work as a *conflict-free replicated data type (CRDT)* (*https://oreil.ly/Zpa-b*). CRDTs, as the name suggests, are data types that are designed to avoid, rather than resolve, merge conflicts.[10] As such, there are some limitations from arbitrary data types, but those can be worked into the design of the backing store without limiting the usability of the DID document. One important thing to keep in mind about CRDTs, and hence DID documents, is that we're after eventual consistency, not the "right answer." In other words, if multiple parties edit the same DID document simultaneously, we want everyone to eventually see the same document, not any specific version of the multiple possible versions. The goal is *agreement*—so that everyone gets the same DID document when it's resolved.

Because of this, two different agents seeing a string of change fragments don't have to receive them in the same order. Figure 14-5 shows the change fragments in Figure 14-4, this time with *delta 3* and *delta 4* being received in reverse order.

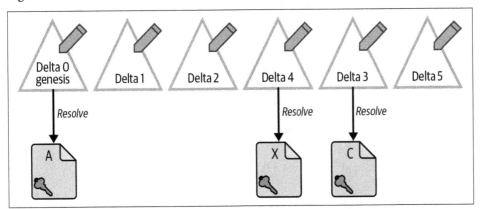

Figure 14-5. Delivering change fragments out of order eventually produces the same resolved DID document (C)

If you were to resolve the change fragments after receiving *delta 4* but before receiving *delta 3*, you'd see a different DID document than any that were resolved in Figure 14-4—the one called *X* in Figure 14-5. But after you eventually receive *delta 3*, the resolved document would be DID document *C*, just as in Figure 14-4.

Peer DID authentication and authorization

Peer DIDs are used as identifiers in a wide range of circumstances. You might be identified by one peer DID to the Swiss bank where you stash your billions and another to the lock on your bike. Because they are used in life-and-death situations as well as those of little consequence, DID documents for peer DIDs go beyond the

---

10 Most people are familiar with CRDT-like structures, if not the underlying technology, thanks to services like Google Docs that allow multiple parties to edit the same document simultaneously without ever getting an error message about merge conflicts.

standard authentication schemes defined in the DID specification and add an `author`
`ization` section for more fine-grained control.[11]

A DID can be associated with more than one set of keys: the `publicKey` section of the
DID document is a list. There are several reasons you might want more than one key
per DID. The most obvious is that putting more than one key in the DID document
allows you to precommit to a backup key in the event the first is compromised. You
can keep the private-key portion of the backup key in cold storage (for example,
printed on paper and stored in a safe) so that it can't be stolen if you're hacked.

Another reason for having more than one key is to associate varying levels of privilege with different keys. For example, one key might have the privilege of exchanging
the DID with another party, another key might have the power to incur nonrepudia-
ble contractual obligations on behalf of the DID subject, and a third might have the
power to manage the DID document by adding authorization rules and rotating keys.
By having different keys for different activities, the DID document allows the DID
controller to manage keys in a way that provides the necessary levels of security for
different tasks. These keys might be held by different controllers who use the DID for
different purposes and have different privileges.

The peer DID specification recommends that the `authentication` section of a peer
DID document should only list keys held by the most trusted controllers, while all
other uses should be governed by the `authorization` section. The `authorization`
section contains two subsections: `profiles` and `rules`.

The `profiles` section declares trust profiles for different keys based on roles that the
key holds. The roles are arbitrary strings that the creator of the DID document
defines to fit its purpose. The `rules` section contains authorization rules written in
Simple Grant Language (*https://oreil.ly/VHk9J*) (SGL), a JSON-based rule language
for granting privileges to actors under specific conditions. The following is an authorization section example from the peer DID specification:

```
"authorization": {
    "profiles": [
        // an "edge" key
        {"key": "#Mv6gmMNa", "roles", ["edge"]},
        // an "edge" and a "biometric" key
        {"key": "#izfrNTmQ", "roles", ["edge", "biometric"]},
        // a "cloud" key
        {"key": "#02b97c30", "roles", ["cloud"]},
        // an "offline" key
        {"key": "#H3C2AVvL", "roles", ["offline"]},
    ],
```

---

11 Recall that the DID specification allows different DID methods to extend the schema for a DID document
beyond the core data model defined in the specification.

```
    "rules": [
        {
            "grant": ["register"],
            "when": {"id": "#Mv6gmMNa"},
            "id": "7ac4c6be"
        },
        {
            "grant": ["route", "authcrypt"],
            "when": {"roles": "cloud"},
            "id": "98c2c9cc"
        },
        {
            "grant": ["authcrypt", "plaintext", "sign"],
            "when": {"roles": "edge"},
            "id": "e1e7d7bc"
        },
        {
            "grant": ["key_admin", "se_admin", "rule_admin"],
            "when": {
                "any": [{"roles": "offline"}, {"roles": "biometric"}],
                "n": 2
            }
            "id": "8586d26c"
        }
    ]
}
```

This example declares four profiles for four different keys, assigning each key a set of roles. The rules then grant privileges based on either profile id numbers or a set of roles.

While roles are arbitrary strings, the privileges are not arbitrary, since they must be understood by the code enforcing the authorizations. The following list is the privilege inventory in the specification, with a brief explanation of each. You can find more information in the peer DID specification (*https://oreil.ly/83a7Y*):

register
: The holder of this privilege is allowed to register the DID as an identifier with another party. Holders of this privilege can exchange DIDs with other agents.

route
: The holder of this privilege is allowed to receive and decrypt DIDComm forward messages encrypted for itself, and to forward the contained DIDComm encryption envelope to another key. This privilege is useful for cloud agents that route messages to edge (device) agents but that shouldn't be able to read the messages (in the interest of security).

authcrypt
: The holder of this privilege is allowed to create messages and send them with authenticated encryption that reveals the identity associated with this DID to the

receiver. Most keys will have this privilege, but you might remove it from IoT devices, for example, to limit the possibility of someone co-opting them to impersonate the DID subject.

plaintext
> The holder of this privilege can see plain-text DIDComm messages intended for an identity owner engaged in a protocol.

sign
> The holder of this privilege can incur nonrepudiable contractual obligations on behalf of the DID subject. This can be used, for example, to authenticate the DID instead of relying on the `authentication` section.

key_admin
> The holder of this privilege can add or remove other keys from a peer DID document's `verificationMethod` section, `authentication` section, or `authorization` profiles list. Because of its power, this privilege should be granted only to keys that are held by trusted controllers.

se_admin
> The holder of this privilege can add or remove items from a peer DID document's `service` section.

rule_admin
> The holder of this privilege can add or remove rules from a peer DID document's `authorization rules` list. Similar to the `key_admin` privilege, this privilege should be granted only to keys that are held by a trusted controller.

rotate
> The holder of this privilege can replace its associated key definition—and all references to that key throughout a DID document—with a new key definition and references, in a single delete-and-add operation.

These authorizations increase the utility and security of peer DIDs. The features and benefits of peer DIDs allow them to scale to support people's many digital relationships.

Key Event Receipt Infrastructure

Key Event Receipt Infrastructure (*https://keri.one*), also known as KERI, is a decentralized system for creating SCIDs and performing all the related key management—including complex, enterprise-grade, multiparty signatures and delegation trees. Now that you understand peer DIDs, the concepts of KERI will feel very familiar; they have much in common. KERI-based SCIDs are more general-purpose than peer DIDs, however, with broader applicability. In this section, I'll discuss the primary features that distinguish KERI from peer DIDs. If you want more information, the KERI technical paper (*https://oreil.ly/XyKVQ*) goes into great depth on its protocol, configuration, and operation.

Self-certifying key event logs

KERI uses a data structure called a *key event log* to record changes to the keys associated with an identifier, rather than recording the changes in DID documents. Each time the controller of a KERI identifier rotates its keys, KERI writes a new digitally signed message to the key event log to record the change. The key event messages in the log are chained together. Each event message (other than the genesis message) contains a digital hash of the immediately preceding key event message.

Anyone in possession of the key event log can cryptographically verify its authenticity by checking the integrity of the final message in the log, then ensuring the digital hash contained in it matches the hash of the preceding message. This process continues, following the chain of message to the beginning. This verifies that no messages have been changed and that nothing has been deleted or inserted.

The controller of the identifier keeps a copy of the key event log. They can also share it with others who need to use the identifier to interact with the controller. In addition, as the controller rotates the keys, they can send the event messages to others so that their copies of the event log are kept up to date.

KERI also allows the controller to use *witnesses*—other digital agents who can validate and sign the key event log. The witnesses also get a copy of the genesis log and all the messages that mark key rotations. They record these and witness them with their own digital signatures to provide additional evidence that the last public key in the log is bound to the identifier and that no one is cheating.

Because KERI identifiers are self-certifying, any system can serve as a witness, including a blockchain, a database, a directory, a filesystem, or a device such as a smartphone. In fact, all of them can serve as witnesses at the same time, meaning the KERI SCID is not dependent on any one of them. KERI calls this avoiding "ledger lock."

Prerotation of keys

KERI includes an ingenious method called *prerotation* to mitigate the damage if private keys are lost or stolen.

Suppose that Alice creates a new KERI identifier and an associated key pair. She shares the public key with Bob and uses the private key as needed. Unfortunately, Malfoy breaks into her computer and steals her private key. What can Alice do? She can't simply rotate the key and start using the new key pair, because Bob has no way to know if the new key in the key event log is from Alice or Malfoy. She and Bob would have to use another channel to share a new key and repair the damage.

But prerotation solves this problem: when Alice creates a KERI identifier and its initial public-private key pair, she can also create the *next* key pair and commit to it cryptographically by writing a hash of it in the key event log. Alice stores this new backup private key offline so that it is secure. If her current private key is lost or stolen, she can share the next public key and use the next private key as needed. Because it's already written to the key event log, Bob will recognize it as Alice's new key without having to take special actions to trust it. Then Alice can prerotate another key and share it using a key event log message, so that she and Bob are prepared for any future catastrophes.

Delegation

You can delegate authority to KERI identifiers by writing delegation events to the key event log of the key doing the delegation. A *delegation event* allows the new key to prove its relationship with its parent identifier; anyone can then use cryptography to verify that the delegation is authentic. The new delegated key is a full-featured KERI identifier, so it has its own key event log and can delegate its authority to other identifiers. The result is a hierarchy of identifiers with their authority stemming from the root identifier.

KERI identifiers and key delegation allow organizations to scale and manage delegation hierarchies of any size or complexity. They also enable individual users of KERI to manage different instances of a digital wallet across multiple devices.

The KERI DID Method

As you've learned, DIDs are a general interface for attaching metadata about keys, services, and other important information to an identifier using a DID document. KERI is a specific technology for attaching slightly different metadata to an identifier. The did:keri specification (*https://oreil.ly/1scy2*) makes KERI identifiers compatible with DIDs by creating a DID method to support them.

The did:keri method defines the DID document that it returns to include the data in the key event log. The did:keri DID document does not include a services section, but it may include a verificationMethod section.

The did:keri method allows software agents that understand DIDs and DID methods to process and use KERI identifiers and keys. Ongoing work promises to make KERI and peer DIDs even more compatible.

Other Autonomic Identifier Systems

In addition to peer DIDs and KERI, researchers are working on several other autonomic identity systems. For instance, Cryptid (*https://oreil.ly/zpIbM*) is working on an authentic data system (*https://oreil.ly/2dYoD*) that uses provenance logs, which are similar to key event logs but include other supporting data. The did:orb method (*https://oreil.ly/PgM-M*) uses self-certifying identifiers and the Sidetree v1.0.0 (*https://oreil.ly/mCs3b*) protocol to encode and propagate DID document updates.

The biggest challenge for various autonomic identifier systems will be interoperability. Schemes like did:keri, which encode the underlying identifier system inside a framework that agents already understand, make it easier to support them. In an ideal world, Alice can use peer DIDs, Bob can use KERI, and Carol can use did:orb and they'll all still be able to interact with each other securely.

Cryptographic Identifiers and the Laws of Identity

Compared to traditional identifiers, cryptographic identifiers comply more fully with the Laws of Identity (from Chapter 4) than do traditional identifiers. Autonomic identifiers are especially adept at creating identity systems that meet the requirements of the laws:

User control and consent
> All the cryptographic identifiers discussed in this chapter are designed to be controlled by their users (or the user's guardian) and to support autonomy for their subject. The specifications for these identifiers create boundaries of control and assign control over various activities to appropriate roles.

Minimal disclosure for a constrained use
> Because autonomic identifiers do not use external systems to operate, they are inexpensive to create and use. As you've seen, it's feasible to create a different identifier for every relationship, reducing correlation and allowing the DID document to be customized to reveal only the information necessary for the relationship to have utility.

Justifiable parties
> Cryptographic identifiers are designed to operate without third-party administrators who intervene in the relationships they support. Only the parties necessary for the relationship to have utility need to be part of the interactions. Also, since the nature of autonomic identifiers allows us to create a different identifier for every relationship, cryptographic identifiers ensure that each party gets only the data they need.

Directed identity
> Public DIDs, like those registered on ledgers, function as omnidirectional identifiers. Peer DIDs and other autonomic identifiers function as unidirectional identifiers.

Pluralism of operators and technologies

The cryptographic identifiers discussed in this chapter are based on standards and aim for interoperability, allowing multiple operators and technologies to function together to meet the identity needs of people, organizations, and things. The realization of that vision is, of course, always in jeopardy, with new technologies constantly being invented and organizations jostling for economic advantage.

Human integration

Cryptographic identifiers are designed to be under the control of the individuals and organizations they identify, without an intervening administrative authority. Consequently, the human controllers are integral components in the creation, management, and use of these identifiers.

Consistent experience across contexts

Cryptographic identifiers put the human controller at the center of the experience and give them choices about the technologies they will use. As a result, the controller sees a consistent user experience, even in vastly differing contexts and uses.

In the discussion of directed identity in Chapter 4, you learned that while identifiers initially seem simple, designing them to have the properties we need can be difficult. Cryptographic identifiers give us the technology necessary to create useful identifiers that respect the Laws of Identity.

CHAPTER 15

Verifiable Credentials

One of the primary duties of an identity system is to allow the transfer of trustworthy, authenticated information. When we log in, the information is minimal—often just a username and password—and the authentication itself is the point. Other times, the identity system may be transferring information like profile information or authorizations.

In Chapter 4 you learned about the identity metasystem and its properties. Recall that an identity metasystem is a system upon which identity systems can be built. The metasystem provides the infrastructure for the identity systems built on top of it so that they have an encapsulating protocol that provides a unified user experience. The metasystem should provide user choice for autonomy, privacy, and flexibility. Modularity and polycentrism (more commonly called *decentralization*) ensure that the metasystem isn't controlled by a single organization. And because the information we need to recognize, remember, and respond to various entities is context-dependent and varies widely from one situation to the next, the metasystem must allow *polymorphic* data records (records that use different data schemas) to be defined.

Clearly, an identity system that is polycentric and polymorphic is much more flexible and capable than the traditional identity and access management (IAM) systems in use today, which provide only authentication and authorization services. But systems with the properties of the metasystem are not unfamiliar to us. We need only look at the rich system of credentials we use to make modern life possible. For example, Alice might have a driver's license and an employee ID. Both function in their specific context (driving or working) but also outside of it: Alice might use them in concert in a context outside driving or work, to prove she's over 21 and employed.

There's no central authority that decides what credentials can exist. Alice's grocery store might issue a loyal shopper card and the volunteer organization she helps with on weekends might give her a badge she can wear so clients know she's someone they can ask for help. When Alice goes to the movies, they issue a one-time use credential we call a *ticket*. A claim stub at the dry cleaner, a medical prescription, and a parking ticket are other examples of credentials. When Alice visits the doctor and fills out (for the thousandth time) her medical history, she's creating a *self-issued credential*.

There's simply no end to the types of credentials organizations or individuals might create for the huge variety of contexts in which they operate. The beauty of a credential-based identity system is its flexibility.

The Nature of Credentials

My use of the word *credential* to describe a movie ticket or medical history might make you scratch your head, if you've been conditioned to think of credentials as formal documents issued by organizations with special authority. A *credential* is a structured document containing claims. *Claims* are name-value pairs representing an *attribute* of some sort. Recall from Chapter 2 that attributes are statements about *what* the subject is, not *who*. A credential can contain many claims. Some claims might have multiple parts.

Figure 15-1 shows a driver's license. The license contains 19 claims, some with multiple parts. For example, claim 2 is the subject's name, Betty Nelson.[1] Claim 4 is a multipart claim that includes the license number and its issue and expiration dates. Claim 12 is restriction code. In this case, *A* means no restrictions, but other restrictions might require glasses or limit driving to daylight only.

In addition to the claims, the license also contains other information. The star in the yellow circle in the upper right corner indicates that the license complies with the US federal government's REAL ID Act, which, among other things, requires identity proofing of some of the claims, like address and date of birth. The picture is a biometric used to authenticate that the person presenting the license is the subject. On the reverse is a set of driving authorizations, which might include endorsements for motorcycle or commercial vehicle operation.

While this driver's license is a document issued by the State of Utah for a specific purpose, there is nothing that keeps Betty from showing it to anyone she wants. And there's nothing to keep others from trusting its claims. As a result, in the US, where there is no national ID credential, a state-issued driver's license is a root identity document that people use in many different contexts to prove things about themselves that have nothing to do with driving.

---

1 Names are attributes, not identifiers, since there can be many people with the same name.

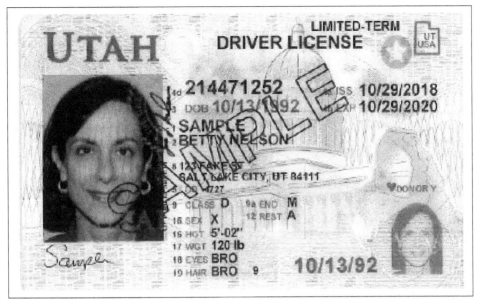

Figure 15-1. A driver's license

Roles in Credential Exchange

When the State of Utah issues a driver's license to Betty and she chooses to show it to, say, her employer so they can verify her address, this makes Utah, Betty, and her employer participants in a process called *credential exchange*.

Figure 15-2 shows the roles in a credential exchange and the relationship each party has with the other. Let's look more closely:

Credential issuer

The *credential issuer* is an entity who knows something about the credential subject and can issue a credential containing claims that encode that knowledge. The credential issuer might be the subject of the credential for self-issued credentials. The credential issuer *issues* the credential to the credential holder, who is usually also the subject.

Credential holder and subject

The *credential subject* is the entity that the claims in the credential are about. The *credential holder* is the entity that the credential is issued to and that keeps the credential for later use. For simplicity, the figure assumes the holder of the credential is also the subject, but it's possible in situations like guardianship, or where the subject is not a person, for the holder to be someone other than the subject.

Credential verifier

The holder shares the credential with the *credential verifier* to transfer the information contained in its claims. The verifier is relying on the claims made by the issuer. Depending on the situation, the verifier may also be concerned with authenticating the holder.

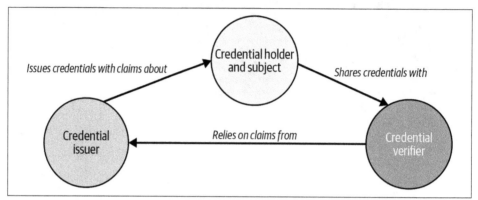

Figure 15-2. Roles in credential exchange

Throughout this chapter and for the rest of the book, I will frequently refer to these roles simply as *issuer, holder, subject*, and *verifier*.

Credential Exchange Transfers Trust

At the start of Chapter 7, I said, "Trust is at the heart of all relationships" and defined *trust* as reliance on the actions of another to benefit or protect the trustor in a specific domain. We must trust others—make ourselves vulnerable and incur risk—for relationships to have utility. People rely on the law, regulation, convention, and past experience to bridge the trust gap when they put themselves at risk.

But we also rely on one other important thing: what others say. Sometimes this is informal. We call that *reputation*. The other way we rely on what others say is using credentials. When Alice gives the ticket taker at the movie theater her ticket, she's providing evidence that the person at the box office says she paid. When she shows her driver's license to the human resources officer (HRO) at her job, she's providing evidence that the state claims she lives at a specific address.

We call these assertions of attributes *claims* because the verifier must believe that the issuer is telling the truth. Recall that in Chapter 7, we discussed *provenance* as the basis for trust. For example, the HRO will want to know who issued the credential, what processes they used to make the claims it contains, what source data they used, and what their reputation is. In the case of a driver's license, most employers will know they can rely on the provenance of its data because of the requirements for collection and the state's reputation.

The verifier will also want to know some specific things about the credential itself:

- That the identity of the issuer is authentic
- That the holder is the subject of the credential or possesses the authority to present the credential on the subject's behalf
- That the credential hasn't been tampered with
- That the credential hasn't been revoked

These properties of the credential and its presentation to the verifier inspire confidence that the credential has *fidelity*. Issuers go to great pains to ensure that credentials like driver's licenses and employee ID badges display who issued them, have pictures or another means to identify the subject, and are tamper-evident.[2] Knowing whether a given credential has been revoked (which is not the same as expired) is more difficult with physical credentials, but not impossible, depending on the degree of risk.

When the credential has fidelity and the verifier believes in its provenance, they can trust the claims it makes. Instead of the HRO trusting Alice to provide her address, the HRO's trust in the issuer of the driver's license allows them to reliably use the address data Alice provides using a credential. They are no longer vulnerable to Alice giving them a false address, and the employer's risk is thus reduced. The verifier's trust in the issuer has been effectively transferred to the holder, who is presenting the credential as evidence of some claim.

Verifiable Credentials

The W3C Verifiable Credential (VC) specification (*https://oreil.ly/_kqQp*) defines standards for creating digital credentials that have the features and convenience of physical credentials. Of course, being digital, they can also do a few things that are impossible for physical credentials to manage. For example, digital credentials can be more easily revoked and are designed to disclose only the information the verifier needs.

A VC is, in its simplest form, a signed JSON document that is structured in accordance with the specification's data model.[3] The data model includes required fields and how optional extensions can be added. In addition to providing the data model for

---

2 For example, driver's licenses used to be laminated in a way so that the top layer could be peeled back, the photo or other information changed, and then relaminated. Newer designs use a process where doing that would result in a license that had obviously been tampered with.

3 The JavaScript Object Notation, or JSON, is the syntax used to represent structured data in JavaScript. JSON has become a widely used method for representing structured data outside of JavaScript as well.

VCs, the specification also contains information about how presentations of the data in the VC are structured.

Because the VC specification provides latitude in how credentials are structured, represented, and understood, various groups have implemented several different credential types. The specification ties them together enough that software can understand and use different types. Daniel Hardman categorizes VCs along five dimensions (*https://oreil.ly/KoDdA*):

Schema

> The *schema* of a credential describes its structure. Is this credential a driver's license or a university transcript? This is an expected and useful difference. Unfortunately, differences might also exist in schema for credentials of the same type. Two universities might use two different schemas for transcripts, with one using a field named surname and the other using last_name. Avoiding a proliferation of schemas for credentials of the same type is a political problem, not a technical one. Schema.org has been standardizing schema for years, and Hyperledger Foundation and others are working on standardizations (*https://oreil.ly/ 8hYM1*).

Rendering

> The VC specification allows credentials to be represented in several formats. The base format, as I mentioned above, is a JSON document. The specification also allows VCs to be *represented*, or rendered as a string, in JSON-LD or JWT format. JSON-LD is a way of adding semantic metadata, using context links, to the fields in a JSON document; recall that you learned about JWT in Chapter 13, where they were used in OpenID Connect to encode claims.

Holder-Subject Relationship[4]

> Recall that a credential holder may or may not be the subject of the credential. For example, Alice would likely hold her own driver's license and thus be both the holder and subject. But she might also hold a credential for some device in her home where the subject is the device itself: for example, Alice might hold a credential for her laptop (more on this in Chapter 20). Credentials can also have more than one subject: for example, a birth certificate might list the baby, mother, father, and doctor as subjects. Again, the holder may or may not be one of the subjects.

Correlation

> You learned about correlation in Chapter 8, where we discussed the risk to privacy when multiple records can be linked to create a more complete picture of

---

4 Hardman calls this dimension the *perspective of the holder.*

their subject. Different presentation methods for credentials impact whether a subject of multiple credentials can be correlated. I'll discuss this in more detail later in this chapter.

Payment

Some credentials are free, and some are paid for. This is true in the digital realm as well as the physical. For example, my employer issues me an employee credential for free. Universities charge the requester (usually the subject) for transcripts. Besides free, there are four different pairwise payment vectors between the different roles in credential exchange: holder-pays-issuer, verifier-pays-issuer, verifier-pays-holder, and holder-pays-verifier. While there are scenarios where each of these may happen, the most common, and most straightforward to implement, is holder-pays-issuer. Figure 15-3 illustrates these potential payment relationships. I'll discuss the implications of this for credential marketplaces later in this chapter.

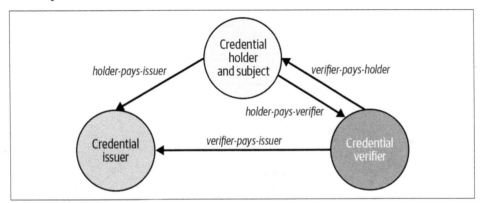

Figure 15-3. Payment relationships in credential exchange.

Different implementations of VCs have made different choices about whether they encourage, exclude, or require the possibilities in these five dimensions. The next section will discuss some of these choices. As you examine different technology stacks for VCs to determine how they mesh with your needs, keep these dimensions in mind.

Exchanging VCs

As you learned above, credential exchange involves three distinct roles: the issuer, the holder, and the verifier. The subject is involved in the exchange only if they also happen to also be the holder. Any party can play any role—and will, in the context of different interactions. In the discussion that follows, I'll use Alice, an individual, as the holder, and two organizations, Attester Org and Certiphi Corp, as the issuer and verifier, respectively. But keep in mind that an organization can also hold credentials and that people can issue and verify them.

Figure 15-4 shows the issuer, holder, and verifier in what's commonly called the *credential trust triangle*. In addition to the three parties I've already discussed, the figure also includes one or more of what's generically called a *verifiable data registry* (VDR). When you read about credential exchange, this is often described as a blockchain or ledger, but there's no requirement that it be a blockchain. Note that the term *verifiable* in the name refers to the data, not the repository. The repository could be a web server, if the data is signed and stored in a way that ensures that entities relying on it can verify its authenticity. The properties of the overall exchange process may vary depending on the architecture and properties of the VDR.

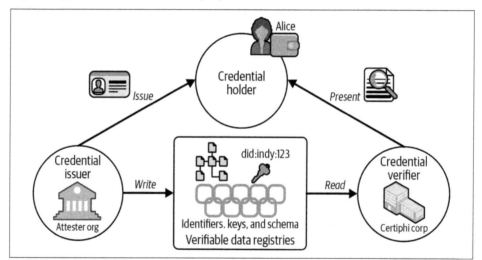

Figure 15-4. VC exchange

Issuing Credentials

Attester Org has written or discovered an acceptable schema for their credential. As you've learned, the schema describes the structure of the credential, including field names and acceptable values. Attester has also created a public DID that identifies Attester as the issuer. Attester may write a credential definition to a VDR that links the schema to the issuer DID it created. The public DID, schema, and definition could be written to different VDRs or the same VDR.

Attester creates a credential for Alice based on the credential definition it has written and issues it to Alice. The issuance ceremony will usually include some interaction with Alice, and Attester will likely need to authenticate Alice before it issues the credential to her. Alice and Attester may have exchanged peer DIDs and have an already established, mutually authenticated DID relationship. If so, Attester would use that

DID relationship to issue the credential to Alice. (I'll discuss the exact mechanism for this in Chapter 19.) Attester also might use more traditional authentication means (which you learned about in Chapter 11) and a TLS-protected channel to issue the credential. In the remainder of this book, I'll presume a DID-based interaction pattern unless otherwise noted.

Attester is issuing a *verifiable* credential. The VC specification requires that credentials include a *proof* that can later be verified by the verifier. The proof is a cryptographic signature. The proof might be *embedded*, meaning the proof is included in the credential, or *external*, meaning it is linked from the credential in some manner. The exact nature of the proof can vary in different representations; the fields in the proof section of the credential can vary as well, so long as they conform to the VC data model.

Holding Credentials

Alice uses a *digital wallet* to collect and hold VCs from various issuers and assemble them into presentations of verifiable data. She also has a software *agent* that engages in the ceremony with the issuer to request and accept the credential when Attester issues it.

The agent is responsible for managing Alice's DID-based relationships, like the one she has with Attester, while the wallet holds the keys for Alice's peer DIDs, public DIDs,[5] and other identifiers. The wallet provides a consistent user experience for Alice across contexts, in keeping with the law of consistent experience you learned about in Chapter 4. Alice doesn't think about keys and DIDs. Instead, her experiences revolve around establishing, maintaining, and terminating relationships and the ceremonies related to credential exchange. Chapter 18 and Chapter 19 discuss wallets and agents in detail. For simplicity, I'll use the term *wallet* for both the wallet and agent in this chapter unless the distinction is important.

Presenting Credentials

At some point, Alice uses her wallet to establish a relationship with Certiphi Corp. As part of bootstrapping or improving this relationship, Alice may need to give trustworthy information to Certiphi. For example, suppose Certiphi needs Alice's home address, and Attester's credential includes that information. The request for the address might happen in person (if Alice is visiting a Certiphi branch office), online (if Alice is filling out a web form), or over the phone (if Alice is talking to a customer support person).

---

5 People may or may not have public DIDs. Organizations will usually have public DIDs and also peer DIDs for each of the many relationships they have.

Regardless of the interaction scenario, Alice's experience is consistent: she gets a pop-up on her smartphone saying that Certiphi is requesting her address and offering a selection of the credentials that Alice holds which contain her address. She picks the one from Attester and her wallet presents the information it contains to Certiphi. Certiphi uses the proof method included in the credential to cryptographically verify the credential's authenticity.

From your experience in the physical world, you may think that the presentation involves Alice's wallet simply transferring the entire credential to Certiphi. After all, if you showed your driver's license to someone to prove your address, you'd hand it to them. The VC specification allows different presentation methods. While a complete transfer of the credential may occur in some presentations, that's not always the case. The next section will explore this in more detail, since it's one of the most important features of credential exchange.

Let's assume that Certiphi needs to know Alice's address and her current salary. She has another credential from her employer asserting salary information. Alice's presentation to Certiphi combines the data from Attester and from her employer to transfer both pieces of information at once.

An obvious question is: how does Certiphi get the required data to verify the credential? For example, if the credential presentation involves a digital signature, how does Certiphi find Attester's public key? This is why the VDR is important. The credential includes references to the information in a VDR, which may include the issuer's public DID and DID document, the credential definition, and the schema, depending on the presentation type (see below). Certiphi reads this information from the VDR and uses it to verify the credential.

The use of a VDR is important because it means that the verifier does not have to have a direct relationship with the issuer.[6] With other data transfer methods, Certiphi might need to have access to an API at Attester, agree to terms and conditions to use Attester's data, or even have a legal relationship with Attester. In contrast, VCs are designed so that the credential verifier needs no relationship with the issuer to verify the credential.

One important consequence of this is that it prevents what is commonly called the *phone-home problem* in privacy circles.[7] By design, Attester does not know where

---

6 The VC specification does *not* require the use of a VDR, but VC methods that do not use a VDR cannot preserve holder privacy as well as those that do.

7 In computer security, *phoning home* is the process of an application contacting its maker's computer to provide information. This might be welcome (your smartphone reporting its location so you can find it if it's missing) or unwelcome, such as hacking (a virus reporting its findings to its creator) or surveillance (like tracking cookies do in ad-supported sites).

Alice presents the credential; it consequently can't track Alice as she uses the credential in web applications and interacts with different people and organizations.

Credential Presentation Types

The nature of credential presentation is an important part of the VC specification. A VC presentation is designed to package and securely transmit data from one or more credentials in a way that allows the verifier to ascertain the authorship of the data. A presentation is usually about one subject, but this need not always be the case: for example, a credential presentation about a development team or board of directors might include information from credentials about different subjects.

A verifiable presentation contains three things:

Presentation metadata
> Metadata includes a required `type` property that identifies the data structure as a verifiable presentation and several optional properties, including an `id` for the presentation and a URI for the `holder` making the presentation.

Verifiable credentials
> The credentials are an optional list of VCs, or data derived from VCs, in a cryptographically verifiable way.

Proofs
> Proofs are included in the presentation so that the verifier can use the proofs to verify the authenticity of the credentials or derived data.

The specification provides many options for how to present a credential. For clarity, I'm going to classify them into two broad categories and discuss the properties of each: *full credential presentation* and *derived credential presentation*.

Full Credential Presentation

As the name suggests, *full credential presentations* include the entire credential. For presentations that involve more than one credential, each referenced credential is included. This is similar to how we present credentials in the physical world. If Alice is taking out a loan at Certiphi Bank, she'll show any documents they require in their entirety: her driver's license, employment verification, and so on.

To see how a full credential presentation works, let's examine how a VC is used in a presentation. Here is an example credential (modified from Example 1 in the VC specification) that asserts that the subject, Alice, is an alumna of Example University:

```
{
  // set the context, which establishes the special terms we will be using
  // such as 'issuer' and 'alumniOf'.
  "@context": [
```

```
    "https://www.w3.org/2018/credentials/v1",
    "https://www.w3.org/2018/credentials/examples/v1"
  ],
  // specify the identifier for the credential
  "id": "http://example.edu/credentials/1872",
  // the credential types, which declare what data to expect in the credential
  "type": ["VerifiableCredential", "AlumniCredential"],
  // the entity that issued the credential
  "issuer": "https://example.edu/issuers/565049",
  "issuanceDate": "2010-01-01T19:23:24Z",
  // claims about the subjects of the credential
  "credentialSubject": {
    // identifier for the subject of the credential
    "id": "did:example:ebfeb1f712ebc6f1c276e12ec21",
    // assertion about the subject of the credential
    "alumniOf": {
      "id": "did:example:c276e12ec21ebfeb1f712ebc6f1",
      "name": [{
        "value": "Example University",
        "lang": "en"
      }]
    }
  },
  // digital proof that makes the credential tamper-evident
  "proof": {
    // the cryptographic signature suite that was used to generate the signature
    "type": "RsaSignature2018",
    "created": "2017-06-18T21:19:10Z",
    // purpose of this proof
    "proofPurpose": "assertionMethod",
    // the identifier of the public key that can verify the signature
    "verificationMethod": "https://example.edu/issuers/565049#key-1",
    // the digital signature value (a JWT)
    "jws": "eyJhbGciOiJSUzI1NiIsImI2NCI6ZmFsc2UsImNyaXQiOlsiYjY0Il19..TCYt5X
      sITJX1CxPCT8yAV-TVkIEq_PbChOMqsLfRoPsnsgw5WEuts01mq-pQy7UJiN5mgRxD-WUc
      X16dUEMGlv50aqzpqh4Qktb3rk-BuQy72IFLOqV0G_zS245-kronKb78cPN25DGlcTwLtj
      PAYuNzVBAh4vGHSrQyHUdBBPM"
  }
}
```

Suppose Alice wishes to use this credential at Example University's website to purchase a T-shirt and receive the alumni discount. If the site, acting as credential verifier, accepts full credential presentations and Alice's wallet supports full credential
presentation, she might present this proof (modified from the VC specification's
Example 2):

```
{
  "@context": [
    "https://www.w3.org/2018/credentials/v1",
    "https://www.w3.org/2018/credentials/examples/v1"
  ],
  "type": "VerifiablePresentation",
```

```
// the verifiable credential issued in the previous example
"verifiableCredential": [{
  "@context": [
    "https://www.w3.org/2018/credentials/v1",
    "https://www.w3.org/2018/credentials/examples/v1"
  ],
  "id": "http://example.edu/credentials/1872",
  "type": ["VerifiableCredential", "AlumniCredential"],
  "issuer": "https://example.edu/issuers/565049",
  "issuanceDate": "2010-01-01T19:23:24Z",
  "credentialSubject": {
    "id": "did:example:ebfeb1f712ebc6f1c276e12ec21",
    "alumniOf": {
      "id": "did:example:c276e12ec21ebfeb1f712ebc6f1",
      "name": [{
        "value": "Example University",
        "lang": "en"
      }]
    }
  },
  "proof": {
    "type": "RsaSignature2018",
    "created": "2017-06-18T21:19:10Z",
    "proofPurpose": "assertionMethod",
    "verificationMethod": "https://example.edu/issuers/565049#key-1",
    "jws": "eyJhbGciOiJSUzI1NiIsImI2NCI6ZmFsc2UsImNyaXQiOlsiYjY0Il19..TCYt5X
      sITJX1CxPCT8yAV-TVkIEq_PbChOMqsLfRoPsnsgw5WEuts01mq-pQy7UJiN5mgRxD-WUc
      X16dUEMGlv50aqzpqh4Qktb3rk-BuQy72IFLOqV0G_zS245-kronKb78cPN25DGlcTwLtj
      PAYuNzVBAh4vGHSrQyHUdBBPM"
  }
}],
// digital signature by Alice on the presentation
// protects against replay attacks
"proof": {
  "type": "RsaSignature2018",
  "created": "2018-09-14T21:19:10Z",
  "proofPurpose": "authentication",
  "verificationMethod": "did:example:ebfeb1f712ebc6f1c276e12ec21#keys-1",
  // 'challenge' and 'domain' protect against replay attacks
  "challenge": "1f44d55f-f161-4938-a659-f8026467f126",
  "domain": "4jt78h47fh47",
  "jws": "eyJhbGciOiJSUzI1NiIsImI2NCI6ZmFsc2UsImNyaXQiOlsiYjY0Il19..kTCYt5
    XsITJX1CxPCT8yAV-TVIw5WEuts01mq-pQy7UJiN5mgREEMGlv50aqzpqh4Qq_PbChOMqs
    LfRoPsnsgxD-WUcX16dUOqV0G_zS245-kronKb78cPktb3rk-BuQy72IFLN25DYuNzVBAh
    4vGHSrQyHUGlcTwLtjPAnKb78"
}
}
```

The structure of the full credential presentation is straightforward. Note that the proof for the presentation is different from the proof for the credential. Both provide a reference to a public key. The credential proof's key is from the DID document associated with the DID for the issuer of the credential. The proof of the credential is a signature over the credential that allows anyone to ensure it hasn't been tampered with.

The key for the presentation is retrieved from the DID document of the holder (who is also the subject in this case). This key also proves ownership of the subject DID, if the signature on the presentation (proof in the preceding example) matches the credential subject. The proof of the presentation allows the verifier to ensure the integrity of the presentation. When the verifier sends for the needed information, they provide additional fields called challenge and domain, which are included in the proof. This helps to prevent other parties from *replaying the presentation*—that is, presenting the credential to someone other than the intended verifier.

To understand the privacy implications of full credential presentation, consider this modification to the credentialSubject field in the example to include other claims:

```
"credentialSubject": {
    "id": "did:example:ebfeb1f712ebc6f1c276e12ec21",
    "overallGPA": {
      "id": "did:example:f4566e12ec21ebfeb1f712abd564",
      "GPA": [{
        "value": "2.43"
      }]
    },
    "degrees": {
      "id": "did:example:bc45afe12ec21ebfeb1f7128fed4",
      "undergraduate": [{
        "BA": "Communications",
        "Honors": "NONE"
      }]
    },
    "alumniOf": {
      "id": "did:example:c276e12ec21ebfeb1f712ebc6f1",
      "name": [{
        "value": "Example University",
        "lang": "en"
      }]
    }
}
```

Now Alice's credential not only identifies her as an alumna but also asserts her grade point average (GPA) and earned degrees. She may not care if the campus website sees her GPA, but she might not want that information revealed to LinkedIn when she uses the credential to prove she has a degree in communications. In a full credential presentation, that data would be included no matter where Alice presents her Example University credential. In the physical world, this is not a big problem, because we don't expect the cashier at the campus store to remember all the data from every ID she checks. But computers have no such limitation.

Not all credentials need privacy protection that individuals require. Suppose Example University has a credential from the state or national government saying it's a legitimate educational institution. Or consider a business with a credential from the state saying it's been legally registered. In these cases, and many others involving organizations, the data in the credential is not private, but public. Example University can share its credential without concern that it's giving away too much data.

Derived Credential Presentation

Recall that one of the Laws of Identity you learned about in Chapter 4 is *minimal disclosure for a constrained use*. This law requires that the verifier constrain their use of the data to those uses to which the holder has agreed. Minimal disclosure also requires that the holder's wallet not reveal any more than the data needed for that use.

Going back to our example, if Alice uses her credential to prove that she's an alumna of Example University at the school's website, her alumna status is the only data that should be revealed, even if more data is included in the credential. When she uses it at LinkedIn to prove she has a degree in communications, there's no need to reveal her GPA, which should be kept back.

Alice can't simply break up the credential, since that will destroy its verifiability via the proof it contains since the proof is based on a digital signature over the entire credential. She could get different credentials from Example University for different purposes, but too many combinations would quickly force Alice's wallet to manage an explosion of credentials as the number of claims in the full credential grows.

Fortunately, you've already learned in Chapter 9 about a technology that can form the basis for a solution to this dilemma: zero-knowledge proofs (ZKPs).[8]

ZKPs and credentials

ZKPs aim to reduce the amount of extra information that the verifier can derive from a presentation. For purposes of applying ZKP to credentials, be aware that we're not usually talking about a pure ZKP, which can be characterized as a *zero-knowledge proof of knowledge* (ZKPOK). For example, Alice could prove she knows the circumference of the earth without disclosing the actual value.

Instead, credential presentations are more often concerned with proving actual values (Alice's birthday), derived values (Alice's age), or even predicates on a value (Alice is

---

[8] This section describes a method of creating derived credentials called *AnonCreds*. AnonCreds are based on a specification (*https://oreil.ly/s9lHF*) developed at Hyperledger as a means of supporting derived credentials in the Indy and Aries projects. Other groups are pursuing other types of derived credentials with technical differences, but the overall design goals are similar. I'll focus on one method here since the point is for you to understand the goals and broad techniques rather than the specific cryptographic methods.

over 18). Recall that techniques like *zkSNARK* allow a prover (the holder) to generate a noninteractive proof that the verifier can authenticate. The proof says that the holder knows a value that satisfies a function, C, that the verifier supplied. This allows for a much broader class of data exchange than a ZKPOK would allow. Note that this technique allows the verifier to state what it wants to know in the function C; the impetus is on the holder to prove the values that satisfy that requirement if they can. This provides bounds for constrained use and evidence of consent.

The use of zkSNARK techniques to produce derived attributes that match exactly what the verifier needs, and no more, is a key method for protecting Alice's privacy and ensuring derived credential presentations meet the law of minimal disclosure for a constrained use.

Correlation and blinded identifiers

One of the privacy risks of full credential presentation is that identifiers are correlatable. In the previous example, the credential's subject is identified by a DID. If Alice is identified in the credential by the peer DID she gave to Example University, then there's no way for the verifier, LinkedIn for example, to verify the signature in the proof. They can't resolve the DID and get the DID document. As a result, full credential presentation requires identifiers that are known to both the issuer and the identifier.

A universal identifier greatly increases an organization's ability to correlate data about an individual, so if credential presentation requires a universal identifier, then we are required to trade away privacy to get authentic data. Minimal disclosure is for naught if the verifiers can simply cooperate behind the holder's back to assemble a dossier.

In Chapter 14, you learned that privacy is enhanced if participants in a relationship use a different identifier for each relationship. Derived credentials can solve this problem using *blinded identifiers*, which ensure the verifier can know that the credential was issued to the presenter, without the issuer and verifier having to share an identifier for the holder.

To use blinded identifiers, Alice's wallet generates a large random string called a *link secret* and wraps it in a cryptographic commitment. Think of the cryptographic commitment as an envelope. Alice can prove she knows the value of the link secret inside the commitment in zero knowledge, without revealing it, similar to how she could prove she knew the code to unlock the door in Alibaba's Cave (see Chapter 9). Alice blinds the commitment by including a random value, called a *nonce*, with the secret when she generates the cryptographic commitment. This means Alice can generate as many different blinded versions of the link secret as needed simply by changing the value of the nonce.

Alice never reveals the link secret to any credential issuers or verifiers. When Example University offers a credential to Alice, she provides them a one-use identifier in the form of a blinded link secret she generates just for Example University. When Alice is offered an employee ID as a VC, she gives her employer yet another blinded version of the same link secret.

The use of blinded identifiers in derived credentials has two purposes. First, when Alice presents information from her credentials, she doesn't provide a raw identifier. Alice can prove, in zero knowledge, that she knows the link secret contained in the blinded identifier that the credential has been issued to. As a result, the verifier gets proof that the credential was issued to Alice. Second, Alice can prove that information from her university credential and her employee ID credential are about the same subject, linking the data in the two credentials. Even though each credential contains a different blinded identifier, Alice can prove that the source credentials are all linked by the same link secret, and thus the same person, without giving the verifier a correlatable identifier.

Figure 15-5 shows the process of presenting a derived credential as a ZKP, based on credentials issued to Alice from Example University and her employer.

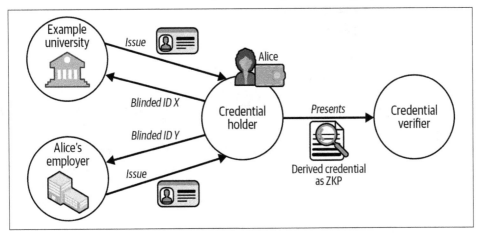

Figure 15-5. Deriving credentials

The derived credential contains only the attributes produced by the ZKP. These attributes might be derived from the data the credential holds (for example, *Alice is over 18*, instead of her actual birthday). Each derived attribute is individually signed so they can be verified and used independently of the overall derived credential.

Combining ZKP with cryptographically blinded identifiers to create a derived credential presentation reduces Alice's privacy risk and allows her to clearly offer her consent to data sharing, without limiting the verifier's ability to get authentic data about her.

Answering Trust Questions

VCs inspire confidence, but many of the transactions people and organizations conduct need more than confidence. This section explores this idea in more detail and shows how verifiers can apply some of the tactics just discussed to gain trust in a transaction.

Suppose Alice's employer uses VCs and issues a credential that includes claims about her employment status and current salary. Later, Alice applies to her bank for a loan. Before the bank processes the loan, she needs to prove to them that she's employed and that she makes at least $75,000 per year. The bank can have confidence in the authenticity of the credential and verify it using cryptography.

But the bank really wants to know whether Alice is actually employed, not just that she has some data, verifiable or not, showing that someone *says* she is. Answering that question requires promises that the credential exchange can't keep. Here are a few things Alice or the bank might want to know:

- Alice is a real person.
- The employer is a real business.
- The bank is a real bank.
- Alice is employed by the employer.
- The salary figure comes from the employer.

Here are some techniques that Alice and the bank can use to answer these questions:

Alice is a real person.
> In this exchange, the bank knows Alice is a real person because they have a relationship with her, memorialized by the exchange of peer DIDs. As part of their new customer process, they performed a Know Your Customer (KYC) process as mandated by law. They associate the results of that with the DID Alice gave them to represent her. So, when Alice contacts them with that DID, they know the account belongs to a real person.

Alice's employer is a real business.
> Knowing the employer is a real business is a little harder. Even if the bank knows the employer by name, how do they know that the credential was issued by that entity? There are several options. For instance, the employer could have published their public DID on their website or some other well-known location, or the employer could provide the bank, or Alice, with a credential proving its business registration status.

The bank is a real bank.

Alice knows the bank is a real bank for the same reason the bank knows Alice is a real person: the DID exchange. One of the important and often overlooked benefits of a DID exchange is that each side can authenticate the other. How did Alice know the bank was a real bank when she opened her account? If she did it physically, then she knew through personal knowledge. If she enrolled online, she might have asked them for a credential or other proof.

Alice is employed by the employer and has a certain salary.

The credential itself is making the claim that Alice is employed by the employer and that her salary is a certain amount. The bank would need to verify the credential by validating the credential schema and definition and understanding what they mean. This validation process is internal to the bank.

Many of the ways the bank and Alice come to trust each other depend on the governance of the identity ecosystems in which they are participating. In Chapter 22, I'll discuss the role governance plays in different identity architectures and how it inspires trust.

The Properties of Credential Exchange

The most important property of VCs is their ability to transmit verifiable data. As you've seen, our physical-world experience with credentials can limit our thinking about what a credential can be. Any structured data can be transmitted in a VC.

Transferring data in a VC provides more authenticity than merely using a secure connection like TLS. TLS can ensure that the transmission is confidential. If certificates are used by both parties, TLS can also give assurance about who sent and received the message. In that sense, it's like interactions supported by DIDs. In addition to those properties, data transmission via VC provides the following assurances that have confidence in the authenticity of the data:

- The data has not been tampered with during, before, or after transmission. The VC represents a verifiable packet of data that protects the integrity of the data regardless of how many times or over what channels it is transmitted.
- The data is about a specific subject.
- The presentation is being made by the holder to whom the credential was issued.
- The data is from a specific issuer who can be identified. The basis for trusting the credential relies on this identification.
- The data is structured according to a schema that can provide help in understanding what the data means.

Credential-based digital identity is *bottom up*. Using credentials, people and organizations can prove things about themselves from what they and others say about them. This is a decided contrast to the *top-down* approach, where people establish an account with an identity provider and then attach attributes to it. The bottom-up approach provides more flexibility and autonomy.

The trust model for VCs has six important characteristics that mirror how credentials work in the offline world:

Credentials are decentralized and contextual.
> There is no central authority for all credentials. Every party can be an issuer, a holder, or a verifier. VCs can be adapted to any country, any industry, any community, or any set of trust relationships.

Credential holders are free to choose which credentials to hold and present.
> People and organizations are in control of the credentials they hold (just as they are with physical credentials), and they determine what to share with whom. This autonomy is a key property of credential exchange. As a result, credential-based identity can be more flexible, more fair, and more inclusive than other forms of identity.

Credential issuers decide on what data is contained in their credentials.
> Anyone can write credential schemas to a VDR. Anyone can create a credential definition based on any of these schemas.

Verifiers make their own trust decisions about which credentials to accept.
> There's no central authority who determines what credentials are important or which are used for what purpose.

Verifiers do not need to contact issuers to perform verification.
> Credential verifiers don't need to have any specific technical, contractual, or commercial relationship with credential issuers. The VDR provides the means to verify the credential without these relationships.

Credential exchange provides for cross-domain authenticity.
> Credential presentation transfers trust from one domain to another. When Alice presents data from her driver's license to the bank, she's giving the bank evidence that they can trust the attributes she's providing because someone the bank trusts, the state, has authenticated them.

Credential presentation allows attributes from multiple sources to be combined at the holder's discretion. For example, in addition to her relationship with her employer and bank, Alice likely has a relationship with the state and holds credentials it issues, such as her birth certificate and driver's license. She might hold credentials from her university representing her transcript. The list of potential credentials that Alice could hold is long and depends on her relationships online and offline. She could have hundreds of relationships and associated credentials in her wallet. She can use any of these, in any combination, to prove things about herself (potentially with minimal disclosure) to any other party who accepts them.

VC Ecosystems

Performing decentralized credential exchange online is novel. As I've discussed, VC exchange gives people and organizations the freedom and autonomy to create authentication, authorization, and data exchange systems that meet their specific needs. The result is a flexible identity architecture that covers thousands of use cases, even ad hoc use cases, while supporting choice and privacy for identity owners.

Chapter 4 defines an *identity metasystem* as a system for building identity systems. DIDs and VCs are the twin pillars of an identity metasystem that has the properties that Cameron said an identity metasystem would provide:

Encapsulating protocol
The DID and VC specifications define protocols for interaction. An *encapsulating* protocol allows other protocols to be defined on top of it. This section will show how a general protocol for credential exchange encapsulates all possible identity systems. Chapter 19 provides details on how protocols can be defined on the metasystem.

Unified user experience
Credential exchange is a familiar ceremony. Regardless of what kind of identity system you build on the metasystem, credential exchange will happen the same way. Consequently, people using an identity system built on the metasystem know what to expect. As a result, they can intuitively understand how to interact in any given context.

User choice
The definition of consistent ceremonies on top of well-defined protocols like DIDs and VCs allows people and organizations to select appropriate service providers and features. The metasystem allows context-specific scenarios to be built and can even support ad hoc interactions that no one anticipated.

Modular
Again, the DID and VC standards and their enabling protocols provide for the rise of interchangeable components that are built and operated by various parties.

Polycentric (decentralized)
As discussed above, the identity metasystem is decentralized. Anyone can generate as many DIDs as they need without anyone's permission. Anyone can function as a credential issuer, holder, or verifier. Each makes their own decisions about how they will use credentials.

Polymorphic (different data schema)

Allowing anyone to define credentials with any schema for any reason ensures that credentials can meet the needs of different contexts and vary according to the needs of the situation.

Figure 15-6 shows the how the metasystem is used to support identity systems built on top of it. This is often referred to as the *self-sovereign identity (SSI) stack*.

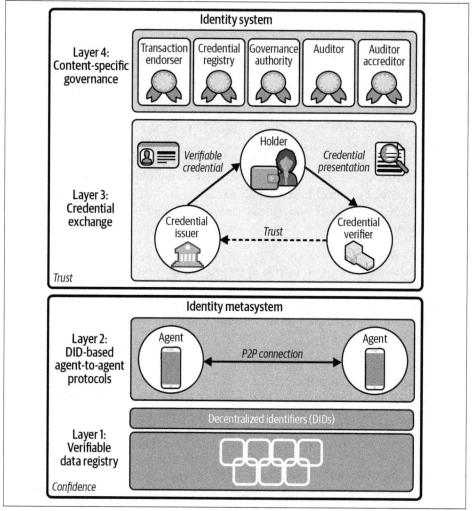

Figure 15-6. SSI stack

The stack in Figure 15-6 is divided into top and bottom halves. The bottom half, labeled "Identity Metasystem," contains two layers. Layer 1 is comprised of VDRs and DID exchange—the foundational cryptographic technologies. Layer 2 is comprised of the DID-based agent-to-agent protocols—including, as you'll learn in Chapter 19, the protocols for credential issuance and presentation. The identity metasystem inspires cryptographic confidence.

The top half of Figure 15-6 represents a single identity system built on the metasystem. Any number of identity systems could be built on the metasystem, but they must all follow the model in this diagram. Each identity system has two layers as well. Layer 3 is a context-specific credential exchange and makes up the schema and credential definition for a specific use case. Layer 4 is the trust framework and may include several actors, as shown in the diagram. These actors all serve to create trust in the identity system, which is defined by the decisions and actions of its architects and operators. The goal is to inspire the required level of trust.

Identity systems are meant to manage relationships. The nature of the relationship determines the precise need for data that must be transferred in a verifiable manner. Businesses define credential-based identity systems all the time, even if they don't think of them as such. Every form or official piece of paper and every bundle of data transmitted in a workflow is a potential credential. Here are a few examples of common credentials, many of which we've used in examples:

- Employee badges
- Driver's licenses
- Passports
- Wire authorizations
- Credit cards
- Business registrations
- Business licenses
- College transcripts
- Professional licenses, both government and private

Here are some others that typically may not be thought of as credentials, but they fit the definition:

- Invoices and receipts
- Purchase orders
- Airline or train tickets
- Boarding passes
- Certificates of authenticity for works of art or other valuables
- Gym (or any) membership cards

- Movie (or any) tickets
- Insurance cards
- Insurance claims
- Titles for real property, vehicles, and so on
- Certificates of provenance for drug ingredients, non-GMO food, ethically sourced coffee, and so on
- Prescriptions
- Fractional ownership certificates for high-value assets
- CO_2 rights and carbon-credit transfers
- Contracts

Since even a small business might issue receipts or invoices, have customers who use the company website, or issue employee credentials, most businesses will define at least one credential. Others will need many more. There are potentially tens of millions of different credential types. Many will use common schemas, but each credential from a different issuer constitutes a different identity credential for a different context.

Beyond the simple credentials listed above, redeemable credentials could allow issuers to ensure that a credential can be presented only N times (a feature often referred to as *double-spend-proofing*). Redemption use cases include clocking in and out of work, voting in an election, posting an online review, or redeeming a coupon.

Alternatives to DIDs for VC Exchange

In my discussions of VCs, I assume DIDs are the underlying identifier in this and later chapters. This implies that DIDComm, the messaging protocol based on DIDs that I'll discuss in detail in Chapter 19, underlies the exchange of verifiable credentials. This does not have to be the case.

The OpenID Foundation has defined protocols on top of OAuth for issuing (*https://oreil.ly/j8-QP*) and presenting (*https://oreil.ly/aHrjZ*) credentials.[9] These specifications support the W3C VC data model specification and support both full credential and derived credential presentations. The OpenID specifications allow for other credential formats as well, such as the ISO mobile driver's license (*https://oreil.ly/cuPmX*).

---

9 Recall that OpenID Connect is based on OAuth.

In addition to defining specifications for issuing and presenting credentials, OpenID for Verifiable Credentials (OpenID4VC) introduces a wallet for holding and presenting credentials.[10] Recall from Chapter 13 that OpenID Connect (OIDC) redirected interactions between the IdP and RP through a user agent under a person's control, but there was never an OIDC-specific user agent. The addition of a wallet allows OpenID4VC to break the link that has traditionally existed between the IdP and RP in the form of federation agreements and an interaction protocol wherein the IdP always knew when a person used OIDC to authenticate at the RP. OpenID4VC offers direct presentation using the wallet.

Extending OAuth and OIDC to support the issuance and presentation of VCs provides for interactions richer than merely supporting authentication. All the use cases we've identified for VCs are available in OpenID4VC as well.

In addition to using the OpenID4VC wallet with a traditional OIDC IdP, OpenID has also added a specification for Self-Issued OpenID Providers (SIOP) (*https://oreil.ly/ tMK-i*). A SIOP is an IdP that is controlled by the entity who uses the wallet. A SIOP might use DIDs, KERI, or something else for identifiers. The SIOP allows Alice to control the identifiers and claims she releases to the RP. As with DIDs, a SIOP-based relationship between the RP and Alice is not intermediated by an external, federated IdP as it is in the traditional OIDC model.

When Alice uses a wallet that supports OpenID4VC and SIOP to present credentials to an RP, the Alice has a relationship with the RP based on a self-issued identity token she creates. SIOP allows Alice to make presentations independent from any specific IdP. As a result, she can present credentials from any issuer to the RP, not just information from a single IdP as is the case in traditional OIDC.

Like any other credential presentation, the RP can verify the fidelity of the credential cryptographically. This can include knowing that it was issued to the wallet Alice is using to make the presentation. The RP also gets the identifier for the credential issuer inside the presentation and must decide whether to trust the information presented.

To make fidelity and provenance determinations for the credential, the RP will need the public key for the credential issuer as is the case with any credential verification. The VDR in an OpenID4VC credential exchange might be a ledger or other decentralized data store if the presentation uses DIDs, or it might be obtained using PKI or web pages accessible under a domain name controlled by the issuer. Depending on how this is done, the credential issuer might or might not know which credentials the

---

10 For details on OpenID4VC, I recommend the introductory white paper from the OpenID Foundation: *OpenID for Verifiable Credentials: A Shift in the Trust Model Brought by Verifiable Credentials* (*https://oreil.ly/ xgf9S*) (June 23, 2022).

RP is verifying. As I mentioned earlier, the design of the VDR plays a large role in whether credential exchange has all the properties I've discussed in this chapter.

OpenID4VC is an important example of alternatives to DIDComm in VC exchange thanks to OIDC's large deployment base and developers' familiarity with its underlying protocols and procedures. Because the W3C specification for VCs does not specify an underlying mechanism for exchanging credentials, others are possible. If you need an alternative, be sure to carefully vet its design to ensure it meets your privacy, authenticity, and confidentiality requirements.

A Marketplace for Credentials

Earlier in this chapter, I discussed payments for credentials. While it's impossible to anticipate every possible credential use case that includes a reciprocal exchange of value, looking at a few use cases is instructive. The following use cases are just for the `holder-pays-issuer` pattern, but other patterns, like `verifier-pays-issuer`, are possible and would expand the list even more.

Driver's licenses
> Driver's licenses are an excellent example of a credential people pay for. There are 112 million licensed drivers in the US alone. If we assume each license costs $30 and is renewed every five years, that's almost $700 million a year in fees for driver's licenses.

Memberships
> Gym memberships are just one example of a membership credential where the credential holder pays the issuer. Gym membership revenues in the US in 2018 were $32 billion, according to Wellness Creative (*https://oreil.ly/d1h0P*). There are many more membership types that could be built on top of the identity metasystem.

Movie tickets
> Movie tickets are another credential that is bought. The *Hollywood Reporter* (*https://oreil.ly/AMfzm*) puts 2021 global box office sales at $21.3 billion, which is 50% less than prepandemic numbers.

Airline tickets
> Airline tickets are a special kind of purchased credential. According to the International Air Transport Association (*https://oreil.ly/--ECv*), there were 4.1 billion airline passengers in 2017. The US Department of Transportation Bureau of Transportation Statistics (*https://oreil.ly/YK4y6*) reports that average airfare was $347 that same year. So, we can estimate that worldwide airfare was about $1.4 trillion in 2017.

Online Sales

Online sales can be accomplished using a holder-pays-issuer credential exchange. If paying for a receipt issues a credential equal to the amount of the order, you could view all ecommerce payments as a form of paid credential issuance. Linking payment to a credential and placing it inside a wallet that emphasizes relationships and credential management may make credential-related payments an important component of online retail—a significant one, given that US online retail sales were $870.78 billion in 2021 (*https://oreil.ly/awfLI*).

These are just a few potential use cases where credentials and value are exchanged. While not all of these will necessarily come to pass, it's easy to conclude that the potential marketplace for credentials is in the trillions of dollars. The identity metasystem, with its mutually authenticated messaging protocol, is an excellent platform for supporting workflows that involve commercial credential exchange.

VCs Expand Identity Beyond Authn and Authz

Physical credentials are indispensable in modern society, and the VC standard brings their power to the digital world. More importantly, when we combine VCs with DIDs, we get an identity metasystem that meets the requirements set out in Chapter 4 and aligns with the Laws of Identity. In the next chapter, we will explore identity architectures to understand the properties of traditional identity systems and the identity metasystem.

CHAPTER 16

Digital Identity Architectures

John Locke was an English philosopher who thought a lot about power: who had it, how it was used, and how it impacted the structure of society. Locke's theory of mind forms the foundation for our modern ideas about identity and independence. He argued that "sovereign and independent" was humanity's natural state and that we gave up freedom, our sovereignty, in exchange for something else: protection, sociality, and commerce, among others. This grand bargain forms the basis for any society.

This question of power and authority is vital in identity systems. You might ask, "What do I give up, and to whom, in a given identity system?" More succinctly: who controls what? Chapter 2 introduced the ideas of *locus of control* and *self-sovereign identity*. An SSI system, you may recall, defines the things over which an entity (person or organization) has complete control, along with the rules of engagement for its relations with other entities. This chapter explores the details of three abstract identity architectures to better understand the locus of control in each.

In addition, we'll consider the legitimacy of each architecture for online interactions. Wikipedia defines *legitimacy* (*https://oreil.ly/gs7fw*) as "the right and acceptance of an authority, usually a governing law or a regime." While the idea of legitimacy is most often applied to governments, I think we can rightly pose legitimacy questions about technical systems, especially those that function in an authoritative manner and have large effects on people and society. If an identity system is not seen as legitimate, the people and organizations using it will be unable to act because others will not recognize their actions as authentic. This is one of the primary reasons identity systems use the authentication methods discussed in Chapter 11.

The Trust Basis for Identifiers

Previous chapters have discussed *identifiers* and their properties. Identifiers help a computer system to remember and discover things—anything from people to devices to database records. You've learned that identifiers are convenient handles that uniquely name the thing being remembered within a namespace. The namespace gives context to its identifiers, since the same string of characters might be a phone number in one system and a product ID in another.[1]

Figure 16-1 shows the relationships between a controller, authentication factors, and an identifier. An identifier is issued to or created by a controller who, by virtue of knowing the authentication factors, can make authoritative statements about it. For example, when Alice authenticates to her employer's financial system, she is claiming an identifier within that system. People, organizations, software systems, devices, and other things can be controllers. The controller might be the subject of the identifier, but not necessarily. As you learned in Chapter 11, the authentication factors might include a password, key fob, cryptographic keys, or something else. The strength and nature of the *bindings* between the controller, authentication factors, and identifier determine the strength and nature of the relationships built on top of them.

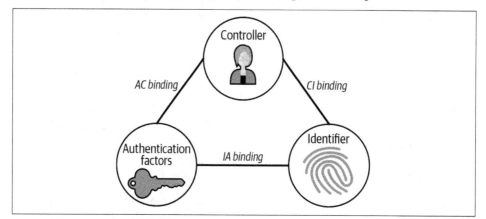

Figure 16-1. Binding of controller, authentication factors, and identifiers in identity systems

To understand why that's so, I introduce the concept of a *root of trust*.[2] A root of trust is a foundational component or process in the identity system on which other

---

1 The terminology and classification of architectures in this section were inspired by Sam Smith's paper "Key Event Receipt Infrastructure" (*https://oreil.ly/ZKfET*).

2 In cryptographic discussions, *root of trust* often refers to a hardware device or some trusted hardware component in the computer. My usage is broader and refers to anything relied on for trust in the identity system.

components of the system rely and whose failure would compromise the integrity of the bindings depicted in Figure 16-1. A root of trust might be primary or secondary, depending on whether it is *replaceable*. Primary roots of trust are irreplaceable. A system may have several roots of trust depending on its architecture. Together, the roots of trust form the *trust basis* for the system.

An identity system's trust basis underlies a particular *trust domain*: the set of digital activities that depend on the binding of the controller to the identifier. For example, binding a customer to an identifier allows Amazon to trust that the actions linked to the identifier are authorized by the customer (controller). Another way to look at this is that the strength of the CI (controller-identifier) binding determines the risk that Amazon assumes in honoring those actions.

The strength of the CI binding depends on the strength of the AC (authorization factor-controller) and IA (identifier-authorization factor) bindings. Attacking either of those bindings reduces the trust we can place in the CI binding and increases the risk that actions taken through a particular identifier are unauthorized.

Identity Architectures

We can broadly classify identity systems into one of three types, based on their architecture and primary root of trust:

- Administrative
- Algorithmic
- Autonomic

Both algorithmic and autonomic are SSI systems. They are distinguished by their trust bases. Some SSI systems use one or the other, and some (like the Sovrin Network (*https://oreil.ly/A53bi*)) are hybrid, employing each for different purposes. We'll discuss the properties of the trust basis for each of these to understand the comparative legitimacy of SSI and traditional administrative ones.

These architectures differ in who controls what. This difference, which is called *control authority*, is the primary factor in determining the basis for trust in each architecture. The entity with control authority takes action through operations that affect the creation (inception), updating, rotation, revocation, deletion, and delegation of the authentication factors and their relation to the identifier. How these events are ordered and their dependence on previous operations is important. The record of these operations is the source of truth for the identity systems.

Administrative Architecture

Identity systems with an *administrative architecture* rely on an administrator to bind the identifier to the authentication factors. The administrator is the primary root of trust for any domain with an administrative architecture. Almost every identity system in use today has an administrative architecture, and their trust basis is founded on the administrator. The administrator is not necessarily a person. Often, it's a software system written to implement rules and policies that the organization controlling it enacts.

For example, when Alice sends an email to *bob@example.com*, she wants Bob to receive it and no one else. She relies on the administrator of *example.com* to ensure the authenticity of the binding between Bob and his email address. In most cases, we are required to *trust* the administrator of *example.com* rather than have *confidence* in the binding, because the system that authenticates Bob is not transparent.

Figure 16-2 shows the interactions between the controller, identifier, and authentication factors in an administrative identity system, including the role of the administrator, and the impact these have on the strength of the bindings. The controller usually generates the authentication factors by choosing a password, linking a two-factor authentication (2FA) mechanism, or generating keys.

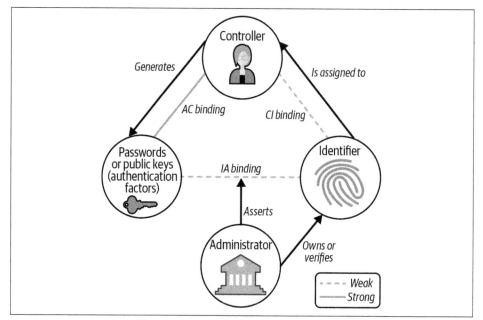

Figure 16-2. The trust basis in administrative identity systems

Even though the identifier might be the controller's email address, phone number, public key, or other ID, the administrator "assigns" the identifier to the controller, because it is their policy that determines which identifiers are allowed, whether they can be updated, and their legitimacy within the identity system's domain. The administrator controls the identifier within the domain. The administrator also asserts the IA binding. An employee's mistake, a policy change, or a hack could affect either the IA or CI bindings. Consequently, these bindings are relatively weak (indicated by the dotted lines in the figure). Only the AC binding is strong—because the controller generates the authentication factors.[3]

The administrator's primary duty is to authoritatively assert the binding between the controller and identifier. Authoritative control statements about the identifier are recorded in the administrator's database, the *source of truth* in the system, and are subject to change by software, employees, and hackers. The administrator might be an ecommerce site that maintains an identity system as the basis for its customers' accounts. In this case, the binding is private, and its integrity is of interest only to the site and its customers. Alternatively, the administrator might provide federated login services. In this case, the administrator is asserting the CI binding in a semipublic manner to anyone who relies on the federated login. A certificate authority is an example of an administrator who publicly asserts the CI binding, signing a digital certificate to that effect (as you learned in Chapter 9).

Because the administrator is responsible for binding the identifier to both the authentication factors and the controller, the administrator is the primary root of trust and thus the basis for trust in the overall system. Regardless of whether the binding is private, semipublic, or public, the integrity of the binding entirely depends on the administrator, the security of their infrastructure, the strength of their policies, the performance of their employees, and their continued existence. The failure of any of those can jeopardize the binding, rendering the identity system unusable.

Algorithmic Architecture

Identity systems that rely on a verified data registry (VDR) have an *algorithmic architecture*. As you learned in the previous chapter, any algorithmically controlled, distributed, consensus-based data store, such as a public or private blockchain, a distributed filesystem, or a database, might serve as a VDR. Of course, the registry is more than algorithms. Algorithms are embodied in code, written by people, running on servers. How the code is written, its availability to scrutiny, and how it is executed all impact the trust basis for the system. "Algorithmic" is just shorthand for all of this.

---

3 Note that this is not making a statement about the strength of the authentication factors themselves—the controller might pick weak passwords. But even with weak passwords, CA binding is still strong because the controller generates them.

Figure 16-3 shows how the controller, authentication factors, identifier, and VDR are bound in an identity system with an algorithmic architecture. As in the administrative identity system, the controller generates the authentication factors, albeit usually in the form of a public-private key pair associated with a DID or other cryptographic identifier. The controller holds, but never shares, the private key. The public key, on the other hand, is used to derive an identifier. Both the public and private keys are registered on a VDR. This registration is the inception of the CI binding, since the controller can use the private key to assert their control over the identifier. Anyone with access to the VDR can determine algorithmically that the CI binding is authentic.

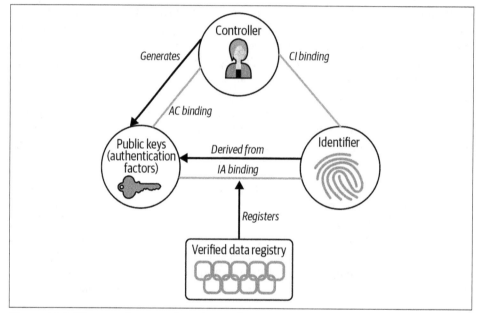

Figure 16-3. The trust basis in algorithmic identity systems

In an *algorithmic* identity architecture, the controller makes authoritative control statements about the identifier using their private key. Events that mark creating, updating, or retiring the keys are recorded in the VDR. For DIDs, these are structured as a DID document, as shown in Chapter 14. The VDR becomes the source of truth for anyone interested in the binding between the identifier and public key.

For VDRs based on public blockchains, no single party has the power to unilaterally decide how to make, modify, or delete the records binding the keys and identifier. Furthermore, as you learned in Chapter 9, the blockchain orders blocks, so that anyone inspecting the blockchain can verify which actions happened first. Public blockchains rely on code executed in a decentralized manner to make decisions about the binding records. The nature of the algorithm, the way the code is written, and the methods and rules for its execution all impact the integrity of the algorithmic identity system and, consequently, any bindings that it records.

Autonomic Architecture

Identity systems with an *autonomic* architecture function similarly to those with an algorithmic architecture. As shown in Figure 16-4, the controller generates a public-private key pair, derives a globally unique identifier, and shares the identifier and the currently associated public key with the other parties in the relationships the controller is joining.

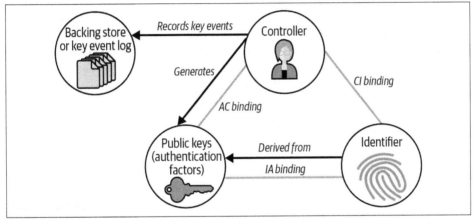

Figure 16-4. Trust basis in autonomic identity systems

The controller uses their private key to authoritatively and nonrepudiably sign statements about the operations on the keys and their binding to the identifier, storing those in an ordered backing store or key event log.[4] One of the important realizations that make autonomic identity systems possible is that the backing store must be ordered *only* in the context of a single identifier, not globally. So, a VDR is not needed to record operations on identifiers that are not public. Remember, the backing store can be shared with and verified by anyone who needs it.

Using a digital signature, the controller can respond to challenges cryptographically, with digital signatures that prove their control of the identifier. As I discussed in Chapter 14, its self-authentication and self-authorization capabilities make the identifier self-certifying and self-managing. As a result, no external third party, not even a VDR, is needed for the controller to manage and use the identifier and prove the integrity of the bindings between themselves and the identifier. Thus anyone (any

---

4 Recall that peer DIDs use a backing store, and KERI uses a key event log. Both are similar in purpose. For simplicity, I'll just say "backing store," since that term is the most generic.

entity) can create and establish control over an identifier namespace in a manner that is independent, interoperable, and portable without recourse to any central authority. Autonomic identity architectures thus rely solely on *self-sovereign authority*.

Autonomic identity architectures have several advantages over algorithmic and administrative architectures. Let's look at them in more detail:

Self-certification
Autonomic identity architectures are self-certifying, so there is no reliance on a third party.

Self-administration
An identity system based on an autonomic identity architecture is administered by the controller. No other parties need to be involved. Even if the controller takes advantage of cloud services for portions of the job, those can be built to be interoperable and substitutable, so that the controller is the sole administrator with access to keys and other vital information.

Low cost
Autonomic identifiers are virtually free to create and manage.

Security
Because the keys are decentralized, there is no trove of secrets that can be stolen. That's not to say that an individual can't be hacked, but there's no large database of secrets to attract hackers like there is for administrative identity architectures.

Regulatory compliance
Since autonomic identifiers need not be publicly shared or stored in an organization's database, regulatory concern over personal data can be reduced. As you learned in Chapter 8, GDPR and other regulatory regimes can significantly increase the overhead cost for identity systems.

Scalability
Autonomic identifiers scale with the combined computing capacity of all participants, not some central system. The decentralized nature of their architectures gives them virtually unlimited scaling capabilities.

Independent
Autonomic identity architectures do not depend on any specific technology. Many different cryptographic algorithms and processes can be used to implement them.

Offline operation
Systems based on an autonomic identity architecture can operate peer-to-peer without the need to be online. The backing store and deltas ensure that peers can operate without relying on an external system. Consequently, Alice can form

an autonomic peer relationship with a door in a basement without WiFi, through Bluetooth, and both Alice and the door can verify the authenticity of their interactions.

Algorithmic and Autonomic Identity in Practice

We are all familiar with administrative identity systems. We use them all the time. Algorithmic and autonomic identity architecture are less familiar.

There are several parallel development efforts supporting algorithmic and autonomic identifiers. As you may recall, the DID specification is the primary guide to algorithmic identifiers that live on a VDR. It provides for many DID methods that allow DIDs to live on a variety of data stores. DIDs have a number of important properties that make them ideal as algorithmic identifiers: they are nonreassignable, resolvable, cryptographically verifiable, and decentralized.

When used as algorithmic identifiers, DIDs allow the controller to cryptographically make authoritative statements about the identifier and the keys to which it is bound by recording statements in the VDR. The VDR provides a record of the key events that anyone with access to it can evaluate. The record is usually public, since the purpose of putting it in a VDR is to allow parties who don't have an existing relationship to evaluate the identifier and its linkage to the controller and public keys.

Most digital relationships are peer to peer and should use autonomic identifiers. Peer DIDs and KERI are two leading proposals for autonomic identifiers that have the required properties to function as the basis for an autonomic identity system.

Recall that verifiable credential (VC) issuers need a public identifier. That public identifier will be algorithmic and stored in a VDR. Algorithmic identifiers allow for public discovery of identifier properties when relationships are not peer to peer.

As an example of how algorithmic and autonomic identity systems interact, consider the Sovrin Network. The Sovrin ledger (serving as the VDR) records public DIDs for VC issuers. But people, organizations, and things form relationships using peer DIDs without a need for the ledger. This hybrid use of both algorithmic and autonomic identity systems was designed so that credential exchange would be practical, secure, and private, while reducing the correlation that might occur if individuals used a few DIDs on a public VDR.

Going one step further, the entities participating in a relationship based on autonomic identifiers will still use an account system to link those identifiers to other information the enterprise needs to remember to give the relationship utility. The account system is, by nature, administrative. Chapters 18 and 19 will discuss the nature and operation of relationships in SSI systems and show how these three architectures work together.

Comparing Identity Architectures

Table 16-1 summarizes the trust bases of administrative, algorithmic, and autonomic architectures. Notice that the locus of control, source of truth, root of trust, and trust basis differ for each.

Table 16-1. Trust bases of administrative, algorithmic, and autonomic identity architectures

Property	Administrative	Algorithmic	Autonomic
Locus of control (control authority)	Administrator	Controller	Controller
Source of truth	Administrative database	VDR	Backing store
Root of trust	Administrator	VDR	Controller
Trust basis	Administrator	VDR/Cryptography	Cryptography

For administrative architectures, the administrator is directly in control of all four of these. In an algorithmic architecture, the controller is the locus of control because the VDR is designed to allow the controller to be in charge of all key operations. Sometimes this is done using special administrative keys instead of the keys associated with the identifier. The organizations or people operating the VDR should *never* have access to the keys necessary to unilaterally change the record of operations. No third party is involved in autonomic identity architecture. The players are all software systems directly under the control of the controller.

Table 16-2 summarizes the architectural properties of administrative, algorithmic, and autonomic identity systems. We can see from the evaluation that algorithmic and autonomic architectures are decentralized while the administrative system has a single point of failure—the third-party administrator. Administrative systems also rely on privacy by policy, rather than on building privacy-preserving features into the architecture. And, as Chapter 8 discussed, all too often, privacy is in direct conflict with the administrator's profit motive. This can lead to weak privacy policies.

Table 16-2. Architectural properties of administrative, algorithmic, and autonomic identity systems

Property	Administrative	Algorithmic	Autonomic
Centralized	Yes	No	No
Relies on human for validation	Yes	No	No
Private by design	No	Yes	Yes
Relies on operational third party	Yes	Yes	No

Power and Legitimacy

I started this chapter talking about power and legitimacy. In a blog post entitled "The Most Important Scarce Resource Is Legitimacy" (*https://oreil.ly/8cuay*), Vitalik Buterin, creator of the cryptocurrency Ethereum, discusses why legitimacy is crucial for the success of any decentralized endeavor, noting that the "Bitcoin and Ethereum ecosystems are capable of summoning up billions of dollars of capital, but have strange and hard-to-understand restrictions on where that capital can go."

These "strange and hard-to-understand restrictions" are rooted in legitimacy. Decentralized systems must be considered legitimate to thrive. Their legitimacy is tied to how well the systems and the people enabling them, like programmers and miners, are seen to be following the rules, both written and unwritten. Legitimacy isn't a technical issue; it's a social one.

With respect to legitimacy, constitutional scholar Philip Bobbitt says:

> The defining characteristic...of a constitutional order is its basis for legitimacy. The constitutional order of the industrial nation state, within which we currently live, promised: give us power and we will improve the material well-being of the nation.[5]

In other words, legitimacy comes from the constitutional order: the structure of the governance and its explicit and implicit promises. People grant legitimacy to constitutional orders that meet their expectations by surrendering part of their sovereignty to them.

From the discussion in the chapter and the summary tables above, you can see that power—their locus of control—is held very differently in these three architectures. In an administrative system, the administrator holds all the power. Chapter 17 will argue that the architecture of an identity system directly impacts the quality and utility of the digital relationships it supports. Specifically, the power imbalance inherent in administrative identity systems yields anemic relationships. In contrast, the balance of power engendered by SSI systems (both algorithmic and autonomic) yields richer relationships, since all parties can contribute to it.

Clearly, administrative identity systems have legitimacy—if they didn't, no one would use or trust them. As new architectures, algorithmic and autonomic systems have yet to prove themselves through usage. But, as Bobbitt says, we can evaluate each architecture in terms of the promises it makes and how well it does in fulfilling the purposes of any identity system: recognizing, remembering, and relying on other parties in the relationship. These are largely a function of the trust basis for the

---

5 Philip Bobbitt, *The Garments of Court and Palace: Machiavelli and the World That He Made* (London: Atlantic Books, 2013).

architecture and the specific choices made when implementing a system within a given architecture.

Administrative systems promise an account that the controller can use to act so long as it's permitted by the administrator. They also usually promise that these accounts will be secure and private. But people and organizations are increasingly concerned with privacy, and seemingly daily news reports of security breaches are chipping away at that legitimacy. The privacy promise is often quite limited. Since the administrator is the basis for trust, administrative systems allow the administrator to recognize, remember, and rely on the identifier, depending on the overall security of the administrator and its systems. But the account holder does not get any support from the administrative system in recognizing, remembering, or relying on the administrator. The relationship is slanted toward the administrator, an idea I'll explore in detail in the next chapter.

SSI systems promise to give anyone the means to create online relationships securely and privately, and to trustworthily share self-asserted and third-party-attested attributes with whomever they chose using VCs. These promises are embodied in the property I've called *fidelity*. To the extent that algorithmic and autonomic identity systems deliver on these promises, they are seen as legitimate.

Both algorithmic and autonomic identity systems provide strong means for recognizing, remembering, and relying on identifiers in the relationship. Participants in an algorithmic system must trust the VDR as the primary root of trust and the trust basis. Clearly, our trust in the VDR will depend on many factors, including the code used to implement it and the governance process that controls its operation.

The trust basis for autonomic identity systems is cryptography. This implies that digital key management is an important factor in their legitimacy. If people and organizations cannot easily manage the keys in such a system, they will not trust it.

Hybrid Architectures

In this chapter, I've explored the high-level architectures of the identity systems in use today, as well as new designs that promise richer, more authentic online relationships, better security, and more privacy. By exploring the trust bases that arise from these architectures, we've analyzed the legitimacy of these architectures as a basis for online identity. A hybrid system that combines algorithmic public identifiers with autonomic private identifiers can provide a universal identity layer for the internet. This could increase security and privacy, reduce friction, and provide new and better online experiences.

CHAPTER 17

Authentic Digital Relationships

How do we change the culture? In a blog post titled "Architecture Eats Culture Eats Strategy" (*https://oreil.ly/0eyca*), Tim Bouma, director of Verification and Assessments, CIO Strategy Council, points out that the old Peter Drucker management chestnut that "culture eats strategy for breakfast" (*https://oreil.ly/rV36C*) leaves this question open. Bouma argues that architecture (in the general sense, not necessarily computer architecture) is an upstream predator to culture, in that it is a powerful force that drives culture and therefore determines what strategies will succeed—or, more generally, what use cases are possible.

Bouma points to examples as diverse as the flying buttress and the printing press to make his point. He says:

> I am of the belief that to focus on real and lasting change, it is little better than a Sisyphean effort to craft a strategy in the hope that it will change the culture. According to our management guru, Peter Drucker (and my own experience), that won't happen. The better approach is to focus on those architecture things (organization-related things) that will force a lasting change. That lasting change will then force a culture change, and strategy will naturally follow.

My thesis in this chapter follows on this insight: since identity systems are the foundational layer of the digital ecosystem we operate in, the architecture of digital identity systems drives online culture, the nature of online relationships, and, ultimately, what we can do and what we can't.

In Chapter 5, I proposed that we build digital identity systems to create and manage relationships—not identities—and discussed the nature of digital relationships in terms of their integrity, life span, and utility. Since identity systems are built to create and manage relationships, their architecture deeply influences the kinds of relationships they support—their culture. And the quality of those relationships determines whether we can live effective lives in the digital sphere.

This chapter builds upon the architectures I just discussed to explore how they can be used to build systems that support authentic digital relationships. Architectures give rise to culture, and culture is foundational to the types of relationships a system nurtures. Authentic relationships are necessary for us to live effective and enjoyable online lives.

Administrative Identity Systems Create Anemic Relationships

In the 1990s I was the founder and CTO of iMall, an early, pioneering ecommerce tools vendor. As early as 1996, we determined that we needed a shopping cart that not only kept track of a shopper's purchases in a single session but knew *who* the shopper was from visit to visit, so we could keep the shopping cart and prefill forms with shipping and billing addresses. These innovations required that we build an identity system. In the spirit of the early web, it was custom-built, written in Perl and storing personal data in Berkeley DB.

Every early web company had the same problem: they needed to know things about people, but there was no reliable way for people to tell the sites who they were. So each of those companies built their own identity system. Thus began my and your journey to collecting thousands of identifiers, as the web expanded and every single site needed its own way to know things about us.

Each of these identity systems is administrative, creating a relationship between the organization operating the identity system and the people who are their customers, citizens, partners, and so on. Administrative identity systems are, as you learned in the previous chapter, federation notwithstanding, largely self-contained and put the administrator at the center. Figure 17-1 illustrates their fundamental structure.

Administrative identity systems are owned. They are closed. They are run for the purposes of their owners, not the purposes of the people or things being administered. They provision and permission. They are bureaucracies for governing. They rely on rules, procedures, and formal interaction patterns. Need a new password? Be sure to follow the password rules. Fail to follow the company's terms of service? You could lose your account without recourse.

As I've discussed in previous chapters, administrative identity systems usually use a simple schema, containing only the attributes that the administrator needs to serve their purposes and reduce their risk. The problem I and others were solving back in the '90s was *legibility*, a term used to describe how administrative systems make things governable by simplifying, inventorying, and rationalizing things around them. Identity systems make people legible to offer them continuity and convenience while reducing risk for the administrator.

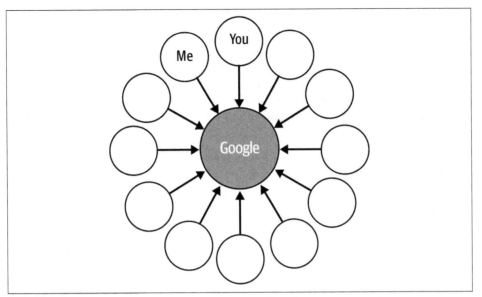

Figure 17-1. Administrative identity systems put the administrator at the center

Venkatesh Rao has written a helpful summary of James C. Scott's important book (*https://oreil.ly/RLdUA*) on legibility and its unintended consequences, *Seeing Like a State*.[1] Scott's book is primarily about the relationship between states and their citizens. But Rao makes the point that Scott's analysis applies to many modern organizations. As organizations seek to know certain, precise things about their customers— and only those things—they necessarily create bureaucratic relationships.

Because of their bureaucratic cultures, administrative identity systems give rise to systematic inequality in the relationships they manage. Every interaction you have online happens under the watchful eye of a bureaucracy built to govern the system and the people using it. The bureaucracy may be benevolent, benign, or malevolent, but it controls the interaction.

Designers of administrative identity systems do the *imaginative work* of assigning identifiers, defining the administrative schemas and processes, and setting the purpose of the identity system and the relationships it engenders. Because of the systematic imbalance of power, administrators can afford to be lazy. To them, everyone is structurally the same, being shoved into the same schema to enhance legibility. This is efficient, because they can afford to ignore all the qualities that make people unique and concentrate on just their business.

---

1 James C. Scott, *Seeing Like a State: How Certain Schemes to Improve the Human Condition Have Failed* (New Haven, CT: Yale University Press, 2020).

Meanwhile, the subjects of these bureaucracies are left to perform the *interpretive labor*, as David Graeber calls it (*https://oreil.ly/SD66a*), of understanding the system: what it allows or doesn't and how it can be bent to accomplish their goals.[2] Subjects have few tools for managing the relationships in administrative systems because each subject is a little different—not only technically, but procedurally. There is no common protocol or user experience, as the Laws of Identity remind us. Consequently, subjects have no way to operationalize the relationship except in whatever manner the administrator allows.

Since the architecture of administrative identity systems gives rise to a bureaucratic culture, you might wonder what kinds of strategies or capabilities that culture engenders. Quoting Graeber, from *The Utopia of Rules*:

> Cold, impersonal, bureaucratic relations are much like cash transactions, and both offer similar advantages and disadvantages. On the one hand they are soulless. On the other, they are simple, predictable, and—within certain parameters, at least—treat everyone more or less the same.[3]

Because of the architecture of current digital identity systems, the internet is best at transactional relationships. Our online relationships with ecommerce companies, social media providers, banks, and others are cold and impersonal, but also relatively efficient. In that sense, the web has kept its promise.

But the institutionalized frame of action that has come to define the modern digital world alienates its subjects in two ways. First, they are isolated and estranged from each other. There is no way for individuals to operate online as themselves—they are not digitally embodied. They are always within someone else's administrative domain. Second, they surrender control over their online activity and associated data within a given domain to its administrator.

The administrative architecture and the bureaucratic culture it creates have several unavoidable, regrettable outcomes:

Anemic relationships
> *Administrative culture creates anemic relationships* that limit the capabilities of the systems they support. For example, social media platforms are designed to allow people to form a link (symmetrical or asymmetrical) to others online—but only within the sphere of the system provider's administrative domain. The relationships in these systems are like two-dimensional cardboard cutouts of the real

---

2 Jack Ozzie called the similar work (*https://oreil.ly/jyk4J*) of weaving meaning around a seemingly disconnected set of messages *context assembly*. *Interpretive labor* emphasizes the real work required of participants.

3 David Graeber, *The Utopia of Rules: On Technology, Stupidity, and the Secret Joys of Bureaucracy* (London: Melville House, 2015), 152.

relationships they mirror. We inhabit multiple walled gardens that no more reflect real life than do the walled gardens of amusement parks.

Surveillance economy

As Shoshana Zuboff writes, administrative systems create a surveillance economy that relies on weak privacy provisions to exploit our online behavior as the raw material for products that not only predict but attempt to manipulate our future behaviors.[4] Many administrative relationships are set up to harvest data about our online behavior. The administrator controls the nature of these relationships, including what is allowed and what behavior is rewarded. The administrator uses that control to maximize its profit.

Single points of failure

In administrative systems, key parts of our lives are contained within the systems of companies that will inevitably cease to exist someday. All companies fail. As Craig Burton, a cofounder of Novell and the Burton Group, told me:[5]

It's about choice: freedom of choice versus prescribed options. Leadership shifts. Policies expire. Companies fail. Systems decay. Give me the freedom of choice to minimize these hazards.

Alternatives to Transactional Relationships

Transactional relationships focus on commercial interactions: usually buying and selling but not always that explicit. Transactional relationships look like business deals. They are based on reciprocity.

My relationships with Amazon and Netflix are transactional. That's appropriate and what I expect. But what about my relationships on Twitter? You might argue that those relationships are between friends, colleagues, or even family members. However, I classify them as transactional as well.

My relationships on Twitter exist within Twitter's administrative control, and Twitter facilitates those relationships to monetize them. Even though I'm not directly participating in the monetization and may even be unaware of it, it nevertheless colors the kind, frequency, and intimacy of the interactions I can have. Twitter builds its platform and makes its product decisions with the aim to facilitate and even promote the kinds of interactions that provide the most profit to it. My attention and activity are the product in the transaction. What I and my friends can do in our Twitter relationship is wholly dependent on what Twitter allows. Given this classification, the bulk of

---

4 This is the central thesis of *The Age of Surveillance Capitalism*, discussed in Chapter 8.

5 Private communication with the author, June 2019.

our online relationships are transactional. Very few are what we might call *interactional* relationships—except for email.

Email is one of the bright exceptions to this landscape of transactional, administrated online relationships. Exploring how email is different can help you to understand what alternatives to transactional relationships might be like. Let's explore what makes email different.

If Alice and Bob exchange emails, they both have administrative, transactional relationships with their respective email providers, but Alice and Bob's interaction does not necessarily take place within the administrative realm of a single email provider. The most obvious difference is that email is based on open protocols. This single, important difference has a profound impact on how email is used:

The user picks and controls the email server
> With an email client, Alice and Bob have a choice of multiple email providers. They can even run their own email server if they like.

The experience is consistent
> Mail client behavior is the same and the user experience is consistent, regardless of what server it connects to. As long as Alice's mail client is talking to a mail server that speaks the right protocol, it can provide her with the same user experience.

The client is fungible
> Alice can pick her mail client based on the features it provides, without changing where she receives email.

People can use multiple clients at the same time
> Alice can use one email client at home and a different email client at work and still see a single, consistent view of her email. She can even access her mail from a web client if she doesn't have her own computer or smartphone handy.

Only an email address is required
> Alice can send Bob email without knowing anything but his email address. None of the details about how Bob receives and processes email are relevant to Alice. She simply sends email to Bob's address.

Mail servers can talk to each other across ownership boundaries
> Alice might use Gmail while Bob uses Yahoo! Mail. Regardless, the mail still gets delivered.

People can change email providers easily
> Alice can use a custom domain even though she uses Gmail. She may have run her own server in the past. If Gmail went away, she could run her own server again. No one else needs to know or care about what server she is using.

In short, email was designed with the architecture of the internet in mind. Email is decentralized. It is open—not necessarily open source, but open in the sense that anyone can build clients and servers that speak its core protocols, IMAP and SMTP. As a result, email maximizes freedom of choice and minimizes the chance of disruption.

The features and benefits that email provides are the same ones we want for every online relationship. If you refer to the properties of the metasystem, outlined in Chapter 4, you'll see that email meets the requirements of a metasystem. These properties allow us to use email to create interactional relationships. An important insight is that systems that support interactional relationships can easily support transactional ones as well, where necessary. But the converse is not true. Systems for building transactional relationships don't readily support interactional ones.

I believe that email's support for richer relationships is a primary reason it has continued to be used despite the rise of social media and messaging platforms like Slack and Teams. I'm not saying email is the right platform for supporting modern, online interactional relationships—it's not. Email has obvious weaknesses: most prominently, it doesn't support mutual authentication of the parties to a relationship and therefore suffers from problems like spam and phishing attacks. Less often noted, but equally disqualifying, is that email doesn't easily lend itself to layering other protocols on top of it—creative uses of Multipurpose Internet Mail Extensions (MIME (*https://oreil.ly/i51KX*)) notwithstanding.

A modern answer to interactional relationships must support all kinds of relationships—from pseudonymous, ephemeral ones to fully authenticated ones. The remainder of this chapter (and, indeed, much of the rest of the book) will explore how we can use identity architectures to support interactional relationships.

The Self-Sovereign Alternative

Self-sovereign identity (SSI) systems offer an alternative to the administrative, transactional model. SSI supports richer, more interactional relationships. Rather than provisioning identifiers and accounts in an administrative system where the power imbalance assures that one party to the relationship can dictate the terms of the interaction, SSI is founded on peer relationships that are coprovisioned by the exchange of autonomic identifiers. This architecture implies that both parties will have tools that speak a common protocol.

In Chapter 16, I discussed how administrative, algorithmic, and autonomic architectures are frequently used together. Figure 17-2 shows this:

- Alice has peer relationships with Attester and Bob based on an *autonomic architecture*.
- Attester, Alice, and Bob use an *algorithmic architecture* for credential exchange.

- The peer relationship between Attester and Alice notwithstanding, Attester uses an enterprise agent and wallet that are *administrative* in nature. Alice's autonomy is enhanced by her standing as a peer, but Attester will still want to make her legible within its domain.

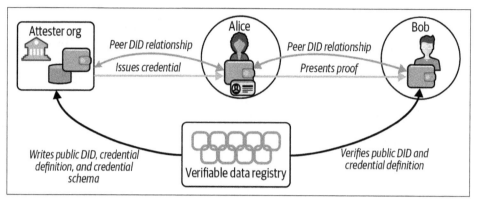

Figure 17-2. A mixed architecture identity metasystem

The interactions shown in Figure 17-2 are happening within the context of the identity metasystem I illustrated in Chapter 15 (Figure 15-6) in the discussion of credential exchange.

The mixed architecture of the identity metasystem has several important features:

It is mediated by protocol

Instead of being intermediated by an intervening administrative authority, activities in the metasystem use a peer-to-peer protocol. As I've discussed, protocols are the foundation of interoperability and allow for scale. By defining the rules for a set of interactions, protocols specify the kinds of interactions that can happen without being overly prescriptive about their nature or content, just as SMTP and IMAP do for email. Consequently, the metasystem supports a flexible set of interactions that can be adapted for many different contexts and needs.

It is heterarchical

Interactions in the metasystem are peer-to-peer rather than hierarchical. They are not just distributed but decentralized. Despite the administrative nature of Attester's system, Alice is largely immune from its effects. Decentralization enables autonomy and flexibility and assures that participants are independent from the influence of any single actor. No centralized system can anticipate all the various use cases, as the next section will discuss in more detail. And no single actor should be allowed to determine who uses the system or for what purposes.

It provides a consistent user experience
Consistent user experiences let people know what to expect so they can intuitively understand how to interact in any given situation, regardless of context.

It is polymorphic
The information you need in any given relationship varies widely with context. As you learned in Chapter 16, the content that the identity metasystem carries is flexible enough to support many different situations.

These architectural features give rise to a culture that I describe as *protocological* (founded on protocols). The protocological culture of the identity metasystem is:

Open and permissionless
The metasystem has the same three virtues of the internet that Doc Searls and Dave Weinberger enumerated as the acronym NEA (*https://oreil.ly/LVIiE*): *No one owns it. Everyone can use it. Anyone can improve it.* Special care must be taken to ensure that the metasystem is resistant to censorship, so that everyone has access. The protocols and code that enable the metasystem must be open and available for review and improvement.

Agentic
The metasystem allows people to act as autonomous agents under their self-sovereign authority. The most vital value proposition of SSI is autonomy—not being inside someone else's administrative system, where they make the rules in a one-sided way. Autonomy requires that participants in the system interact as peers, which the architecture of the metasystem supports.

Inclusive
Inclusivity is more than being open and permissionless. Its design must ensure that people are not left behind. For example, some people, like minors, cannot act for themselves for legal reasons. Others, like refugees or people with some disabilities, may need help from guardians. Support for digital guardianship ensures that those who cannot act for themselves can still participate.

Flexible
The metasystem allows people to select appropriate service providers and features. No single system can anticipate all the scenarios that will be required for billions of individuals to live their own effective digital lives. A metasystem allows for context-specific scenarios.

Modular
An identity metasystem can't be a single, centralized system from a single vendor with limited pieces and parts. Rather, the metasystem will have interchangeable parts, built and operated by various parties. Protocols and standards enable this. Modularity supports substitutability, a key factor in autonomy and flexibility.

Universal

Successful protocols eat other protocols until only one survives. An identity met-asystem based on protocol will have network effects that drive interoperability, leading to universality. This doesn't mean that one organization will have control; it means that one protocol will mediate all interaction and everyone in the eco-system will conform to it.

Supporting Authentic Relationships

SSI envisions a digital life that cannot be supported with traditional, transactional identity architectures. The mixed architecture of SSI and the culture that springs from it supports richer, more authentic relationships. SSI provides people with the means to operationalize their online relationships by providing them the tools to act online as peers and to manage the relationships they enter. I will explore how SSI allows people to operationalize digital relationships in detail in Chapter 19.

Furthermore, SSI, through protocol, allows ad hoc interactions that were not or can-not be imagined *a priori*. The following subsections give several examples.

Disintermediating Platforms

Many real-world experiences have been successfully digitized, but the resulting inter-mediation opens us to exploitation despite the conveniences. We need digitized expe-riences that respect human dignity and don't leave us open to being exploited for a company's advantage. For example, consider how the identity metasystem could be the foundation for a system that disintermediates food-delivery platforms.

Platforms service two-sided markets. We're all familiar with platform companies like Uber, Airbnb, Monster, eBay, and many others. Visa, Mastercard, and other credit card systems are platforms. Platforms are a popular Web 2.0 business model because they create an attractive way for the provider to extract service fees from one side, and sometimes both sides, of the market. They can have big network effects and tend toward natural monopolies.

Platform companies have been very successful in intermediating these exchanges and in charging exorbitant rents for what ought to be a natural interaction among peers. That's not to say platforms provide no value. The problem isn't that they charge for services, but that their intervening position gives them too much power to make mar-kets and set prices. Platforms provide several things that make them valuable to par-ticipants: a means of discovering relevant service providers, a system to facilitate the transaction, and a trust framework to help participants make the leap over the trust gap. Like compound interest, small advantages in any of these roles can have huge effects over time, as network effects exploit the advantage to drive participants to a particular platform.

During the 2020 COVID-19 lockdowns, the *New York Times* ran an article headlined "As Diners Flock to Delivery Apps, Restaurants Fear for Their Future" (*https://oreil.ly/ ukFE0*). This highlights the power that platforms have over their users:

> But once the lockdowns began, the apps became essentially the only source of business for the barroom restaurant he ran with a partner, Charlie Greene, in Columbus, Ohio. That was when the fees to the delivery companies turned into the restaurant's single largest cost—more than what it paid for food or labor.
>
> Pierogi Mountain's primary delivery company, Grubhub, took more than 40 percent from the average order, Mr. Majesky's Grubhub statements show. That flipped his restaurant from almost breaking even to plunging deeply into the red. In late April, Pierogi Mountain shut down.
>
> "You have no choice but to sign up, but there is no negotiating," Mr. Majesky, who has applied for unemployment, said of the delivery apps. "It almost turns into a hostage situation."

The standard response to these problems is more regulation. The article discusses some of the attempts that cities, counties, and states have made to rein in the fees that food delivery platforms charge. A better response is to create marketplaces that don't require an intermediary.

An identity metasystem supporting SSI provides a universal trust framework for building systems that can serve as the foundation for creating markets without intermediaries.

Figure 17-3 shows how different strategies for food distribution emerge from centralized or decentralized architectures for the underlying identity system. Disintermediating platforms requires creating a peer-to-peer marketplace on top of a metasystem. While the metasystem provides the means of creating and managing the peer-to-peer relationship, defining this marketplace requires determining the messages to be exchanged between participants and creating the means of discovery: how customers find a take-out restaurant, for example.

These messages might be simple or complex, depending on the market, and could be exchanged using verifiable credential (VC) exchange or something more specific to the problem. There might be businesses that provide discovery but don't intermediate, sitting to the side of the interaction and providing a service. For example, such a business might provide the service of allowing a restaurant to define its menu, create a shopping cart, and provide for discovery. However, the merchant could replace this service with a similar one, providing competition, because the trust interaction and transaction are happening via a protocol.

Building markets without intermediaries greatly reduces the cost of participating in the market and frees participants to innovate. Because these results are achieved through protocol, there's no need to create new regulations that stifle innovation and lock in incumbents by making it difficult for new entrants to comply. And these systems preserve human dignity and autonomy by removing administrative authorities.

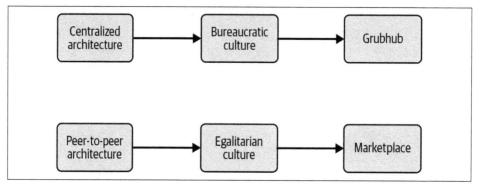

Figure 17-3. How architectures influence culture and strategy

Digitizing Auto Accidents

The interactions that occur after an auto accident are an excellent example of everyday activities that are difficult to bring into the administrative sphere. Because these interactions are ad hoc, large parts of people's lives have yet to be digitized. The identity metasystem enables the kinds of ad hoc, messy, and unpredictable interactions that happen all the time in the physical world.

I hope you've never been in an automobile accident, but even if you haven't, you know that this scenario involves a number of credentials as it plays out over days or even weeks. The following diagram shows some of the credentials that would be used in the initial investigation following a serious accident.

In this scenario, two drivers, Alice and Bob, have had an accident. Fortunately, no one was hurt, but the Highway Patrol has come to the scene to make an accident report. Figure 17-4 shows the interactions, mostly credential exchanges, that might happen.

Both Alice and Bob have several credentials in their digital wallets that will be important in creating the report. These include:

- Driver's licenses, issued by the Utah Department of Public Safety (DPS) in Alice's case and the California Department of Motor Vehicles (DMV) in Bob's
- Proofs of insurance issued by their respective insurance companies
- Vehicle origination documents issued by each vehicle's manufacturer
- Vehicle registrations issued by the Utah and California DMVs

In addition, the police officer has a badge from the Highway Patrol.

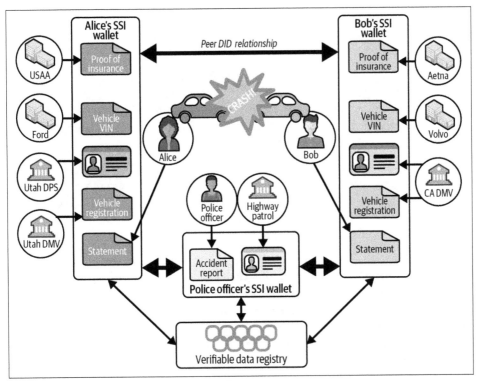

Figure 17-4. Credential uses in a car accident

Alice and Bob must make and sign statements, and the police officer creates an accident report.

Typically, each of these documents is on paper, or at best PDF. They are exchanged, copied, and filed away. The thought of doing it all digitally conjures visions of complex, special-purpose software systems with uneven acceptance by the various players and jurisdictions.

The SSI metasystem changes that by providing an open, decentralized system that supports the flexible exchange of standards-based VCs. Each of the credentials mentioned can be independently created by the appropriate issuer; held by Alice, Bob, and the patrol officer; and presented to any party they desire.

Here's how it would play out in an SSI metasystem. After the accident, Alice and Bob would use the SSI wallets on their phones to create a relationship.[6] When the officer arrives on the scene, Alice and Bob would each also create a relationship with the officer. They can use these relationships to exchange information based on the

---

6 The next two chapters discuss wallets and agents and the ways they interact in detail.

credentials they each hold. Alice and Bob create statements about what happened. The highway patrol officer creates an accident report. These are also credentials that can be shared between the parties.

Later, Alice and Bob will use credential exchange to share the accident report and information about one another with their respective insurance companies. They may enlist the services of mechanics and auto body shops, who will need to get information from the accident report. In turn, they will provide attestable statements about repair quotes and completion of repairs to the insurance companies.

The decentralized nature of the SSI metasystem allows all this information to be exchanged regardless of the fact that Alice and Bob are from different states that have different government organizations and structures. The exchange works even though Alice and Bob use different insurance companies. The exchange works regardless of whether they're in or out of their home states.

As you learned in the discussion of VCs, the receiver of each credential can verify that it hasn't been altered, that it is about the party who presented it, and that it was issued by a specific entity. Standards ensure that each party can issue their own credentials and that others can understand them. Standards and protocol allow the exchange to happen without anyone building a special-purpose vehicle accident reporting system and convincing all the players to participate in a closed ecosystem. The standards that enable the SSI metasystem allow each participant to work through an ad hoc scenario with finesse.

This scenario gets even more interesting if the cars are connected to the internet and have identities of their own. Data from a connected car may be relevant to the accident: for example, an accelerometer in Bob's car could have measured data points before and during the accident. This data might be included in his statement or the police officer's accident report. The vehicles themselves can have agents and consume, hold, or generate VCs. But the vehicles' identities are owned and controlled by the vehicle's owner—who might not be the driver involved in the accident. (Chapter 20 will discuss identity on the Internet of Things.)

Real life is complicated and messy. The only hope we have of enabling digital interactions that mirror activities in the physical world is with decentralized systems that allow each person, organization, and thing to act independently and autonomously.

Taking Our Rightful Place in the Digital Sphere

Devon Leffreto, developer and founder of kidOYO, said something in a 2020 blog post (*https://oreil.ly/p7APQ*) that made me think: "You do not have an accurate operational relationship with your Government."

My thought was "not just government." The key word is *operational*: people don't have many operational relationships at *all* online, except perhaps email. An operational relationship allows all parties to function independently. We have plenty of online relationships, but they are not operational because we are prevented from acting autonomously by their anemic natures. Our helplessness is the result of the power imbalance that is inherent in bureaucratic relationships.

The solution to the anemic relationships created by administrative identity systems is to provide people with the tools they need to operationalize their self-sovereign authority and act as peers with others online. Scenarios like the ones I just envisioned happen all the time in the physical world—in fact, they're the norm. When you dine at a restaurant or shop at a store in the physical world, you are not acting within some administrative system. Rather, as an *embodied agent*, you operationalize your relationships, whether long-lived or nascent, by acting for yourself. An identity metasystem provides people with the tools they need to be embodied in the digital world and act autonomously.

Time and again, various people have tried to create decentralized marketplaces or social networks, only to fail. I believe these systems fail because they are not based on a firm foundation that allows people to act in relationships with sovereign authority, mediated through protocol rather than platforms. We have a fine example of a protocol-mediated system in the internet, but we've failed to take up the daunting task of building the same kind of system for identity. Consequently, when we act, we do so without firm footing or sufficient leverage.

No one could live an effective life in an amusement park. Similarly, we cannot function as autonomous agents in the digital sphere within the administrative systems of the current Web 2.0 internet, despite their attractions. Ironically, in the 1990s the internet broke down the walled gardens of CompuServe and Prodigy with a protocol-mediated metasystem, but surveillance capitalism has rebuilt them on the web. The emergence of SSI, agreements on protocols, and the creation of a metasystem to operationalize them promises a digital world where decentralized interactions create lifelike online experiences. The identity metasystem, and the richer relationships that are its result, promise an online future that gives people the opportunity to act for themselves as autonomous human beings and supports their dignity so that they can live effective online lives.

CHAPTER 18

Identity Wallets and Agents

In the previous chapter I spoke of being *digitally embodied*. That phrase may strike you as odd. After all, the point of the internet is to move beyond the physical world. To understand what I mean, recall the example I've used elsewhere in this book to contrast our physical and digital experiences: eating at a restaurant.

The primary point I've made with that example is that in the physical world we function as peers, autonomously interacting with staff, our fellow diners, and the objects in the restaurant without the aid of an overarching administrative system that grants us those powers. In the digital world, we rarely interact as true peers.

If you're familiar with user experience (UX) design, you might be familiar with the term *embodied experience*. Designing for embodied experiences focuses on the kinds of interactions people have with computer systems that are based on nontraditional input and output methods: for example, a smartwatch responding to hand gestures or using haptics to signal the wearer. When I say *digital embodiment*, I'm speaking of something more fundamental than this. In digital embodiment, the embodied person (or organization) is an autonomous peer of other people, organizations, things, and systems in the digital world.[1]

Embodiment is related to the ideas in substance theory that I discussed in Chapter 1. Recall that substance theory holds that attributes are borne by an entity that doesn't depend on another entity to exist. Embodied digital beings—with substance—cannot

---

1 That said, these two ideas are not unrelated. As computing systems become more pervasive and the user experience becomes more ambient, the need for digital embodiment will become more and more critical.

arise from an administrative system because entities in such a system depend on the administrator for their existence.[2]

Embodiment requires tools. The primary tools we use to act in the digital world—browsers and apps—are not sufficient because of their underlying architecture. In the same way that the architecture of identity systems gives rise to bureaucratic culture, the architecture of the web—client-server—leads to inherent power imbalances. Peer-to-peer architectures may sometimes behave like client-server systems, but the reverse is not true. Client-server architectures are difficult to use to support peer-based relationships. The client is always, structurally, at the mercy of the server.

Chapter 16 discussed the concepts of *locus of control* and *control authority*: contrasting identity architectures, in part, by where the locus of control resides. This is another way to think of digital embodiment. Where can you exert control authority? Do you exert it using a single tool or many, creating fractured experience that you knit together only in your head? *Digital embodiment provides consistent ways for people to exercise control authority*. With the proper tools, people may be able to finally develop tacit knowledge in the digital world, overcoming one of the core problems of online identity that you learned about in Chapter 3.

This chapter discusses identity wallets and agents that are architected to support peer-to-peer relationships. I'll start by discussing the nature of wallets and agents, explore their security properties, and then show how the interaction patterns they support give people a locus of control with the power to create peer relationships and act autonomously online.

Identity Wallets

Our physical wallets are, historically, for holding currency. But that may be the least interesting use case for wallets. Many of the things people put in their wallets represent relationships they have and authorizations they hold. Most people don't often leave home without their wallet.

But the analogy to a physical wallet can only take us so far,[3] because as physical beings, our natural capabilities are multitude. In the digital world, we need tools for accomplishing almost anything useful. The name *wallet* for the software we use to interact digitally doesn't do the tool justice. In Chapter 15 I distinguished wallets from *agents*, tools for taking action. This chapter will further distinguish between these two tools and discuss how they work together.

---

2 Marshall McLuhan recognized this problem (*https://oreil.ly/HQOwA*) with respect to electronic media in general as early as 1977. He called it being *discarnate*.

3 I've heard various people object to the term *wallet*, but so far, no one has come up with anything else that has stuck, so for now, *wallet* is the word the industry uses.

A *digital identity wallet* is a secure, encrypted database that collects and holds keys, identifiers, and verifiable credentials (VCs). The wallet is also a digital address book, collecting and maintaining its controller's many relationships. The wallet is coupled with a software agent that speaks the protocols necessary to engage with others. Elsewhere in this book, I've used *wallet* as a shorthand for both *wallet* and *agent*, not distinguishing carefully between them. In this chapter, I'll be more specific about which tool performs which actions.

Alice's digital wallet might contain many things that she, in her capacity as controller, needs to store securely, including:

- Decentralized identifiers she has created or received, including public DIDs, peer DIDs, and KERI identifiers
- The backing store (or key event log) she uses to manage peer relationships
- Keys related to DIDs but perhaps others as well; SSH keys, for example, could be securely managed in a digital wallet
- PKI digital certificates and the private keys associated with them
- Keys and addresses for cryptocurrency
- VCs that Alice holds
- Receipts, warranties, and titles (some as VCs)
- PDFs or other digital representations of physical credentials for which Alice doesn't have proper VCs
- Usernames and passwords
- Personal data of all kinds that Alice uses to create self-issued VCs, fill out web forms, or simply store securely

Many people store these kinds of data in password managers or operating-system-specific tools like Apple's Keychain. People who hold cryptocurrencies also have one or more *cryptowallets* to store keys and addresses. These various *protowallets* suffer from several problems:

- They are often *proprietary systems*. As such, they suffer from many of the problems that I've delineated for administrative identity systems. The most limiting is that they can be used for only the purposes their owners allow.
- While they might be open, allowing other parties to store things in them, the types of use cases are *tightly controlled*.
- They use *inflexible data schemas* that limit the kinds of data they can store.
- They aren't built on open standards and thus *lock people into a specific platform*. I'd hate to reenter all the login data I have stored in my password manager, for example.

- They *lack consistent user experiences*. My password manager, keychains, smartphone wallet, and cryptowallets all behave differently. Sometimes even the same tool, like a keychain, differs from platform to platform despite being created by one organization.

An identity wallet overcomes these problems and has the added advantage of putting all of your important documents and relationships in one consistent place. Thus, many people will opt to move sensitive data from protowallets into identity wallets.

Other terms you might hear in the context of identity wallets are *personal data store* and *vault*. The variety of information that might be stored in an identity wallet may feel like a loose grab bag of digital stuff. The line between an identity wallet, a personal data store, and a vault is blurry, but they are distinguished by both their sizes and the types of data they contain. A vault might be a secure place to store *all* my digital stuff, while a personal data store holds all the information I have *about me* and an identity wallet is just the information I use to recognize, remember, and interact with others.

Another key distinction between these three stores is the level of protection they must offer. Figure 18-1 illustrates the levels of protection we might require for various kinds of personal information.[4] Information like my cryptocurrency keys needs much stronger and more robust security protection than the messages I've exchanged with Amazon or my friends. Personal data stores and vaults may get by with weaker protections for the data they hold than an identity wallet would. These distinctions provide guidance on the design and implementation of an identity wallet.

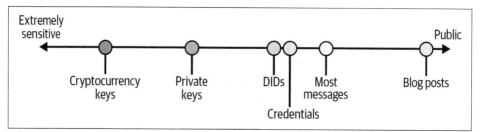

Figure 18-1. Relative protection requirements for personal data

Platform Wallets

The two big smartphone platform vendors, Apple and Google, each have a wallet built into the operating system and available to all users of the system. Since they're part of the platforms, I've labeled them *platform wallets*. These wallets suffer from

---

4 I adapted this figure from "Aries RFC 0050: Wallets" (*https://oreil.ly/52Pc3*) from the Hyperledger Aries Project, October 2021.

many of the same problems that browser keychains and password managers do, but they have some advantages and can provide increased utility since they're built in.

Platform wallets allow third parties to place their credentials from apps on the phone in the wallet.[5] For instance, they have provided the means of securely storing and using credit cards for many years now. Some of the first and most widely used third-party credentials for platform wallets were airline tickets. Figure 18-2 shows an airline boarding that Delta placed in my Apple Wallet.

Figure 18-2. An airline boarding pass

Boarding passes in a platform wallet offer great utility because travelers can present them in hurried, and harried, situations. The wallet can push notifications to the lock screen that make accessing them nearly instantaneous. I find this very convenient.

---

5 I refer here to credentials in the general sense; these are not compliant with the VCs standard.

Other businesses, even small ones like my local theater company, have started using similar tickets and passes.

The primary disadvantage of these wallets is that they are proprietary. While they are open, they are also administered. Anyone can place credentials in them so long as they follow the rules of the platform vendor. Their proprietary nature locks people into a specific platform.

Platform providers like Apple and Google recognize the importance of wallets both for enhancing the user experience and for locking people into their platform. Other app vendors will as well. There will likely be a significant competition in the market for digital wallets in the coming years.[6]

The Roles of Agents

Identity agents are software services that manage all the stuff in the wallet. Agents store, update, retrieve, and delete all the artifacts that a wallet holds. Beyond managing the wallet, agents perform many other important tasks:[7]

- Sending and receiving messages with other agents
- Requesting that the wallet generate cryptographic key pairs
- Managing encrypted data interactions with the wallet
- Performing cryptographic functions like signing and verifying signatures
- Backing up and retrieving data in the wallet
- Maintaining relationships by communicating with other agents when DID documents are updated
- Routing messages to other agents

Figure 18-3 shows the relationship between an agent, a wallet, and an underlying operating system. While most current implementations pair a single agent with a single wallet, the presence of an API means that it's possible for one agent to use several wallets, or for multiple agents to access one wallet. Some specialized agents might not even need a wallet, such as those that just perform routing, although most will at least need to store their own keys.

---

6 For more on the marketplace for wallets, see Darrell O'Donnell, "The Current and Future State of Digital Wallets" (*https://oreil.ly/aP_kK*) (white paper, Continuum Loop, April 2019).

7 Beyond these identity-specific functions, agents can also play a role in payments (see Chapter 15). Building payments into an identity wallet would make the exchange of value for identity data easier and more secure, whether this is in the form of credentials or not. I will not discuss incorporating payments into an agent in detail here, because it's outside the scope of this chapter.

The key-management function in the wallet includes events for cryptographic keys like generation, storage, rotation, and deletion. Key management is performed in cooperation with the operating system and underlying hardware. Ideally, the operating system and hardware provide a secure enclave for key storage and a trusted execution environment for performing key-management functions.

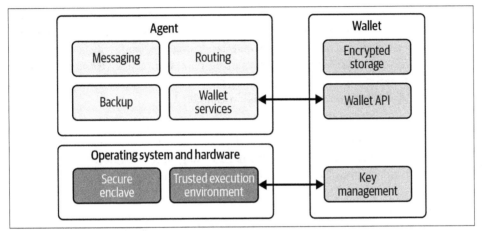

Figure 18-3. The relationship between identity wallets and agents

The basic functions shown in Figure 18-3 might not seem to have much to do with identity. Identity-related activities like authentication and credential exchange are built on top of these basic functions. The agent can issue, request, and accept VCs. The agent also presents and verifies credentials. Specialized messages perform these activities (see Chapter 19).

Properties of Wallets and Agents

The identity wallets and agents discussed above have several important properties that distinguish them from the protowallets that most people use now:

Open, substitutable, and portable
> The discussion of the properties of email in Chapter 17 showed the important features that result when a system is based on a standard set of protocols. Alice should see similar benefits from her identity wallet and agent that she enjoys in email: choice, consistent user experience, and flexibility—all design features of an identity metasystem.

Secure by design
> Security is a nonnegotiable feature for identity wallets and agents. Some security features are the result of mutually authenticating DID exchange as the basis for relationships that natively support confidential messaging. Some security features

depend on good engineering of things like the wallet's encrypted storage or the wallet API. Still others result from governance of the overall ecosystem, a topic I'll return to in Chapters 21 and 22.

Private by design

As you learned in Chapter 8, privacy by design doesn't layer privacy onto an already built system. Rather, it uses specific design principles to ensure privacy is the default. Identity wallets and agents provide privacy in their design by supporting minimal disclosure of personal data using *zero-knowledge proofs* (ZKPs) and other techniques, properly encrypting data so that it's visible only to the intended party, and engineering anticorrelation into the system with techniques like blinded identifiers, as you learned in Chapter 15.

Autonomous

As key components in algorithmic and autonomic identity system architectures, agents and wallets give people tools for exercising control authority over identifiers and personal data. This control is the basis for autonomy in digital relationships.

Consistent and familiar in their user experience

There's a saying in security: "Don't roll your own crypto." I think we need a corollary in identity: "Don't roll your own interface." By supporting the exchange of data based on VCs, identity wallets and agents provide a single means of accomplishing many tasks. One of the important UX features of identity wallets and agents is that people do not manipulate cryptographic keys and DIDs; rather, they manage relationships and credentials. These are familiar artifacts that people understand.

SSI Interaction Patterns

Agents, supported by wallets, enable three simple authentication and authorization patterns used in self-sovereign identity. All three are just specializations of the standard VC exchange pattern. Understanding them can help you understand the requirements for wallets and agents.

DID Authentication Pattern

The simplest authentication pattern uses autonomic identifiers to establish a peer relationship. Because of their mutual authentication capabilities, relationships based on autonomic identifiers can be used for authentication.

Figure 18-4 illustrates the DID authentication pattern. This pattern has two parties, both of whom employ agents:

- Alice has an SSI agent on her mobile phone.

- Bravo Corp has an enterprise agent tied to an IAM system that is protecting some resource.

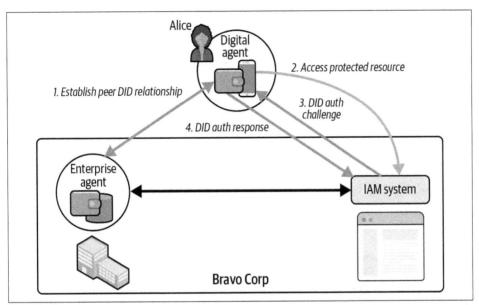

Figure 18-4. Simple DID authentication interaction pattern

The interaction pattern has the following steps:

1. Alice and Bravo establish a peer DID relationship. This means that each agent generates a peer DID and sends it to the other, along with the associated DID document, which contains a public key and service endpoint URI that identifies how to contact the DID controller. As you've learned, autonomic identifiers are self-certifying, and each party can use the information associated with the DID to authenticate the other.

2. Alice tries to access the protected resource. The request is intermediated by Bravo's IAM system. As part of this request, Alice transmits her DID to Bravo's IAM system. There are several subscenarios for the different ways this may happen. For example, she could scan a QR code or enter an associated human-readable identifier that is linked to her DID in Bravo's system.

3. The IAM system, working in concert with Bravo's enterprise agent, issues a DID-based authentication challenge to Alice's wallet through her phone. This is a form of challenge-response authentication (see Chapter 11).

4. Alice is notified by her agent of the challenge and instructs her agent to issue a response to Bravo's challenge.

Having received Alice's response, Bravo verifies it and allows or disallows the access.

There are several things to note about this interaction. First, because Alice and Bravo are using peer DIDs, no verifiable data registry (VDR) is involved in the authentication. As you know, in a peer DID relationship, both parties are obliged to keep the other informed of relevant key events such as key rotation and store updates in a cryptographic backing store. This pattern is just authentication, not authorization. Any authorization would have to be done based on information the IAM system has from another source. For example, if the peer DID relationship were established within a different authenticated context, Alice could have been assigned a group for role-based access control (RBAC) or the IAM system could use policy-based access control (PBAC) using attributes it has associated with Alice's DID.

The interaction pattern described here leaves out several details. Markus Sabadello identifies 10 different variations of this pattern in his talk "Introduction to DID Auth for SSI" (*https://oreil.ly/GQllU*). I encourage you to review it for details relevant to specific authentication scenarios.

Single-Party Credential Authorization Pattern

While the DID authentication pattern is simple, it is not as flexible as some situations require. For more complicated scenarios, a digital wallet and agent can use VCs to provide evidence the controller is authorized to take some action. The first scenario I'll consider is where the same organization is issuing and verifying the credential.

Figure 18-5 shows the pattern for authorizing a single party. The parties in this scenario are the same: Alice and Bravo Corp. The interaction pattern is as follows:

1. Since Bravo Corp will be issuing a credential, it writes a public DID and credential definition to a VDR. It might also write a schema and revocation registry, if necessary. Storing these in a VDR is not strictly necessary if Bravo Corp never plans to use the credential externally. But it's a good idea to do so, since it's a relatively cheap and easy step that enables future use cases that weren't anticipated when the credential was planned.

2. Alice and Bravo establish a peer DID relationship as before. Note that the DID that Bravo uses for this relationship is not the public DID that it created in step 1. Instead, Bravo creates a peer DID specific to the relationship with Alice. Doing this allows Bravo to easily update or terminate the relationship without affecting the public DID. Since peer DIDs are free, there's little reason not to use them wherever needed.

3. Bravo issues a credential to Alice. The nature, content, and context of this credential issuance depend on Bravo and Alice's specific needs. Bravo is the credential issuer and Alice is the credential holder.

4. Alice tries to access a protected resource. The request is intermediated by Bravo's IAM system. Like the DID authentication pattern shown above, the IAM system is working in concert with an enterprise agent and its wallet.

5. I'll assume that Bravo is using a PBAC system that relies on knowing attributes about Alice. The IAM system makes a credential request to Alice's agent using its agent. The request asks for just the specific attributes needed by the policy protecting the resource Alice is attempting to access.

6. Alice sees the request and authorizes her agent to issue a proof of attributes based on the credential she holds. The response contains only the attributes that Bravo needs, not the entire credential, to minimize the information that is shared.

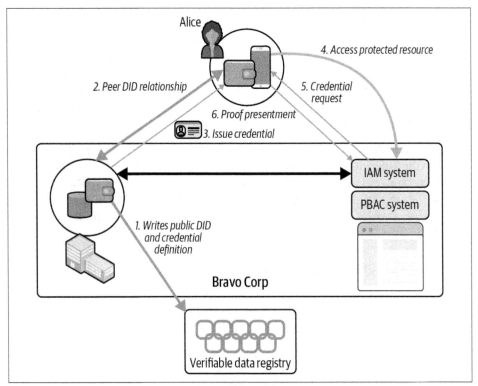

Figure 18-5. Single-party credential-based authorization pattern

The PBAC system uses the attributes in the proof presentation to authorize Alice's access.

There are several things to note about this interaction. First, Bravo does not necessarily need to access the VDR to verify the credential since they own it. They already know the information necessary to validate it. But others might access it if Alice decides to present it somewhere other than Bravo.

In addition, for Bravo, using a credential held by Alice to validate her authority to access the protected resource is more flexible and potentially more reliable than a centralized attribute store. Using a VDR minimizes centralized data requests and single points of failure, since suborganizations within Bravo can verify the credential no matter who issued it. And rather than building a central attribute store for Bravo's PBAC system and linking every system in the enterprise to it, each system can stand alone and make decisions based on its own policies. As a bonus, this means that Bravo stores less personal data, reducing its risk.

Using minimal disclosure reduces risk even further, since other services at Bravo don't need access to all the data Bravo keeps about Alice. And since presenting trustworthy attributes using credentials is quick, these services don't need to store the data themselves. They can simply ask Alice whenever she needs the service, cache the data for the duration of the service interaction, and then delete it, confident they can access it again if necessary.

Astute readers will read the last two paragraphs and ask, "But don't they all have to be linked to the same digital agent and wallet to take advantage of the peer DID relationship?" The answer is no. Each service can have its own peer DID relationship with Alice, verify the attributes from the credential, and know it's Alice. The only thing they need to know is the public DID that their organization uses and the credential definition.

Multiparty Credential Authorization Pattern

We can extend the single-party pattern to include multiple parties. In this pattern, one entity, Bravo Corp, is issuing credentials, but another entity, Certiphi Corp, is verifying the credential and using its attributes to authorize Alice's access to a resource.

Figure 18-6 shows how Certiphi Corp can use attributes asserted by Bravo Corp as part of its authorization of Alice. The interaction proceeds as follows:

1. Since Bravo Corp is issuing a credential, it writes a public DID and credential definition to the ledger. Again, it might also write a schema and revocation registry, if needed.

2. Alice and Bravo establish a peer DID relationship.

3. Bravo issues a credential to Alice.

4. Alice and Certiphi establish a peer DID relationship.

5. Alice tries to access the protected resource at Certiphi. The request is intermediated by Certiphi's IAM system.

6. Certiphi is using a PBAC system, so the IAM system makes a credential request to Alice that asks for the specific attributes the policy needs to grant access to the resource.

7. Alice sees the request and authorizes her agent to present those attributes based on the credentials she holds. The agent gives Alice the option to use the credential from Bravo, since it has the attributes needed to satisfy Certiphi's request.

8. Certiphi cryptographically validates the *fidelity* of the presentation to ensure it's from Bravo, is about Alice, hasn't been tampered with, and hasn't been revoked. They might also need to validate the *provenance* of the attributes in the proof. Certiphi is the credential verifier in this pattern.

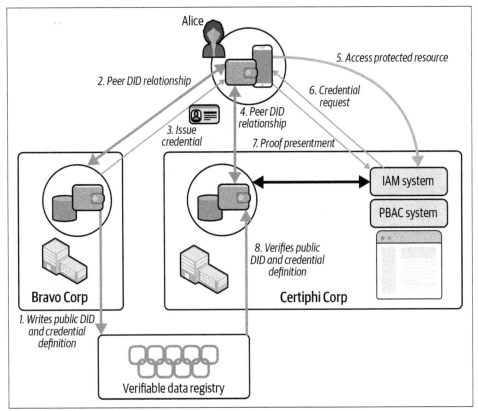

Figure 18-6. Multiparty credential-based authorization pattern

Certiphi's PBAC system uses the attributes in the proof presentation to authorize Alice's access.

There are several things to note about this pattern. First, the DID relationship Alice and Certiphi create in step 4 could be ephemeral; it needn't be permanent unless the parties need it to be. The relationship between Alice and Bravo is likely long-lived, since Bravo has issued a credential asserting something about Alice.

Second, there is no direct connection or link between Bravo Corp and Certiphi Corp. They needn't have any preexisting business or technical relationship. Certiphi needn't connect to a Bravo Corp API. The VDR allows Certiphi to know important things about the credential without a direct connection.

Third, the primary difference between the single-party and multiparty patterns is step 8: checking the fidelity and provenance of the credential. The fidelity check can be done automatically using cryptography. But, as you learned in Chapter 15, determining provenance is not a trivial thing, since it involves Certiphi determining that it can trust attributes attested by Bravo.

Provenance is a governance issue, not a technical one. The governance issue could be simple or complex, as Chapter 15 discussed. Chapter 22 takes this up again in more detail.

Revisiting the Generalized Authentic Data Transfer Pattern

All the previous interaction patterns are specializations of the general data transfer pattern that should be familiar to you from Chapter 15. I'll discuss the general pattern again here so you can place the three previous patterns inside it. The general data transfer pattern shown in Figure 18-7 moves beyond simple authentication and authorization patterns to using identity data in workflows.

In this pattern, all the interactions are identical to the pattern for multiparty authorization in the last section, with a few exceptions. One is that Alice is accessing a general web service in step 5 that needs data to proceed, rather than a protected resource. The web service might be an IAM system, but it needn't be. The other is that the web service uses the data from the proof presentation as part of its workflow, such as filling out a form.

We can view all the previous patterns as specializations of this pattern. For instance:

- The peer DID relationship provides a mutually authenticated communications channel in every case. You can always use this to know that you're talking to the entity with whom the relationship was originally established—the core requirement for any authentication system.

- Transferring attributes using VCs for PBAC is just a special case of transferring attribute data in a trustworthy manner.

- As you learned in Chapter 15, there's no need for the data transferred in the general pattern to come from a single credential. In fact, the service can ask for

---

attributes without knowing what credentials Alice holds. Alice's agent will match the requested attributes to the credentials Alice holds. Alice can choose which credentials to use for specific attributes if she wants.

- While Figure 18-7 shows Alice accessing a web service, this can be further generalized beyond the web. Any data needed for an online workflow can be transferred using VCs. The next chapter will discuss how DID-based messaging can be the basis for this.

- While this pattern involves Alice and two organizations, there's no reason why people can't be credential issuers and verifiers. Any party in these diagrams could play any of the roles.

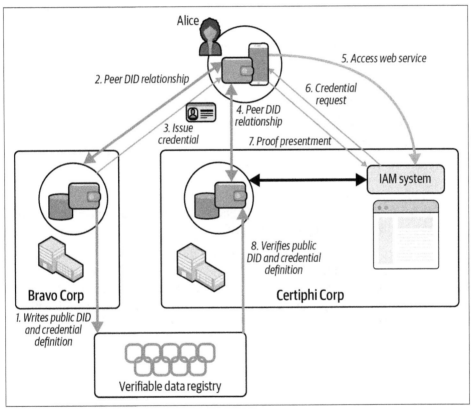

Figure 18-7. Credential-based data transfer pattern

Viewing traditional IAM functions like authentication and authorization as special-purpose authentic data transfers significantly broadens identity beyond its traditional bounds. While this expanded view of digital identity may make some uncomfortable, I think it is perfectly aligned with the realization that we build identity systems to manage relationships rather than identities. Every relationship is unique. Flexible, trustworthy VCs uniquely serve those relationships and introduce the means of moving digital identity beyond just authentication and authorization.

What If I Lose My Phone?

If people are storing all their important, sensitive data in an identity wallet, protecting that information from the disasters that will inevitably occur becomes critical. One of the chief concerns for any system using cryptographic keys is making them not just easy to use but protecting them from attackers or even simple loss. Many cryptographic systems have failed the test of time because of the poor user experience around key backup, recovery, and security. I believe it's one of the things holding back cryptocurrencies from more widespread adoption. So, how do identity wallets and agents avoid this same fate?[8]

There are many scenarios that could pose a problem:

- Alice loses her phone
- Alice can't unlock her phone
- Alice loses or forgets a cryptographic key
- Alice's laptop is hacked
- Alice is the victim of a ransomware attack

The common denominator in these is that Alice has lost control of the agent that manages her identity wallet. Fortunately, Alice can prepare for this possibility, making recovery possible and keeping her secrets safe.

At this point in the book, you are familiar with the basics of DIDs, VCs, and their cryptographic underpinnings.[9] That understanding will help as we follow along with Alice, who has just discovered her phone was stolen from a park bench by Malfoy. To start, let's assume Alice's phone has only weak protection, in the form of a PIN to unlock it.[10] Alice takes two steps as soon as she's aware of the loss.

---

8 The material in this section is based on the excellent Sovrin Foundation paper (*https://oreil.ly/Qbii5*) by Daniel Hardman.

9 For this discussion, I assume Alice's agent has many of the features in the Hyperledger Aries reference agent. This grounds the discussion in several specific features that are helpful in Alice's predicament. There's nothing about these features that couldn't be built into other agent software as well.

10 For this discussion, we'll ignore the help Alice's smartphone operating system may provide, like the ability to wipe the phone remotely. Alice may have to avail herself of that remedy, but Alice should be able to recover control of her identity assets without resorting to that.

Step 1: Alice Revokes the Lost Agent's Authorization

Alice's first move upon discovering her phone is missing should be to cancel its permissions to represent her. By revoking the agent, Alice limits how Malfoy can use it, should he get past the device's PIN. Impersonating Alice requires more than her keys, credential, and link secret—it also requires that the derived credential presentation be done from an agent Alice has authorized to represent her.

Alice revokes the device using some other agent she controls. That might be an agent on her laptop or one she controls in the cloud. This requires, of course, that she's made these provisions and prepared for the possibility that she might lose her phone. She could even require control of more than one additional agent to revoke agents so that losing control of one doesn't risk having an attacker revoke the others she still controls if they gain access before she realizes what's happened.

Alice can revoke her agent because she's using agents and VDRs that support this feature. The agent authorization is stored on the VDR and the derived credential presentation protocol her agents run requires that presentations be made from agents that have not been revoked. When Alice revokes an agent, the revocation is written to the VDR and anyone verifying a credential presentation will see that the agent has been revoked. Even if Malfoy is extremely sophisticated and can remove the cryptographic secrets from the phone's secure enclave, he will not be able to use them to impersonate Alice in a credential presentation.[11] Writing a revocation to a VDR can be nearly instantaneous and is globally visible.

Note that unlike schemes that rely on deleting or erasing a device, revoking the agent doesn't require that the agent be online. Alice can revoke the agent even if Malfoy has turned off the phone and removed the SIM chip.

One of the most important features of agent revocation is that it's reversible. If Alice later recovers her phone, she can unrevoke its agent and continue using the keys and credentials it contains. This allows Alice to be aggressive and err on the side of caution. Anytime she feels like she might have lost control of an agent, she can revoke its authorization to represent her until she's convinced that she's back in control.

Step 2: Alice Rotates Her Relationship Keys

Revoking the agent means that Malfoy can't impersonate Alice in any credential presentations. But if he can break in, he could still use the keys underpinning Alice's peer relationships to sign and encrypt messages with Alice's contacts. Protecting against this requires that Alice rotate her private keys. One of the advantages of autonomic

---

11 For more on the technology underlying these capabilities, see "DKMS (Decentralized Key Management System) Design and Architecture V3" (*https://oreil.ly/O5XKa*) by Drummond Reed, Jason Law, Daniel Hardman, and Mike Lodder.

identifiers like peer DIDs and KERI identifiers is that they make it possible to rotate keys without needing to change the identifier that is the basis for the relationship.

Alice's user experience to rotate all her keys could be as simple as a single button press. Behind the scenes, the agent Alice has control of and is using to perform revocations must rotate the keys underlying each DID she's shared and update the DID documents for each DID-based relationship. If the DID is public, that would require writing to the VDR. If it's a peer DID, then Alice's agent would use the normal method for notifying other parties in the peer relationship of DID document changes based on deltas.

What Alice Has Protected

By taking the two simple steps of revoking the agent and her relationship keys, Alice has accomplished a lot:

- Malfoy can't use the contents of the stolen wallet and agent to impersonate her in an existing or new relationship.
- Alice can use other agents she controls to continue using her existing relationships and credentials.
- Alice can establish new relationships using her existing credentials without fear that Malfoy will misuse them in another context.
- Malfoy can't request new credentials in Alice's name because he has no control of her credentials or relationship keys.
- Alice can buy a new phone, install an agent on it, and use it the same way she did her old phone, with the same relationships and credentials.

As a result, Alice's immediate risk is mitigated and there are few long-term impacts to having her phone stolen—at least for her SSI-based relationships and credentials.

Protecting the Information in Alice's Wallet

Earlier, I assumed that Alice's phone has only weak protection in the form of a PIN to unlock it. That raises the question of how the secrets in Alice's wallet are protected. Identity wallets are encrypted and, in best practice, the unlock keys are stored separately. Because of that encryption, Malfoy might see the metadata about items stored in the wallet like creation or modifications dates, size, and data types.

The protections that the unlock key provides are largely a function of features of the underlying operating system. If Alice's device has a secure enclave protected with biometrics rather than a simple PIN, and the wallet is designed to store sensitive data in the enclave, then Malfoy may have a very hard time breaking into Alice's wallet.

Suppose that's not the case, and Malfoy manages to break into the wallet. Malfoy can now see every DID, key pair, and credential that Alice knows about. He could find out private information like Alice's birthday, her driver's license information, or sensitive information stored in credentials, like account numbers. But, presumably, Alice's bank accounts and credit cards are protected by her ability to respond correctly to credential challenges. Thus getting the account number isn't very useful, since Malfoy can't use the keys and credentials to access the account.

If you recall our discussion of noncorrelating credential presentations in Chapter 15, there is a piece of information in Alice's wallet called a *link secret*. The use of "secret" in the name may give you the idea that its exposure has dire consequences for Alice, but such is not the case. The link secret is used to create blinded identifiers when credentials are issued to Alice, and she uses ZKPs in derived credential presentations to prove she knows the value of the blinded identifier without revealing it. Alice has revoked the agent, and Malfoy can't use the link secret to request new credentials or make presentations. He can't correlate it to any of Alice's credential presentations in the past or future, since it's always used in a blinded fashion. Alice can continue to use her link secret and the credentials based on it *even though Malfoy knows it*.

In short, even if Malfoy gets into the wallet, he can't do Alice much harm.

Censorship Resistance

Censorship is the act of preventing someone from speaking. As you learned in Chapter 8, speech is defined as any data packet communicated on behalf of a speaker. Since Alice's agent is doing the speaking on her behalf, the best way to censor Alice is to control her agents.

As I just discussed, a hacker would have little chance of upsetting Alice's communications by stealing Alice's device—she could use agents on other devices just as easily. A hack that embeds itself on her device might be able to block her from speaking altogether, something she'd undoubtedly notice, but it can't single out specific messages or recipients since messages are encrypted and sent on secure channels. Even if the hacker could see the DIDs, they don't identify who Alice is speaking to—they are *private*, as I defined the term in Chapter 8.[12]

The best way to censor Alice's communications using her identity agent is to be embedded in the agent itself. Protecting against this is a software security issue, and the answers are familiar: using software from trusted sources, conducting code and operation reviews, and ensuring that installed apps haven't been tampered with. None of this is specific to identity agents or wallets.

---

12 This assumes that the DIDs are peer, not public. Privacy is one of the big advantages of using peer DIDs instead of public DIDs for relationships.

The biggest threat to Alice is from governments or other actors who can control or coerce ecosystems, so that all agents are spying on the people and organizations who use them. This is not a problem that can be solved with cryptography; the issue here is one of governance and human rights.

Web3, Agents, and Digital Embodiment

As I write this in 2022, *Web3* is a hot topic. One definition of Web3 that I'm particularly fond of looks like this:

Web1: read

Web2: read, write

Web3: read, write, own

I don't know if the name "Web3" will continue to be used. And I don't know that *own* is the right word; *autonomy* isn't as pithy, even if it is more appropriate. But I do think the ideas behind Web3 resonate with many people, well beyond the cryptocurrency phenomenon that started it.

In late 2021, Tim O'Reilly published "Why It's Too Early to Get Excited About Web3" (*https://oreil.ly/hBF-E*), an excellent discussion on the role of bubbles in industrial transformation. He uses this historical lens to look at Web3 and where it stands in its developmental arc. One of O'Reilly's points is that our architectures tend to fluctuate between decentralized and centralized models. He uses Clayton Christensen's law of conservation of attractive profits (*https://oreil.ly/X2xyy*) to show why this happens. O'Reilly says:

> I love the idealism of the Web3 vision, but we've been there before. During my career, we have gone through several cycles of decentralization and recentralization. The personal computer decentralized computing by providing a commodity PC architecture that anyone could build and that no one controlled. But Microsoft figured out how to recentralize the industry around a proprietary operating system. Open source software, the internet, and the World Wide Web broke the stranglehold of proprietary software with free software and open protocols, but within a few decades, Google, Amazon, and others had built huge new monopolies founded on big data.

O'Reilly's broader point is that while there's a lot of promise, the applications that deliver a decentralized experience for most people just aren't there yet. Enthusiasts like to focus on decentralized finance, but I don't think that's enough (nor, I think, does O'Reilly). While centralized payments are a big part of the problem, I don't think it's the most fundamental. The most fundamental problem is that people have no place to stand in the modern web. They are not *digitally embodied*, as I've termed it.

In "Why Web3?" (*https://oreil.ly/rlBF1*) Fred Wilson, who has as deep an understanding of how the underlying technology works as anyone, explains it like this:

It all comes down to the database that sits behind an application. If that database is controlled by a single entity (think company, think big tech), then enormous market power accrues to the owner/administrator of that database.

This should resonate with what you learned about the locus of control and identity architectures in Chapter 16. With algorithmic and autonomic identity architectures, Wilson's application databases are decentralized. As I discussed, companies will continue to have systems for keeping track of who they interact with. But people will also have software—*identity agents*—to keep track of their relationships with these companies. More importantly, agents allow us to interact with each other without having to be controlled by someone else's administrative system. *That's the most important benefit of identity agents: digital embodiment.*

In the next chapter, I'll explore how agents and the protocol at the heart of agent interactions, DIDComm, create a secure, identity-enabled, privacy-respecting messaging overlay on top of the internet.

CHAPTER 19

Smart Identity Agents

Previous chapters have discussed agents and their capabilities without saying much about how they work, other than to say they exchange messages. This chapter will discuss the protocol that agents use, DIDComm, and its importance in creating a self-sovereign internet. DIDComm is an *encapsulating protocol*—you can define other protocols that run in it. While I've focused on the role agents play in credential exchange, DIDComm's properties make agents useful for more than that. I call agents that are used to participate in arbitrary protocol interactions *smart agents*.

I begin with a discussion of self-sovereign authority and its relationship to self-sovereign communication. Next you'll learn about DIDComm messaging and its inherent support for defining protocols. Credential exchange protocols are just two of many possible protocols. The final part of the chapter discusses smart agents and their role in helping people operationalize their online relationships.

Self-Sovereign Authority

You might hear people talk about *decentralized identity* instead of using the name *self-sovereign identity* (SSI). The word *sovereign* has some negative connotations for some, and others just don't understand what it means. Personally, I don't like the word *decentralized* to describe identity systems, since decentralization is an implementation strategy, not an outcome or feature. In an answer I authored on Quora about Web3 (*https://oreil.ly/BELbP*), I said:

> While people often talk about decentralization as an unalloyed good and the answer to every ill, the truth is that decentralization is just an implementation strategy. The goals of Web3 include self-sovereignty (autonomy and independence) and censorship resistance. Decentralization is a good way to achieve these things, but I can imagine decentralized services (in the technical sense) that don't achieve either of these. It's ok to use

"decentralization" as shorthand for these goals, but recognize the goals, not the implementation technique.

Decentralization isn't the goal. The goals are much grander and include nothing less than a digital world that respects *human dignity and autonomy*.

In "Web3 Is Self-Certifying" (*https://oreil.ly/-QCaB*), Jay Graber defines Web3 as *user-generated authority, enabled by self-certifying web protocols*. This is more nuanced than the definition I gave at the end of the previous chapter. I like *self-sovereign* better than *user-generated* because I think it speaks better to the source of our authority to act. Besides, *user* makes me think of a drug addict, dependent on someone for their next fix. *Sovereign* is the right word for describing the essential distinction between our inalienable self and the administrative identifiers and accounts endemic in Web2. Even so, I like Graber's work to define Web3 in terms of sovereign-source authority and self-certifying protocols.

Figure 19-1 distinguishes Web 1.0 from Web 2.0 and Web 3.0 based on Graber's discussion. The axes of the matrix differentiate between who generates content and who has authority.

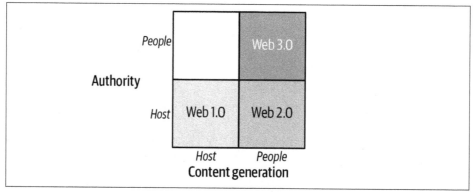

Figure 19-1. Comparing Web 1.0 versus 2.0 versus 3.0

In this figure, a *host* is some server, somewhere. In Web 1.0, it was just the machine under my desk, with no notion of users other than me. In other words, the website I hosted had no logins, no authentication, no identities. That didn't matter, because it was public and read-only for anyone besides me. Web 2.0 separated the need to host the content from the desire to generate it: for example, blogging on platforms like Radio, Typepad, and WordPress. Later, Twitter, Facebook, and other social media platforms filled this role and became behemoths. All these systems use administrative identity to provide *multitenanted web services*. In Web 3.0, people are returning to generating content (broadly defined) under their own authority.

You learned about self-certification in Chapter 14. A closely related idea is *self-administration*. Self-administration means that something is independently administered by the controller—not just in the Web 2.0 sense of "I have a password," but in the sense that there *is* no administrator other than the controller.

Here's an example of what I mean. I've created a completely self-administered blog using IPFS (*https://ipfs.tech*) and *No*FILTER (*https://nofilter.org*). IPFS is a decentralized file storage system that addresses files using their hash as the address. *No*FILTER brands itself as "the world's first unstoppable, uncensorable, undeplatformable, decentralized freedom of speech app." There's no server storing files, just a set of JavaScript files that run in your browser. Identity is provided via MetaMask (*https://meta mask.io*), a JavaScript application that runs in the browser and uses an Ethereum address as your identifier.

I created some posts using *No*FILTER to demonstrate how it works. My *No*FILTER blog can be accessed here:

```
https://nofilter.org/#/0xdbca72ed00c24d50661641bf42ad4be003a30b84
```

The portion after the # is the Ethereum address I used at *No*FILTER.[1] If you look at a single post, you'll see a URL like this:

```
https://nofilter.org/#/0xdbca72ed00c24d50661641bf42ad4be003a30b84
    /QmTn2r2e4LQ5ffh86KDcexNrTBaByyTiNP3pQDbNWiNJyt
```

Note the additional identifier following the slash after my Ethereum address. This is the IPFS hash of the content of that post and is available on IPFS directly. What's stored on IPFS is the JSON of the post:

```
{
   "author": "0xdbca72ed00c24d50661641bf42ad4be003a30b84",
   "title": "The IPFS Address",
   "timestamp": "2021-10-25T22:46:46-0-6:720",
   "body": "<p>If I go here:</p><p><a href=\"https://ipfs.io/ipfs/
QmT57jkkR2sh2i4uLRAZuWu6TatEDQdKN8HnwaZGaXJTrr\";>..."
}
```

JavaScript running in the browser renders that JSON human readable.

As far as I can tell, this system is completely decentralized. The identity is just an Ethereum address that anyone can create using MetaMask. The files are stored on IPFS in a decentralized manner, by providers around the internet. They are rendered into blog posts using JavaScript that runs in a browser, not on a server. So long as you have access to the JavaScript files from somewhere, you can write and read articles without relying on any central server. There are no third parties (hosts or platforms)

---

1 Recall that the fragment portion of a URL (everything after the #) is used only in the browser and never sent to the server identified in the URL. So, the Ethereum address is not sent to *No*FILTER. It is only used by the JavaScript running in the browser.

to say what I can or can't post, censor me, surveil me, or otherwise intermediate me and my posts.

While I control my *NoFILTER* blog using an autonomic identifier in the form of an Ethereum address, the MetaMask wallet is less sophisticated than most password managers. The agent in this scenario is weak and isn't delivering a truly self-sovereign experience. I can't easily rotate keys or use credentials to provide trustworthy information. For that, I would need a *smart identity agent* like the one discussed in the previous chapter.

Principles of Self-Sovereign Communication

In "Self-Sovereign Communication" (*https://oreil.ly/ETIei*), Oskar van Deventer discusses the communications layer enabled by DIDs. This is the same layer that I discussed in the last chapter when I said that agents exchange messages based on DIDs. Van Deventer lays out nine requirements for self-sovereign communications:

1. The communication channel shall be usable for machine-readable issuer-holder-verifier interactions.
2. The communication channel shall be protected against eavesdropping, impersonation, message modification and repudiation.
3. Parties shall be able to digitally find each other and to establish a communication channel.
4. The communication channel between counterparties shall be persistent.
5. The communication channel shall be intrinsically symmetrical.
6. The communication channel shall not unnecessarily disclose information between counterparties or to third parties.
7. The communication channel shall be unilaterally closable.
8. The communication channel shall not depend on third parties more than needed.
9. The communication channel shall enable compliance with legal requirements, like legal intercept.

These are important properties that we need in a self-sovereign messaging system like the one used by smart agents.

Reciprocal Negotiated Accountability

Van Deventer's last point is likely to be the most controversial. Indeed, when I read it, my first reaction was to start arguing. One common answer to giving law enforcement access to encrypted communication involves creating technical "backdoors" that provide someone other than the principal the means of decrypting the message. If complying with legal requirements means creating backdoors to smart agent messaging, I'd oppose it. The problem with using backdoors for complying with legal requirements is that they require developers and cloud operators to determine who the good guys are. The whole point of decentralized communication systems is to avoid the kind of centralized single points of failure that backdoors imply.

One answer is provisional authenticity, which you learned about in Chapter 8. The only way to hold people accountable while protecting their privacy is to make the authenticity of a message provisional through agreement.

To that end, Daniel Hardman proposes what he calls reciprocal negotiated accountability (*https://oreil.ly/YVzVW*). Hardman's idea is to combine two capabilities—digital watermarks and provisional anonymity—to create a decentralized system that enables accountability. Let's look more closely.

The first capability is *digital watermarks,* which specify terms of service for the data. The watermark is a cryptographically signed addition to the original document that states the terms behind the sharing. For example, a sales agreement could include data-sharing terms stating that the recipient may not disclose named aspects of the document except under legal subpoena.

The second is *provisional anonymity,* where identifying information is encrypted and the encrypted packaged is shared with the recipient. The keys to decrypt the identifying information are shared with a third party under escrow, with legal requirements that the keys only be revealed to the recipient under specific conditions.

Hardman's proposal combines these into a decentralized system of opt-in agreements between parties that are tailored to the context and circumstances of the specific communications channel and data sharing. The legal agreement, a form of governance, defines the requirements that must be met for access. He calls this "reciprocal negotiated accountability" because both parties negotiate an agreement about how shared data will be treated.

Reciprocal negotiated accountability won't please those who wish for unfettered access to communications channels. But it represents an alternative to backdoors that solves many of the problems backdoors present while protecting privacy for legitimate uses—as negotiated by the parties that are sharing data.

DID-Based Communication

DIDs and DID-based communication, or *DIDComm,* form the second layer of the SSI stack, providing a secure communications layer for the exchange of identity information via verifiable credentials (VCs). Because of DIDComm's flexibility and the ability to define protocols on top of DIDComm messaging, it promises to be as important as the identity layer it enables.

Figure 19-2 shows the now-familiar identity metasystem stack. Layer 2, the DID-based agent-to-agent messaging system, is enabled by DIDComm messaging. The DIDComm protocol is governed by the DIDComm specification (*https://oreil.ly/ZX-Np*), hosted at the Decentralized Identity Foundation. The current ratified version is 2.0.

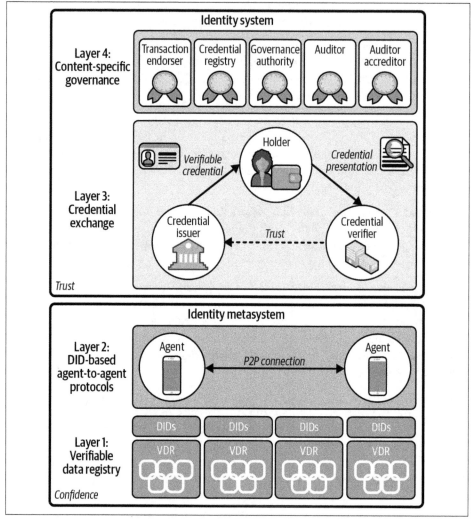

Figure 19-2. The identity metasystem stack

The specification's opening sentence states that "the purpose of DIDComm Messaging is to provide a secure, private communication methodology built atop the decentralized design of DIDs."

Note that the specification describes DIDComm as a communications *methodology*. This means that DIDComm is more than just a way to send a message or chat with someone else. DIDComm messaging allows individual messages to be composed into application-level protocols and workflows. This makes DIDComm messaging a foundational technology for performing different kinds of interactions within the framework of trust that a DID-based relationship implies.

Exchanging DIDs

I've previously talked about Alice exchanging DIDs with people and organizations several times, but I haven't discussed how that happens. You could imagine that Alice generates a new peer DID and emails it to Bob, who replies with one he's created for Alice. But that leaves both of them entangled in the details of how DIDs work: how they're created, stored, validated, and so on.

Hyperledger Aries RFC 0023 (*https://oreil.ly/gyNhs*), entitled *DID Exchange Protocol 1.0*, is a protocol for exchanging DIDs that allows the process to be automated by smart identity agents working on Alice and Bob's behalf.[2] Figure 19-3 shows a DID exchange.

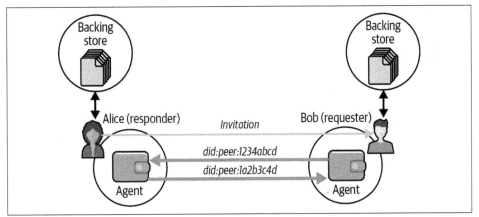

Figure 19-3. Alice and Bob exchange DIDs

---

2 DIDComm v2 builds DID exchange into the protocol. Each DIDComm v2 message contains both the sender's DID and public key. As a result, the exchange of DIDs and keys that occurs using the DID Exchange Protocol described here happens each time a message is transferred in DIDComm v2. I include a discussion of the explicit exchange protocol because it's useful to understand exchanging DIDs explicitly as well.

The DID Exchange Protocol uses two roles: *requester* and *responder*. In Figure 19-3, Bob is the requester and Alice is the responder.

The interaction begins with Alice sending Bob an explicit invitation message using the process described by Aries RFC 0434 Out-of-Band Protocol (*https://oreil.ly/DrFCY*). Alternately, Bob might use an implied invitation from a public DID. For example, Bob might be verifying a credential. His agent could resolve the DID in the credential to get the DID document. Information in the DID document would give his agent what it needs to initiate an exchange.

The Out-of-Band message specification is important because Alice may want a new connection to Bob. If so, she can't use an already established DIDComm connection to message him. The Out-of-Band message is plain text and could be sent as a QR code or clickable URL, in an email message or any other convenient channel. Alice will usually already possess smart agents with DIDComm capabilities, but Bob might not. The invitation gives him the opportunity to get one.

Using the invitation, Bob's agent has the necessary information to generate a DID and send it with the initial DID document as a request to Alice. Alice's agent evaluates the DID in Bob's request using its specific DID method. The request includes information about the invitation so that Alice's agent can evaluate whether it should accept the request or not. Her agent persists Bob's DID and DID document in its backing store. Finally, it generates a DID and formulates a response for Bob.

Bob processes Alice's response by evaluating the DID Alice gave him and its DID method and persisting the information to his backing store.[3] Having completed these steps, Alice and Bob have exchanged DIDs and are ready to begin using DIDComm messaging to communicate with each other.

DIDComm Messaging

Once Alice and Bob have exchanged DIDs, they have a DID-based relationship that they can use to exchange messages using the DIDComm protocol. Suppose Alice wishes to send a message to Bob: an invitation to dinner, a job offer, an invoice, or almost anything else. Alice's smart agent composes the messages as a plain-text JSON message. Alice's agent resolves Bob's DID to get his DID document and retrieves two important pieces of information:

- The public key that Bob's agent is using for the `Alice:Bob` relationship

---

3 There are several places things can go wrong and errors can be generated and communicated. The specification provides full details on these and state machine diagrams for understanding the exact interaction steps.

- The service endpoint where messages can be delivered: this could be web, email, or almost any other transport that Alice and Bob agree on

Alice uses Bob's public key to encrypt the plain-text message and signs it using the private key she created for the Alice:Bob relationship. The agent arranges delivery to Bob. This might be a direct connection to Bob's agent or involve routing through intermediaries. Figure 19-4 shows the exchange of messages using the Alice:Bob relationship.

Bob's smart agent receives Alice's message. He looks up the public key Alice uses for this relationship in the DID document he gets by resolving Alice's DID. Using the public key in the DID document, Bob authenticates the sender as Alice using the signature, then decrypts it using the private key he created for the Alice:Bob relationship. Bob's agent can send a response using a reciprocal process.

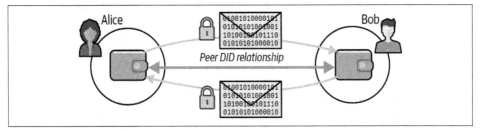

Figure 19-4. Alice and Bob exchange messages

DIDComm interactions are inherently asynchronous. So, while the exchange shown in Figure 19-4 is typical, other variations are possible:

- DIDComm supports occasionally connected endpoints because the asynchronous and simplex nature of the protocol doesn't require turn-taking or request-response.
- DIDComm interactions can include more than two parties.
- JSON isn't the only format allowed for messages.

Properties of DIDComm Messaging

The DIDComm Protocol is designed to have the following properties:

Secure
> Message security is achieved through the protocol's support for heterarchical (peer-to-peer) connections and decentralized design along with its use of end-to-end encryption.

Private

Message privacy is built on the exchange of peer DIDs that are created on a per-relationship basis to reduce correlatability and increase privacy.

Decentralized

The decentralization of DIDComm rests on the decentralized properties of DIDs. DIDComm messaging does not require specific intermediaries, oracles, or platforms.

Interoperable

As an interoperable protocol, DIDComm is not dependent on a specific operating system, programming language, vendor, network, hardware platform, or verifiable data registry (VDR).

Transport-agnostic

In addition to being interoperable, DIDComm can use any transport mechanism including HTTP(S) 1.x and 2.0, WebSockets, Internet Relay Chat (IRC), Bluetooth, Near Field Communication (NFC), Signal, email, push notifications to mobile devices, ham radio, multicast, snail mail, and more.

Routable

Like email, Alice and Bob can talk to each other without having a direct connection because it supports routing messages through intermediaries. A single message might be routed over different transports for different legs of its journey.

Extensible

The JSON data structure in the plain-text message can contain other data to support higher-level protocols riding on top of DIDComm. I'll return to this in a later section.

Message Formats

The use of plain text to describe the messages Alice and Bob exchange doesn't imply that the message is unstructured. DIDComm messages are based on JWM, the JSON Web Message specification (*https://oreil.ly/r2wY6*). The following example message from the DIDComm specification shows the common elements of a DIDComm plain-text message:

```
{
  "id": "1234567890",
  "type": "<message-type-uri>",
  "from": "did:example:alice",
  "to": ["did:example:bob"],
  "created_time": 1516269022,
  "expires_time": 1516385931,
  "body": {
    "message_type_specific_attribute": "and its value",
```

```
        "another_attribute": "and its value"
    }
}
```

Most of these are self-explanatory, but a few deserve additional comment. Everything but the body is header information. The id is the message identifier and must be unique to the sender across all messages they send. The type is a URI that identifies a published schema describing the structure of the body. The to field is an array to accommodate multiple recipients. The body can be structured, as JSON in this case, depending on the specific type of message being sent.

Messages can also have attachments to supplement the message with other, arbitrary data. Attachments are contained in a key-value pair where the key is attachments and the value is an array of JSON objects containing the data for the attachment. These work much like attachments in email, including support for MIME types.

Supporting structured bodies and attachments is what makes DIDComm suitable for issuing and presenting credentials. But its extensibility is useful for more than just credential exchange.

Figure 19-5 illustrates a signed and encrypted DIDComm message. The plain-text message includes both data and metadata and can be wrapped in a signature envelope (identified by the media type JWS [JSON Web Signature]) and an encryption envelope (identified by the media type JWE [JSON Web Encryption]).

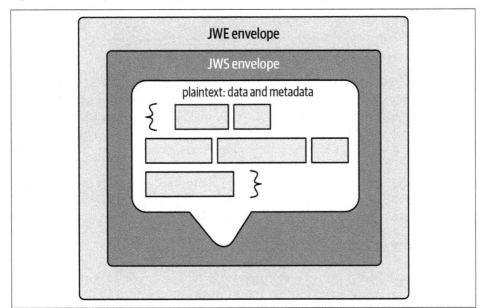

Figure 19-5. DIDComm message formats

DIDComm puts messages in a JWE envelope by default to hide content from unauthorized recipients and provide integrity guarantees. The JWE envelope also ensures that only authorized recipients know who the sender is.

Because DIDComm communications occurs within the mutually authenticated and encrypted DIDComm channel, the signature envelope isn't necessary for the recipient to know who the sender is. Rather, signed messages are used when the origin of the plain-text message needs to be proven to third parties.

Recall, from Chapter 8, that a key factor in message privacy is repudiability: if Alice sends a private message to Bob, he shouldn't be able to prove to Carol that Alice sent the message. Because signing messages needlessly can allow the recipient to prove to others who sent the message, signing should be used only when necessary. As a result, DIDComm messages are not often signed.

Protocological Power

DIDComm is designed for extensibility, allowing for protocols to be run on top of it. By using asynchronous, simplex messaging as the lowest common denominator, you can build almost any other interaction pattern on top of DIDComm. Application-layer protocols running on top of DIDComm allow extensibility in a way that also supports interoperability.

Protocols describe the rules for a set of interactions, specifying the kinds of interactions that can happen without being overly prescriptive about their nature or content. Protocols formalize workflows for specific interactions like ordering food at a restaurant, playing a game, or applying for college.

The Hyperledger Aries project has a collection of RFCs (*https://oreil.ly/FuQ1C*) that describe adopted, accepted, demonstrated, and proposed protocols that can be encapsulated in a DIDComm message. While we frequently think of smart agents being strictly about exchanging peer DIDs to create a connection, request and issue a credential, or prove attributes using credential presentation, these are merely specific protocols defined to run inside the DIDComm messaging protocol. RFC 0036 (*https://oreil.ly/wlIYG*) is the protocol specification for requesting and issuing credentials. RFC 0037 (*https://oreil.ly/rf1Qf*) is the protocol specification for presenting credentials. Dozens, even hundreds, of other protocols are possible.

Playing Tic-Tac-Toe

Daniel Hardman has provided a comprehensive tutorial on defining protocols that use DIDComm (*https://oreil.ly/S-qE-*). Hardman gives a sample definition of a protocol for playing tic-tac-toe (*https://oreil.ly/ez0H-*) over DIDComm messaging.

The tic-tac-toe protocol defines types of messages that are allowed, the game state, and what messages are allowed in each game state. I recommend it for understanding DIDComm protocols, since it's familiar and easy to understand.

Protocols are defined by a state machine for each role. In the case of tic-tac-toe, there's just one role, player, although it's held by two parties. Figure 19-6 shows Alice and Bob playing tic-tac-toe using a DIDComm relationship. Each keeps track of the game state locally and sends messages allowed by the protocol to play the game.

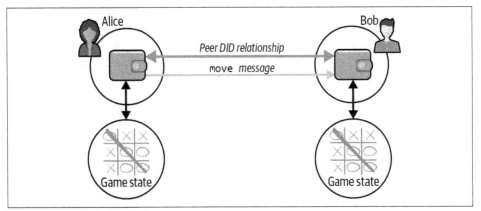

Figure 19-6. Alice and Bob play tic-tac-toe

The columns in Table 19-1 represent the events (sending and receiving for each of the two allowed message types, move and outcome). The rows are the allowed states. Each cell indicates the state to transition next, an error, or unreachable state.

Table 19-1. State machine for player role in tic-tac-toe

	Send move	Receive move	Send outcome	Receive outcome
my-move	Transition to their-move or wrap-up	Error; send problem-report	Transition to done	Transition to done
their-move	impossible	Transition to my-move or wrap-up	Transition to done	Transition to done
wrap-up	impossible	Error; send problem-report	Transition to done	Transition to done
done	impossible	Error; send problem-report	(ignore)	(ignore)

This table allows us to understand the possible actions a player might make in any allowed state. For example, if the player is in the my-move state, they could send a move message and then transition to either the their-move or wrap-up state depending on whether the game is continuing or over. They could also simply transition to done if they wish to abandon the game.

A move message is a JSON structure that specifies the type of message. It uses a DID-based URI, an `id` to establish a message thread, a field called `me` to identify the mark (X or O) the player is using, a list of `moves` so far, and an optional `comment`:

```
{
  "@type": "did:sov:SLfEi9esrjzybysFxQZbfq;spec/tictactoe/1.0/move",
  "@id": "518be002-de8e-456e-b3d5-8fe472477a86",
  "me": "X",
  "moves": ["X:B2"],
  "comment": "Let's play tic-tac-toe. I'll be X. I pick cell B2."
}
```

The `outcome` message is a JSON structure that identifies the message `type` using a DID-based URI, a `thread` identifier, a `winner`, and an optional `comment`:

```
{
  "@type": "did:sov:SLfEi9esrjzybysFxQZbfq;spec/tictactoe/1.0/outcome",
  "~thread": { "thid": "518be002-de8e-456e-b3d5-8fe472477a86", "seqnum": 3 },
  "winner": "X",
  "comment": "You won!"
}
```

You should be able to use the state table given in Table 19-1 and these sample messages to imagine the message flow necessary for a game to proceed from start to finish. The protocol says what messages and transitions you can legally make and describes all the possible outcomes of a game of tic-tac-toe.

Protocols Beyond Credential Exchange

DIDComm can be used to transport specialized protocols for all kinds of interactions that people might want to undertake online, including:

- Delegating
- Commenting
- Notifying
- Buying and selling
- Negotiating
- Enacting and enforcing contracts
- Putting things in escrow (and taking them out again)
- Transferring ownership
- Scheduling
- Auditing
- Reporting errors

All of these would be more complicated than the tic-tac-toe protocol I discussed in the last section; they would have more roles, and each role would have its own state table and more message types. But all would be specified in a similar manner to allow scripted interactions.

As you can see from this partial list, DIDComm is not just a secure, private way to connect and exchange credentials. Rather, it is a foundation protocol that provides a secure and private overlay to the internet for carrying out almost any online workflow. DIDComm qualifies as the encapsulating protocol of the identity metasystem I discussed in Chapter 4.

Smart Agents and the Future of the Internet

Equipped with the ability to support additional protocols like the ones discussed in the last section, smart agents can mediate many of the workflows that make up our digital lives. At their core, agents provide the following capabilities:

Identity and trust establishment
> By exchanging DIDs and VCs, agents can establish your identity and provide other reasons to trust you in the form of VCs, even if the entire interaction is digital and remote.

Relationship management
> Exchanging DIDs establishes a relationship, but relationships change over time. New information and interaction patterns emerge. An ephemeral relationship may become more permanent after repeated interactions, necessitating new services. Agents manage these changes on behalf of their controllers.

Secure, confidential, and structured message sharing
> DIDComm provides a basic messaging protocol that ensures the confidentiality of messages based on the keys associated with the exchanged DIDs. Messages are structured so that other protocols can be wrapped in a DIDComm message. Put another way, DIDComm is a transport protocol. Agents that understand those protocols can exchange messages and engage in structured workflows.

Using the protocols that I just discussed, smart agents can aid in many of the tasks people face daily:

Payment and value exchange
> Not all relationships are transactional, but many are. Agents need to mediate value exchange on behalf of their controllers to simplify digital interactions.

Private, secure, trustworthy data sharing
> Through their ability to issue and use VCs, agents provide private, secure, authentic data sharing. I think most people only poorly understand the magnitude of this capability. When people think about VCs, they fall back on the

familiar: driver's license, university transcripts, employee IDs, movie tickets. But as I discussed in the previous chapter, any structured data can be shared as a VC with the attendant trust and confidence that the exchange provides for more traditional credentials.

Buying and selling
Building on payment and value exchange, agents can be smart digital assistants for commerce with companies or individuals, managing the workflow of the entire transaction.

Ownership transfer
Agents can play an important role in simplifying the transfer of property. Selling a car, for example, may involve interacting with banks, insurance companies, and the DMV. The agent can help mediate the interactions on these different relationships. I'll give a detailed example of this in Chapter 20.

Interacting with things
Agents can carry out tasks that make our interactions with the Internet of Things easier and more rewarding. Again, I'll discuss this more in Chapter 20.

There are many more. In fact, *any* workflow can be defined as a protocol on top of DIDComm, allowing multiple parties to work together with the help of their agents.

Operationalizing Digital Relationships

Smart agents are tools for people to operationalize their digital relationships. Let's review what you've learned in the preceding four chapters and pull it all together to understand how Alice can operationalize her digital relationships. Figure 19-7 illustrates Alice and her relationships.

In the diagram, Alice has a smart agent. She uses the agent to manage her relationships with Bob and Carol as well as a host of organizations. Bob and Carol also have agents. They have a relationship with each other, and Carol has a relationship with Bravo Corp, just as Alice does. These relationships are enabled by autonomic identifiers in the form of peer DIDs (blue arrows). The agent used by each participant provides a consistent user experience, like the browser did for the web. People using agents don't see the DIDs (identifiers), but instead the relationships they have with other people, organizations, and things.

As you've learned, these autonomic relationships are self-certifying, meaning they don't rely on any third party for their trust basis. They are also mutually authenticating; each of the parties in the relationship can authenticate the other. Further, as you've just learned, these relationships use a secure communications channel based on the DIDComm protocol. Because of built-in mutual authentication, Alice has trustworthy communication channels with everyone with whom she has a peer-DID-based relationship.

Alice, as mentioned, also has relationships with various organizations. Each of these organizations uses an *enterprise agent* that is integrated with other enterprise systems. One of them, Attester Org, has issued a VC to Alice (green arrows) using the DID-Comm issue credential protocol (*https://oreil.ly/8xbmv*). That protocol runs on top of the DIDComm-based communication channel enabled by Alice's peer DID relationship with Attester.

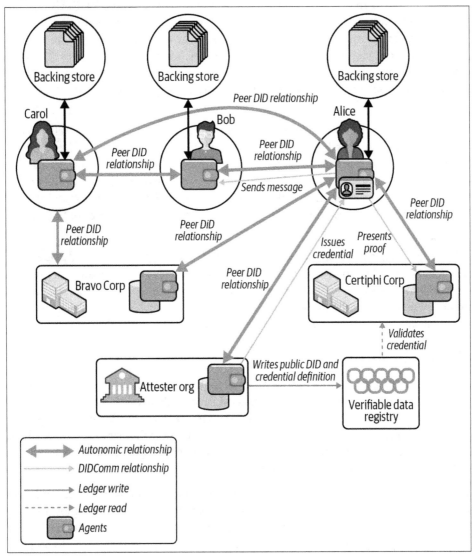

Figure 19-7. Agents in digital relationships

When Alice later needs to prove something, like her address, to Certiphi Corp, she presents a DIDComm-derived credential proof (*https://oreil.ly/_D0av*), again enabled by the peer DID relationship she has with Certiphi Corp. Certiphi can validate the fidelity of the credential using the VDR.

Alice has relationships with five different entities: her friends Bob and Carol, and three organizations. Each relationship is based on autonomic identifiers in the form of peer DIDs. All the organizations use agents to manage *autonomic relationships* with each other and their customers. As a credential issuer, Attester Org has an *algorithmic identifier* in the form of a public DID that has been recorded on the VDR. Using algorithmic identifiers on a VDR allows discovery of the credential definition and the public DID by Certiphi Corp when it validates the credential. As you learned in Chapter 15, you need to use a public VDR for this purpose unless you're willing to give up the loose coupling it provides. Remember, loose coupling provides scalability, flexibility, and isolation. Isolation is critical to the privacy protection promises of VC exchange.

Each company tracks the attributes and other properties it needs for the relationship to provide the promised utility. These are *administrative systems,* since they are administered by the organization for their own purpose and their root of trust is a database managed by the organization. The difference between these administrative systems and those common in online identity today is that only the organization is depending on them. Alice, Bob, and Carol have their own autonomic root of trust in their agents.

Alice might employ multiple agents (even though the diagram shows only one). Alice's agents allow her to create, manage, and utilize secure, trustworthy communications channels with anyone online without reliance on any third party. As we've seen, Alice's agents are also the place where specific, protocol-enabled interactions happen. Alice's agents are flexible tools that she uses to manage her digital life.

Multiple Smart Agents

As peer-DID-based relationships become more and more common, people won't just have a single agent. They will have agents on each of their edge devices and several (perhaps many) in the cloud. Some agents will serve as routers, automatically getting messages to the agents that can process a specific request or carry out a specialized task. Some agents will control things like a car or smart home. Some will employ automated reasoning to carry out their work.

But regardless of its capabilities and assigned operations, every agent works on behalf of the entity who controls it. The enterprise agents that organizations employ are connected to their internal IT systems, the customer relationship management (CRM) system, the IAM system, and any other part of the enterprise that needs to securely share structured information with others.

As I've discussed, people will also have agents, called *smart agents*, that work on their behalf, digitally embodying them so they can act autonomously, as peers, with other entities online. As you saw in the auto accident example in Chapter 17, smart agents will play an important role in helping people manage everyday tasks. Imagine having a smart agent that can help you schedule doctor's appointments or buy a motorcycle.

Smart agents allow people to create peer networks with their friends and with businesses they use without an administrative intermediary (like Facebook, Signal, or WhatsApp). Smart agents allow people to exchange signed bundles of structured data in the form of credentials. Alice could use her smart agent to share a blog post or a picture. A network of smart agents, exchanging trustworthy structured data among peers, forms a decentralized social graph that provides safety, security, and privacy on top of the value we all recognize in being able to connect with others online.

Realizing the Smart Agent Vision

Some of the work necessary to realize the vision for smart agents is already done. Several companies already offer agents and associated wallets that speak the necessary DIDComm messaging protocol and support protocols for exchanging DIDs and VCs. The problem is that these, like the name "verifiable credential," are limited—based on a vision of agents that are merely software for exchanging credentials. The vision that people working in SSI have for smart agents is much more expansive.

To fulfill that vision, agents will need to be extensible so that they can adapt to the multitude of needs a diverse set of users will have. You can't hardwire the capabilities needed to function as a smart agent into a piece of software, any more than you could lump people's needs for credentials into a few popular types. Smart agents must have the following capabilities and attributes:

- Smart agents must be computational nodes that can represent or model anything: a person, place, or organization, a smart thing, a dumb thing, a concept, even a pothole.

- Smart agents must employ a substitutable hosting model. Not only will Alice have multiple agents, but she will also host them at different places. Her new car, for example, may come with an agent that is hosted by the manufacturer. She must be able to choose to leave it there or move it somewhere else.

- Smart agents must use an extensible service model onto which new functionality can be layered. The functionality within a smart agent should use a programming model that ensures its services are loosely coupled. Isolating state changes inside the smart agents will allow for adding new services without interfering with existing services.

- Smart agents must provide better control over terms, apps, and data than current systems. Smart agents cleanly separate the data for different entities. Agents, representing a specific entity, and services, representing a specific business capability within it, provide fine-grained control over data and its processing. For example, if you sell your car, you can transfer the vehicle's smart agent to the new owner, after deleting the trip service, and its associated data, while leaving untouched the maintenance records, which are stored as part of the maintenance service in the agent. I'll discuss this more in Chapter 20.

Digital Memories

Real life is complicated and messy. The only hope we have of enabling digital interactions that mirror activities in the physical world is with decentralized systems that allow each person, organization, or thing to act independently and autonomously.

I began the chapter with a discussion about what differentiates what people are calling Web3 from what came before. The foregoing discussion of smart agents and the DIDComm protocol has given you a foundation for understanding how digital relationships can be operationalized and the capabilities such smart agents might afford people in their digital lives.

Marshall McLuhan wrote extensively of how our things become extensions of ourselves.[4] A driver might speak of "my engine" or "my wheels," and a pilot might say "my wings" or "my rudder." In Chapter 3 I discussed Polanyi's ideas on tacit knowledge as a fundamental limitation of the digital world. That tacit knowledge is gained through what he calls *indwelling*: our senses dwell in the car, the plane, the shoes, the hammer, or the bike.[5] Smart agents extend people in the digital sphere, letting us dwell in the virtual tools of the digital world in the same way we naturally extend ourselves into our tools in the physical.

Memories of our physical interactions with people, places, and things play a big part in our ability to interact with them—tacitly, without significant conscious effort. Suppose I go to the corner store to buy a Coke with a credit card. In this situation, the cashier, others in the store, and I all share a common experience. No one participating would claim to *own* the interaction. But we all retain memories that are our own. There is no single *true* record of the interaction. Every participant will have a different perspective (literally).

On the other hand, the store, as an institution, might retain a memory of having sold a Coke and of the associated credit card transaction. This digital memory of the transaction can easily persist longer than any of the analog memories of the event. Because it is a digital record, we trust it and consider it to be *true*. For some

---

4 Marshall McLuhan, *Understanding Media: The Extensions of Man* (New York: Signet Books, 1964).

5 Michael Polanyi, "Tacit Knowing: Its Bearing on Some Problems of Philosophy," *Reviews of Modern Physics* 34, no. 601 (October 1962).

purposes—say, proving in a court of law that I was in the store at a particular time—that record is useful. But for other purposes, such as recalling whether the cashier was friendly or rude, the digital memory is woefully anemic.

Online, people only have digital memories. And we have very few tools for saving, managing, recalling, and using them. I think digital memories are one of the primary features of digital embodiment—giving people a place to stand in the digital world, with their own perspective, memories, and capacity to act. We can't be peers online without having our own digital memories.

One of the recent trends in application development is microservices, with an attendant denormalization of data. The realization that there doesn't have to be—indeed, often *can't* be—a single source of truth for data has freed application development from the strictures of centralization. This has led to more easily built and operated distributed applications that are resilient and scale more easily. I think this same idea applies to digital interactions generally. Freeing ourselves from the mindset that digital systems can and should provide a single record that is *true* will lead to more autonomy and richer interactions.

StJohn Deakins calls this the "analog-digital memory divide." (*https://oreil.ly/wnJDT*) This divide is one source of the power imbalance between people and administrative entities (for instance, anyone who has a record of you in an account). In addition to all the other capabilities of smart agents that I've discussed in this chapter, smart agents must also provide tools for people to manage their digital memories holistically and comprehensively, if they are to be the basis for digital embodiment.

Smart agents provide a foundation for our digital personhood and allow us not only to take charge of our digital memories but to operationalize all of our digital relationships. Enriching our digital memories of events by allowing everyone their own perspective will lead to a digital world that is more like real life.

CHAPTER 20

Identity on the Internet of Things

I use a Philips Sonicare toothbrush. One of its features is a little yellow light that comes on to tell me to change the toothbrush head. The first time the light came on, I wondered how I would reset it once I replaced the head. I even googled it to find out.

Turns out I needn't have bothered. Once I changed the head, the light went off. This didn't happen when I simply removed the old head and put the same one back on. Each toothbrush head has a unique identity that the toothbrush recognizes. This identity is used to signal head replacement as well as to put the toothbrush into different modes based on the type of head installed.

Philips calls this technology BrushSync, but underneath the branding it's using RFID (radio frequency identification). Each head has an RFID chip embedded in it. The toothbrush body reads the data off the head and adjusts its internal state in the appropriate way.

I like this RFID use case because it's got clear benefits for both Philips and its customers. Philips sells more toothbrush heads—so the Internet of Things (IoT) use case is clearly aligned with business goals here. Customers get reminders to replace their toothbrush heads and can reset the reminder by simply doing what they'd do anyway—switching the head.

There aren't many privacy concerns at present—the toothbrush doesn't connect to the internet and phone home to Philips. But as more and more products begin to include RFID chips, you could imagine scanners on garbage trucks that correlate chipped items that are used and thrown out with an address. Maybe there will be a market for garbage cans that can disable RFID chips when they're thrown away.

A friend of mine, Eric Olafson, is a founding investor in a company called Riot. Riot is another example of how thoughtfully applied RFID-based identifiers can solve business and customer problems. Riot creates tech that companies can use for

RFID-based in-store inventory management. This solves a big problem for stores that often don't know what inventory they have on hand. With Riot, a quick scan of the store each morning updates the inventory management system, showing where the store's inventory data is out of sync with its physical inventory. I often go to physical stores because the parent company's app tells me that a specific location has the product I want, so it would be nice to know the app isn't lying. Riot puts the RFID on the product tag, not in the product, sidestepping many of the privacy concerns that arise if people are walking around with lots of RFID chips in their clothing.

Both BrushSync and Riot assign identities to physical things to solve business problems, showing that unique identifiers on individual products can be good for business and customers alike. This speaks to the breadth of identity and its importance in areas beyond associating identifiers with people.

This chapter starts with a discussion of the models and protocols that enable identity in the current IoT. I'll explore the limitations of, and discuss alternatives to, the current model. The chapter concludes with a discussion of how the SSI technologies and protocols you've learned about in the last six chapters provide a new, better model.

Access Control for Devices

Managing who can control a device is a fundamental capability for the IoT. Devices—things—are not (yet) autonomous and are therefore always under the control of a person or organization. As you learned in Chapters 11 and 12, authentication and authorization underpin access control. Securely connecting devices to each other, to APIs, and to the owner's computer systems is not an easy task. Connected devices carry personal information, and as such devices become more ubiquitous, the aggregation of that data can represent significant elements of a person's life, posing potential privacy problems. A connected car, for example, knows its current location and speed, all the trips it's been on, perhaps who was driving, and even its fueling and maintenance records. That's a treasure trove of personal data that has legitimate and illegitimate uses.

The most common pattern for connected devices is shown in Figure 20-1. Suppose Alice buys a new connected Bravo lightbulb. In the figure, Alice is using an app on her phone to access servers and APIs operated by Bravo, the maker of the connected lightbulb.

The lightbulb is also connected to the internet and is using Bravo's API to send data. In some cases, the data being produced by the lightbulb and stored on Bravo's servers contains Alice's personal information or information that might be sensitive—like when a room is occupied. Consequently, the channels between Alice's phone, the lightbulb, and Bravo's servers should be secure and authenticated.

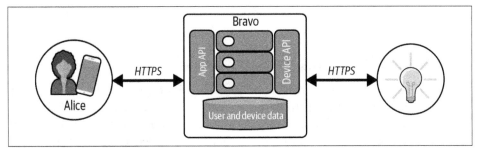

Figure 20-1. Relationships in the IoT

In addition to the pattern shown in Figure 20-1, sometimes Alice's phone might serve as a network proxy for a Bluetooth-connected device rather than the device connecting directly to Bravo. Often, simple, low-power devices will have a smart hub that serves as their proxy.

Supporting connections with devices and ensuring that their owners control the data associated with that device assumes the manufacturer can do at least the following:

- Ensure the device has a unique identifier
- Register the device over a secure channel
- Authenticate the device
- Create an association or relationship between the owner and their device

There are various ways to implement a system that fulfills these requirements. This section will discuss using OAuth as a way of meeting the last two. I discussed the basics of OAuth in Chapter 13. As the sales of connected devices have increased, APIs for personal data have become more widely used and OAuth has become the protocol of choice for letting device owners choose what applications access their data. OAuth's flow makes people part of the process that determines what data is shared and with what applications.

As you learned in Chapter 13, OAuth was designed for a very specific purpose: to allow people to control access to their resources (like an API) without requiring that they share their usernames and passwords. Before OAuth, if Alice wanted Bravo to have access to her data on Attester, she'd have to give Bravo her username and password on Attester. Bravo would store the username and password and impersonate Alice each time they needed to access Attester on her behalf. By using Alice's username and password, Bravo would demonstrate they had Alice's implicit permission to access her account at Attester.

Recall that the OAuth protocol, in contrast, does not give Alice's username and password to Bravo. Instead, it provides an access token that Bravo can use to access an

API at Attester. Alice or Attester can expire the token anytime they no longer want Bravo to have access to Alice's data.

Using OAuth with Devices

In 2013, I launched a connected-car project called Fuse (*https://oreil.ly/lQhAG*) on Kickstarter that followed the pattern in Figure 20-1. Fuse used an off-the-shelf OBD-II device (*https://oreil.ly/DH_at*) that had a cellular connection.[1] The devices were supplied by a company called Carvoyant, which also provided a cloud-based API that served as the online proxy for the device. The Carvoyant-supplied devices were pre-provisioned with cellular service on a virtual mobile network that provided connectivity to Carvoyant's servers.

Carvoyant authorized access to its API for the car using OAuth. Using the terminology of Chapter 13: Fuse, a cloud service with a mobile app, was the client; the Carvoyant account system was the authorization server (AS); and the Carvoyant API was the resource server (RS). Fuse asked car owners to create a Carvoyant account and then authorize access to data about their car in the API using OAuth. The interaction was a standard authorization code grant.

Fuse helped me understand the pros and cons of using OAuth for connecting devices to the internet and the importance of ensuring that vehicle data ends up in the right hands. For the most part, OAuth was a great choice for connecting the Fuse system to the Carvoyant API while allowing owners to maintain control of how their data is used. Its big advantage is that the process is well understood, and numerous libraries and API platforms provide support for API providers and client developers alike. But OAuth is far from a complete solution. Let's see why.

OAuth's Shortcomings for the IoT

OAuth has several limitations that make it less than ideal as a universal solution to device authorization. I think of them in two categories: device limitations and owner autonomy.

Device limitations

From the preceding discussion, you can see that one almost universal element of current connected devices is that they do not interact directly with the client. Instead, something else—a cloud-based service, a gateway, or a phone—is acting as a proxy. This is often necessary (or at least desirable) for reasons beyond access control, such as interdevice coordination. Devices often have small microcontrollers instead of

---

1 OBD, or on-board diagnostics, provides a standard hardware interface port on every vehicle sold in the US since 1996. The port has access to events on the vehicle's internal CAN bus (*https://oreil.ly/Y-mCd*).

---

full-blown microprocessors, and most don't have the memory or processing power to even parse a JSON object, let alone handle HTTP with TLS.

Furthermore, devices often don't have displays, making configuration and other interactions difficult. This limitation restricts the utility of OAuth flows, since the device is unlikely to have a web browser available to process redirects. These limitations apply whether the device or the client is providing the API.

There are several ways to mitigate these issues. The most obvious way is to use the pattern in Figure 20-1, where a more powerful computer or smartphone sits between the device and its owner and serves as a proxy for the physical device.[2] That still leaves the problem of securely connecting the device to the proxy. For the most part, this latter process is ad hoc, with few standards. As a result, the user experience of connecting and using a device varies widely. What's more, the security of these ad hoc mechanisms depends on the abilities of the programmers creating them.

Another approach is to make it easier to connect to lower-powered devices. Alternative transport protocols such as MQ Telemetry Transport (MQTT (*https://oreil.ly/ QFzd2*)), interaction protocols like the Constrained Application Protocol (*https:// oreil.ly/xu23s*), and security protocols such as Datagram Transport Layer Security (*https://oreil.ly/-TWy7*) are potential fixes, by themselves or in combination. Unfortunately, I've not seen much uptake on any of these in commercial IoT products.

When the lack of a display is the primary problem, most devices provide some way of using Bluetooth, WiFi, or QR codes to connect to a phone or other device and complete the configuration.

Where's the owner?

OAuth's flows were designed for systems where a person is available to approve the initial connection. I've already discussed the problems of low-powered devices not being powerful enough to support web-browser-based flows, but there's another problem.

As you learned in Chapter 13, OAuth supports refresh tokens. Refresh tokens are meant to be used by the client with the AS to get a new access token when the old one has expired. Normally this isn't a problem for a connected device, since the owner doesn't need to reauthorize access to use a refresh token. The problem occurs when the refresh token fails for some reason and the owner needs to regrant access.

---

2 You'll sometimes hear this proxy called a *device shadow* or *digital twin*. I prefer Bruce Sterling's name (*https:// oreil.ly/IH1Qk*): *spime*, a neologism combining the words *space* and *time*. But regardless of what you call them, the need for some computational node that is separate from, but representing, the device is a reality.

In the web and mobile interactions envisioned by OAuth's original framers, this wasn't a big concern since the need to access the API would be driven by a person interacting with the application. Hence, someone would be available to approve access again, if necessary.

Devices are another matter. Devices are often reacting to their environment, not by a direct command, so the owner isn't available to handle problems with access control. I had this problem with Fuse. The OBD-II device reacted to vehicle events such as the ignition being turned off or on. When that happened, the Fuse system processed the event and sometimes needed other information from the device and its API. All of this happened in the background, without human involvement. Consequently, if the refresh token failed, Fuse had no recourse except to notify the owner (using email or some other means) that an access control problem had occurred and that they would need to log in and fix it. In the meantime, Fuse was disconnected from the API and unable to carry out its expected tasks.[3] Note that this problem isn't mitigated by the device having a proxy.

Connected-car scenarios also point to other problems with connected devices and OAuth's dependence on a person being present. For example, what happens if Alice lets Bob borrow her car? How does she grant him access? Can she limit what Bob can do? What happens if the device can't communicate with the AS? These problems can be solved in a variety of ways, but if every device manufacturer solves them differently, the IoT won't be interoperable.

Magically working together

Even with the preceding problems, OAuth presents a viable solution to a lot of present-day IoT challenges. Still, supporting a world where dozens or even hundreds of connected devices easily connect with each other to get things done for their owners will need more than what present-day OAuth is prepared to provide.

Mike Schwartz of Gluu calls this the "magically working together" problem (*https://oreil.ly/IxBVa*). Schwartz uses the example of a connected lightbulb and light switch. He says, "If you buy a light switch and a lightbulb, they need to magically work together." In this scenario the lightbulb is the RP and the switch is the client.

Getting connected devices to directly work together is difficult. Commercial connected lightbulb products, like Philips Hue, use a hub and a proprietary connection system. Others, like TP-Link's Kasa, use WiFi-enabled devices, forgoing the hub but still placing everything inside a single app, disconnected from other manufacturers'

---

3 Much of the Fuse code was involved in solving this problem by recognizing when data was missing and syncing the Fuse application with the data at Carvoyant. In fairness to OAuth, even if refreshing access tokens hadn't been a problem, significant error-handling code would still have been needed to ensure the systems were consistent.

---

devices. It seems unlikely that any of us will be willing to buy all our lightbulbs and switches from a single vendor, let alone every connected device we might ever own.

The CompuServe of Things

If you're anything like me, you've got a collection of connected devices—everything from Kasa-connected outlets to Nest thermostats. The problem with all these devices is that they are all quite antisocial. That is, they don't easily talk to each other.

Nearly every connected device currently for sale asks buyers to follow the same process: download the mobile app, create an account on the manufacturer's server, and connect your new device to your account. There are variations in how this happens, but, in the end, you have a device you can control with your phone.

Most current IoT business models focus on cloud-based strategies that place the vendor at the heart of the data architecture (as shown in Figure 20-1). If the IoT is going to come to fruition, we're going to need better ways of connecting devices. Merely connecting them to a network and then to an account under the manufacturer's administrative control isn't enough. Devices need to be connected to each other and to services that the owner uses. Owners want to coordinate their interactions, and this requires having devices connect to more than just their makers.

Here are some of the reasons devices need rich connections:

- To discover contextual and other data, such as weather or price data, through APIs
- To coordinate with other devices and systems to achieve a goal, such as reducing peak electric power usage in a home
- To integrate with systems that can automatically represent the owner's intent, such as reducing the thermostat only if the house will be unoccupied for more than eight hours

Richer connections require that we move from the current manufacturer-centric connected device ecosystem to a true IoT. Making these interactions secure and protecting owners' privacy will require more sophisticated access control methods than are currently employed.

Online Services

Back in the day, by which I mean 1986, I was lucky enough to be at a university and have early access to the internet as I entered graduate school at UC Davis. In those days, if you weren't one of the lucky few with an internet connection and you wanted to communicate with friends online, you used CompuServe, Prodigy, America Online (AOL), or some other proprietary *online service*. Each of these offered a way to send email, but only to people on the same service. They had forums where you could discuss various topics. And they all had what we'd call *apps* today. These services were silos. Each was an island that didn't interoperate with the others.

In the mid-1990s, popular interest in the web caused many companies to get into the dial-up internet service provider (ISP) business. Once connected to the internet, you could email anyone, participate in forums anywhere, look at any website, shop from any online store, and so on. While AOL successfully made the transition from online service business to ISP, the rest of the online services of the early '90s did not.

Online 2.0: The Silos Strike Back

Each of these online service businesses sought to offer a complete soup-to-nuts experience. They all capitalized on their captive audiences to get businesses to pay for access. In fact, you don't have to look very hard to see that much of what's popular on the internet today looks a lot like more sophisticated versions of these online service businesses. Web 2.0 isn't so much about the web as it is about recreating the online business models of the '80s and early '90s. Maybe we should call it "Online 2.0" instead.

To understand the difference, consider Gmail versus Facebook Messenger. As I discussed in Chapter 17, because Gmail is really just a massive web client on top of internet mail protocols like SMTP and IMAP, you can use your Gmail account to send email to any account on any email system on the internet. And, if you decide you don't like Gmail, you can easily switch to another email provider (at least if you have your own domain).

Facebook Messenger, on the other hand, can only be used to talk to people using the means Facebook allows. Not only that, but you only get to use the clients that Facebook chooses for you. Facebook is going to make those choices based on what's best for Facebook. Most Web 2.0 business models ensure that the interests of Web 2.0 companies are not necessarily aligned with those of their users. Companies don't decide not to make their products interoperable out of ignorance, but on purpose. For example, WhatsApp uses an open protocol (XMPP [Extensible Messaging and Presence Protocol]) but chooses to not interoperate with other XMPP clients.[4]

Which brings us to the IoT. The IoT, as it works today, isn't a real internet. It's a collection of silos, built by well-meaning companies repeating the errors of history, giving us the modern equivalents of isolated mainframes, incompatible LANs, and siloed

---

4 I'm not making a "Google good, Facebook bad" argument, merely comparing Gmail to Facebook Messenger. Many Google products have their own forms of lock-in and are every bit as much re-creations of the 1980s "online service" business model as Facebook.

networks like those of AOL, CompuServe, and Prodigy. What we're building might more properly be called the CompuServe of Things.

A Real, Open Internet of Things

If we were really building the Internet of Things, with all that that term implies, there would be open, decentralized, heterarchical systems at its core, just like at the core of the internet itself. There aren't. Sure, we're using TCP/IP and HTTP, but we're doing it in a closed, centralized, hierarchical way, with only a minimal nod to interoperability using APIs.

We need the IoT to be the next step in the series that began with the general-purpose PC and continued with the internet and general-purpose protocols—systems that support personal autonomy and choice. The IoT envisions computing devices that will intermediate every aspect of our lives. I strongly believe that this will provide the envisioned benefits—or even be tolerable—only if we build a true Internet of Things rather than a CompuServe of Things.

When I say the internet is "open," I'm using that as a key word for the three key concepts that underlie it: decentralization, heterarchy (what some call peer-to-peer connectivity), and interoperability.

As you learned in Chapter 2, decentralization and heterarchy are not the same. To recall how they differ, consider two examples: DNS, the Domain Name System you learned about in Chapter 10, and Facebook. DNS is decentralized but hierarchical. Zone administrators update their zone files and determine, in a completely decentralized manner, which subdomains inside their domain correspond to which IP addresses (among other things). But the way DNS achieves global consensus about what these mappings *mean* is hierarchical. A few well-known servers for each top-level domain (TLD) point to the servers for the various domains inside the TLD, which in turn point to servers for subdomains inside them, and so on. There's exactly one hierarchical copy of the mapping.

Facebook, on the other hand, is heterarchical but centralized. The Facebook Open Graph relates people to each other in a heterarchical fashion—peer-to-peer—but, of course, it's completely centralized. The entire graph resides on Facebook's servers under Facebook's control.

Interoperability allows independently developed systems to interact. It provides for substitutability, allowing one system or service to be substituted for another without loss of basic functionality. As previously noted, even though I use Gmail as my email provider, I can talk to people who use Hotmail and I can, if I'm unhappy with Gmail, substitute another email provider.

These three concepts aren't optional. We won't get the real IoT unless we develop open systems that support decentralization, heterarchy, and interoperability. You might well ask: where are the protocols underlying the IoT? Protocols like TCP/IP, HTTP, and MQTT aren't enough because they work at a level *below* where the IoT's things need to interoperate. Put another way, they leave unspecified many important processes (like discovery).

Alternatives to the CompuServe of Things

In "Peloton Bricks Its Treadmills" (*https://oreil.ly/Rdo6f*), blogger and journalist Cory Doctorow discusses fitness equipment manufacturer Peloton's response to a product recall on its treadmills. Part of that response was a firmware upgrade. Rather than issuing the firmware upgrade to all treadmills, Peloton bricked all the treadmills and then only updated the ones whose owners were paying for monthly subscriptions to Peloton's service.[5]

This points to a bug in the current architecture for IoT. Even though you bought a connected thing, you're really *renting* it. You don't own it, despite paying hundreds, even thousands, of dollars up front. The terms and conditions on accounts usually allow the manufacturer to close your account for any reason and without recourse. Since many products cannot function without their associated cloud service, this renders the devices inoperable.

If Peloton decides to revoke my account, I will probably survive. But what if, in some future world, the root certificate authority of the identity documents I use for banking, shopping, travel, and a host of other things decides to revoke my identity for some reason?[6] Or if my car stops running because Ford shuts off my account?

I've discussed the need for autonomy in identity systems. Autonomy is just as important in those identity systems that underlie the IoT. People must be in control of the connected things in their life. There will be systems and services provided by others and they will, of necessity, be administered. But those administering authorities need not control people and their lives.

The architecture of the CompuServe of Things looks like Figure 20-2. This is Figure 20-1, but I've added a box to show where authority and control lie.

---

5 The term *brick* is used to describe a piece of hardware that becomes useless because of a firmware update—it no longer has any more smart functions than a brick.

6 This is the underlying scenario of one of my favorite science fiction books, *Rainbows End* by Vernor Vinge. I ask all my students to read *Rainbows End* because I think it does a good job of taking current ideas and technology and asking where they might end up in 30 or 40 years' time. I do this as part of asking them to consider how they can build the world they want to live in.

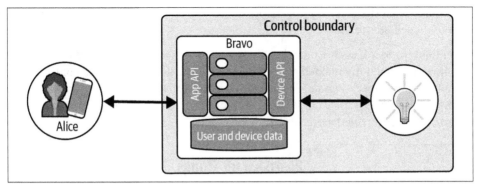

Figure 20-2. *The architecture for the CompuServe of Things*

As noted above, Alice uses an app on her phone to control her connected lightbulb through the manufacturer's API. Everything is inside the administrative control of the device manufacturer (indicated by the gray box).

There is an alternative model shown in Figure 20-3 that I call the *self-sovereign Internet of Things*.

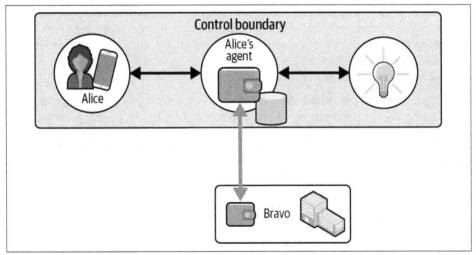

Figure 20-3. *A self-sovereign IoT architecture*

In this model, the device and data about it are controlled by Alice, not the manufacturer. The device, and an associated smart agent that Alice uses to interact with it, have a relationship with the manufacturer, but the manufacturer is no longer in control. Alice is in control of her device, the data it generates, and the agent that processes the data. Note that this doesn't mean Alice has to code or even manage all that. She can run her agent at a cloud service (called an *agency*), and the code in her agent is likely from the manufacturer. But it *could* be other code, instead of or in addition to what she gets from the manufacturer. The point is that Alice can decide. A true IoT is self-sovereign.

You might wonder if such a model could work. Fuse, which I introduced earlier, used this model and still maintained the familiar user experience of a device controlled by an app on the owner's phone. The agent was not a DIDComm agent (like we talked about in Chapter 19), since DIDComm did not yet exist in 2013. Instead, it was based on an open source, rule-based agent called a *pico*.

Picos: SSI for Things

Picos are an open source project (*https://oreil.ly/JtmQY*) I run to explore programmable smart agents. While a detailed discussion of picos is beyond the scope of this book, they have been the basis for my work in decentralized identity and IoT for many years.

Picos can be arranged in networks supporting peer-to-peer communication and computation. A cooperating network of picos is an actor-model distributed system, reacting to messages from other picos, changing state based on those messages, and sending messages to other picos. Picos have an internal event bus for distributing those messages to rules installed in the pico. Rules are selected to run based on declarative event expressions. The pico matches events on its bus with event scenarios declared in each rule's event expression. The pico engine schedules any rule whose event expression matches the event for execution. Executing rules may raise additional events, which are processed in the same way.

Picos provide a programmable SSI agent system that is capable of supporting complex IoT applications. Vehicle owners in Fuse controlled their data. While the picos (acting as agents) were hosted in an agency that I provided for Fuse, someone else could have set up an alternative pico agency or hosted their own. The Fuse picos would have run there just as well without loss of functionality.

Picos allowed Fuse to easily provide an autonomous processing agent for each vehicle and to organize those into fleets. Because picos support peer-to-peer architectures, putting a vehicle in more than one fleet or having a fleet with multiple owners was easy.

The Self-Sovereign Internet of Things

Through Fuse and other projects, I've been working toward a self-sovereign Internet of Things (SSIoT) for over a decade.[7] In an SSIoT, Alice has direct relationships with her things or a proxy she controls. In Figure 19-7, I showed a diagram where Alice has relationships with people and organizations. But the diagram did not show *things*. Figure 20-4 is largely the same, but with a Bravo lightbulb.

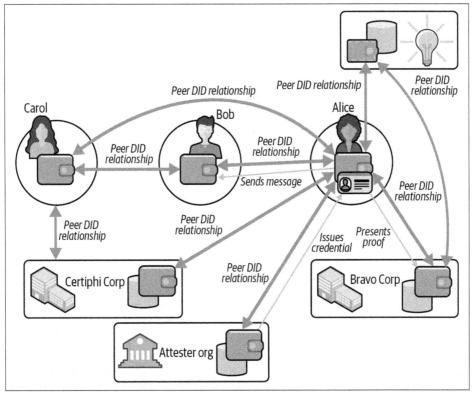

Figure 20-4. Alice forms a relationship with her lightbulb

In Figure 20-4, the lightbulb is a fully capable participant in Alice's relationship network. Either the lightbulb is powerful enough to run an edge agent or the lightbulb is being proxied by a *device shadow*, *spime*, or *pico* that serves as its agent. Alice has a DID-based relationship with the lightbulb's agent. She also has a relationship with the

---

7 Since things can't be sovereign or autonomous, the term *self-sovereign IoT* shouldn't be taken to mean autonomous things, but rather that the boundary of control is under the umbrella of the owner's self-sovereign authority.

company who makes it, Bravo, as does the lightbulb. Those last two are optional, but useful—and, importantly, fully under Alice's control.

DID Relationships for IoT

Let's focus on Alice, her lightbulb, and Bravo to better understand the contrast between the CompuServe of Things and an SSIoT.

In Figure 20-5, rather than being intermediated by the lightbulb's manufacturer, Alice has a direct, DID-based relationship with the lightbulb. Both Alice and the lightbulb have agents and wallets. Alice also has a DID-based relationship with Bravo, which runs an enterprise agent. Alice interacts with her lightbulb and Bravo as she sees fit, even serving as the intermediary if that suits her purposes.

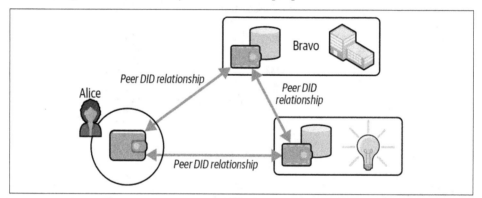

Figure 20-5. Alice's relationships with her lightbulb and its manufacturer

Figure 20-5 also shows a DID-based relationship between the lightbulb and Bravo. In the CompuServe of Things, Alice might be concerned with the privacy of her data. But in an SSIoT, Alice controls the policies on that relationship and thus what is shared. She might, for example, authorize the lightbulb to share diagnostic information when she needs service. She could also issue a credential to Bravo that allows them to service the lightbulb remotely, then revoke it when they're done.

The following sections describe three of many possible use cases for the SSIoT.

Use Case 1: Updating Firmware

One of the problems with the CompuServe of Things is securely updating device firmware. There are many ways to approach secure firmware updates in the CompuServe of things—each manufacturer does it slightly differently. The SSIoT provides a standard way for the lightbulb to determine that the firmware update is from the manufacturer and not a hacker.

As shown in Figure 20-6, Bravo has written a public DID to a verifiable data registry (VDR). They can use that public DID to sign firmware updates. Bravo embedded its public DID in the lightbulb when it was manufactured. The lightbulb can resolve the DID to look up Bravo's current public key on the VDR and validate the signature. This ensures that the firmware package is from Bravo. And DIDs allow Bravo to rotate its keys as needed without invalidating the DIDs stored in the devices.

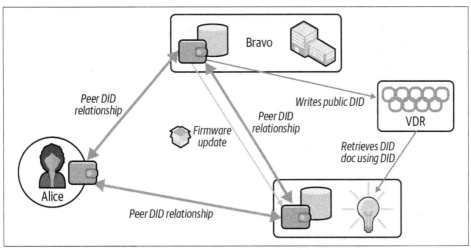

Figure 20-6. Updating the firmware in Alice's lightbulb

Of course, digital certificates could also solve this problem.[8] So, this example is about achieving parity. The advantage of using SSIoT for secure firmware updates instead of digital certificates is that if Bravo is using it for other things (see below), it gets this for free without also having to support the certificate code in its products or pay for certificates and the inevitable updates.

Use Case 2: Proving Ownership

Alice can prove she owns a particular model of lightbulb using a verifiable credential. Figure 20-7 shows how this could work.

The lightbulb's agent is running the DIDComm Introduce protocol (*https://oreil.ly/bO7zr*) and has introduced Alice to Bravo. This allows her to form a relationship with Bravo that is more trustworthy because it is based on an introduction from something she trusts.

---

8 The problem with using digital certificates for this is that certificates expire, as you learned in Chapter 9. A manufacturer would manage that by building devices that can update their certificates, but this complexity is enough that certificates are rarely used in IoT devices.

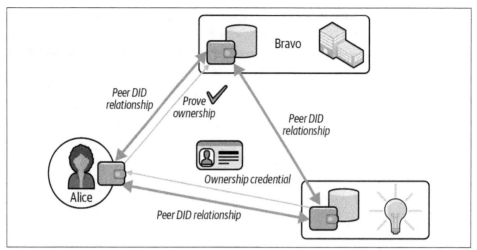

Figure 20-7. Alice uses a credential to prove she owns the lightbulb

Furthermore, Alice has received a credential from her lightbulb stating that she is the owner. This is a kind of imprinting. While it may not be secure enough for some use cases, for something like a lightbulb it's probably secure enough. Once Alice has this credential, she can use it to prove she's the owner. The most obvious place to do so would be at Bravo's website, to receive support, rewards, or other benefits. But other places might be interested in seeing it as well: "Prove you own a Bravo lightbulb and get $10 off your purchase of a Certiphi light switch."

Use Case 3: Real Customer Service

Nearly everyone's experienced customer service hell: you call a company, get put on hold, get asked a bunch of questions to validate who you are, recite serial numbers or model numbers to one agent and then another, and then lose the call and have to start all over again. Or you might have been trapped in a seemingly endless automated response loop trying to even get to a human.

The DID-based relationship Alice has created with Bravo does away with that, because DIDComm messaging creates a mutually authenticated communication channel where each participant knows they are communicating with the right party without the need for further authentication, thus reducing effort and increasing security. Furthermore, as we saw in the last section, Alice can prove she's a bona fide owner of a Bravo lightbulb.

But because DIDComm messaging can support higher-level application protocols, the experience can be much richer. Figure 20-8 provides a simple example.

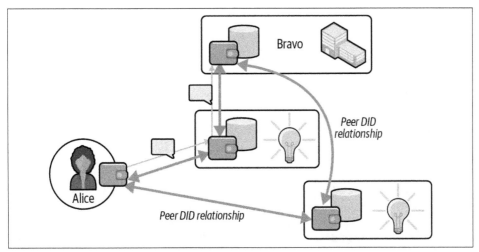

Figure 20-8. Alice uses a specialized smart agent to manage the things she owns

In Figure 20-8, Alice has two Bravo lightbulbs. Let's further assume that Alice has a specialized smart agent to interact with her things. Alice's smart agent does all the things a normal agent can do, but it also has a user interface for managing all the things she owns and her relationships with them.[9]

Having two things manufactured by Bravo presents a problem when Alice wants to contact them if she is serving as the intermediary between the thing and its vendor—she'll have to juggle serial numbers and other identifiers to get the right information from the right device to Bravo. But if we flip that model around and let the thing be the intermediary, the problem is easily resolved. Now when Alice wants to contact Bravo, she clicks one button in her agent and the lightbulb she's chosen intermediates the transaction. The lightbulb can interject relevant information into the conversation, so Alice doesn't have to.[10]

Alice's agent has relationships with each of her things' agents, which might have relationships with each other if that is useful. These agents could be running an application protocol for vendor message routing. The protocol is using subprotocols that allow the lightbulb to act on Alice's behalf in customer support scenarios. CRM tools could be fitted out to understand these protocols as well.

---

9 The idea of things as the conduit for customer service interactions has been on my mind for a while. This blog post I wrote in 2013, "Facebook for My Stuff" (*https://oreil.ly/qICSV*), discusses it in the social vernacular of the day.

10 Doc Searls does a great job of describing why the *thing as conduit* model is so powerful in his article "Market Intelligence That Flows Both Ways" (*https://oreil.ly/frG5b*).

Vic Cooper, the CEO of HearRo, a company working on this idea, told me:

> Most communications happen in the context of a process. [Customers] have a vector that involves changing some state from A to B. "My thing is broken, and I need it fixed." "I lost my thing and need to replace it." "I want a new thing and would like to pay for it, but my card was declined." This is the story of the customer service call. To deliver the lowest effort interaction, we need to know this story. We need to know why they are calling. To add the story to our context we need to do two things: capture the intent and manage the state over time. SSI has one more superpower that we can take advantage of to handle the why part of our interaction. We can use SSI to operationalize the relationships. [11]

As you saw in Chapter 19, operationalized relationships provide persistence and context for any relationship. When we include the product itself in the conversation, we can build customer service applications that lower the effort for the owner because the trustworthy connection can include not only the *who* but also the *what* to provide a more complete story, as the example with two lightbulbs shows. Automatically knowing which lightbulb Alice needs service for is a simple bit of context, but one that reduces effort, nonetheless.

Going further, the interaction itself can be a persistent object with its own identity and DID-based connections to the participants.[12] Now the customer and the company can bring tools to bear on the interaction. They can invite others to join the interaction as necessary. The interaction itself now becomes a persistent nexus that evolves as the conversation does. I recently had a monthlong customer service interaction involving a few dozen calls with the financial services company Charles Schwab. Most of the effort for me and for them was repeatedly reestablishing context. No CRM tool can provide that, because such tools are entirely one-sided. Giving *customers* tools to operationalize their customer relationships solves this problem.

Relationships in the SSIoT

The last section introduced the idea of Alice having a relationship with a device she owns, her lightbulb. Many of the devices we attach to the IoT will be fairly simple, with limited use cases. But some offer much richer possibilities. One of the lessons I took from Fuse is that vehicles are complex devices in a rich ecosystem. In this section, we'll explore Alice's relationship with her Ford F-150 truck in a future SSIoT.

---

11 Private communication with the author.

12 The idea that an interaction might itself be a participant in the DID relationships may take some time to process. Once we create a true IoT, it's not just material, connected things that will be on it. The interaction object could have its own smart agent to store credentials and allow all participants to continue to interact with it over time. It could maintain context, provide a workflow, and serve as a record that everyone involved can access for as long as they need to.

Figure 20-9 shows a few of the relationships a vehicle might have. The most important relationship that a vehicle has is with its owner. But there's more than one owner over the vehicle's lifetime. At the beginning of its life, the vehicle's owner is the manufacturer. Later the vehicle is owned by a dealership, and then by a person or finance company. And, of course, vehicles are frequently resold. Over the course of its lifetime a vehicle will have many owners. Consequently, the vehicle's agent must be smart enough to handle these changes in ownership and the resulting changes in authorizations.

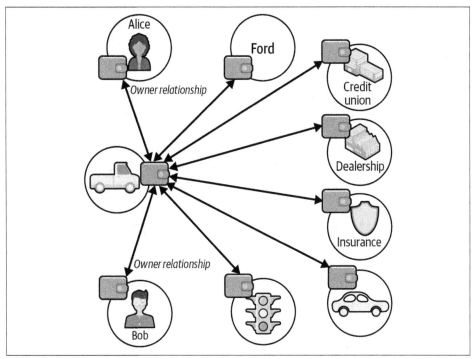

Figure 20-9. Vehicle relationships

In addition to the owner, the vehicle has relationships with other people: drivers, passengers, and pedestrians. The nature of relationships changes over time. For example, the vehicle probably needs to maintain a relationship with the manufacturer and dealer even after they are no longer owners. With these changes to the relationship come changes in authorizations.

In addition to relationships with owners, vehicles also have relationships with other players in the transportation ecosystem: repair shops, gas stations, insurance companies, finance companies, and government agencies. Vehicles might exchange data and money with these players over time. And the vehicle might have relationships with other vehicles, traffic signals, the roadway, and even potholes.[13]

The following sections discuss three scenarios involving Alice, the truck, and other people, institutions, and things.

Multiple Owners

One of the relationship types that the CompuServe of Things fails to handle well is multiple simultaneous owners. Some companies try; others just ignore the whole question. The problem is that when the service provider intermediates the connection to the thing, it must account for multiple owners and allow those relationships to change over time. For a high-value product, the engineering effort is justified, but for many others, it simply doesn't happen.

Figure 20-10 shows the relationships of two owners, Alice and Bob, with their truck. The diagram is simple and hides some of the complexity of the truck dealing with multiple owners. The biggest hurdle is ensuring that developers don't assume a single owner when they develop services to run in the truck's agent. The infrastructure for supporting it is built into DIDComm, including standardized support for subprotocols like Introduce.

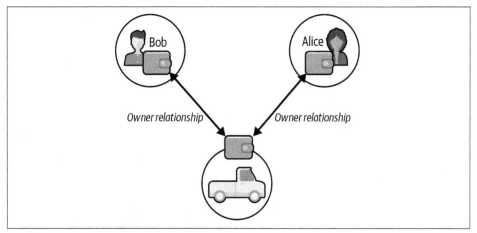

Figure 20-10. Multiple owners

---

13 Again, you might wonder why a pothole would be on the IoT. In my blog post "Pot Holes and Picos" (*https://oreil.ly/AyEJH*), I explain how nonconnected things like potholes might come to have and use a presence on the internet when we imagine it as a digital world that mirrors the physical one. A well-designed IoT can become a true metaverse.

Lending the Truck

People lend things to friends and neighbors all the time. And people rent things out. Platforms like Airbnb, Vrbo, and Outdoorsy are built to support high-value rentals. But what if you could lend or rent anything at any time, without an intermediating platform? Figure 20-11 shows the relationships between Alice and her friend Carol, who wants to borrow Alice's truck.

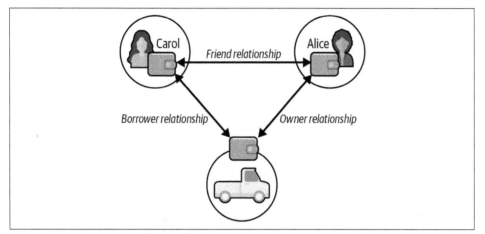

Figure 20-11. Borrowing the truck

Like the multiple-owner scenario, Alice would first have a connection with Carol and introduce her to the truck using the Introduce protocol. The introduction would give the truck permission to connect to Carol and tell the truck's agent what protocols and data to expose to Carol's agent. Alice would also set the relationship's longevity. The specific permissions that the borrower relationship enables depend, of course, on the nature of the thing.

The data that the truck stores for different activities depends on these relationships. For example, the owner is entitled to know everything, including trips. But someone who borrows the car should be able to see their trips, but not those of other drivers. Relationships dictate the interactions. Of course, a truck is a very complicated thing in a complicated ecosystem. Simpler things, like a shovel, might simply involve keeping track of who has the thing and where it is. But, as you learned in the last section, there is value in having the thing itself keep track of its interactions, location, and status.

Selling the Truck

Selling the vehicle is more complicated than the previous scenarios. In 2012, my company Kynetx prototyped this scenario for Swift's Innotribe innovations group and presented it at their Sibos conference. Heather Vescent of Purple Tornado (*https://oreil.ly/hrFtL*) created a video that visualizes how a sale of a motorcycle (*https://oreil.ly/m_fpT*) might happen in a heterarchical DIDComm environment.[14]

In Figure 20-12, Alice is selling her truck to Doug. (I'm ignoring how Alice and Doug got connected and negotiated a price; this example focuses on the sale itself.) To complete the transaction, Alice and Doug create a *sale relationship*. They both have relationships with their respective credit unions or banks where Doug initiates and Alice confirms the transaction. At the same time, Alice introduces the truck to Doug as the new owner.

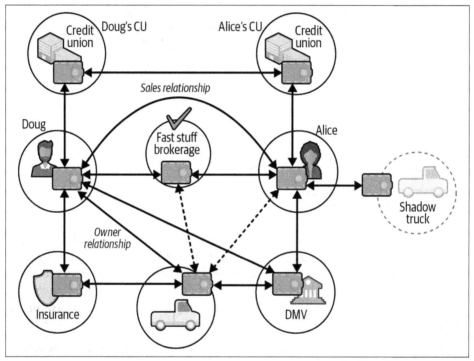

Figure 20-12. Alice sells her truck to Doug

Alice, Doug, and the truck are all connected to the DMV and will use these relationships to transfer the title. Doug can use his agent to register the truck and get plates. Doug also has a relationship with his insurance company. He introduces the truck to the insurance company so it can serve as the service intermediary for the policy issuance.

---

14 In 2012, DIDComm didn't exist, of course. We were envisioning something that Innotribe called the *Digital Asset Grid* (DAG) and used the term *personal clouds* instead of agents, but the envisioned operation of the DAG was very much like what exists now in a DIDComm-enabled peer-to-peer network enabled by DIDs.

Alice is no longer the owner, but the truck knows things about her, like trip and maintenance information, that Doug shouldn't have access to and that she wants to maintain. Alice creates a digital twin of the truck that is no longer attached to the physical device but has a copy of all the information Alice cocreated with the truck over the years she owned it. This digital twin has all the same functionality for accessing and using this data that the truck did. At the same time, Alice and Doug can negotiate what data also stays on the truck. Doug likely doesn't get data about Alice's trips and fuel purchases, but he might want the maintenance data.

Unlocking the SSIoT

DIDComm-capable smart agents can be used to create sophisticated relationship networks that include people, institutions, things, and even soft artifacts like interaction logs. The relationships in that network are rich and varied—just like relationships in the real world. Things, whether they can run their own agents or employ a digital twin to host them, are much more useful when they exist persistently, control their own agent and digital wallet, and can act independently. Things now react and respond to messages from others in the relationship network as they follow the rules their owner has specified.

While the examples in this chapter may not be in production now, everything I've discussed is doable using technologies that already exist. By removing the intermediating administrative systems that make up the CompuServe of Things and moving to a decentralized, peer-to-peer architecture, we can unlock the tremendous potential of the self-sovereign Internet of Things.

CHAPTER 21

Identity Policies

Previous chapters have discussed identity technologies of various kinds. But running an effective and secure identity system requires more than just technology. Doing so requires what we might broadly call *governance*.

This chapter will focus on identity policies, the basic tools for governance. While we typically think of policy as a tool of hierarchical organizations, markets and networks often use policy as well. Chapter 22 will discuss applying policies and other tools for effectively governing identity ecosystems.

Policies and Standards

Let's take a moment to distinguish between policies and standards. *Standards* stipulate specific levels of performance, specify certain goods or services, set quality requirements, or describe best practices. *Policies*, on the other hand, are rules of conduct and behavior. Policies often refer to standards but go beyond them, governing or even mandating their use in specific contexts.

Throughout this book I've referred to standards of various sorts. Some of the standards I've discussed include OAuth, SAML, OpenID Connect, various encryption algorithms, WebFinger, LDAP, DNS, TLS, FIDO's CTAP and WebAuthn, decentralized identifiers (DIDs), verifiable credentials, and DIDComm. Standards are necessary, but often insufficient, for interoperability. Most standards have enough wiggle room to allow for incompatible or incomplete implementations. Implementation leeway is a necessary part of getting standards accepted and ensuring they are resilient to changes in technology.

As a result, many identity policies will reference standards but include details about how the standard is used. For example, in Chapter 14 you learned about the DID specification and that there are various DID methods to choose from. Each of those

DID methods makes choices about things like cryptographic signature suites and, importantly, the verified data registry it uses. An organization using DIDs can't just refer to the DID specification itself; it must pick a method and then create a policy about how the organization or group will use DIDs.

In addition to external standards, most implementations of an identity system also make choices about software and execution environments. Often these choices are turned into explicit internal standards or architectural decisions.

The Policy Stack

Many organizations have a collection of security policies in place, and some of these touch on identity issues. I'm an advocate for separating out the identity aspects of those policies and creating a holistic approach to identity on which to build not only security policies but also other important aspects of the business.

A good way to determine what policies you need and which standards you support is to consider what the organization does and where identity impinges on its activities. Figure 21-1 shows an identity policy stack. Policies, in the center, rest on decisions about standards and architectural decisions. In turn, they provide a foundation to govern activities. A top-down approach ensures that you don't waste time creating policies that don't matter.

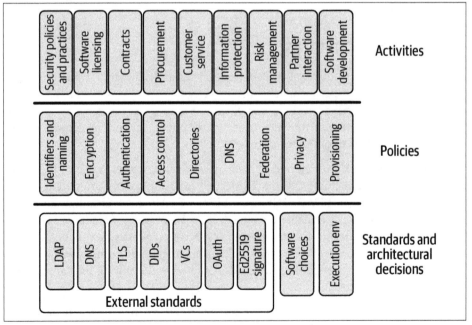

Figure 21-1. The policy stack

Figure 21-1 includes policies for identifiers and naming, encryption, authentication, access control, directories, DNS, federation, privacy, and provisioning. These are just examples; you may need different policies depending on what activities are being governed. The top layer of the stack records activities that are important to the organization, such as software development, security practices and policies, software licensing, contracting, procurement, customer service, information protection, risk management, and partner interactions.

Attributes of a Good Identity Policy

Since policies define appropriate behavior and form the basis for enforcement, they must have several important qualities:

Implementable
> Good policies should be realizable given existing technology and resources. Technical controls are not always possible. Policies should be made by teams that include subject-matter experts. You *will* discover problems that could keep the policy from being implementable during the review process, when you work to get buy-in from various groups.

Enforceable
> Enforcement is not a tool to force compliance so much as a tool for ensuring uniformity and gathering feedback. *Enforceability* requires that the policy contanes clear guidelines on what to do and that enforcement procedures are clearly spelled out. I'll discuss enforcement more later in this chapter.

Understandable
> The people who must live by the policies should be able to understand them. You can't use the internet without running into unreadable terms and conditions in multipage agreements. These are universally derided, because they are not written to be understandable; perhaps they are even written to *not* be understandable. Writing good policies requires walking a fine line between formal and informal language. Users often perceive formal language as "stuffy" or "officious," but informal language often lacks the precision to clearly say what needs to be said. Regardless, the tone should be straightforward and clear, using short sentences and bulleted lists for ease in reading. Paragraphs (and subparagraphs) should be numbered so that they can be referenced easily. Policies should avoid passive voice wherever possible because it can obfuscate *who* is responsible for acting. Most organizations will likely want to adopt a template as one of their first actions in creating policies, so that subsequent policies share a common format.

Guided by the organization
> Policies should be tied to the organization's goals and represent a consensus. Nothing is more important than creating consensus among the influencers in

your organization around each policy. Some policies will need consensus from people outside a single organization. I'll discuss this more in the next chapter.

Practical

People trying to "just get the work done" will circumvent policies that are too restrictive, not understood, or perceived as being impractical. One of your primary goals should be to avoid creating policies that don't work. Remember that no matter how important you may think a particular policy is, it will be a waste of time if most people do not voluntarily adopt it.

Recording Decisions

Creating and maintaining policies will require many significant decisions. Wikipedia defines *architectural decisions* (*https://oreil.ly/QVPr2*) as "design decisions that address architecturally significant requirements; they are perceived as hard to make and/or costly to change." The word *architecture* may make you think of software or hardware decisions, but you can apply the architectural decision methodology to other significant decisions. For example, if you are implementing an administrative architecture for the company you work for, there will be numerous policies, which reflect countless decisions, within that overall architecture.

Rather than thinking of policies as places to *record* such decisions, I think it's better if policies *reflect* and *reference* those decisions. You might be tempted to create a policy that says, "We will use the Ed25519 Signature Suite," and that certainly will govern (the purpose of a policy) how people develop software. But I'm a fan of recording these decisions separately in architectural decision records (ADRs) (*https://oreil.ly/hI6nw*).

Understanding the motivation behind decisions helps the people affected by them. ADRs are a process for systematically recording significant architecture decisions. They capture the context and intended consequences of decisions in versioned documents that later groups can use to understand why decisions were made when they need to be justified, updated, or retired. A lightweight ADR consists of an identifier, title, status, context, decision, and consequences.

With a process for recording ADRs in place, policy writers can refer to decisions by ADR number (and hyperlink), giving people who read the policy a place to go for history and context on decisions that affect them and their work. For example, a policy that depends on an architectural decision on cryptographic signatures might have a section referencing relevant ADRs. Be aware that sometimes architectural decisions are made by referencing policy. The policy and architectural decision processes are mutually reinforcing.

Determining Policy Needs

Identity policies will typically come from one of six places:

- Business-inspired projects and processes
- Security considerations
- Privacy considerations
- Information governance
- External demands
- Feedback on existing policies

This section will examine each in turn.

Business-Inspired Projects and Processes

When I was the CIO for the State of Utah, we undertook a statewide metadirectory project. This project was driven by a clear business need: the governor and others wanted a better URL for state websites and shorter email addresses for employees. Accomplishing this was a big effort involving hundreds of people, and it inspired policies about naming conventions and directory interaction.

To some, driving policies from business projects and processes may seem somewhat less than pure.[1] But that's the point. The policy stack in Figure 21-1 is meant to inspire a top-down approach. By tying your policies to the places where they are needed, you'll get better policies and avoid creating policies you don't use.

As an example, say you're looking at updating your identity infrastructure. You determine that the update would save enough money on password reset calls to justify the cost. Such a project would generate several significant architectural decisions and associated ADRs. Perhaps you're going to move to FIDO, necessitating architectural decisions about hardware tokens, platform authenticators, supported browsers, vendors, and integration methods. These decisions provide a perfect opportunity to create or update your naming, identifier, and authentication policies. Even then, you might opt to create just the parts of those policies that you need to complete the password reset project, leaving other parts of those policies for another time.

The danger in this approach is that sometimes business requirements will force you to make decisions faster than your existing policy creation process can. You can mitigate this problem in one of three ways:

---

1 The word *business* in this section doesn't imply only for-profit, hierarchical organizations; it also encompasses the more general idea of things a group or organization needs to get done to meet its goals.

1. Separate decisions from policies and use a nimbler ADR process when applicable. Some business requirements can be met with architectural decisions that are followed up with a policy.

2. Proactively create policies or ADRs in primary areas before you need to use them. For example, because of a security breach you might need to make decisions about encryption in a matter of a few days. If you wait until the decision is needed to create the policy or make a decision, you won't have enough time.

3. Create an expedited procedure for solving policy questions. Use this process to create point policies on specific questions that need to be answered immediately, then use the longer policy process, including its built-in feedback mechanism, to iterate this point policy to a more general solution.

In any event, you want to avoid two extremes. On one extreme, your policy process is so slow that it delays those making and implementing important business decisions. This is certain to breed discontent and force people to work around the system, rather than within it. On the other extreme, people make decisions without any guidance from the policy process, and your identity infrastructure suffers from *ad hoc* decisions and no structural context.

Amazon uses the metaphor of one-way and two-way doors to approach decisions. A one-way door decision is one that can't be easily reversed. These should be done carefully since the consequences of a bad decision are large. A two-way door decision, on the other hand, *can* easily be reversed. These can be made quickly, in the spirit of experimentation. This metaphor is useful for guiding the level of deliberation you use to make policies.

In the password reset example I gave above, deciding to move to hardware tokens and get rid of passwords completely is a one-way door decision due to the expense and difficulty in going back to passwords. Thus, policy questions surrounding it will need to be done carefully. But you might start by updating your password requirements policy to make resetting them less onerous. Such a policy change is a quick, inexpensive, two-way door decision that can be monitored and easily reversed if needed.

Security Considerations

One of the most important roles for identity policies is to secure resources for an organization or network. Much has been written about information security, and most large organizations have people dedicated to this important task. You may already have security policies that touch on some of the identity issues that your policies will need to address.

Identity enables information security but is not subsumed by it. Indeed, there are significant security considerations that have little to do with identity. This implies that security policies should be separate from and built on identity policies, as shown in the policy stack in Figure 21-1.

Traditional security policies, such as network security, acceptable use, and firewall requirements, typically use concepts such as naming, authentication, encryption, and access control. However, policies on those issues are frequently not aggregated together. You may find, when you review your organization's security policies, that they even contradict each other on these issues.

Separating identity policies from security policies requires that you rewrite each security policy to remove more general identity issues and reference the identity policies instead. As you do this, the requirements of your security policies will drive the contents of your identity policies.

The governance process for policies should always include subject-matter experts on security, so that they can speak to information security needs as policies are developed and implemented. While the needs of information security should play an important role in creating identity policies, they should not overshadow other important needs in the organization.

Privacy Considerations

Like security policies, privacy policies depend on your identity policies—even more so. While security policies are usually separate from identity policies, privacy considerations are often tightly wrapped in identity policies to ensure that the identity infrastructure they govern meets privacy needs.

Chapter 8 contains significant information on how privacy can impact an organization's identity decisions. Do your identity policies support privacy by design principals? Do they ensure your organization complies with the various relevant regulations and laws? Is the business need for data collection clear and reflected in decisions and policies? Are you making good trade-offs between the value of data and the cost of privacy? Most importantly, are you treating information about your customers, partners, and employees the way you would want your own data to be handled? These and other questions can guide your identity policies in support of good privacy practices.

Information Governance

Many organizations have information governance processes in place to protect sensitive information. Some of this is privacy related, but personally identifying information is not the only information that needs to be protected. Trade secrets, corporate performance numbers, and other critical data all need protection from disclosure to unauthorized parties.

Information governance has the biggest impact on access control decisions and policies. Critical questions in information governance that will drive requirements for identity policies iinclude: Where is information stored? Who has access? How long is it retained? How it is destroyed?

If your infrastructure supports policy-based access control (PBAC), many information owners and stewards will be able to write access control policies directly in the PBAC tool. These small, automatically enforced access control policies must comply with larger, more general policies. For that to happen, identity policy must be clear and complete.

Meeting External Requirements

External sources such as government regulators and large partners frequently place requirements on identity infrastructures. These requirements germinate identity policies. Chapter 8 discussed several legal and regulatory requirements, such as GDPR, CCPA, HIPAA, Sarbanes-Oxley, and the Gramm-Leach-Bliley Act. Any of these that apply to your organization will influence the policies you put in place.

Some external requirements are developed by an industry group and have the force of law for all intents and purposes (such as "generally accepted accounting principles"). Others are voluntary, but the organization has concluded that it will abide by them for some reason.

In any event, your organization probably already meets, or attempts to meet, these requirements. Doing so places a burden on the identity infrastructure. Identity policies can codify and normalize these requirements as well as provide a process for meeting any external identity requirements that others place on your organization.

Feedback on Existing Policies

Determining what policies are needed in your organization is an iterative task, not an event. Like any good business process, your policy process should have a defined feedback mechanism. If properly implemented, this feedback mechanism will give you information about which policies are working and which are not. The process will also point to policies that need to be developed to answer questions that arise in the application or enforcement of existing policies.

Writing Identity Policies

We've already discussed five important attributes of a good identity policy. In addition to those specific attributes, these important guidelines will help ensure that your policies are implementable, enforceable, understandable, practical, and guided by the business:

Never release a policy that you can't or won't enforce.
Creating policies that people ignore weakens the process.

Build a policy review framework.
The review framework is a document containing a table that gives status information and a review schedule for each policy.

Good policies are general enough that they do not need frequent updating.
Policies should be unambiguous, without being so specific that they lose their relevance with every change to the business operations of the organization.

Avoid referencing specific standards or products in your policies.
Instead, use an interoperability framework, which can be a collection of ADRs, to call out specific products and standards. Merely reference specific decisions from the interoperability framework in the policy. This will ensure that you don't have to continually update policies as new products and standards are released.

Policies should not specify processes or best practices.
Put another way, policies should talk about "what," not "how." ADRs are a good place to record process and practice decisions.

Policies should not contain confidential or proprietary information.
Policies usually need to be widely distributed to be effective. If you can't avoid including confidential information, be sure that the policy is properly classified by your information governance process and that the chosen classification ensures everyone who needs to see it has access.

Break policies into short, modular documents.
Don't write large, monolithic policies. Develop modular policy structures just as you would modular software, and cross-reference specific sections when needed. The benefits are similar. Short modular policies:

- Can be reused by reference from multiple places
- Benefit from being written by an expert in that specific area
- Are relevant for a longer period
- Are easier to maintain

Include the HR and legal teams in the review process.

This is especially important where enforcement is concerned. Without proper review, you likely will not be able to take action against individuals who break the policy.

Use a document management or version control system for managing the policy-writing process.

This same system can be used to distribute and version policies when they are complete. A workflow that involves writing policies in a word processor, using email for workflow, and putting together a simple website for distribution will work for a small number of documents that are modified infrequently, but it becomes unwieldy for more active policy-maintenance processes.

Rather than starting from scratch, consider buying policy templates from one of the many vendors or consulting companies who service this market.

Alternately, hiring a consultant to put together an identity-policy suite specific to your organization may jump-start the process and give you several workable policies in short order.

The specific policies you develop may have all or only some of these sections depending on the circumstance.

Policy Outline

What should a policy look like? Typically, identity policies have a set of sections that follow an identifiable outline. Each policy should have a title and identifier.[2] I recommend the following sections:

Section 1: Purpose

This section is typically just a paragraph or two long and answers the question, "Why is this policy needed?"

Section 2: Scope

This section is also generally short and identifies what the policy covers.

Section 3: Status

This section identifies the status of the policy. For example, it might be "in development," "under review," "approved," "sunset," or "revoked."

Section 4: Definitions

This section is simply a list of definitions of terms used in the rest of the document. Clear definitions are important in avoiding ambiguity in later sections and

---

2 Don't overthink this. If you're using a version control system like GitHub, for example, the document URI can serve as its identifier and has the bonus of allowing the policy to be easily retrieved using a hyperlink.

avoiding lengthy explanations of concepts in the main body of the policy. Note that the point of this section is not to give dictionary definitions so much as to give definitions specific to the organization and how the words are used in the policy.

Section 5: References

This section is a list of other policies, standards, architectural decisions, and documents that are used in the body of the policy.

Section 6: Policy

This section is the main body of the document and describes in detail the requirements of the policy.

Section 7: Enforcement

This section describes what actions will be taken when the policy is violated. Some enforcement actions may be against personnel such as an HR action, and others may be against organizations such as a budget action. In the case of personnel actions, you typically won't include them in the policy directly, but by reference to the appropriate HR policy.

Section 8: Contacts

This section lists who is responsible for the policy and its review, modification, and enforcement. Specify this by title and position, not name, so that the policy is not outdated by personnel actions.

Section 9: Revision History

This section documents each revision by date and the primary changes. The version control system you use will likely include this automatically in the metadata, and that may be good enough for many actions. If policy changes require approval from other parts of the organization, the Revision History section could include that information.

I recommend that you develop a policy template for your organization and use it for every policy, so the policies have a consistent style and format.

The Policy Review Framework

You should include a policy review framework in the policies that you develop. The framework is really nothing more than a schedule. Consequently, it is generally short and relatively uncontroversial. The review framework consists of the following parts:

- An introduction stating the purpose of the document.
- A table that serves as a schedule of policies. The table should include columns for policy identifier, policy title, responsible person or group, status (for example,

Approved, Final Draft, Draft—RFC), date approved, review cycle (for example, yearly, biannual, etc.).

- A table that serves as a calendar for the current year, showing which policies will be reviewed in any given month.

- Guidelines for how frequently different types of policies should be reviewed, to guide policy writers in proposing a review schedule.

The schedule itself should be reviewed the last month of the calendar or fiscal year and a new review calendar created for the coming year.

Assessing Identity Policies

Policies should be assessed when they are initially created, and again when they come up for review or modification. This process will be most effective when done as a routine, semiformal procedure with a brief report to the reviewing body. Policies of any sort can be difficult to assess. Here are several criteria you might want to use to review and assess your policies:

Completeness

Ideally, policies would cover every situation that might come up. That isn't practical, for reasons of cost and because no one can foresee every possible problem. The best approach is to create a policy that is complete for a specific context and then add to it as unforeseen circumstances arise. The building trades use this approach to create building codes, and it has served them well. The reviewing body should review any incident reports that bear on the policy and make recommendations about changes that would have prevented or lessened the severity of any related incident.

Effectiveness

To gauge a policy's effectiveness, the organization must have some goal that they want the policy to accomplish and must understand how the policy being reviewed contributes to meeting that goal.

Cost

This can be difficult to assess, but it's worth at least estimating so that you can make a case for or against a policy (or changes to an existing policy). The estimate should include the cost of complying with the policy *and* the cost of not implementing the policy. Cost estimates are usually easier to make for components of a policy rather than the entire policy.

Risk

Policies can be hard to compare for relative risk. For example, is a periodic forced password reset better than letting people choose when to update their passwords? Often, the best you can do is to estimate risk. The most important thing is to use the process to build consensus among key players about risk. As a result, everyone will approach policies and their enforcement from a similar perspective.

Enforcement

There is little point in creating policies if they are not enforced. Just imagine how ineffective building codes would be if they were not enforced. Enforcement is not a duty that can fall to a committee. Neither should the same operational group that is supposed to be providing service also enforce policy. It's difficult to provide good customer service and be the police force at the same time.

Make sure policies are promulgated effectively to those who need to see them. As part of this effort, you might consider developing a training program around your policy suite and make sure you include this program in new employee orientation, management training, and other meetings as appropriate.

How strictly you want to enforce policies depends on how costly the consequences of noncompliance are. For example, if your organization is subject to regulatory oversight with potentially large fines, then you may be obligated to strictly enforce policies related to compliance with external regulations.

You might consider including an acknowledgment statement in important policies. This can be as simple as a signed statement saying that the responsible person asserts that they (or their organization) are in compliance with the policy. If they can't sign a compliance statement, be sure to have a program for helping them develop a roadmap that takes them to compliance and require milestone reporting for major milestones in the roadmap.

One of the most effective techniques for measuring and encouraging compliance is to conduct periodic audits. Here are some important points to remember when planning and carrying out audits:

- Make sure you have approval to conduct the audit.
- Don't exclude groups or individuals, such as the IT department or executive management, from audits.
- Don't announce the audit ahead of time.
- Find creative ways to make audits nonpunitive where possible. As silly as it sounds, just leaving candy or rocks in someone's office after an audit as a measure of their compliance can alert people to problems in a nonthreatening way.
- Develop standard audit forms.
- Develop custom audit procedures for each type of policy. For example, a password audit is very different from an audit of coding practices.

- Develop processes for conducting audits and reference them in the policy.
- Document and share audit results.

Penalties for noncompliance should also be included in the policy where applicable. Creating workable enforcement provisions will usually require having legal and HR subject-matter experts review and comment on the policy. Be careful not to make policies so strict that they create deadlock when important work can't get done while remaining in compliance. And provide some means of granting exceptions for exigent circumstances.

Remember that the point of policies and enforcement is to create a context within which a working digital identity infrastructure can be built and operated. Enforcement actions should consequently be aimed at helping projects, organizations, and employees come into compliance rather than extracting punishment.

Procedures

Closely related to policies are procedures. Where policies define "what," procedures define "how." Procedures can be recorded in ADRs. A proper policy suite serves as the basis for creating procedures. Procedures outline specific actions to take in specific situations and give instructions for how to handle events and incidents—even those that are unanticipated. Procedures are just as important as policies, because properly defined procedures lead to repeatable results.

Procedures can be created proactively under authority granted in a policy. More often, though, they will spring up to fill a need without any specific authorization. That's natural and proper. What's important is that the policy should provide the context within which the procedures are created. Returning to an analogy, building codes don't have to authorize a contractor to create their own building procedures, but the best builders create procedures with the building code in mind.

One of the most important general procedures you can create is an incident-handling procedure. The incident-handling procedure is a preplanning document for common, foreseeable incidents. The procedure should define areas of responsibility, actions to take, and the escalation process. Other organizations within the enterprise may define specific incident-handling procedures for their areas of responsibility, but they should be done under the umbrella of a general incident-handling procedure so that nothing falls through the cracks.

Policy Completes the System

Functional systems are more than technologies and architectures. Policies provide the structure, guidance, consistency, and control to solve problems that technology alone cannot.

This chapter has outlined in some detail how to create policies and has given specific examples of what your organization might want in the policy suite that undergirds its identity architecture. The next chapter will take up the reason for policy: governance.

CHAPTER 22

Governing Identity Ecosystems

Starting in 2016, I was the founding chair of the Sovrin Foundation (*https://sovrin.org*), a nonprofit organization created to provide governance for the identity metasystem known as the Sovrin Network. I, and a handful of like-minded people, started the foundation because we knew that an identity ecosystem that aimed to provide *identity for all* (the foundation's vision) would need governance. The irony of decentralized systems is that they often need *more* governance than centralized systems, which can often get by with ad hoc or just-in-time decisions about how they will operate. Decentralized systems must figure that all out ahead of time or they fall apart.

In Chapter 7 I discussed confidence and trust, ending with an exploration of social cohesion. Cohesion enables a group of people to operate with one mind about some set of ideas, processes, and outcomes. You might have wondered how the four types of organizations I discussed create cohesion; the answer is, in short, governance.

When you hear the word *governance*, you might first think of presidents, legislatures, courts, and other apparatuses of governments. In his excellent (and short) introduction to governance, philosopher Mark Bevir defines *governance* as "all processes of social organization and social coordination."[1] While most people typically think of governance as a process undertaken by hierarchical, bureaucratic organizations, Bevir's definition also includes the processes for social coordination and organization used by tribal groups, markets, and networks. In Bevir's words:

> Governance refers, therefore, to all processes of governing, whether undertaken by a government, market, or network, whether over a family, tribe, formal or informal organization, or territory, and whether through laws, norms, power, or language.

---

1 Mark Bevir, *Governance: A Very Short Introduction* (Oxford: University of Oxford Press, 2012).

The word *social*, in Bevir's definition of governance, refers to interactions between people and/or organizations. So, governance is any activity or process aimed at organization or coordination. Bevir points out that things like social norms, raw power, the way we speak and write, and even coercion are all part of governance. Invoking a social norm by saying "That's rude!" is often just as effective as an actual law in regulating people's behavior.

Throughout this book you've learned about many technologies for accomplishing specific goals. These goals are often about organization and coordination. Governance, especially in technical realms like digital identity, often involves both social and technological processes or controls, but its end goal is always coherence. This chapter will explore the processes, both social and technological, that govern identity systems and create coherence. The identity architectures you learned about in Chapter 16 are all governed differently. I'll start the chapter with a section describing governance in each of these. Next, I'll discuss governing hybrid architectures, since most interesting metasystems will be mixtures of all three types. Then I'll turn to governing credential ecosystems that depend on the metasystem. I conclude by exploring how the governance of an identity system promotes or detracts from its legitimacy.

Governing Administrative Identity Systems

You have been involved in administrative organizations of one kind or another for most of your life. Schools, universities, and companies are all hierarchically organized institutions that administer things. As a result, you've likely absorbed a lot of ideas about governance from watching (or being subjected to) how these kinds of institutions work. Creating, promulgating, and enforcing policies are social processes.

Chapter 17 discussed the bureaucratic culture that is endemic in administrative identity ecosystems. This culture leads to a clear power imbalance. In an administrative identity ecosystem, there is a person or an organization that makes decisions and forms policy. Consequently, policies are one of the principal tools administrative organizations use to govern. You probably read the discussion in the last chapter on policy through that lens. Indeed, I find it hard to write about policy without giving it a hierarchical spin. Good policy practice is often synonymous with good corporate governance. While leaders can certainly make ad hoc decisions when unforeseen problems arise, policy is the tool that ensures consistency in how the identity system operates: preventing mistakes, increasing security, and reducing costs.

An important goal of administrative identity system governance is to *create a clear and comprehensive set of policies that will guide its use and operation.* These policies let employees, partners, and customers know what is and is not allowed, and they create coherence by ensuring that everyone's behavior is consistent with the overall goals of the identity system. For example, if your customers or partners agree to terms and conditions as part of creating an account, those should be based on policy.

Federated identity systems make good policy even more important. As you learned in Chapter 13, *federation* is the process of outsourcing some of your identity decisions to another organization. When you use social login to authenticate customers on your site using Google's identity system, you are outsourcing the authentication question to Google. Google is the service provider and thus sets the terms for the federation. Signing up to use Google for your authentication will require that you accept Google's terms and conditions—guided by its policies. Policies can help determine where and how social login is appropriate and what terms your organization is willing to accept.

Other types of federation, like that between an employee portal and a benefits provider, usually require negotiated agreements. In these situations, both participants' policies come into play. They may govern activities such as session length, data sharing and retention, and access control.

Architectural decisions about technology and standards also play a role in governing administrative identity systems. Choosing an IAM system, for example, involves making choices about what the identity system can and can't do. Different systems from different vendors have different features, so making a vendor choice is an act of governance: it sets a boundary for what is possible and what is not. After the choice is made, your organization might decide to turn off some features, or enable others that are not on by default—determining what is permissible within the set of possibilities. Again, each of these choices changes the boundary of what's possible and what's not.

Similarly, federated identity interactions are governed by protocols defined in standards. For example, federation protocols like OpenID Connect, OAuth, and SAML govern the interaction and the roles that each participant plays. Making protocol choices is an act of governance since it ultimately amounts to limiting the possible interactions and controlling them by protocol.

Many of the tasks required to securely operate an administrative identity system can be controlled using technical systems that are integrated with IAM infrastructure. Systems that perform these tasks go by the name *identity governance and administration* (IGA). IGA systems typical provide tools that allow identity and security teams to review and control access automatically, with segregation of duties, roles, and workflows in mind. By administering the IAM system according to rules, IGA systems can automate audits, reviews, and checks that might be mandated by policy. The result is a simpler, error-resistant access control system that can provide alerts about anomalous activity and ensure policy compliance.

Governing Autonomic Identity Systems

Since autonomic identity systems (discussed in Chapter 16) are self-certifying, they are governed almost exclusively through technology rather than by policy. Identity ecosystems based on autonomic identifiers are peer-to-peer, with each participant exercising self-sovereign authority to make choices about technology and how to employ it.

Autonomic identifiers are self-certifying because of the cryptography that underlies them. The cryptography provides confidence (in the sense defined in Chapter 7) about the relationship between the controller, their public key, and their identifier. The controller can use their private key to authoritatively and nonrepudiably sign statements about the operations on the keys and their binding to the identifier. With the proper implementation, another party can use the public key and identifier to check those statements.

Professor Lawrence Lessig's famous essay "Code Is Law" (*https://oreil.ly/0N1mI*) explores what it means for a system to be regulated by the developers who write the code. He says:

> The code regulates. It implements values, or not. It enables freedoms, or disables them. It protects privacy, or promotes monitoring. People choose how the code does these things. People write the code. Thus the choice is not whether people will decide how cyberspace regulates. People—coders—will. The only choice is whether we collectively will have a role in their choice—and thus in determining how these values regulate—or whether collectively we will allow the coders to select our values for us.

When I say that autonomic identity systems are *almost* exclusively governed through technology, my *almost* refers to the space where Lessig's *collective "we"* might enter in.

Other parties might raise questions about the controller and their keys, the implementation, the integrity of the codebase, and choices about standards. For example, suppose Alice and Bob exchange autonomic identifiers as the basis for a digital relationship. When Bob receives a signed communication from Alice, how does he know it's really Alice and not someone who has gained control of her keys through nefarious means? If he tries to validate a signed message and it fails, is that because the signature is bad or because his implementation of the signature validation algorithm is buggy? Did someone plant a bot in Alice's digital agent? Does the algorithm have a fundamental flaw?[2]

The answers to these questions are social, not technical. For example, Bob might verify it's Alice by asking her something an impersonator wouldn't know. Or he might trust the agent Alice uses because he's reviewed its security features. That agent is an implementation of a set of algorithms. Its developers made choices about how to implement it (also a social phenomenon). The algorithm might have been subject to

---

2 TLS has suffered from all of these at one time or another. For example, Heartbleed was a bug in the OpenSSL code base that introduced a security hole in millions of servers around the web. TLS 1.0 protocol was found to be vulnerable to man-in-the-middle attacks. TLS 1.2 does not have that vulnerability and has been formally verified to provide greater assurance about its design.

peer review or analysis by formal methods. These are all social processes that affect whether Alice and Bob can have a private, authentic, and confidential conversation.

All these processes combine to provide governance for the algorithmic identity system. Its governance is more patchwork than that of an administrative system, where there is a person or an organization making decisions. For example, protocol standards are heavily controlled by governance processes; standards bodies go to great length to formalize and ensure committees adhere to these processes. The code may be developed in a closed or open process (the latter is commonly called *open source*). You might trust an open process more, even if you are not a developer, because its transparency makes it possible to watch what's happening and expose flaws. Third parties might certify the agent explicitly, using a certification process, or implicitly, by including it in their product offering.

Bob might know all of this or none of it. But his confidence in the authenticity and confidentiality of Alice's messages rests on it. You might feel uncomfortable placing your trust in a patchwork of processes, but in large part, that's the basis for how the internet works. Few people understand, for example, how TLS works, but it protects them nonetheless. In the end, governance of an autonomic identity system relies on lots of parties worrying about lots of issues to ensure there are no major gaps in the algorithms, protocols, and implementations that make it work.

Governing Algorithmic Identity Systems

The distinguishing feature of an algorithmic identity architecture is the verifiable data registry (VDR), where public DIDs are associated with DID documents and other information related to the credential may be stored, like the schema, credential definition, and revocation registry. So the nature of the VDR's governance is an important pillar in the trustworthiness and legitimacy of an algorithmic identity system.

Figure 22-1 classifies a few popular VDRs (or ways VDRs might be implemented) on two axes based on their read and write permissions. A VDR can be public or private for reading and permissioned or permissionless for writing. Being permissionless and private doesn't make much sense, so that square is red.

VDRs based on Bitcoin, Ethereum, and many other blockchains are public: anyone can read any record stored on them (although the record may be encrypted) and anyone can write a record. Recall, from Chapter 9, that permissionless blockchains are designed to overcome Byzantine faults and prevent double spending, protecting records from being written fraudulently so long as the writer is firmly in control of their private keys.

VDRs based on *public-permissionless ledgers* are not without governance. But their governance is created through interactions between interested parties. For example, in the case of Bitcoin, there are developers who can propose changes, node operators (*miners*) who decide whether to accept the code changes, and people who decide whether to use Bitcoin for their use case (like a VDR). Each of these parties makes individual decisions every day about the ongoing legitimacy of the Bitcoin blockchain and applications that run on it. That is a social process governing the network.

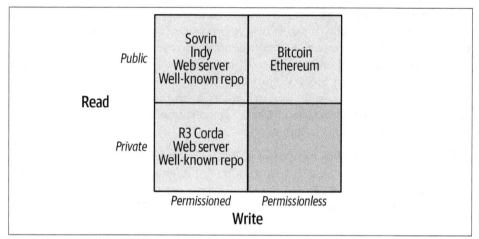

Figure 22-1. Classifying algorithmic identity systems

R3's Corda, an open source distributed ledger usually run by a consortium of companies for their own purposes, is an example of a *private-permissioned VDR*. Only the organizations that control a specific instance of Corda can say who is allowed to read and write to the ledger. The consortium makes these decisions using an administrative corporate governance process.

VDRs based on HTTP or on well-known repositories may be centralized and governed by a single organization.[3] The governance of a private-permissioned ledger is like the governance of a federated identity system in that it's negotiated between parties in the consortium that runs the VDR. The legitimacy of this governance model rests on the legitimacy of the consortium and how it is run.

That brings us back to the Sovrin Network—a network running the Hyperledger Indy codebase, which represents a *public-permissioned* model. Anyone can read the VDR, but writing is controlled by a set of nodes that operate according to the extensive governance documents of the Sovrin Network (*https://oreil.ly/qODvu*), which are based on the broad, open input of participants in the Sovrin ecosystem.

Other public-permissioned VDRs, based on other ledgers or HTTP-based systems, might have similar governance models—or they could be more centralized. The

---

3 For example, RFC 5785 (*https://oreil.ly/KcIGx*) specifies a path, ~/.well-known/, that can be used in URIs as an aid for discovering well-known information.

legitimacy of a public-permissioned system depends on its governance policies and the integrity of the node operators in following them.

Beyond normal operational issues that any online system must deal with, like reliability and scalability, *censorship* is a key question that VDRs must address. Each of the three models handles this differently:

Public-permissionless VDRs

Proponents of public-permissionless VDRs often tout censorship resistance as a primary feature because their operation is dictated by the code implementing the algorithms. But the devil is in the details. For example, the integrity of most permissionless blockchains depends on no single person or organization controlling a majority of the nodes operating the chain. Large mining pools could threaten that because they represent a cartel that operates as a bloc. For similar reasons, well-known, heavily used blockchains like Bitcoin and Ethereum are more trustworthy than lightly trafficked systems, where theoretical guarantees about censorship resistance are overcome by the practical reality of not very many nodes maintaining the chain. Nevertheless, public-permissionless VDRs have the strongest claim to censorship resistance of any of the three models.

Private-permissioned VDRs

These usually have the weakest guarantees on censorship resistance, since the organization running the VDR network can make any decisions it wants regarding its operation, including whom and what to censor. It usually isn't a concern for the members, since there's a clear use case for the VDR and who's using it, and a private VDR will be used in a completely closed ecosystem.

Public-permissioned VDRs

These VDRs, like the Sovrin Network, depend on public pronouncements about their governance to guarantee censorship resistance. No single node operator can decide independently to censor a record. The public nature of the ledger allows outside parties to check for censorship, since changed or removed records would be noticed. The legitimacy of a public-permissioned VDR thus depends on the neutrality, transparency, and perceived fairness of its governance, similar to how the legitimacy of modern democratic nation-states is judged.

Governance in a Hybrid Identity Ecosystem

In "Digital Ecosystems: Evolving Service-Oriented Architectures,"[4] Briscoe and De Wilde describe digital ecosystems that mimic the properties of biological ecosystems:

---

4 Gerard Briscoe and Philippe De Wilde, "Digital Ecosystems: Evolving Service-Oriented Architectures" (Conference on Bio-Inspired Models of Network, Information and Computing Systems, IEEE, 2006).

they are distributed, adaptive, diverse, self-organizing, and scalable. Many successful identity systems in the physical and digital worlds have similar properties. Figure 22-2 reproduces Figure 19-7, which illustrates the mixed architectural nature of an operational identity ecosystem as the basis for discussing how governance functions in this hybrid system.

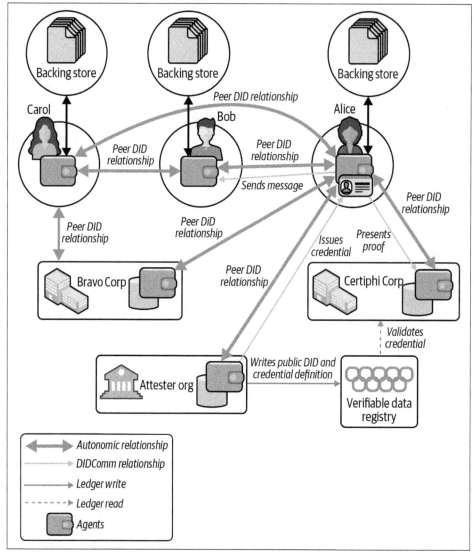

Figure 22-2. Agents in digital relationships

Alice, Carol, and Bob share relationships with an autonomic identity architecture. Similarly, Alice has peer DID-based relationships with Attester, Bravo, and Certiphi.

But the IAM systems that manage Alice's accounts with these three organizations will be administrative. Finally, Attester is a credential issuer, Certiphi is a credential verifier, and Alice is a credential holder. So, each party is participating in one or more algorithmic identity systems.

The identity ecosystem pictured in Figure 22-2 is a form of networked organization with multiple participants in a governance patchwork. Each of the administrative identity systems is likely governed differently from all the others. The diagram shows only peer DID relationships, but it's possible that some of these relationships are based on KERI-compliant autonomic identifiers. In this figure, with just one VDR, Alice, Attester, and Certiphi are participants in only one set of VDR governance policies. But Alice could have credentials on different VDRs and thus be subject to each, forcing verifiers like Certiphi to participate in them in turn if they want to accept credentials issued on those VDRs.

The range of governance models in the ecosystem and the plurality of stakeholders are realities in an identity metasystem. The stakeholders in a networked ecosystem are interdependent, and governance policies in the patchwork will necessarily influence others in the ecosystem. As they respond with their own changes, the ecosystem adjusts again. Actors in a network generally learn to trust each other through these interactions.

Networked ecosystems are more likely to end up with stable governance relationships when all the participants have equal resources. That's not usually going to be the case in identity metasystems, since some participants (like the VDR) will be in positions of relatively greater power. Fairness and stability in these situations will depend on the VDR's choice of partners and on any public commitments to specific policies to inform those choices. Even so, this is a dangerous area and all participants, especially those designing governance policies for potentially powerful actors like a VDR, must pay attention to it.

Governing Individual Identity Ecosystems

Consider your daily interactions that use a credential of some sort. Whether it's a movie ticket, a loyalty card, a credit card, or a government ID like a driver's license, each represents an identity ecosystem that was designed for a specific purpose. Some of those credentials have broad uses outside their intended purpose because of who the issuer is and the strength of the governance that underlies them.

The marketer at the grocery store chain who thinks up and designs a loyalty card, for example, may not think that they are building an identity ecosystem, but they are. Much of what you've learned in this book comes into play in creating a loyalty program or any other successful credential use case. In Chapter 7, I distinguished between confidence and trust, with confidence being based on fidelity and trust being based on provenance. These concepts are useful for understanding the need for credential governance, which the following sections examine.

Credential Fidelity and Confidence

The processes for issuing and presenting credentials impact people's *confidence* in the result. These processes are controlled by decisions about architecture and standards that govern the operation of the VDR and agents. The following are all questions you can ask about the *fidelity* of a credential:

- How are this credential's DIDs resolved? Put another way: Do I trust the DID method?
- Do I have confidence that the resulting DID document is the one that the purported controller of the DID intends me to receive?
- Has the definition for the credential been tampered with?
- Has the schema referenced in the definition been tampered with?
- Can the verifier validate the credential has not been tampered with?
- Was the credential issued to the subject who is presenting it?
- Is the presentation made by a holder with whom the verifier has a relationship?
- Has the issuer revoked the credential?

The answers to these questions are all knowable based on the technology, architecture, algorithms, and protocols used to issue and present the credential. With the right choices for the VDR and proof methods for the credential, you can evaluate the technology stack and cryptographically verify the credential to gain confidence in its fidelity.

Credential Provenance and Trust

Determining the *provenance* of a credential and whether you can *trust* it is a more difficult problem than credential fidelity. Note that the list of questions in the previous section didn't include *Is the DID controlled by the party that I think it is?* For example, if Alice presents a derived credential based on credentials she received from her university and employer, how can the verifier trust that the information actually comes from those institutions?

Each credential includes an identifier for the issuer, usually a public DID. The verifier can resolve the DID and retrieve the DID document. The DID document will contain public keys and service endpoints. The verifier could use any or all of the following methods to determine the *provenance* of the issuer's identifier and develop trust in it:

Personal knowledge

The identifier might be known to the verifier through other interactions outside of the credential exchange. For instance, the verifier of Alice's credential might have had other business with her university or employer. Verifiers (whether institutions or people) will build up personal address books containing the public identifiers of parties with whom they interact.

Out-of-band verification

The verifier might be able to use the service endpoints in the DID document, along with a well-known discovery scheme like the one described in RFC 5785 (*https://oreil.ly/N9dCB*), to check that the identifiers are claimed by an entity otherwise identified using PKI. For example, if the university's DID document includes a web server protected using TLS, the digital certificate authenticating the domain will likely also identify that server's owner. As you saw in Chapter 9, depending on the type of certificate, that *might* lead the verifier to believe that the identifier is associated with Alice's university. They must evaluate, for their particular purpose, the level of proof they need and whether the certificate provides that proof.

Web of trust

The issuer's identifier could be introduced to the verifier by someone it trust, or who can be transitively associated with someone it trusts. This category is similar to the web of trust model (*https://oreil.ly/-_xh9*) that Pretty Good Privacy (PGP) and other public-key cryptography systems use to establish the authenticity of the binding between an identifier and a public key. In this case, however, the verifier already has confidence in the binding to the public key. Instead, the verifier would be interested in the binding between the identifier and a domain or some other well-known public identifier for the issuer.

Verifiable claims

The identifier could be verified by reliance on other trustworthy claims in verifiable credentials (VCs) issued to the issuer. This is analogous to how banks use other documents that they can trust (like a driver's license or passport) to establish the identity of a new account holder.[5] They trust those documents because they know the issuer.

While personal knowledge, out-of-band verification, and webs of trust can all be used to develop trust in credential issuers, relying on VCs is the most scalable and automatable. Figure 22-3 contains the familiar trust triangle of Figure 15-3 and illustrates how this works.

---

5 In the case of banks, this process is highly regulated by Anti-Money-Laundering laws and goes by the moniker Know Your Customer (KYC).

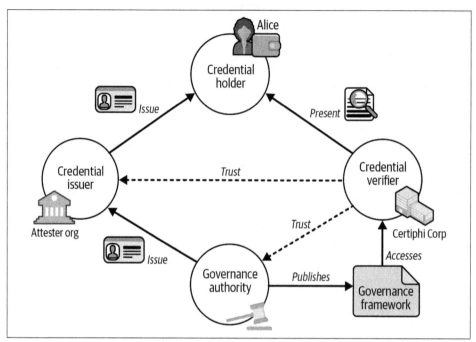

Figure 22-3. The credential exchange diamond

In Figure 22-3, I've left out the VDR for clarity and added a second credential exchange triangle on the bottom to create a diamond. In this example, Alice has a credential issued by Attester Org and is presenting it to Certiphi Corp. Attester also has a credential issued by a *governance authority*. The governance authority has published a *governance framework*, a document that binds it to operating in a specific way and according to published policy and rules.

For example, if Attester is a US-based bank, the governance authority might be the Office of the Comptroller of the Currency (OCC), which charters, regulates, and supervises all national banks and federal savings associations in the US. Certiphi can know the public identifier of the OCC and access its governance framework. This allows them to trust the provenance of the credential Alice presents to them, because they know that it comes from a chartered bank.

How does Certiphi come to trust the OCC? In the words of the old joke, it's turtles all the way down (*https://oreil.ly/KmJ7t*). The OCC will have credentials from the US Department of the Treasury. At some point, Certiphi will run into an organization that represents the final authority in a credential chain. In this example, the Department of the Treasury serves that function since its authority ultimately rests on the US Constitution, it is readily identifiable, and its authority to regulate financial institutions in the US is established in US law.

As I mentioned earlier, organizational credentials are usually public and can thus be freely shared in a public directory. Organizations don't usually need minimal disclosure for these kinds of credentials, so full credential presentation is appropriate for them. Attester could, for example, not only issue its own credential to Alice but also give her its credential from the OCC. Alice could use both in her credential presentation to prove the data Attester has claimed and that it comes from a chartered national bank.

Domain-Specific Trust Frameworks

Domain-specific trust frameworks (as discussed in Chapter 7) provide the means to help people and organizations answer trust questions. The governance framework in Figure 22-3 is part of an overall trust framework provided by the governance authority.

A governing authority does *not* need to be a government body. In fact, most will be private organizations. Anyone determining the rules, procedures, and technology for a given use of a VC is that credential's governing authority. In the example I gave earlier about a loyalty card program, the company issuing the loyalty card is the credential's governing authority. In addition to governance documents in Figure 22-3, a trust framework for a given domain might include the technology, business processes, and legal agreements necessary to trust the claims in the credential. The decisions of this authority create the trust framework for a given domain.

A trust framework can be ad hoc. For example, in the loyalty program, the grocery store issuing it might make most of its decisions without regard to how others will interact with the credential and thus never publish them. Only the grocery store needs to know how it is governed because no one else is relying on the loyalty card.

But a trust framework for an identity ecosystem used by interacting partners must be more formal. This is as true for federated identity ecosystems as it is for a credential-based identity ecosystem. Designing a trust framework can seem daunting at first, but remember that there are many real-world examples. Governing and regulating bodies for banks, universities, sports leagues, credit cards, and many other organizations have been doing this for decades, even centuries in some cases. What's new is that digital capabilities provide many organizations with the technical means to easily create networks that might be useful to others using credentials, forming an ecosystem.

The Trust Over IP Foundation (ToIP) (*https://oreil.ly/miZF7*) is a nonprofit subsidiary of the Linux Foundation that aims to help organizations understand, build, and deploy trust frameworks. ToIP promotes global standards that provide confidential, direct connections between parties. It does this by helping people and organizations understand and exploit opportunities for interoperable digital wallets and credentials. Among other activities, ToIP provides example processes, governing documents, and legal structures. If you find yourself designing an identity ecosystem, ToIP can help.

The Legitimacy of Identity Ecosystems

I said in Chapter 16 that an identity system's legitimacy comes, in part, from the structure of its governance. After this discussion of governance, you are prepared to analyze the legitimacy of all the parts of an identity ecosystem.

Figure 22-4 reproduces the SSI stack that I've discussed several times throughout the book. The identity metasystem that underlies each ecosystem depends on one or more VDRs, shown in Layer 1. Each VDR will be governed in the ways I discussed earlier for algorithmic identity systems, including the choice of standards and technologies that define its operation.

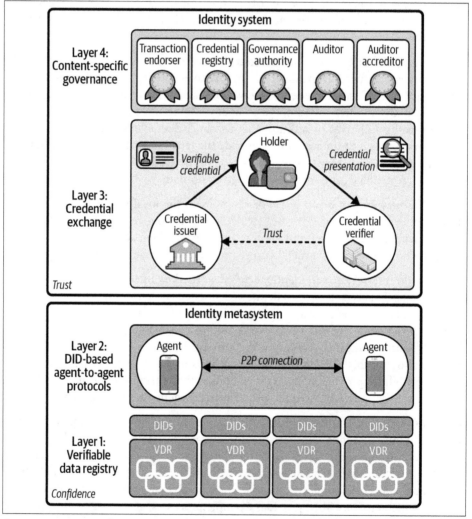

Figure 22-4. SSI stack

The peer-to-peer connections in Layer 2 are governed through the standards and implementation code of the autonomic identifiers on which they depend. Even though there may not be any overt governance other than the standard documents defining the operation, the choices developers and people make about agent implementations provide networked governance for this layer. The technical choices and governance of Layers 1 and 2 inspire confidence in the metasystem, leading ecosystem architects to recognize its legitimacy and use it.

Each identity ecosystem will define credentials and schema, choose credential presentation models, and, possibly, provide governance frameworks for the interactions that take place within the ecosystem. Each organizational participant will usually have policies that govern how they act. Individuals will not usually have formal policy documents but will have a collection of agreements they have made and records of what they have consented to. Their participation may be regulated by the governance framework of the ecosystem, the regulations and laws of their specific government jurisdiction, and their personal value system. In addition, as you learned in Chapter 8, their participation may place obligations on other actors in the ecosystem through laws like GDPR and CCPA.

The explicit and implicit technical choices of an ecosystem, including choices of metasystem, and governance are designed to inspire trust in the authenticity of the actors in that ecosystem and the authenticity of the data they share. These choices directly impact the legitimacy of the ecosystem and thus its adoption. Even if people are unaware of the Laws of Identity (introduced in Chapter 4), I believe that the degree to which identity ecosystems respect and follow these laws affects whether or not an ecosystem enjoys legitimacy. For example, given a choice, people and many organizations will opt for systems that respect privacy through *minimal disclosure*, including only *justifiable parties*, and using *directed identity*. Similarly, the interoperability required by the law of *pluralism of operators and technologies* will drive network effects that grow ecosystems that offer it. And, as I've discussed many times in the book, the laws of *user control and consent, human integration*, and *consistent user experience across contexts* engender identity ecosystems that support respect for autonomy and human dignity and in which people can live effective online lives.

Some identity ecosystems are inconsequential, and thus people make few demands concerning their legitimacy. Other ecosystems are significant, with regional, national, and international impact. Some, like national identity cards, passports, and driver's licenses, are obvious. Others, like the trust models underlying things like the financial system and university transcripts, are less well understood and appreciated. Combining the technology underlying the identity metasystem with governance models appropriate for digital identity ecosystems provides solutions for moving these vastly important ecosystems (and others) firmly into the digital realm.

CHAPTER 23

Generative Identity

Each semester, I challenge my students to "build the world you want to live in." I believe that as technologists we have a duty to create systems that respect people, give them better lives, and help them realize their dreams. The designers, architects, product managers, and developers of identity systems make choices each day that impact the lives of the people who use them. Sometimes that impact is trivial or mundane, but often it is not.

As I said at the close of the last chapter, I take an optimistic view that people will choose systems that respect the Laws of Identity, and that the network effects of interoperable ecosystems will ensure their growth beyond those of systems that do not. But current implementations of digital identity have their dangers, especially when it comes to enabling a surveillance economy that commands enormous resources and reaps tremendous profits. The result is that technical systems have encroached on our private lives and administer the means by which we interact with each other. We cannot dismiss this as we contemplate what kinds of identity systems we should build.

Throughout this book, I've been asking you to consider how an identity metasystem that conforms to the Laws of Identity could overcome the problems of identity. Having read this far, you have learned a great deal about the philosophies, architectures, protocols, technologies, and social context comprising modern notions of digital identity. If you've learned only one thing, I hope it's that identity is more complex and nuanced than people usually give it credit for. This misunderstanding of identity's subtleties sits at the heart of many of the security, privacy, and autonomy problems that people experience online.

This chapter closes the book by describing two identity metasystems, one that exists today and another that is emerging. I introduce the concept of generativity and use it to explore the properties of self-sovereign systems that make them generative and the consequence of that for our digital future.

A Tale of Two Metasystems

The identity technologies you've learned about give rise to two different views of how the metasystem can be architected. I call these the Social Login (SL) Metasystem and the Self-Sovereign Identity (SSI) Metasystem.

The Social Login Metasystem

First, let's look at the system in place now. The SL Metasystem is composed of the various "Log in with…" identity systems that large companies like Facebook, Google, Apple, Twitter, and Amazon support. SL rests on a foundation created using the OAuth and OpenID Connect (OIDC) protocols and uses an administrative architecture. Of course, the large companies aren't the only ones that support authentication in the SL Metasystem, but they have the largest number of accounts and thus are attractive to organizations looking to outsource their authentication.

Figure 23-1 shows the relationships in the SL Metasystem. Alice has an account at Attester, the *identity provider* (IdP), which offers SL services. She also has accounts with Bravo and Certiphi, which have relationships with Attester. The relationship between Alice and Attester was likely created for some purpose other than providing authentication services; that is, Attester provides authentication as a sideline, not as its primary business. The relationships that Bravo and Certiphi have with Attester are not negotiated but based on a set of terms and conditions to which Attester requires all their partners agree. In the SL Metasystem, Attester is the center of attention, since everyone has a relationship with it and depends on it.

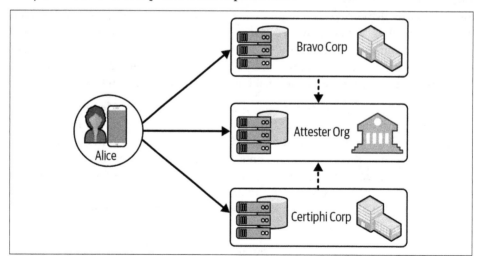

Figure 23-1. Relationships in the SL Metasystem

The SL Metasystem stacks up pretty well when we evaluate it against the Laws of Identity. (If you need a refresher on the Laws, see Chapter 4.) Let's take a look:

User control and consent

Alice chooses "Login with Attester" on Bravo and Certiphi's websites or in their apps, so she's in control of the authentication choice and is implicitly consenting to those relying parties (RPs) using Attester. Bravo and Certiphi likely support more than one IdP, to ensure broad coverage for the largest possible number of accounts, providing Alice with a choice, albeit limited by their decisions.

Minimal disclosure for a constrained use

If authentication is the primary use, then the information disclosures are small but important: Bravo and Certiphi know that Alice uses Attester and Attester knows that Alice uses Bravo and Certiphi. Whether that use is constrained or not depends on the terms and conditions Alice agrees to (if she even reads them). If their use involves access to other data about Alice at Attester, then the scopes of these terms and conditions (see Chapter 13) clearly indicate to Alice what's being shared with Bravo and Certiphi.

Justifiable parties

You could argue that Attester is a justifiable party, since its authentication service is needed to complete the transaction. You might consider the fact that Alice and Bravo have consented to this arrangement as evidence that they see Attester as a justifiable party. But Attester, from its central position, doesn't *just* see that Alice is logging into Bravo; it also knows about everyone else who logs into Bravo using its login service, as well as all the other sites Alice logs into using its service. In addition, Bravo learns something about Alice it doesn't necessarily need to know: that she has an account at Attester.

Directed identity

SL uses omnidirectional (what I've called *public*) identifiers almost exclusively. Attester can correlate Alice's activity across the web because the relationships she's creating are not based on unidirectional, or peer, identifiers.

Pluralism of operators and technologies

Using an underlying protocol like OIDC allows SL to be used on the web, in apps, and in other browsers or browser-like interactions. But OIDC has traditionally been limited in the kinds of data it can transport. Recent innovations to transport credentials over OIDC fix this, as you learned in Chapter 15.

Human integration

Because of how OAuth and OIDC are designed, Bravo and Certiphi can leverage Attester's authentication service by redirecting through Alice's browser. She's integrated with the flow by construction and is a necessary part of the interaction.

Consistent experience across contexts

The redirection experience from one website to another, or from inside an app to another website, can feel a little clunky, but it *is* consistent. Once Alice is familiar with the process, she can follow what's happening and know that she's logging into Attester, a site she trusts. If she uses more than one IdP, her interactions with those different IdPs may differ quite a bit. For example, one may use FIDO while another uses passwords with SMS-based MFA. The user experience with authentication can be rather inconsistent, but that's more a problem the SL Metasystem inherits from the web on which it relies.

The SL Metasystem's two biggest problems with the justifiable parties and directed identity laws may seem small, but they limit how and where SL is used.

Because its architecture is largely administrative, SL doesn't easily support peer relationships between people. It has thus been limited to transactional relationships with organizations. People have no specific tools for interacting other than the IdPs' various websites, which don't support anything other than authentication with partner web services and apps. Thus, SL has *not embodied people or given them autonomy*. The very name of Attester's role, *identity provider*, speaks to the fact that Alice is not the source of her own identity in the SL Metasystem.

Despite recent work to provide ways of transporting richer, more authentic data over OIDC using verifiable credentials (VCs), SL's use has been largely limited to authentication. That's an important part of digital identity, but it isn't enough on its own to support rich relationships.

Because the architecture of SL puts the IdP in the middle, SL has been unable to gain acceptance in some industries, like banking, where organizations are unwilling to give up their primacy in the relationship with their customers.

Finally, some people, like me, prefer to use the RP's authentication system over SL because of concerns about privacy. The primary benefit of SL—fewer passwords to remember—isn't as important when you're using a good password manager, but the threat of surveillance is all too real.

Even with these limitations, there's no denying that the SL Metasystem is a huge success that is providing significant utility to companies and people alike. Next, let's examine the SSI Metasystem.

The Self-Sovereign Identity Metasystem

The SSI Metasystem is based on cryptographic identifiers and VCs and uses a hybrid of administrative, algorithmic, and autonomic architectures. (The discussion of operationalizing digital relationships in Chapter 19 exemplifies this metasystem.)

Figure 23-2 shows the relationships in the SSI Metasystem. Alice has relationships with Attester, Bravo, and Certiphi. Attester has issued Alice a credential that she can present to Bravo and Certiphi as her needs dictate. In the SSI Metasystem, Alice is at the center.

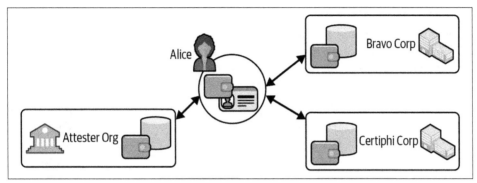

Figure 23-2. Relationships in the SSI Metasystem

The SSI Metasystem conforms well to the Laws of Identity:

User control and consent
Alice is choosing with whom she has relationships, what credentials she holds, and what data she shares from her credentials to others.

Minimal disclosure for a constrained use
Alice can make derived credential presentations, disclosing only the data necessary for a given request. Her consent to the disclosure is implied by that sharing.

Justifiable parties
If Alice shares data from her credential with Certiphi, Attester will not know what she shared or with whom she shared it.

Directed identity
SSI, as you've learned, uses both public and peer identifiers in different contexts, limiting the ability of the parties to the transactions (or anyone else) to correlate Alice's activities.

Pluralism of operators and technologies
Autonomic identifiers can support both ephemeral and long-term relationships. VCs are a flexible and trustworthy method of sharing data. DIDComm, as an encapsulating protocol, allows any workflow to be defined as its own protocol on top of the messaging platform through smart agents. The combination of these three capabilities ensures that the SSI Metasystem can be used in an incredibly diverse range of applications.

Human integration
> The smart agent that sits at the heart of the SSI Metasystem and provides all players with tools for operationalizing their online relationships ensures that people are integrated with the system in ways that give them full control over their relationships.

Consistent experience across contexts
> Regardless of application, the underlying experience in the SSI Metasystem is one of managing relationships and credentials. Both are familiar experiences to most people and can be used in a variety of contexts.

Because it conforms so well to the Laws of Identity, the SSI Metasystem more closely aligns with the ideal metasystem Cameron defined (see Chapter 4). The flexible nature of the SSI Metasystem's architecture allows decentralized players to define, build, and deploy identity systems that match their needs. This is called *generativity*.

Generativity

In 2006, Jonathan Zittrain wrote a compelling and prescient examination of the generative capacity of the internet (*https://oreil.ly/4N9r6*)[1] and its billions of attached personal computers, tablets, and smartphones. He defines *generativity* as "a technology's overall capacity to produce unprompted change driven by large, varied, and uncoordinated audiences," adding, "Generativity is a function of a technology's capacity for leverage across a range of tasks, adaptability to a range of different tasks, ease of mastery, and accessibility."

Zittrain masterfully describes the extreme generativity of the internet and its attached computers, explains why the openness of both the network and the attached computers is so important, discusses threats to the generative nature of the internet, and proposes ways that the internet can remain generative while addressing some of those threats. I recommend you take some time to explore Zittrain's paper in detail, since its applications are broader than just identity systems.

Generative systems use a few basic rules, structures, and features to yield behaviors that can be extremely varied and unpredictable. Zittrain lays out four important criteria for evaluating the generativity of a technology:

Capacity for leverage
> Generative technology makes difficult jobs easier—and sometimes even possible. *Leverage* is measured by the capacity of a device to reduce effort.

---

1 Jonathan Zittrain, "The Generative Internet," *Harvard Law Review* 119, no. 7 (2006): 1974.

Adaptability

Generative technology can be applied to a wide variety of uses with little or no modification. Where leverage speaks to a technology's depth, *adaptability* speaks to its breadth. Many useful devices, such as airplanes, saws, and pencils, have good leverage but are nevertheless narrow in their scope and application.

Ease of mastery

Generative technology is easy to adopt and adapt to new uses. Many billions of people use a PC, tablet, or smartphone to perform tasks important to them without understanding the details about how they work. As they become more proficient at using a technology, they can apply that learning to an even wider variety of tasks.

Accessibility

Generative technology is easy to come by and to access. Access is a function of cost, deployment, regulation, monopoly power, secrecy, and anything else that introduces artificial scarcity.

I will use Zittrain's framework, outlined above, to explore the generativity of two layers in the SSI Metasystem: the secure overlay network formed by DIDComm, in Layer 2, and the credential exchange that happens in Layer 3.

The Self-Sovereign Internet

Generativity provides decentralized actors the means to create cooperating, complex structures and behavior. No one person or group can or will think of all of its possible uses, but each is free to adapt the system to their own use. The architecture of the self-sovereign internet exhibits several important properties on which its generativity depends. The true value of the self-sovereign internet is that it provides a leveragable, adaptable, usable, accessible, and stable platform upon which others can innovate.

The network of relationships created by the exchange of decentralized identifiers (DIDs; Layer 2 in SSI stack) forms a new, more secure layer on the internet (see Chapter 19). Moreover, the protocological properties of DIDComm make that layer especially useful and flexible, mirroring the internet itself.

This kind of "layer" is called an overlay network. An *overlay network* comprises virtual links that correspond to a path in the underlying network. Secure overlay networks rely on an identity layer based on asymmetric-key cryptography to ensure message integrity, nonrepudiation, and confidentiality. TLS (HTTPS) is a secure overlay, but it is incomplete because it's not symmetrical. Furthermore, it's relatively inflexible, because it overlays a network layer that uses a client-server protocol rather than a peer-to-peer protocol.

Figure 23-3 illustrates an overlay network of messaging nodes (smart agents) riding atop the routing infrastructure of the internet itself. In "Key Event Receipt Infrastructure (KERI)" (*https://oreil.ly/hoRmK*),[2] Sam Smith makes an important point about secure overlay networks:

> The important essential feature of an identity system security overlay is that it binds together controllers, identifiers, and key-pairs. A sender controller is exclusively bound to the public key of a (public, private) key-pair. The public key is exclusively bound to the unique identifier. The sender controller is also exclusively bound to the unique identifier. The strength of such an identity system-based security overlay is derived from the security supporting these bindings.

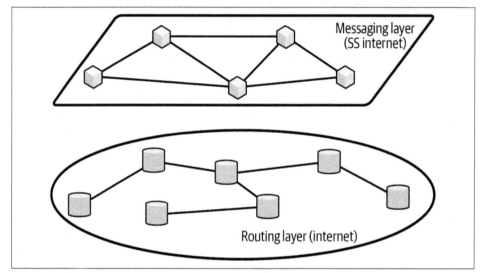

Figure 23-3. The self-sovereign internet as an overlay on the existing internet

Figure 23-4 (reproduced from Chapter 16) shows the critical bindings between the three components of the secure overlay that Smith mentions.

The important point here, from the standpoint of generativity, is that the peer-to-peer network created by peer DID exchanges constitutes an overlay with an autonomic architecture, providing the strongest possible bindings between the controller, identifiers, and authentication factors (public-private keys). In addition, this network doesn't need an external trust basis (like a VDR) because autonomic identifiers are self-certifying.

DIDs allow us to create cryptographic relationships, solving significant key management problems that have plagued asymmetric cryptography since its inception.

---

2 Samuel M. Smith, "Key Event Receipt Infrastructure (KERI)," arXiv, October 11, 2021.

Consequently, a regular person can now use a general-purpose secure overlay network based on DIDs and smart agents. As you learned in Chapter 19, the DID network that is created when people use these relationships provides a protocol, DIDComm, that is every bit as flexible and useful as TCP/IP.

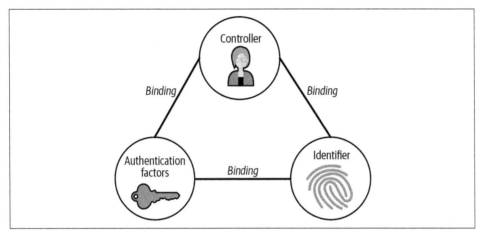

Figure 23-4. Binding of controller, authentication factors, and identifiers in identity systems

Because DIDComm provides the same features as TCP/IP does, communications over a DIDComm-enabled peer-to-peer network are as generative as the internet itself. Thus, the secure overlay network formed by DIDComm connections represents a *self-sovereign internet*, emulating the underlying internet's peer-to-peer messaging in a way that is both secure and credible, without the need for external third parties.[3]

Properties of the Self-Sovereign Internet

In "World of Ends" (*https://oreil.ly/Q8KTK*), Doc Searls and Dave Weinberger enumerate the internet's three virtues:

- No one owns it.
- Everyone can use it.
- Anyone can improve it.

---

3 Admittedly, the secure overlay is running on top of a network with many third parties, some benign and others not. Part of the challenge of engineering a functional secure overlay with self-sovereignty is mitigating the effects that these third parties can have on the self-sovereign internet—engineering against censorship, for example.

These virtues apply to the self-sovereign internet as well. As a result, the self-sovereign internet displays important properties that support its generativity. Here are the most important:

Decentralized
> Decentralization follows directly from the fact that "no one owns it." This is the primary criterion for judging the degree of decentralization in a system.

Heterarchical
> In Chapter 2 you learned that a *heterarchy* is an organization where the nodes are unranked (nonhierarchical). This is colloquially called a *peer-to-peer organization*. Nodes in a DIDComm-based self-sovereign internet relate to each other as peers. This is a heterarchy because there is no inherent ranking of nodes in the architecture of the system.

Interoperable
> Regardless of what providers or systems you use to connect to the self-sovereign internet, you can interact with anyone else who is using it, so long as they follow its protocols.[4]

Substitutable
> Substitutability is an outgrowth of interoperability. The DIDComm protocol defines how systems that use it must behave to achieve interoperability. Thus, anyone who understands the protocol can write software that uses DIDComm. This ensures that people can choose from different software, hardware, and service offerings without fear of being locked into a proprietary system. Usable substitutes provide choice and freedom.

Reliable and censorship resistant
> People, businesses, and others must be able to use the self-sovereign internet without worrying that it will go down, stop working, go up in price, or get taken over by someone who would do harm to it and those who use it. This is larger than mere technical trust that a system will be available; it extends to the issue of censorship.

Nonproprietary and open
> No one has the power to change the self-sovereign internet by fiat. Nor can it suddenly go out of business and stop operating, since its maintenance and operation are distributed, not centralized in the hands of a single organization. Because

---

4 Interoperability is, of course, more complicated than merely following the protocols. Daniel Hardman does an excellent job of discussing this for VCs (a protocol that runs over DIDComm), in "Getting to Practical Interop With Verifiable Credentials" (*https://oreil.ly/bhyFK*).

the self-sovereign internet is an *agreement* rather than a technology or system, it will continue to work so long as there are enough people who want it to work.

The next section analyzes how these properties combine to create a secure network overlay that is as generative as the internet it relies upon.

The Generativity of the Self-Sovereign Internet

Applying Zittrain's framework for evaluating generativity is useful for analyzing the generative properties of the self-sovereign internet.

Capacity for leverage

In Zittrain's words, leverage is the extent to which an object "enables valuable accomplishments that otherwise would be either impossible or not worth the effort to achieve." Leverage multiplies effort, reducing the time and cost necessary to innovate new capabilities and features. Like the internet, DIDComm's extensibility through protocols enables the creation of special-purpose networks and data distribution services on top of it. By providing a secure, stable, trustworthy platform for these services, DIDComm-based secure overlay networks reduce the effort and cost associated with these innovations.

Like a modern operating system's API, DIDComm provides a standardized platform supporting message integrity, nonrepudiation, and confidentiality. Programmers get the benefits of a trusted message system without need for the expensive and difficult development work needed to create it.

Adaptability

Adaptability can refer to a technology's utility for multiple activities without change, as well as its capacity for modification in service of new use cases. Adaptability is orthogonal to capacity for leverage. An airplane, for example, offers incredible leverage, transporting goods and people over long distances quickly. But airplanes are neither useful in activities outside transportation nor easily modified for different uses. A technology that supports hundreds of use cases is more generative than one that is useful in only a few.

Like TCP/IP, DIDComm makes few assumptions about how the secure messaging layer will be used. Consequently, the network formed by the nodes in a DIDComm network can be adapted to any number of applications (as you learned in Chapter 19). Moreover, because a DIDComm-based network is decentralized and self-certifying, it is inherently scalable for many uses.

Ease of use

Ease of use refers to how readily, easily, and broadly a technology can be adapted and adopted. Having a secure, trustworthy platform supporting the self-sovereign internet allows developers to create applications without worrying about the intricacies of the platform's underlying cryptography or key management.

At the same time, because of its standard interface and protocol, DIDComm-based networks can present people with a consistent user experience that reduces the skill they need to establish and use connections. Just like a browser presents a consistent user experience on the web, a DIDComm-based smart agent can present people with a consistent user experience for basic messaging, as well as specialized operations that run over the basic messaging system.

Of special note is key management, which has been the Achilles' heel of previous attempts at secure overlay networks for the internet. As you learned in Chapter 14, DIDs reference their associated public keys indirectly, so that the keys can be rotated, when necessary, without also needing to refresh the identifier. This greatly reduces the need for people to manage or even see keys. People focus on the relationships, and the underlying software manages the keys for them.

Accessibility

Accessible technologies are easy to acquire, inexpensive, and resistant to censorship. DIDComm's accessibility is a product of its decentralized and self-certifying nature. Peer DIDs are free to create, requiring only a little computation on devices that people already own. Their protocols and implementing software are freely available to anyone, without intellectual property encumbrances. Multiple vendors, and even open source tools, can easily use DIDComm. You don't need any central gatekeeper or other third party to initiate a DIDComm connection and form a digital relationship. Moreover, not requiring specific third parties makes censorship more difficult.

Generative Identity

One of the key features of the self-sovereign internet is that it is protocological—its messaging layer supports the implementation of protocol-mediated interchanges on top of it. This extensibility underpins its generativity. Two of the most important protocols defined on top of the self-sovereign internet support the exchange of VCs. Together, these protocols work on top of the self-sovereign internet to give rise to a global identity metasystem that provides generative identity.

The preceding chapters have given you a deep understanding of how credential exchange works, the support DIDs and DIDComm provide for credential exchange, and its nature and properties. There's no need to repeat that here, but if you need a refresher, review the "Operationalizing Digital Relationships" section of Chapter 19.

The properties of credential exchange (enumerated in Chapter 15) underlie several important characteristics that support its generativity. Credential exchange also inherits important characteristics from the SSI Metasystem: it is decentralized, open, permissionless, inclusive, agentic, flexible, and universal (see Chapter 17). Several other characteristics deserve mention because of the ways credential exchange supports them. Credential exchange is:

Private
Privacy by design is baked deep into the architecture of the SSI Metasystem. This is reflected by several of its fundamental architectural choices, including using peer DIDs that can't be correlated, using derived credential presentations for minimal disclosure, and isolating the verifier from the issuer.

Interoperable
VCs have a standard format, readily accessible schemas, and standardized protocols for issuance, presentation, and verification. Credential exchange isn't a single, centralized system from a single vendor with limited pieces and parts. Rather, interoperability relies on interchangeable parts, built and operated by various parties.

Reliable and censorship resistant
Resisting censorship is part technical and part governance. People, businesses, and others must be able to exchange credentials without worrying that the infrastructure will be unavailable. Substitutable tools and credentials, combined with autonomy, make the system resistant to censorship. The biggest threat of censorship lies in the VDR, which allows verifiers to ensure the fidelity of the credential presentation. Governance, as you learned in Chapter 22, is a key factor in supporting VDRs that resist censorship.

Because of these properties, credential exchange can be used to build millions of different identity systems matching many specific contexts and use cases. The next two subsections analyze the generativity of credential exchange and its role in generative identity.

The Generativity of Credential Exchange

To better understand the generative properties of the SSI Metasystem, it's instructive to apply Zittrain's framework for evaluating generativity to credential exchange. This section spends some time on each of his four criteria.

Capacity for leverage

Traditional identity systems have been anemic, supporting simple relationships focused on authentication and a few basic attributes their administrators need. They can't easily be leveraged by anyone but their owners. Federation through SAML or

OIDC in the SL Metasystem has allowed users to leverage the IdP's authentication expertise in a standard way, but authentication is just a small portion of the overall utility of a digital relationship.

Credential exchange's capacity for leverage could be the foundation for a system that disintermediates platform companies like Uber, Airbnb, and Grubhub, as I discussed in Chapter 17. Because platform companies build proprietary trust frameworks to mediate transactions between parties, they can charge exorbitant rents for what ought to be a natural interaction among peers. Credential exchange can open up these trust frameworks, creating open marketplaces for services.

Credential exchange on the SSI Metasystem supports all of the use cases I described in Chapter 15, with minimal development work on the part of issuers, verifiers, and holders. And because the underlying system is interoperable, an investment in the tools necessary to solve one identity problem with credentials can be leveraged by many others without new investment. The cost to define a credential is very low (usually less than $100), and once the definition is in place, there is no cost to issue credentials against it. A small investment can allow an organization to issue millions of credentials of different types for different use cases.

Adaptability

Identity systems based on credential exchange provide people with the tools for acting online as peers, for managing their relationships and interacting through them—in short, for operationalizing their online relationships. In addition, credential exchange allows for ad hoc interactions that were not or cannot be imagined *a priori*.

The wide variety of credential use cases I've discussed speaks to the flexibility of credentials. Every bundle of data transmitted in a workflow is a potential credential. Since credentials are just trustworthy containers for data, there are many more use cases that might not typically be thought of as credentials.

The information needed by the participants in any given relationship varies widely with context. Credential exchange protocols must be adaptable enough to support many different situations, including context-dependent, ad hoc situations.

Ease of use

One of the core features of credential exchange on the SSI Metasystem is that it supports the myriad use cases I've discussed *without* requiring new applications or user experiences for each one. The smart agent at the heart of credential exchange activities on the self-sovereign internet supports two primary artifacts, along with the user experiences to manage them: relationships (via DID-based connections) and credentials. Even though multiple vendors provide smart agents, the underlying protocol informs a common user experience (much as a web browser does). Consistent user experiences let people know what to expect, so they can intuitively understand how to interact in any given situation regardless of context.

Accessibility

Because it is open, standardized, and supported by multiple vendors, credential exchange is easily available to anyone with access to a computer (or other device with an internet connection). But its use shouldn't be limited to individuals who have digital access and legal capacity. Ensuring that technical and legal architectures for credential exchange support guardianship and use on borrowed hardware can ensure SSI is accessible by almost everyone in the world.

Self-Sovereign Identity and Generativity

In a 2020 blog post called "What Is SSI?" (*https://oreil.ly/hXtDb*), I made the claim that SSI requires DIDs, credential exchange, and autonomy for participants. Dick Hardt,[5] CEO of Hellō, pushed back on that a bit and asked me if DIDs were really necessary. We had several fun discussions on that topic.

As I thought about Dick's comments, I realized that the issue isn't DIDs and VCs—those are implementation choices. The important thing is their properties. For example, OpenID4VC and SIOP (discussed in Chapter 15) might be used to form an SSI Metasystem with the same properties as one built on DIDs.[6]

I also realized that administrative identity systems *can't* provide generative identity. Self-sovereign identity is generative not only because of the credential exchange protocols but also because of the properties of the self-sovereign internet, upon which credential exchange protocols are defined and operate. Without the self-sovereign internet, enabled through DIDComm, you might implement something that exchanges credentials like SSI, but it wouldn't provide the leverage and adaptability necessary to create a generative ecosystem or the network effects to propel it to ubiquity.

The approach to digital identity that is common on the internet has put us in a difficult position: people's privacy and security are threatened by the administrative identity architecture being imposed on them. Moreover, limiting its scope to authentication and a few unauthenticated attributes, repeated across thousands of websites with little interoperability, has created confusion, frustration, and needless expense. None of the identity systems in common use today offers support for the kind of ad hoc attribute sharing that happens every day in the physical world. The

---

5 Private communication with the author.

6 What's missing in an OpenID4VC-based SSI Metasystem is the secure network overlay that DIDComm provides. But that's not strictly necessary for autonomous, private, and effective credential exchange.

result has been anything but generative. Entities that rely on attributes from several parties must perform custom integrations with the APIs for each of them. This is slow, complex, and costly, so it typically happens only for high-value applications.

An identity metasystem that supports protocol-mediated credential exchange, running on top of the self-sovereign internet, solves these problems and promises generative identity for everyone. By starting with people and their innate autonomy, generative identity supports online activities that are lifelike and natural. Generative identity allows us to live digital lives with dignity and effectiveness, contemplates and addresses the problems of social inclusion, and supports economic access for people around the globe.

Our Digital Future

I opened this chapter with a discussion of two metasystems, the SL Metasystem and the SSI Metasystem. The SL Metasystem, which represents business as usual on the internet, has provided significant utility and made Web 2.0 possible. But it has come at a cost.

In the book *Age of Surveillance Capitalism*, Shoshana Zuboff asks: "Can the digital future be our home?" The answer comes down to who will determine and control the experiences available to us. Will our experiences be predicated on our own goals, desires, and needs, or those of the companies that control Web 2.0?

The SSI Metasystem offers a different choice, one where people act autonomously as digitally embodied agents to live effective online lives. The architectural differences between these two metasystems, which I've discussed at length, illustrate why. Remember: *architecture eats culture and culture eats strategy*. The generativity of the SSI Metasystem gives rise to an online ecosystem of decentralized actors in which *all of us can find a digital home.*

Index

Hypertext Transfer Protocol (HTTP), 150

About the Author

Phil Windley is a development manager for AWS Identity. He's also cofounder and organizer of the Internet Identity Workshop, one of the world's most influential and long-lived identity conferences, and the author of *Digital Identity* (O'Reilly) and *The Live Web* (Course Technology). Previously, he was a principal engineer in the Office of Information Technology at Brigham Young University and founding chair of the Sovrin Foundation. In addition, Phil was chief information officer for the State of Utah and founder and chief technology officer of iMALL, Inc., an early creator of ecommerce tools.

Colophon

The animal on the cover of *Learning Digital Identity* is a nankeen night heron (*Nycticorax caledonicus*), also known as a rufous night heron. *Nycticorax* means "night raven" in Ancient Greek, and was used to describe birds of ill omen. In 1555, the term was applied to the night heron.

Nankeen night herons can be found all over Australia, generally in areas where there is permanent water. They like to roost in tall trees and foliage during the day near heavily vegetated wetlands, river margins, floodplains, swamps, parks, and gardens. They breed in colonies that can contain hundreds to thousands of breeding pairs. The largest of these colonies can be found in the Murray-Darling Basin. At twilight, they feed on insects, crustaceans, fish, and amphibians in shallow waters.

The name rufous (reddish-brown) night heron comes from the rich, cinnamon-colored upper parts of the birds. They have white undersides, a black beak, and a black crown on their large heads. Their relatively short legs are yellow, as are their feet and eyes. Compared to other herons, they are stocky and medium-sized.

Populations of nankeen night herons remain stable, so they are listed as a species of least concern on conservation lists. Many of the animals on O'Reilly covers are endangered; all of them are important to the world.

The cover illustration is by Karen Montgomery, based on an antique line engraving from *Cassell's Natural History*. The cover fonts are Gilroy Semibold and Guardian Sans. The text font is Adobe Minion Pro; the heading font is Adobe Myriad Condensed; and the code font is Dalton Maag's Ubuntu Mono.

Printed in the USA
CPSIA information can be obtained
at www.ICGtesting.com
JSHW050246090424
60798JS00010B/186

9 781098 117696